UP WITH THE TIMES

UP WITH THE TIMES

CONOR BRADY

Gill & Macmillan

Gill & Macmillan Ltd
Hume Avenue
Park West
Dublin 12
with associated companies throughout the world
www.gillmacmillan.ie

0 7171 3961 1
Index compiled by Cover To Cover
Print origination by O'K Graphic Design, Dublin
Printed by Creative Print and Design, Wales

The paper used in this book is made from the wood pulp
of managed forests. For every tree felled, at least one
tree is planted, thereby renewing natural resources.

A catalogue record is available for this book from the
British Library.

5 4 3 2

For Ann, Neil and Conor

CONTENTS

ACKNOWLEDGEMENTS

This book would not have come into being without the encouragement and enthusiasm of Michael Gill, of Gill & Macmillan and long a friend and collaborator of *The Irish Times*. I am grateful to him for the care and interest with which he shepherded the idea from its beginning. He took me to lunch at Jacob's Ladder, in Nassau Street, in Dublin shortly after I had stepped down as editor. At that point, delighted with my new-found freedom from the responsibility of turning out nightly editorials, the last thing I felt I wanted to do was to start writing. 'But you *will* want to, sometime,' he said. 'Call me when you do.' He was right. And I did.

I would also like to thank and to acknowledge the professionalism of Aoileann O'Donnell, Managing Editor and her team at Gill & Macmillan, all of whom, in this project, manifested qualities of patience to which a former newspaper editor is largely, by definition, a stranger. In particular I would like to thank Eleanor Ashe for her painstaking editing and proofing.

The library at *The Irish Times* responded with its legendary efficiency and courtesy to the publisher's request to access its photo-files. I would like to express my thanks to the staff there. I would also like to thank the various members of the newspaper's Photographic Department down the years who recorded events and personalities within the newspaper and who sometimes presented me with copies of prints. Some of these also appear in the following pages.

Many colleagues and former colleagues, both within *The Irish Times* and elsewhere, helped me in sifting through our varying recollections of events. Editorial decisions are generally made on the run in newspapers and the reasons for them are rarely recorded. But this is not a history. It is my view—my account—of how things were. Thus I will not ask any of them to carry any share of responsibility for its content by naming individuals. Any errors of fact or judgment are, of course, mine alone.

Some of what appears in the following pages, especially in relation to the earlier years of the newspaper, is *Irish Times* lore. It should be read as such. Most of the company records were destroyed in the fire of 1950. Thus documentary sources are few. Where I use quotations from the newspaper or from other publications or sources, I indicate this in the text. I have consciously eschewed the use of footnotes and annotations.

There are no words sufficient to acknowledge the contribution, encouragement and advice of my family. The years of my editorship of *The Irish Times*, in particular, were also a big part of their lives. They have been unfailingly supportive, caring and—where necessary—challenging of my account of events which, in many instances, they also witnessed at first hand. I have been blessed by their wisdom, love, good humour and resilience.

Conor Brady
Dublin
June 2005

INTRODUCTION

Comment is free but facts are sacred . . . It is well to be frank, it is even better to be fair.

—C.P. SCOTT, *The Manchester Guardian*

Nobody really controls a great newspaper. Not an editor; not a manager; not a proprietor. People who think they do, fail to understand that it has something akin to a life-force of its own. The writer Maeve Binchy once told me how she found this out when she first worked as a journalist at *The Irish Times.* 'Before I was a journalist I used to think that you'd see the editor rushing out of his office, shouting "Hold the front page." I only ever saw him coming out, pointing at something in the paper and demanding to know "How the hell did this get in?"'

A great newspaper has an identity and a personality that constantly evolve, drawing upon the past while being shaped by the present. It has its accumulated values and weaknesses. It has its own culture. By definition, it must include, among its journalists anyway, the broadest spectrum of talent and ability, of human oddity and frailty. Otherwise it will die of sameness and predictability. Trying to run an enterprise made up of such people can be a challenge—to put it mildly. Will Thorsell, the former editor of the *Globe and Mail* of Toronto, once described it to me as 'like trying to herd cats'.

A newspaper is an organism that is greater than the totality of the human effort at work within it at any given time—the whole is greater than the sum of its parts. And it has strengths that can survive short-sighted editors, domineering proprietors, profit-obsessed management and the myopia of trade unions. Proprietors, editors, managers and staff come and go. Each puts something of himself or herself into the organism. And the organism generally leaves a lasting impression on them too.

I had the privilege of editing one of the great newspapers of the English-speaking world, *The Irish Times,* for a period of 16 years—from 1986 to 2002. Over that period, the circulation of the newspaper grew from around 85,000 to a historic high in excess of 120,000 daily average.

Not many people are neutral about *The Irish Times.* Some think it is a dreadful thing and a wicked influence on society. One lady who telephoned me regularly was convinced that I was in the grip of Satan—or at least the Freemasons. Others think it is wonderful. There are some cherished myths about it. 'The *Irish Times* is the best *Times* on this side of the Atlantic,' the British politician Richard

Crossman once said.

The myth of the excellence of *The Irish Times* is somewhat like the myth about the best English in the world being spoken in Dublin. Or the myth that the Irish are the world's greatest newspaper readers. (In fact they are about half way down the league for newspaper circulation per 100,000 of population.)

The Irish Times is not something unique in world terms. Many other countries, including small countries, have newspapers that are as good as, or better than, *The Irish Times* in their own communities. Indeed, some of them leave *The Irish Times* behind in certain respects.

But most countries do have a 'newspaper of reference'. That is the newspaper to which people turn when serious issues are at stake. They may not agree with the newspaper's line on events. But they know that they will get a serious, considered appraisal, with accurate, fair reporting. That is what *The Irish Times* is about in the society it serves.

This book is an attempt to chronicle some of the events of a momentous period of Irish and world history, as they appeared from within the newspaper. It also aims to set out how the newspaper itself evolved and how it handled both opportunities and challenges during this period.

A newspaper is a collaborative effort of ordinary men and women to attempt something that is extraordinary. It seeks to give the community a mirror in which it can view itself. And it seeks—or certainly should—to give a window onto worlds beyond the community as well.

Throughout my time as editor I was conscious that what I was doing was part of this collaborative effort. The newspaper that came out of the printing hall at D'Olier Street, and latterly at Citywest, was the product of many minds and many hands.

Nor were these newspapers the product simply of those engaged in the task here and now. They were shaped by the legacy of generations gone before, by long-departed men and women who were the spirit of *The Irish Times* of yesteryear.

Newspapers are only newspapers. By definition, they are imperfect products. Newly-made each morning, against a deadline, they are often in error both in detail and in overview. But each new day offers an opportunity to put right, or to amplify, what has been done imperfectly the day before.

These recollections are presented with an acceptance that *The Irish Times* got it wrong, and that I as editor got it wrong, from time to time. But we also got it right—a great many more times. We produced some very bad newspapers. But we also produced many more good ones.

Various metaphors are employed to define the thing that is a newspaper. Phil Graham of the *Washington Post* called it 'the first draft of history'. Arthur Miller said a good newspaper is a 'nation talking to itself'. The great Irish parliamentarian Edmund Burke, speaking in Parliament of the Three Estates of the realm, said: 'In the Reporters' Gallery yonder, there sits a Fourth Estate more important than they all.'

There have been many attempts at describing what a newspaper does. I think no editor can do better than read and take to heart the centenary essay penned by C.P. Scott in 1921. Scott was editor for 54 years of the then 'Manchester' *Guardian*. As a very old man, he was still a familiar figure on the streets of Manchester, cycling to the newspaper office. He is my hero-editor—for the clarity of his understanding of what a good newspaper should be in the society it serves. Scott wrote:

> A newspaper has two sides to it. It is a business, like any other, and it has to pay its way in the material sense in order to live. But it is much more than a business; it is an institution . . . Between its two sides there should be a happy marriage, and editor and business manager should march hand in hand, the first, be it well understood, just an inch or two in advance . . .
>
> In all living things there must be a certain unity, a principle of vitality and growth. It is so with a newspaper, and the more complete and clear this unity the more vigorous and fruitful the growth. I ask myself what the newspaper stood for when I first knew it, what it has stood for since and stands for now . . . it plays on the minds and consciences of men. It may educate, stimulate, assist or it may do the opposite. It has therefore a moral as well as a material existence and its character and influence are in the main determined by the balance of these two forces. It may make profit or power its first object, or it may conceive of itself as fulfilling a higher and more exacting function . . .
>
> . . . A newspaper is of necessity something of a monopoly and its first duty is to shun the temptations of monopoly. Its primary office is the gathering of news. At the peril of its soul it must see that the supply is not tainted. Neither in what it gives nor in what it does not give, nor in the mode of presentation must the unclouded face of truth suffer wrong.
>
> Comment is free but facts are sacred. 'Propaganda' so called by this means is hateful. The voice of opponents no less than of friends has a right to be heard. Comment also is justly subject to a self-imposed restraint. It is well to be frank, it is even better to be fair. This is an ideal. Achievement in such matters is hardly given to man. Perhaps none of us can attain it in the desirable measure.
>
> We can but try, ask pardon for our shortcomings, and there leave the matter.

1

EDITOR AS EXPRESS TRAIN DRIVER

Give Charlie a few years as his own man and you won't know what's happened to this country.

—JOHN HEALY

Bruce Williamson sat at the desk under Willie Conor's portrait of R.M. ('Bertie') Smyllie and told me that a new world order was coming. It was Christmas week 1986. The winter solstice was darkening the windows on to Fleet Street outside. A few days earlier I had been appointed editor of *The Irish Times*.

It was the most prescient of a number of conversations that framed the 16-year period in which I did the job.

Bruce was the former deputy editor and was still serving as a member of the board. He had retired a year previously but continued to watch international news developments for the newspaper, producing two or three editorials each week, always well-informed and exquisitely written.

He was a huge man—perhaps six feet, three inches, with a chest like a barrel. 'I'd have made a great County Inspector of the RUC,' he used to say. 'My mother always regretted I didn't.' It required no great leap of the imagination to visualise him in uniform with a blackthorn stick and gold braid across his cap.

But Bruce became a newspaper man and a poet. He was proud of his published poems, including two that had appeared in *New Irish Poets*, published in 1948 by the Devin-Adair Company of New York. He lived in Donnybrook and he had a wonderful collection of Dinky and Corgi toys. He had fire-brigades and Churchill tanks; Cadillacs and Jaguars. Occasionally he would bring one in to the office and give it to me to take home to my boys.

His routine was to take a taxi from his home in Donnybrook and to present his hand-written copy after the morning conference in the editor's office. He would then sit and chat for perhaps half an hour during which he would occasionally reach into the pockets of his overcoat to present chocolate bars to anyone who happened to be around.

'Russia is done for,' he announced to me one morning, dropping a giant Mars bar on my desk. 'Put it in the drawer, Old Chap,' he advised. 'You'll have lots of long days and late nights by the time this fellow Gorbachev is done. You'll never know when you'll need an energy boost.'

'My editorial for Saturday is on Sakharov,' he said. 'If Gorbachev allows him to be rehabilitated, he's renouncing 70 years of Communism. Mark my words. We're seeing the beginning of the end of the Soviet Union as we know it.' Over the previous 48 hours the international news agencies had been running reports confirming that the Soviet leader was to allow the dissident intellectual Andrei Sakharov to return to Moscow from exile.

The beginning of the end of the Soviet Union? To someone of my generation, it was an unimaginable prospect. We had grown to adulthood in a world divided between two superpowers, facing each other across the oceans with nuclear arsenals capable of destroying the planet many times over.

But here was the judgment of a veteran editor who had been monitoring and analysing international relations since the rise of Hitler and Mussolini. I thought a great deal about its implications. Over Christmas, I immersed myself in one or two of the biographies of Mikhail Gorbachev and in some of the new political analyses of the USSR that were coming on to the bookshelves in increasing numbers.

———

On a wet and freezing January night two weeks later, Charles Haughey told me that a new Ireland—a land of economic success—was on its way. It was a prediction that seemed no less fanciful at the time than Bruce Williamson's anticipation of the end of the Soviet empire.

That week the Labour leader and Tánaiste, Dick Spring, had led his Ministers out of government, bringing the Fine Gael-Labour coalition led by Garret FitzGerald to an end. In spite of lengthy wrangling and negotiation, the two parties had failed to agree a Budget for the coming year.

The Fine Gael Minister for Finance, John Bruton, had proposed extensive cuts in government spending while raising taxes. Labour was unwilling to support the proposed measures. The government had been on a life-support system provided by the Dáil's Christmas recess. Now an election was inevitable and the polls showed that Charles Haughey would once again be Taoiseach at the head of a Fianna Fáil administration.

I drove to Haughey's home at Abbeville for a working dinner, accompanied by *The Irish Times* political columnist, John Healy. The hail sweeping in across Dublin Bay was a metaphor for the mood of the country. The unemployment figure that month had passed 250,000. Each day's newspapers brought reports of factory closures and cutbacks. Interest rates were in double-digit figures and rising, putting pressure on businesses and young home-owners. Payments on the national debt, built up by successive governments over the previous decade, were soaking up taxation revenues. A mood of deep pessimism hung over the country.

The state of the economy was mirrored in the news from the North. With the implementation of the 1985 Anglo-Irish Agreement (the Hillsborough Agreement) the Dublin government had been given a formal role in monitoring events within Northern Ireland. Irish civil servants now worked alongside their UK counterparts within Northern Ireland, at a complex known as 'the Bunker' at Maryfield, near Belfast.

But unionist reaction had been implacable. No progress had been made towards political co-operation across the community divide. The paramilitary organisations continued their campaigns. The nightly news brought details of assassinations, bombings, arson attacks and intimidation.

Healy, who had contributed the influential 'Backbencher' column, first to the *Sunday Review* and later to *The Irish Times*, had been a long-time supporter of Charles Haughey. When Douglas Gageby was appointed for his second term as editor in 1977, he contracted Healy to write a new, twice-weekly column, 'Sounding Off'. Week after week, Healy poured out paeans of praise to Haughey, to the infuriation of most of the staff and many readers of the paper. As soon as my appointment as editor was announced, he proposed that we should have dinner together with Haughey. 'No strings attached, Star.' It was a term of affinity that he liked to use, softening the 's' in the West of Ireland pronunciation and lengthening the word so that it came out 'Shhtaa...ar'.

It was my one and only visit to Abbeville. Healy and I were greeted pleasantly by Haughey's wife, Maureen. She sat with us for a drink, along with her husband and his political ally Brian Lenihan. The eighteenth-century house was not as grand in scale as I had anticipated. A number of portraits and busts of our host were displayed around the beautifully proportioned reception rooms.

Maureen Haughey retired and Brian Lenihan went home. Haughey, Healy and I then had a working dinner during which Haughey spoke at length about his hopes and plans for his upcoming period as Taoiseach and for the formation of his new government.

I put it to Haughey that such was the disastrous state of the economy that recovery might be impossible during the lifetime of the incoming government. What could he do that Garret FitzGerald had been unable to do over the previous three or four years?

'Oh, things will change. You'll see,' he replied with apparent confidence. 'I've got two or three things to move on immediately. The key is to find a way to restore a bit of national spirit, let people see that things can happen. Make a few investments that will pay off. That's how you start the ball rolling. Then we can get growth of maybe two and a half per cent per annum over three or four years.'

Wasn't there the problem that State finances were so tight there simply was no money to invest? Reductions rather than increases in State spending seemed to be in order.

'Not at all,' he waved a hand airily. 'MacSharry will cut back a bit here and there. There's always waste. We'll find the cash.' Ray MacSharry, Dáil member for

Sligo-Leitrim and a former Minister for Finance, was generally—and correctly—expected to be re-appointed to that portfolio in the incoming administration.

Haughey had a habit of narrowing his eyes and slightly cocking his head to make a point of emphasis. 'And interest rates are going to come down internationally. I'm quite certain about that. There'll be money to spare for what we need to do,' he said quietly.

'Talk about the projects you have in mind, Charlie,' Healy said. Haughey went on to outline three proposed initiatives that were indeed to impact on the Irish economy and on Irish public life over the next decade. 'I want to get an international financial centre going in Dublin,' he said. 'Something akin to what Maggie Thatcher did in the Docklands in London. There's a very imaginative proposal in from a fellow ... what's his name?' 'Dermot Desmond,' Healy chimed in. Haughey nodded. 'That's him. Desmond. Bright young fella. Mara introduced him.'

P.J. Mara was Haughey's media adviser and was to become Government Press Secretary in the incoming administration. He had been a central figure in Haughey's rehabilitation within the Fianna Fáil party, culminating in his election for the first time as Taoiseach in 1979.

'Then we've got a scheme in from another bright young one, [Laura Megahy],' Haughey continued. 'Do you know Temple Bar—just there off the Liffey Quays? CIÉ wanted to put a big bus dépôt there a few years back?' I did. The Temple Bar district was partially bisected by Fleet Street, which extended across Westmoreland Street where it flanked the offices of *The Irish Times*.

'With a little bit of investment we could turn that whole area into a new cultural district. We'd have artists, studios, galleries, restaurants—all that kind of thing. Revitalise the place. Get a bit of a buzz going.' It seemed improbable, I thought to myself. The area was thoroughly run down, with little commercial activity beyond a few small stores and dusty workshops.

'Then we've got a very promising concept to reorganise the Irish beef processing industry,' he added. 'This country won't ever make it in international markets if we have dozens of different brands competing. We're too small. Yet we've probably got the best beef in the world. If we bring the entire beef industry under one brand or umbrella we could really make an impact in the export markets. There's a fella called Goodman up in County Louth who could do it if we give him the backing.'

We finished our dinner and talked on for perhaps an hour. Since I was driving, I had had little or no alcohol. But Healy had a few glasses of wine and a couple of stiff brandies after the meal. He was in good spirits and in expansive mood as we drove back to the city.

'He needs a good run at things now. He's never had that before. Give Charlie a few years as his own man and you won't know what's happened to this country, Star.'

Healy was right in more ways than he could ever have imagined.

In March, with Fianna Fáil back in government—albeit in a minority administration—and Haughey once again Taoiseach, I went to talk to Pádraic White, the head of the Industrial Development Authority (IDA), the State's inward investment agency.

The IDA had a lengthy and successful track-record of persuading overseas companies to invest in Ireland. Hundreds of thousands of jobs in cities and towns across the country had been provided by foreign industry, lured by promises of start-up grants, generous tax-breaks and the availability of a reasonably well-educated workforce, in a low-pay economy.

But, much of what had been built up in the 1960s and 1970s had been dissipated during the 1980s. Many of the factories that came in from the US and Europe were little more than assembly lines or simple production units. They turned out electronic components, machine parts, raw textiles or bulk chemicals, while higher-value functions such as research, development and marketing were carried out from corporate headquarters elsewhere.

Conditions in Ireland for many of these enterprises grew less attractive as the 1980s went by. Labour costs increased, industrial disputes were frequent, automation and new technologies meant that workforce numbers could be substantially reduced in many instances. All of this was bad news for the IDA and for Ireland. By the end of the 1980s, many of the big enterprises that had started up in the 1970s were winding down. Some were gone.

I was anxious to hear from White and his senior team at the IDA how they saw the future. I was certain the picture they would paint would be fairly grim. The US economy which had fuelled much of the 1970s investment in Ireland was chugging along but America had not yet begun to experience the huge markets uplift that was to endure through the 1990s. The UK, or more accurately the South of England, was doing well, enjoying the fruits of Thatcherism. But Ireland appeared to be trapped in the economic ideologies of an earlier age, crippled with debt and with the second highest rate of unemployment in Europe.

The invitation to the IDA had come from White within a couple of weeks of my appointment. But I had been faced with urgent organisational problems at the paper and I had deferred it. By the time the meeting took place, Haughey's Minister for Finance, Ray MacSharry, had already begun to wield the axe over public spending, announcing substantial reductions in the numbers of civil servants and a range of cutbacks in public services.

Pádraic White put on lunch at the IDA headquarters at Wilton Place, by the Grand Canal. We were joined by Kieran McGowan, his deputy, who later succeeded him as head of the organisation. Some other heads of functions were also present. It was a 'dry' lunch. That is to say, no alcohol was served or offered. Not even a glass of wine. It was the first time I had ever encountered this at a working lunch in Dublin. It was a harbinger of change, of a new era of determination in business. Sparkling Ballygowan suited me just fine.

I was wholly mistaken in expecting to hear a tale of gloom and doom from White and his lieutenants. Yes, they agreed, the past few years had been extremely difficult. And yes, many of the industries established in the 1970s—and even some set up in the 1980s—were not going to be there for much longer. But the IDA had a well-informed vision of what was coming up for the future—and it looked good.

White explained that the IDA would be concentrating on high-value activities. They would be seeking to attract enterprises that perhaps employed fewer people but at much higher levels of skill and remuneration. They would be aiming to identify companies that wanted to hire Irish scientists, engineers, computer experts, statisticians and other professionals.

In the past the emphasis (mainly for political reasons) had been on job numbers. For the future it would be on the value of jobs. Ireland's attractions would be its favourable tax regime, its location within the European Community and the availability of a highly-educated workforce.

'It sounds fine in theory,' I ventured. 'But where are these jobs going to come from? And who's going to ensure they land in Ireland?'

'They're going to come in the main from the United States,' White said. 'The whole microchip industry is going to take off over the next few years. The mobile telephone is going to be commonplace. New generations of computers are going to be developed. Every business, every organisation will be computerised. The personal computer will start appearing in homes as well as offices. We're going to make Ireland the Number One destination in Europe for American microchip companies.'

With the daily headlines filled with closures, cutbacks, emigration and ever-rising unemployment, I was sceptical.

'We haven't just come up with this overnight,' McGowan said. 'We've put some of our best people into our North American offices and we've done an enormous amount of groundwork. When the US economy begins to move forward—and we know it will—we'll be well placed. The colleges and the universities have done their part. We have the skilled graduates and workers. We have a Single Market coming into operation in Europe in 1992. We can put really attractive propositions to the boards of these corporations.'

I finished my lunch and went back to the newspaper to chair the afternoon conference, wondering if these people weren't rather disconnected from reality.

———

In June 1987, John Hume told me that there would be a new settlement and a cease-fire in Northern Ireland. The future Nobel laureate and architect of the Northern Ireland peace process usually stayed at Jury's Hotel in Ballsbridge when he came to Dublin and after I was appointed editor at the end of 1986 I would meet him there regularly.

As 1987 went by, the political outlook in the North was as bleak as it ever had been. The year had opened with a series of 13 murders arising from a feud between members of the extremist Irish National Liberation Army (INLA) and a breakaway group styling themselves the Irish People's Liberation Organisation. Two INLA members were shot to death with automatic weapons in a hotel lobby near Drogheda. In February, the wife of the INLA leader, Dominic McGlinchey, was shot dead while she bathed her young children at their home in the town.

In March a civilian prison worker and two Royal Ulster Constabulary (RUC) officers were assassinated at Magee College in Derry. In April, one of Northern Ireland's most senior judges, Lord Justice Gibson, and his wife were murdered by a 500-lb Irish Republican Army (IRA) bomb as they drove their car just north of the border, near Killeen. In May, the IRA sustained its heaviest casualties in a single incident during the Troubles when eight members of the East Tyrone Brigade were shot dead by the Special Air Services (SAS) in an ambush as they attacked the RUC station in the small village of Loughgall. A ninth man, an innocent driver passing through the village, was also shot dead by the soldiers.

By the summer, it was generally accepted that the unionists were either incapable of or unwilling to make a political response to the Hillsborough Agreement. A unionist 'task force' comprising Frank Millar, general secretary of the Ulster Unionist Party (UUP) and Peter Robinson, deputy leader of the Democratic Unionist Party (DUP), had been set up to make proposals for action. The report would finally be delivered in July but it was effectively renounced by the two party leaders, James Molyneux (UUP) and Ian Paisley (DUP).

I met Hume over breakfast in Jury's Coffee Dock. He looked stressed and his mood was low. I said to him that I reckoned he had good reason to be depressed. 'You know,' he said, 'I think the IRA would call a ceasefire if the conditions were right.'

It was the first time he had mentioned any such possibility. But it was something to which he would return again and again over coming months. None of the regular commentators, including my own immediate colleagues, would have given the idea any serious consideration. All of the IRA's rhetoric promised a 'long war' that would only end when the British would leave Ireland. There was no hint of compromise. Moreover, the struggle was too bitter, the price already paid in blood too high, for such a prospect in the foreseeable future.

'I know the Brits would respond,' Hume said. 'If the killings stopped, anything would be possible. I think the Provos know that too. The trouble is that even if they want to, they're just not capable of doing it at the moment.'

It was not until August 1994, more than 7 years later, that the IRA called its first ceasefire—apart from brief cessations at Christmas time. But what very few people knew in early 1987 was that almost a year previously, the Belfast Redemptorist priest Fr Alec Reid had come to visit Charles Haughey in Dublin. Fr Reid's mission was to seek to open dialogue between the Fianna Fáil leader and Sinn Féin's Gerry Adams.

And within a few months of that breakfast meeting with John Hume in Jury's Coffee Dock, he was himself leading colleagues from the Social Democratic and Labour Party (SDLP) in secret discussions with the Sinn Féin leadership at Father Reid's Redemptorist retreat house, St Gerard's, on the Antrim Road in Belfast.

The peace process was in embryo—even though few people outside of the immediate participants in these discussions knew about it.

———

After three hectic months in the job, I took a couple of weeks holiday with my family in Lanzarote. I reckoned, rightly, that there would be little prospect of a summer vacation as such, that year.

On my return, I called Fr Dermod McCarthy, a well-known priest of the Dublin Archdiocese, then Administrator attached to the Pro-Cathedral. Dermod had been an early member of *Radharc*, the adventurous religious programming unit in RTÉ. We had come across each other over the years and got on well. We had a common bond in that we had both been at school at the Cistercian College in Roscrea, although Dermod was some time ahead of me.

Dermod had written to congratulate me on my appointment at Christmas and I had called him to acknowledge that. 'So, how's it going for you?' he inquired. 'Busy,' I replied. 'I'm doing a lot of reorganising and I'm trying to get back to all the people who want to open up lines of communication.'

I had been somewhat taken by surprise at the great volume of letters and messages that had landed on my desk in the weeks after my appointment. Mostly they were simple expressions of good will. But a great many were from individuals, organisations or groups that wanted to have the new editor of *The Irish Times* aware of their viewpoint, their ambitions or their concerns. These ranged from ambassadors, to small community groups around the country, to professional lobbyists. In time, I did get back to every one of them. But it was to be quite a few months before I got through them all.

'Is there any communication from any of our people?' Dermod asked tentatively. I was momentarily unsure what he had in mind. Then I realised he meant the Catholic hierarchy. Up to that point it had not struck me as significant that while I had a great many communications from Protestant church figures of various denominations, I had heard nothing from any of the leaders of my own church.

'No, I'm afraid not,' I replied. He sighed, audibly. 'That's a pity. They need to be more in dialogue. You'd think that with one of their own sitting in the editor's chair at *The Irish Times* they'd see an opportunity,' he said. There had been some focus on the fact that I was the first Catholic to be appointed as editor in a newspaper and organisation that were traditionally seen as Protestant-dominated. It was not regarded as an especially significant matter within the newspaper itself, and certainly not among the journalists. But it had been commented upon in some other media.

Dermod was silent for a moment. 'They've got very little idea of where this society is going . . . of what's happening in this society. They need to be in touch. Or they'll wake up one morning and find it's all a bit too late.'

Dermod McCarthy was right, of course. Within a few short years, the slippage in the traditional authority of the Irish Catholic church had become an avalanche. The revelations that two prominent churchmen, supposed celibates, had fathered children, were sufficient to send tremors of doubt throughout the faithful.

But the unmasking of extensive sexual abuse by priests and clerics, especially against children, unleashed undreamt-of anger. From a condition of widespread religious conformity and loyalty, urban Ireland in particular changed to a largely secular, post-religious set of values in a short space of a few years. By the end of the 1990s it was reflected in dwindling congregations, a big drop in the numbers of vocations in every diocese and the withdrawal of religious from many institutions around the country.

Some historians have argued that the twentieth century ended, for most practical purposes, in the early 1990s and not in the millennium year 2000. The American analyst Francis Fukuyama memorably coined the phrase 'The End of History' as the title for his book, chronicling the events of the 1980s and 1990s.

The global power balance between the United States and the Soviet Union came to an end, leaving the US as the sole superpower. The wealth of the twentieth century was largely founded on manufacturing industry. But by the early 1990s, the primacy of information-based wealth had been confirmed with the spread of the internet. The separate economies of the developed world merged into one, as the process known as globalisation gathered momentum.

Yet scarcely had the threat of nuclear war between east and west receded than it had been replaced by the reality of random terrorist attack from a radicalised Islamic world.

Little of this was apparent in 1986 when I was appointed. But by 2002, when I stepped down, the wider world had altered extraordinarily and Ireland, along with the Europe of which it had become a part, had also changed.

In 1986 it seemed that there could be no end to the large-scale violence of the North. Both parts of Ireland, Britain and sometimes locations further afield were subject to terrorist violence. By 2002, the Belfast Agreement—in all its imperfections, its violations and its exploitations—had been in place for four years and the IRA's ceasefire had held for more than eight years.

Years of tortuous and inconclusive negotiations were yet ahead in the North and a functioning executive and power-sharing assembly were to operate only briefly. The Sinn Féin/IRA 'axis', as I referred to them in leading articles during my editorship, was to prove itself intractable, seeking the benefits of democratic participation while maintaining a private paramilitary organisation, deeply enmeshed in crime. But the other elements of the Agreement, notably those providing for all-Ireland co-operation and cross-border liaison, were well-secured. Attitudes had changed too. As David Trimble put it in 2004, 'the extremes were not what or where they had once been.'

From a position in which it languished close to the bottom of the EEC's wealth leagues in 1986, Ireland by 2002 had gone to the top of those leagues, with virtually no unemployment, and significant inward migration taking the place of the mass emigration of the 1970s and 1980s. By 2002 Ireland was a multi-cultural society with Chinese, Nigerians, Romanians, Russians and people of many other races settling in the cities and towns.

Europe had moved from a loose trade and industry arrangement to a union, bound together by a series of treaties and shortly to be expanded to 25 nations, with a population of almost 600 million.

In retrospect, one can readily identify the period of which I write as one of concentrated and historic change. But of course that perspective is only possible with hindsight.

Editing a daily newspaper like *The Irish Times* in a period such as this is something akin to driving an express train. The forward dynamic is all. Newsrooms and printing halls may fall silent in the dead hours before a new day begins. But these are only intervals pending the next dash forward. There is no time or opportunity to dwell on the wonders of the landscape or the novelty of the events that have just passed by. Nor is there much time to assess the hazards that one has skirted. They have been left behind. What is important is what lies ahead, in the next immediate stretch.

I was editor over a period that encompassed 4,752 publishing days—from December 1986 to October 2002. But if I try to identify the most memorable days and nights of a 16-year editorship, I find myself struggling to isolate them.

My sense now is of a ceaseless torrent of events, one succeeding another. There were wars, famines, atrocities, natural disasters. Governments came and went. New, powerful personalities emerged to change the history of Ireland and of the world. Various protective myths with which we had surrounded ourselves in Ireland were swept away. Tribunals sitting in Dublin Castle tore away the mask of respectability that had disguised corruption in business and in public life. Extraordinary changes in technology, in values, in popular culture took place. Random chance and misadventure shaped the headlines from time to time.

Certain events and moments do stand out. But for a newspaper editor, important events and moments of historic significance will invariably be tested against one criterion. Did we do a good paper that night?

2

FIRST LESSONS

Make the call . . . always make the call.

—DAN DUFFY

The newsroom of *The Irish Times*, into which I arrived in October 1969, seemed to me the most exciting, the most vibrant place in which I could ever hope to be. It was also an excellent training ground for good journalism.

Its appeal did not lie in its aesthetics. It comprised a single, open space, running the length of the third floor of the steel-frame building. The four-storey block had been put up by Cramptons, the Dublin building firm, following the fire that destroyed the old *Irish Times* premises in 1951.

The 'Front Office' stood on Westmoreland Street, almost facing Bewley's café. Other commercial departments faced on to D'Olier Street. But the editorial departments and the Caseroom, where the compositors worked setting type and making up pages, looked on to the narrow Fleet Street through iron-framed windows.

Across Fleet Street lay the Pearl Bar, Bowe's and the Fleet Bar—three oases to which *Irish Times* staffers would have recourse, depending on their disposition, their credit-worthiness and their taste. The Pearl was patronised by editorial only. The Fleet's clientele included journalists, sales staff, printers and others. Bowe's was where *Irish Times* journalists tended to take visitors. High above them all, over a bookie's was The Irish Times Club. Of this last institution—more anon.

There was little natural light in the editorial offices fronting onto Fleet Street. Fluorescent strips burned night and day, suspended among Cramptons' open steel beams. The walls were an oily green with a permanent patina of nicotine, dust and particles of ink and newsprint from the press hall on the ground floor. The place was always pleasantly warm, although in high summer it could become stuffy.

Reporters were located at one end of the floor, grouped around plain wooden tables that seated four people. Sub-editors were at the other end, working at a series of similar tables, arranged in a hollow rectangle. Telephone wires dangled from the ceiling, one to each reporter's desk so that four reporters shared a telephone.

I was on my way to my first day's work as a trainee reporter, complete with spiral-bound notebook and pencil. It was 10 o'clock in the morning. As I crossed Westmoreland Street under the Tom Moore statue, three Dublin Fire Brigade tenders, along with a rescue unit, swept around the corner of College Street, sirens wailing and blue lights flashing. I saw the tense, grim faces of the firemen as the powerful vehicles thundered past Trinity College.

A man crossing the street with me nodded knowingly towards the screaming convoy. 'Shockin' news, isn't it?' 'What do you mean?' I asked. 'Oh, I hear the Liberties is ablaze. It started in a factory or somethin',' he shrugged. I could scarcely believe my luck. My first day on the job and the city was in conflagration! I raced into the building and flew up the two flights of concrete stairs to the newsroom.

A frail-looking gentleman of perhaps 60 years of age, wearing a tweed jacket, with rimmed glasses perched on his nose, sat at the newsdesk, reading *The Irish Press*. I had expected to find Donal Foley, the news editor. I went over to the gentleman who was peering at me over the rim of his glasses.

'I'm Brady, the new trainee,' I said, trying to sound calm even though I had first-hand information that Dublin was burning outside.

'Who?'

'Conor Brady. I'm the new trainee reporter. Mr Foley told me to start this morning.'

The elderly gentleman chuckled and put down his *Irish Press*. 'It's the first I've heard about that. I'm Dan Duffy, assistant news editor. I'm afraid Mr Foley is on holidays. In the Balearic Islands.' He enunciated the words 'Balearic Islands' slowly, emphasising each syllable, as though he required me to appreciate that the news editor was a man who would be found only at a holiday destination so exotic.

'Well, he told me to turn up today,' I hurried my response. 'And, by the way, Mr Duffy, there's some sort of big disaster just taking place right now. There's a convoy of fire engines gone screaming down Dame Street with a rescue unit. Shouldn't I get out there, grab a taxi or something and follow them?'

Dan Duffy raised his eyebrows. 'Then, it's a good job we have a fine young fella like yourself here to help out.' He gestured with a thumb towards an empty desk. 'Before you rush off in all directions, just put a call through to the Brigade Headquarters and see what the story is.'

Pulse racing, I dialled Tara Street fire station. A broad Dublin accent answered. 'Good mornin' . . . Fire Brigade.'

'Conor Brady, *Irish Times* newsroom here.' (It felt wonderful to hear myself say that.) 'Is there something big happening?'

'Naw. Hardly turned a wheel all mornin' since the shift started.' I was baffled. 'But you've just sent three engines and a rescue unit up Dame Street with sirens and lights?' 'Ah, that?' came the reply. 'It's just some oul' wan in Pimlico with a saucepan on fire. The husband had it out in the yard by the time our lads got there.'

I put the 'phone down and went back dejectedly to Dan Duffy who had resumed his study of *The Irish Press*. 'It's only a saucepan fire . . . and it's been put out.'

'It's just as well you made the call, then, isn't it,' he said. 'Make the call, Mr Brady . . . always make the call,' he repeated, not unkindly.

It was my first lesson in real journalism. Never assume. Always make the call.

————

The first half of the day is generally quiet in a morning newspaper. But by mid-afternoon on my first day, the *Irish Times* newsroom was hectic. Reporters jostled for chairs and typewriters (there was never enough of either). They bawled into the telephones—when they could get their turn at these precious instruments from their colleagues. The racket from the typewriters was frightful. Most of the men and all of the women were smoking ceaselessly.

Everybody seemed pretty old, I reckoned, certainly over 25. I was confirmed in that estimate a couple of days later when I discovered a message on the notice board, announcing that Maeve Binchy, John Horgan and Mary Maher were all celebrating their thirtieth birthdays. And all were invited to a party at the Four Courts Hotel.

People rushed in and out of the newsroom all the time, carrying notebooks and bits of paper. Copy boys were ferrying files and photographs from one area to another. In a row of booths along the wall, three or four women with headphones worked the copy-telephones, typing reports from correspondents around the country and abroad. When they were not taking copy, one or two of them knitted, their needles click-clacking through the din.

Things seemed to reach a peak just before 5 o'clock. This was the appointed hour for the main editorial conference of the day. The newsdesk staff were frantically typing copies of the evening schedule—a full list of the content for the next day's editions, department by department.

At 5 o'clock, the heads of the various departments would troop into the editor's office, just off the newsroom, for a meeting that might last anything up to half an hour or even three quarters. It was unheard of for junior staffers like myself to venture in there. I wondered what went on.

The two potentates of the newsroom, the news editor and the chief sub-editor, had their command posts at opposite ends of the floor. I was to learn that reporters and sub-editors were the two irreconcilable elements of a common enterprise—getting the paper out. Tensions were often apparent. Sub-editors had the ultimate power to determine how and where a reporter's copy might appear. But it seemed to me that reporters had all the fun, out on stories and following the excitement.

My first few days were spent under the watchful eye of Gerry Mulvey, the deputy news editor who was in charge of the newsdesk in Foley's absence. Gerry Mulvey was a veteran newsman, conscientious, informed and demanding. He had a perpetually worried look about him and he had a habit of chewing paper clips. I learned much from him and later we became good friends even though he was old enough to be my father. If Dan Duffy's motto was 'always make the call,' Gerry's was 'check the file.' He had an encyclopaedic memory. But he never trusted memory alone.

The emphasis in the newsroom was on accuracy, accuracy and accuracy. Gerry Mulvey, Dan Duffy and Jack Fagan—the youngest of the team of news editors—were stern taskmasters.

That emphasis was matched at the other end of the room where the sub-editors held sway. The chief sub-editor was Noel Fee, a serious man of few words, with the eye of a hawk. He presided like a stern magistrate at the top of the rectangle of tables where his underlings sat, processing the copy that had been typed by the reporters. He rather frightened me. But young sub-editors who worked under him spoke of his kindness.

Many of the sub-editors appeared to be quite a bit older than the reporters. They included veteran journalists who had retired on small pensions or none and who were employed under contract to do a limited number of nights each month at *The Irish Times*. Most of the subs (the abbreviation was universally applied) were people with well-stocked minds. They were highly literate and conscientious to a fault.

There was a marked contrast between the working atmosphere of the reporters' area and that of the subs' area. The reporters were noisy, garrulous and hurried. They had a fairly relaxed relationship with their newsdesk supervisors. The subs, in contrast, were low-key, concentrated and generally calm—at least until final deadlines drew near. Their relationship with their boss, Noel Fee, was closer to that of apprentices with their master.

The subs seemed a disciplined lot, compared to the rather rumbustious reporters. They worked quietly, intently. Noel Fee's senior deacons, assistant chief subs, were Peter Tynan O'Mahony, Niall Fallon and Michael Devine. Peter's father, 'Pussy' O'Mahony (so called because he liked to keep a cat in his office), was for many years general manager of *The Irish Times*, and his brother was Dave Allen, the comedian.

There were other keen and intent young men who were to go on to senior rank—Pat O'Hara, Gerry Smyth, Malachy Logan and Joe Breen.

Most of the subs brought their own dictionaries to work. They used the Oxford and Webster's dictionaries and some would carry a Roget's *Thesaurus*. But their bible was the Style Book which laid down rules for the use of English in *The Irish Times*.

I never learned the authorship of the Style Book that was in use when I joined the paper. It ran to about 200 pages and set out everything an *Irish Times* journalist should know about the preparation of copy for publication in the newspaper.

It laid down the correct style for describing the various functionaries of Church and State. An *Irish Times* report could not open with the words, 'Taoiseach Seán Lemass . . .' The correct form was 'The Taoiseach, Mr Lemass . . .' One could not refer to 'The Irish Army . . .' It was simply 'The Army . . .' There were precise instructions on how honours, decorations and academic distinctions were to be described. Nobody was ever 'conferred with' a degree in *The Irish Times*. The degree was 'conferred upon' the person.

A separate section set out the correct usage of words that were commonly misspelled elsewhere or misused. 'Apprise' was not the same as 'appraise'. A convoy of motor vehicles was not a 'cavalcade' but a 'motorcade'. To 'decimate' was not the same as to 'devastate'. The capital of Malta was not 'Valetta' but 'Valletta'.

Too many reporters, I learned in time, were free and easy with the Style Book rules. In fact very few reporters even had a copy. Some seemed to make it almost a badge of honour to ignore the rules and to 'let the subs clean it up'. Over the years, my sympathies increasingly lay on the side of the subs.

George Burrows was one of the subs. He was a learned man. He was the Ireland correspondent of *The Daily Telegraph* and he spent much of his time filing copy to London. But he was a master at his craft. He was well-known as a writer and broadcaster on wildlife and on fishing in particular.

Peter Tynan O'Mahony was a dour perfectionist, obsessed with accuracy and, in particular, geographical accuracy. I saw him explode one night when he received a piece of copy that purported to locate the town of Buttevant in Co Limerick. 'The most ignorant peasant in the slums knows that Buttevant is in Cork,' he hissed at the guilty reporter.

Peadar O'Curry was one of the veteran subs. He had been editor of *The Irish Catholic*, was fluent in Irish and had a reputed full mastery of Latin and Greek grammar. By the time I joined the newspaper he had already sustained a stroke which left his face partially paralysed and he was obliged to walk with a stick.

———

One day during my first few weeks I was assigned to cover the funeral of a man who had been a prominent member of the Dublin business community. Gerry Mulvey patiently instructed me in the protocol of reporting a funeral. The first sentence always began: 'The funeral took place yesterday, at such-and-such a cemetery, of Mr So-and-so, who died in such-and-such a hospital . . .' etc. Next had to come the details of the eminence, celebrity or public stature that had warranted the report of his obsequies in the newspaper. 'The late Mr So-and-so was for many years a director of the Acme Trading Company and was prominent in Dublin golfing circles,' or whatever. There followed a list of those who had attended the service, carefully arranged in precedence and rank but beginning with the next-of-kin and the name of the celebrant or minister. Finally, one then added details of the service.

The day was wet and I was thoroughly soaked at the funeral. But I completed my report, assiduously ranking colonels ahead of commandants and monsignors ahead of parish priests and put it in the copy box on the newsdesk. Gerry Mulvey passed it for accuracy and a copy boy transported it to the chief sub who, in turn, sent it to Peadar O'Curry for final editing.

A few minutes later I heard O'Curry's distinctive Northern accent calling from the subs' area. 'Mr Brady. A moment, if you please.' I left my desk and walked down to where he sat. 'Yes, Mr O'Curry.'

'Mr Brady, you have prepared an excellent account of this funeral.'

'Thank you.'

'Save for one matter.'

'What's that, Mr O'Curry?'

'You say the choir sang a hymn called "The Lord is My Shepherd."'

'Yes, Mr O'Curry, I heard them sing it.'

'I doubt it very much, Mr Brady. I doubt it. Now would you kindly go to the library upstairs and bring down a copy of *Hymns Ancient and Modern*.'

I went to the third floor and signed out a copy of the book. O'Curry opened it, glanced at the index and turned to the relevant page. 'Now, Mr Brady, you'll see that there is indeed a hymn that you may have heard. But it is not called "The Lord *is* my Shepherd". It's called "*The Lord's* my Shepherd".'

I admit that I got angry. 'Ah, for the love of God, just change the bloody thing. You're not the one who was out in the rain. Who'll notice it?'

O'Curry leaned over the page and made the change with a heavy pencil. 'That's not the point, Mr Brady. It would be wrong. And nothing should be wrong in *The Irish Times* if a little bit of extra effort can make it right.'

3

| EARLIER *TIMES*

In The Irish Times, *the excesses of language too common in Irish journalism have been sedulously avoided.*
  —*The Progress of British Newspapers in the Nineteenth Century*

In the 1950s, the heyday of the satirical magazine *Dublin Opinion*, there were occasional, gently–mocking references to *The Irish Times*. One hilarious, full-page cartoon purported to depict life in the editorial offices. Everyone wore a silk top hat. The messenger boys all had MA after their names. One was reading Ovid. A huddle of sub-editors was conversing in Latin. And a liveried functionary was telling a gentleman visitor that, no, he could not see '*the editah*' because '*the editah*' had 'gone out to Kingstown'.

There were many aspects of *The Irish Times* organisation that evoked its Protestant heritage when I joined in 1969. Perhaps half the company's senior business staff and about one third of the editorial staff were Protestant. The principal shareholders were Protestant. Journalists' duties included detailed coverage of the doings of Protestant-endowed institutions and charities like the Liberty Creche, Simpson's Hospital and the wonderfully-named Sick and Indigent Roomkeepers' Society.

By the time I arrived there was no discernible denominational bias. Catholic, Protestant and Dissenter (and there were plenty of those) mingled happily. There was a lively social scene, including a cricket club, a bridge club and—for a while —mixed football leagues. That meant males and females, as well as Catholics and Protestants. Some of the young Protestant men on the commercial staff were enthusiastic organisers for parties and for club events. I liked the sense of fun I found in people like Derek McCullagh, a young accountant and Iain Pratt, who went on to become company secretary.

At a time when few university graduates entered journalism, *The Irish Times* always had a few Trinity men. Others had come through the English public school system. Some had served as officers in Her Majesty's forces. George Leitch, who had been chief photographer, had served as an aerial reconnaissance officer with the Royal Flying Corps in World War I.

There had always been a few titles among the journalists through the middle decades of the century. Patrick Campbell was to become Lord Glenavy. Hugh

O'Neill was heir to the title of Lord Rathcavan. Sir John Arnott, whose family had controlled the newspaper for more than 70 years, had been London editor.

An *Irish Times* had been published briefly in Dublin between 1823 and 1825. But it did not endure. In March 1859, however, the title was revived as a thrice-weekly publication by 29-year-old Major Lawrence E. Knox. In its first editorial it committed itself to 'faithfully reflecting the opinions of the most independent, intelligent and truly progressive portion of Irish society . . .'

The Irish Times had been a Protestant newspaper since its foundation in 1859. But contrary to latter-day belief, its influence and support did not lie primarily among the landed classes. It was more likely to be read in the vicarage or the bank manager's residence than in the big house. Nor was it always a unionist newspaper. Its founder, Major Knox, had stood for the Westminster parliament as a candidate for Isaac Butt's Home Rule Party.

The first two editors were doctors of divinity from Trinity College and both were Fellows of the College. Dr George Frederick Shaw held the editorship for no more than the first three issues. As a thrice-weekly publication, this would have meant that his editorship lasted just a week. He was a close friend of Abraham ("Bram") Stoker, the creator of *Dracula*. It was said of Shaw that although he added greatly to the entertainment at Trinity College, he added little to its learning.

He was immediately succeeded by his brother-in-law and 'best substitute', Dr George B. Wheeler. Wheeler held the editorship until his death in 1887. He was also Church of Ireland minister at the parish of Ballysax, near the Curragh, in Kildare. Unhappily, he was killed when his carriage overturned one evening near Newbridge as he returned from his parish to take up his other occupation of 'labouring at the press'. Pride of place was apparently given at his funeral to the recently-formed 'Irish Times Brass Band'.

Wheeler was succeeded as editor by Robert Scott who, in turn, was succeeded by Algernon Lockyer. Lockyer was editor until 1904 when John Edward Healy took over the chair.

After Major Knox's early death from scarletina in 1873, the newspaper was sold by his widow to Sir John Arnott, MP, former Lord Mayor of Cork and eponymous proprietor of the department store. The sale price was an impressive £35,000. Arnott committed the newspaper to the inculcation of 'union, peace and goodwill amongst all creeds and classes', and to 'laying the foundation of well-grounded hopes for our country's future'.

In March 1882 Arnott transferred the newspaper from its original home in No 4 Lower Abbey Street to the address at 31 Westmoreland Street which location—albeit with different frontages and variations in curtileges—remained the home of *The Irish Times* for the next 100 years.

After its takeover by Sir John Arnott and his descendants, it became the newspaper of the Dublin mercantile and administrative class—by definition, predominantly Protestant and unionist. At least one Arnott remained on the board until 1958 with the death of Sir Lauriston Arnott. It lost its liberal, Home Rule ethos under the Arnotts. But it maintained its cosmopolitan, international outlook—from an imperial perspective, of course.

The fortunes of *The Irish Times* had declined once the new Irish state came into existence in 1922. The Protestant population of the Free State (the Republic from 1949) dwindled steadily and with it the natural readership of the newspaper. It was quipped in the 1950s that if one wanted to measure the falling readership of *The Irish Times* on any given day, one simply counted the names in the deaths column. Advertising dropped too. As business and industry moved increasingly into the hands of the expanding Catholic middle-classes, *The Irish Times* had fewer friends in the boardrooms where advertising budgets were decided.

In 1954, the bulk of the Arnott shareholding was sold to a number of Dublin businessmen that included Frank Lowe, George Hetherington and Ralph and Philp Walker. Ralph Walker was a partner in Hayes and Sons, the firm of solicitors that still handles litigation for *The Irish Times*. Frank Lowe became chairman of the company.

In spite of changes of proprietorship and, in the years after World War II, adverse trading conditions, it remained a fine newspaper. The editor from 1904 to 1934 was John Edward Healy, who succeeded Algernon Lockyer. Healy was a barrister and a former teacher at Alexandra College.

He steered *The Irish Times* through the turbulent years of the Great War (1914-1918) and the upheavals that created two new states on the island of Ireland. His editorial policy was staunchly conservative and pro-British but he simultaneously adapted the newspaper to the new realities. He ensured full coverage of the new Dáil and Senate and of the other institutions and trappings of the new state.

———

When he died in 1934, Healy was succeeded by his deputy, Robert Maire ('Bertie') Smyllie. Smyllie was also staunchly pro-British but he had an unconventional, artistic streak that gave the newspaper a vigour and vitality that often challenged the establishment values of two increasingly inward-looking, sectarian states, North and South. Like his predecessor and mentor, John Edward Healy, he also recognised the importance of world news coverage, albeit from the perspective of a Britannia that still had an empire and whose navy still ruled the waves—or some of them.

Smyllie's *Irish Times* was beset by difficulties. War-time censorship imposed enormous burdens and placed daily frustrations before the editor and his senior staff. There was little money to develop the newspaper. Indeed, a fire that destroyed much of the premises in 1950 was something of a godsend, since it enabled the company to re-build and to acquire a new press.

Two brief editorships, those of Alec Newman and Alan Montgomery, followed Smyllie's tenure which ended with his death from diabetes and heart-failure in

1954. He had suffered from poor health since his days in a German internment camp during World War I and he was worn out from wrangles with the military censors who scrutinised the pages nightly, excising anything they considered inimical to Ireland's neutrality or constituting 'intelligence' that could be of use to one or other of the warring sides.

Smyllie was happiest in literary and artistic circles. Paradoxically, he knew W.B. Yeats well but never got on with him. Smyllie was much the younger man —by 30 years. Both had Sligo connections. Smyllie's Scottish father had started his working life as a printer and became editor of the Unionist *Sligo Times*. Yeats's poetry was informed by the landscape, the traditions and the people of Sligo. But their perspectives on the evolution of the Irish State and the upheavals that preceded its foundation were very different.

Smyllie was sorely traduced by Yeats in the poem *Why Should Old Men Not Be Mad?*

> Why should old men not be mad?
> Some have known a likely lad
> That had a sound fly-fisher's wrist
> Turn to a drunken journalist.

According to Norman Jeffares and Augustine Martin, two of the leading authorities on Yeats, 'Bertie' Smyllie was the 'drunken journalist'. Certainly he was a regular, nightly drinker. And there is no doubt that he was frequently diminished in his capacity due to alcohol. But it was not simply a question of drink. His health was such that he was often exhausted. He was overweight and he was diabetic. He laboured to get through his daily and nightly routine. He was sometimes incoherent but it was more often as a result of over-exertion with limited physical resources.

Yeats may never have forgiven him for telling the tale of the poet's response when Smyllie, in 1923, had been deputed to tell him Reuters was reporting that he had won the Nobel prize. 'This is a great honour for Ireland,' Smyllie had said, 'a wonderful day for us all . . .' 'For God's sake Smyllie, get to the point,' came the response from Yeats. 'How much is it worth?'

In August 1996, Michael Keohane, who was president of the Yeats Society, invited me to perform the official opening at the 37th Yeats Summer School in Sligo. I took particular care, in my address, to put the record straight about the poor health of the maligned 'drunken journalist' who was one of my predecessors in office.

By the end of Smyllie's editorship, the fortunes of the company and the newspaper were approaching their nadir. Official circulation figures show the paper selling around 35,000 copies each day. But on some days it may have been as low as 25,000. Advertising revenue had dried to a trickle. *The Irish Times*, it was quipped, had become the house journal of the 'stranded gentry'.

Independent Newspapers Ltd, owned by the Murphy family and The Irish Press Ltd, controlled by the De Valeras, were strong and prosperous by the standards of the day. But The Irish Times Ltd, and with it, Dublin's longest-established daily newspaper appeared to be in terminal decline. However, when it seemed as if the lights would probably have to be turned out, two men arrived whose individual acuity and whose pragmatic collaboration were to turn *The Irish Times* around and start it on the road back to stability.

——

Thomas Bleakley McDowell was 38 when he became a director of The Irish Times Ltd. From a middle-class, Ulster background, McDowell had been commissioned into the Royal Ulster Rifles and assigned to the British Army's legal services, serving in the department of the Judge Advocate General. He qualified as a barrister. After the war, promoted to captain, he served in Austria with the occupying allied forces.

When he left the British army in 1955 he took his majority and for the rest of his life he was '*Major* McDowell'. The business world beckoned to a young man with energy and talent, albeit with little money, and he secured a post with Great Universal Stores. He saw business opportunities in Dublin and moved there to operate a clothing company—Two Owls Ltd.

Some time later, he had an opportunity to buy shares in The Irish Times Ltd. It was a high-risk proposition. The company was teetering and the investment must have appeared hazardous in the extreme. But he put his money and his confidence into the newspaper. In 1962 he became chief executive of the company.

Robert John Douglas Gageby was also of Northern background. Five years older than McDowell, he had been raised in Belfast. Before the advent of the Irish Free State, his father had been a junior-ranking civil servant in Dublin, where Douglas was born. After the new State came into existence, the family moved to Belfast where the father enrolled in the Northern Ireland Civil Service.

Douglas Gageby came back to Dublin as a student at Trinity College and on the outbreak of World War II joined the Irish army as a private soldier. He was commissioned, given the rank of lieutenant and assigned to the Intelligence Corps because he had read German at Trinity.

When the war ended, he went to work for The Irish Press Ltd and began his career as a journalist. Meanwhile, he married Dorothy Lester, daughter of a successful Irish diplomat (and former journalist), Seán Lester, who had been the League of Nations High Commissioner in the Polish city of Danzig (Gdansk).

Gageby was deeply patriotic, embracing with an almost religious zeal the Irish State that his father had left behind. He worked on the newly-launched *Sunday Press* and when the company decided to build on its market success by launching an evening newspaper, he was appointed as the first editor of *The Evening Press*. He brought extraordinary energy and a sense of modernity and style to the newspaper, overshadowing the staid *Evening Mail* and the *Evening Herald*.

In 1959, Gageby left The Irish Press Ltd and transferred to The Irish Times Ltd where he initially held the position of Joint Managing Director along with George Hetherington. Thus the point of convergence began between the talents of Gageby and McDowell. Gageby also invested in the company, buying a one-fifth share of the ordinary stock.

In 1963 Alan Montgomery vacated the editorship to become press relations manager with Guinness's, the brewing company. He had been asked to sit on the interview board, screening applicants for the job. When no fully suitable candidate emerged, somebody suggested that Montgomery himself might be interested. When he learned that it paid a great deal more than the editorship of *The Irish Times*, he readily departed Westmoreland Street for St James's Gate.

Gageby, championed by chief executive McDowell, was appointed editor by the board. He already held a directorship and made it a condition of his appointment that he would retain it as editor. That was unique in Ireland at the time, although it was common practice in London and in the leading European newspapers.

McDowell ran the business side of the organisation, while Gageby set about reinventing the newspaper. It was a successful synergy. Both agreed that the best way forward was to put every available pound into developing the content of the newspaper.

Ireland was changing. The initial shoots of growth had appeared as the first and second programmes for economic expansion, devised by T.K. Whitaker and driven by Seán Lemass, stimulated the economy. The educational system was expanding and university enrolment was increasing.

There was a growing conviction in political and administrative circles that Ireland had to define its future within the framework of the European Economic Community.

Traditional values, unchallenged for decades, were coming under scrutiny. The Second Vatican Council, called by Pope John XXIII, was changing the face of Catholicism across the world. Irish television—Telefís Éireann—had started in 1961 and was opening up debate on issues of personal morality and received social values.

Ireland was taking early steps in a great journey of transition. It was about to leave behind values, institutions, class-structures and authority systems that had been in place since after the Famine. It was crying out for a newspaper that would chronicle and reflect these changes while providing a forum for dialogue. *The Irish Times* was ideally placed to meet these needs.

Gageby set about modernising the newspaper, modelling it in part on the London broadsheets and in part on serious German and French titles. His design and layout sense was informed by *The Times* and *The Daily Telegraph*. He liked the way in which *Frankfurter Allgemeine* and *Le Monde* provided daily platforms for intellectual discourse and argument.

The advent of Telefís Éireann was a challenge to the advertising revenues of *The Irish Times*, as it was to all Irish newspapers. But it was a boon for Gageby's and McDowell's plans to revamp the newspaper's team of journalists. Perhaps a dozen senior reporters left the newsroom to join the television channel's news operation. Lesser editors would have regarded this as a problem, but Gageby saw it as an opportunity to bring in fresh talent.

He was fortunate in having as his news editor, Donal Foley, a creative, garrulous and iconoclastic career journalist, from Waterford. A fluent Irish speaker, Foley had an enormous sense of the country in all its moods and flavours. He was a passionate follower of Gaelic games. He loved Irish literature, music and dance. He had an instinctive interest in politics with a decidedly left-wing perspective. A spell in London, during which he had served in the newspaper's Fleet Street office, had yielded formative friendships with British labour party luminaries and trade unionists.

Gageby worked closely with Foley in selecting the talent that would make the new *Irish Times*. Together, they carefully used their resources to assemble a team that reflected a much broader Ireland than that of Protestant, middle-class Dublin. They aimed for a spread of backgrounds and a variety of interests. They recruited some from the better provincial papers, North and South. Others were spotted and recruited from the university newspapers such as *Trinity News* or, as in my own case, *Campus UCD News*. Over the years, quite a few migrated, like Gageby himself—and Donal Foley—from *The Irish Press*. Some came from the *Cork Examiner*.

The Irish Times had always had a scattering of women writers since the 1930s. But they were not numerous and they tended to be allocated to what were assumed to be areas of female interest, such as social diaries. Foley was particularly adept at spotting potential in female journalists. He had an easy, comfortable rapport with women that was not universal in Irish men of his generation. Women generally liked him and were willing to push themselves to great lengths to get a story or to complete an assignment. The women journalists of *The Irish Times* became a powerful cohort within the institution. They were energetic, courageous and assertive and they contributed greatly to the newspaper's success in this period.

Gageby's strategy for the newspaper was grounded on four or five principles.

The newspaper had to have spread or reach. That is, it had to broaden its range of content. There had to be something in there for everyone. Thus, new sections were added, such as an Irish language news section, *Tuarascáil*, under Foley's hand.

The newspaper had to have depth and authority. So he extended the numbers of specialist correspondents, appointing bright people, often but not always young graduates, to cover subjects such as religion, education, science and so on.

The newspaper had to have strong, clear editorial positions. These did not have to be conclusive or indeed consistent. But they had to say something about the issues of the day. 'Readers should always be able to pick up the newspaper, no matter what's going on, on a given day, and say "I wonder what *The Irish Times* is saying about that?'" he used to insist.

The newspaper's first duty was to print the news. But it also had to entertain and stimulate. Gageby expanded coverage of literature and the arts. He would frequently give over a valuable news page for pictures of the Paris Spring or Autumn collections.

His one blind spot was sport in which he had not the remotest interest, beyond rowing—a hangover from Trinity days. The sports editor was not expected to attend the full daily conference and when he did he was not allocated a seat. Nor was his schedule of content read out. Gageby would growl at Paul McWeeney, the sports editor. 'Well, how much space do you want, Paul?' The gentlemanly and diffident McWeeney had a slight stammer. "I wa..was hoping for th..th....three p..p...pages, Douglas.' 'Three pages? Jesus Christ, you'll get two if you're lucky.'

It was also a cardinal tenet of Gageby's editorship that any given day's newspaper, once printed and on the streets, should be put out of mind. Celebrations of triumph or inquests into failure should be as brief as possible. What always mattered was the next day's editions.

———

With the strengthening of the editorial team, with the broadening of content and with a new, vigorous, thrusting attitude infusing the columns, Gageby began to reverse the circulation decline of his newspaper. By the end of 1964, it was comfortably back above 35,000. By 1965 it had reached 40,000. By 1968 it had gone past the magical 50,000 figure. Gageby bustled excitedly around the newsroom the day the 55,000 figure was breached. 'Jesus, we'll have to hold it above 55,000. And we can charge two bob for it!'

Any spare funds were to be put into editorial developments and initiatives. McDowell and Gageby were well served in the implementation of this approach by a young trainee accountant, Louis O'Neill, who later became Managing Director and then Group Chief Executive of The Irish Times.

McDowell and O'Neill managed the finances to ensure that Gageby had the resources he needed. The company had no capital reserves and very little liquid cash. But it was also in the happy position that it had no borrowings. Working conditions were not a priority, so facilities such as canteen, washrooms and toilets were generally poor. McDowell's and Gageby's own offices were also fairly basic and remained so.

O'Neill was not drawn from the Protestant business *cadre* that gave the company many of its business staff. A Catholic and a quiet, sharp-eyed Dubliner, he put himself through his accountancy articles and worked long hours to keep the books balanced, keep the cash flowing and build up the systems and operations that were required in a modern newspaper company. At the end of his career, unhappy differences were to arise between him and McDowell.

But in these years of consolidation his role was vital. He knew the company inside out and often came up with ingenious solutions to problems that arose in the funding of Gageby's editorial plans. Money was found so that foreign coverage was enhanced by taking the wire services of *Agence France Presse* and *The New York Times*. These were in addition to *The Press Association* (PA) and *Reuters* which were London-focused and which viewed events through British eyes.

The newspaper could not aspire to a fulltime staff position in the United States but Gageby contracted Seán Cronin, a New York-based journalist and lecturer, to provide an Irish perspective on American issues. Cronin was a former Irish Army officer who had later become chief-of-staff of the IRA and who had been active in the shambolic Border campaign of the late 1950s. He had a good mind and a fine writing style and he did the newspaper much service.

The newspaper had no staff in mainland Europe. But when Paris erupted in the student-led riots of 1968, Gageby sent Dermot Mullane from the newsroom to cover *les evenements*. In 1971, when Ireland's second application to join the EEC was in train, Fergus Pyle was sent to Paris to open the newspaper's first fulltime bureau outside of Ireland and Britain.

Earlier, in 1966, Pyle had been sent to Belfast and styled with the title 'Northern editor'. It was unheard of at this time for any Dublin newspaper to allocate a journalist of Fergus Pyle's profile and experience to Belfast. Gageby was passionately interested in the North and he may have sensed something of the coming storm, although I am certain that he did not anticipate the thirty year descent into violence that was to follow.

Pyle, who was to succeed Gageby as editor in 1974, blazed a trail of reportage in the North. His great energy and capacity for detail yielded nightly avalanches of copy. It was said that his reports of the parliament at Stormont were longer than the official Hansard version.

It seemed as if *The Irish Times* was doing something new and exciting every day. The other Dublin newspapers seemed conservative and lacking in inspiration by comparison with what was happening in Westmoreland Street.

The Irish Times team of specialists led the field. And even where they were matched by able counterparts in other newspapers, they seemed somehow to have a *cachet* about them, as part of a newspaper that was seen to be on the move.

John Horgan was the guru of both religious and educational coverage. Later, the paper's educational coverage was led by the indomitable, committed and hugely-energised Christina Murphy.

John Healy's 'Backbencher', an irreverent, provocative 'insider's guide to politics' was a national talking point. More conventional political coverage was provided by Michael McInerney and Dick Walsh.

The irrepressible Maeve Binchy was women's editor. Her turn of phrase and her effervescent writing style presaged her later emergence as one of the most successful and prolific writers of popular fiction in the twentieth century.

Foley had a talent for coming up with simple but compelling ideas for the content of the paper. He hired Nell McCafferty from Derry and sent her to do a personalised daily diary of what was happening in the Dublin criminal courts. Her coverage broke all the long-standing conventions that had sanitised courts coverage. It shocked and disquieted readers and helped to stimulate important reforms in the way the courts and the criminal justice system were operated.

Terence De Vere White was literary editor. He built a coterie of critics and reviewers that made the weekly books page essential reading among the literary community. He also directed the fine arts coverage.

Michael Browner, who died while still in his thirties, was the quiet, authoritative expert on agriculture. The larger-than-life Michael Dillon covered the agricultural markets.

A young Englishman, Michael Viney, began to explore Irish social issues such as poverty, domestic violence, juvenile crime and unemployment. His reports were far out of the ordinary run of Irish journalism, drawing on sociological research and other sources, mainly from the UK. He also shared the editing of the features pages with Donal O'Donovan and Fergus Linehan.

The business pages had an authority and *panache* about them that reflected the personalities of successive editors—Hugh O'Neill, Valentine Lamb and Andrew Whittaker. Later, both Richard Keatinge and Bill Murdoch served as Business Editors under Gageby.

Irish Times critics and contributors became household names. Charles and Carol Acton on music. Theodora Fitzgibbon on food. Brian Fallon on art. Marian Fitzgerald on household affairs. Terry Keane and later Gabrielle Williams on fashion. Ken Gray was television critic. Another ex-army man, Séamus Kelly, a one-time actor who played a bit-part in *Moby Dick* took over the daily 'Irishman's Diary'.

Gageby appointed David Nowlan, a medical doctor, recently returned from abroad, as medical correspondent. Nowlan was a natural-born journalist and his professional qualifications brought authority to the role. His principal interest in coming the The Irish Times, he later acknowledged, was to write about theatre, which he loved. He later served for many years as the newspaper's chief theatre critic, succeeding Séamus Kelly.

A young Irish-American journalist, Mary Maher, arrived from *The Chicago Tribune*, and enlivened the news pages with her combination of lyrical prose and sharp-eyed analysis of Irish social conditions.

Although it rarely got sufficient credit for it, the paper's sports section was staffed with fine writers that included Edmund Van Esbeck, Paddy Downey, Peter Byrne and Paul McWeeney. Later they were joined by writers like Dermot Gilleece, Seán Kilfeather and Michael O'Farrell.

With the advent of the troubles in Northern Ireland, a new dimension of news coverage began. The newspaper's reportage of events in the North became widely recognised as comprehensive and generally even-handed. It absorbed enormous resources however. Significantly, and perhaps as a result of the commitment to the North, *The Irish Times* never sent staff correspondents to the Vietnam war or to cover the 'Prague Spring' in Czechoslovakia over these years. In 1970, I was assigned to travel to Vietnam with Seán MacBride but that assignment foundered. It was the only attempt by the newspaper to put a reporter into the field in what was undoubtedly the world news story of the day.

By the early 1970s, the resuscitation of *The Irish Times* and its place in a newly-emerging Ireland were assured. Circulation, though small by comparison with the *Irish Independent* or *The Irish Press*, was climbing, while the others were static or falling. Circulation numbers were crucial to the newspaper. But what confirmed *The Irish Times* as a valuable property by this time was its penetration of the influential and affluent middle classes—the ABC1s as they were categorised by the advertising and marketing industries.

In April 1974 it was announced that the ordinary shareholders, McDowell, Gageby, George Hetherington and Ralph and Philip Walker, had sold their shares to a newly-created entity, The Irish Times Trust Ltd. The aim of the Trust, it was declared, was to maintain *The Irish Times* as an independent newspaper and to ensure that it could not be bought by any commercial interest, whether Irish or foreign. Each shareholder received £325,000, a sum equivalent to perhaps €10 million in today's money values.

The Trust was to be chaired by McDowell who would continue to hold the functions of chairman and chief executive of The Irish Times Ltd, the company that operated *The Irish Times*. A number of trustees were to be appointed, drawn from various sectors of Irish society, North and South. These would hold the ordinary voting shares collectively. Nobody could buy or sell the shares.

However, The Irish Times Trust Ltd had no money. In order to acquire the ordinary shares from their five owners, it had to borrow from the Bank of Ireland. The bank advanced a loan that would be equivalent to perhaps €30 million in today's values. It was a large sum. Even if the newspaper were to make profits at the rate of £400,000 a year, it would be more than a decade before the debt would be paid back. And the onus would be on the operating company to pay it off.

Staff reaction to the setting up of the Trust was generally favourable. Things were good and getting better at *The Irish Times*. Pay was rising in real terms for all and conditions and opportunities, especially for journalists, were improving. A partially discordant note was struck by the newspaper's own business editor, Andrew Whittaker, who raised questions about the wisdom of taking on the indebtedness.

The Trust structure was to shape *The Irish Times* for the remainder of the century and see it into the twenty-first century, albeit with very significant modifications in 2002. It was the framework within which I was to operate as editor when I succeeded Gageby as the eleventh person to hold the editorship.

4

'IT SURE BEATS HONEST WORK'

—*Washington Post* editor, BEN BRADLEE, on journalism, in the film *All the President's Men.*

I did not set out to be editor of anything. But I was very fortunate. Some good opportunities came my way and sometimes I realised I could hardly turn them down—although there were one or two that I did.

There was some newspapering in the family. My mother's cousin and friend, Gertie Harrington from Castletownbere in West Cork, married Michael Spillane, a journalist on *The Freeman's Journal* who later became Clerk of the Dáil. Two of his sons—by extension, my cousins—went into newspapers. Des was a reporter and later chief librarian at the *Irish Independent.* Terence worked in *The Irish Times* advertising department and later became proprietor and editor of a successful magazine serving the hardware trade. A third Spillane brother, Eimear, worked in advertising.

Although my cousins were older, I always enjoyed meeting them and in particular loved to hear Des tell newspaper stories. As a schoolboy I would often visit him at the cuttings library at Independent House and I would spend hours poring through old files. I found myself fascinated by the sheer volume of news—things that happened, made the headlines and were then forgotten about.

There were teachers, doctors, religious and lawyers in the family. My father was one of a small group of young men brought in to be commissioned as Garda superintendents after the civil war. He had trained at the Marino Institute to be a teacher. He taught French, Irish and English. Then he became a member of the Irish Volunteers. His file in Garda Headquarters says he was in 'Intelligence'. I never found out what that involved. He did not take either side in the Civil War.

My mother, Amy (née MacCarthy), set out to be a pharmacist. But, as was customary in that era, became a full-time housewife on her marriage.

My father's health was poor and he died in 1962 when I was 13. I went to boarding school at Mount Saint Joseph Abbey, the Cistercian College in Roscrea, after he died. I had thought I might go to college and study architecture but I was hesitant about imposing the costs of a lengthy course on my mother. So I opted for a shorter course in arts at University College Dublin, though without any idea of how I might make a career.

Mount Saint Joseph Abbey was a fine school, the only full secondary school in the world run by Trappist monks. Not being very good at sports, I drifted to other interests. The school had a thriving magazine, *The Vexillum*, run by boys of the senior house through the school *praesidium* or branch of the Legion of Mary.

I have to admit that I was not too enthusiastic about the Legion's spiritual activities. But I thought *The Vexillum* might be fun and I offered my services there. When they turned me down, I went with a couple of other juniors to the President, Fr Patrick, to ask if the junior house could start its own magazine. With remarkable broadmindedness for the time, Patrick agreed. He arranged for us to have use of *Vexillum's* Gestetner copying machine and even offered to pay a local woman who would type the stencils for us.

Alas, *The Junior Journal* did not survive. Four editions were published that year. We rotated the tasks among us. Joe Hayes, who later went on to a distinguished career in the diplomatic service, was the first editor. My turn came in the Easter term of 1963. I still have my copy—the first publication I ever edited. When I reached the senior house I was asked to become editor of *The Vexillum*, by the young monk in charge, Fr Cathaldus. Again, remarkably for the era, there was no censorship or screening of content by the monks either in *The Junior Journal* or *The Vexillum*.

Mount Saint Joseph Abbey also had a quarterly publication, *The Roscrea Review*. Fr Cathaldus was the editor and in my fifth year he asked me to write an account of events in the school for the *Review*. To my astonishment he paid me ten shillings. It was the first time I had been paid for writing and it struck me as odd that one should be paid for doing something one enjoyed so much.

———

UCD in the late 1960s was a vibrant, sometimes turbulent place. The 'Gentle Revolution' was under way. Women students were agitating against the prohibition on their wearing trousers in the libraries. A group calling themselves Students for Democratic Action (SDA) was protesting against the college's authorities about virtually everything. They linked up with a socialist group called the Dublin Housing Action Committee which, in turn, was linked with Sinn Féin. There were daily meetings, speeches, petitions and at one stage the administrative offices of the college were occupied.

The activities of the SDA held little interest for me. But I was interested in the college newspapers, of which *Campus UCD News* was by far the more serious and professional. I offered my services and immediately found myself doing everything from writing news reports to putting up sales posters on Earlsfort Terrace.

Campus, as it was known, was established by John Crimmins, a student from Cork. John had some money and invested it in the newspaper. The chairman of the board was Christina Murphy, who later became education editor and duty editor at *The Irish Times*. Both John and Christina were a little older than the rest of the *Campus* staff and we school-leavers were impressed by what we saw as their more extensive worldly experience. Christina had gone from secondary school in Castlebar, Co Mayo to work in Germany, in order to finance her college education. She was one of the most principled persons I met in journalism.

In my second year, the board offered me the job of editor—unpaid—which I accepted with alacrity. I edited the newspaper through the academic year 1967–1968, being succeeded by Maurice Sweeney who went on to work with *The Irish Press*.

I was fortunate in that my subjects introduced me to three of the best departments in the university—political science, history and (for my first year) English. The Political Science department was especially vibrant, with a cohort of lively, engaged young academics. They included Maurice Manning, later Fine Gael leader in the Seanad and, subsequently, President of the Irish Human Rights Commission, who became a life-long friend.

Being editor of *Campus* opened some unexpected doors. I was telephoned by Ciaran Carty, features editor at the *Sunday Independent* who offered me a bi-weekly column, contributing notes of happenings at UCD at the generous rate of five guineas a time. Some time later, I received a similar call from Michael O'Kane at the *Evening Press* newsdesk who asked me if I would be interested in filing news reports to be paid for on a usage basis. I was and I did.

There was plenty of news in college. Apart from the 'Gentle Revolution' there was a variety of political clubs and societies. Controversial or prominent speakers were regular. The student body also numbered many young men and women who were to figure prominently later in politics and public life—John Bruton, Ruairí Quinn, Eithne FitzGerald (*neé* Ingoldsby), Tony Gregory, to name a few.

Other contemporaries who went on to media careers included Henry Kelly, Gerald Barry, Vincent Browne, Renagh Holohan, Kevin Myers, Frank McDonald, Maurice Sweeney, John Feeney. UCD was then a relatively small campus, based at Earlsfort Terrace, and everybody seemed to know everybody else.

When it came to final year, I still had no firm career plan. I thought the diplomatic service might be interesting so I inquired and they sent me the application forms.

———

One day in Grafton Street I met Henry Kelly, who was a year ahead of me. Tall, thin as a pencil, flamboyant and brimming with confidence, he had been recruited by *The Irish Times* after graduation. He asked me what I was planning to do. I said I thought journalism might be interesting. 'Why don't you go and see Donal Foley, the news editor at the *Times*?' Henry asked. 'I'll tell him you're interested. Telephone him later this week.'

The Irish Times was expanding its editorial staff very rapidly. The Northern troubles were placing heavy demands on newsroom resources. Ireland was now firmly on course to join the EEC. Areas like education, health, justice, social welfare were all in flux. The churches were trying to absorb the aftershocks of Vatican II.

I telephoned Foley who asked me to come and meet him. At the same time, prompted by Michael O'Kane at the *Press*, I sent in a job application to Tim Pat Coogan, the editor of *The Irish Press*. RTÉ was also advertising for news reporters and I applied there too.

I went for interview at RTÉ. It was a daunting experience. The interview panel was chaired by Jim McGuinness, a former IRA man, turned journalist, who had now become head of news. I don't think he liked me one bit. They gave the job to Liam Hourican who went on to become one of the station's most distinguished correspondents. They were right. He was considerably more mature and better-versed in current affairs than I.

Coogan asked me to come down and see him at *The Irish Press*. We had some pleasant exchanges. Then he handed me over to Bill Redmond, the general manager. It did not go well. Redmond clearly did not like me—any more than McGuinness at RTÉ—and I did not take to him. He was a heavy-set man with a jowly face and he did not smile.

He lounged back in his chair behind his desk and peered at my application form, holding it out from him, as if it were coated with some dangerous substance.

'It says here, Mr Brady, that you're studying "political science" above at UCD.'

'I am, Mr Redmond.'

'Well, will you tell me please what use that would be to you here?'

'I suppose it would show I've got some sort of a mind, Mr Redmond.'

He dropped the form on the desk. 'The only thing I'd ask you to show me, Mr Brady, is if you could make me a good pot o' tea.' That ended my career discussions with The Irish Press Ltd.

A few days later, I went to *The Irish Times* to meet Foley. He was mumbling and vague. But as I was to learn, Foley was often like that. A lively imagination and a mind that could move from one issue to another with astonishing alacrity were trapped behind a larynx that only seemed to achieve full elasticity with a few pints on board. 'Better go in and see Douglas, anyway,' he said.

The contrast with *The Irish Press* could not have been greater. Gageby was behind his desk in a sharp blue, tailored shirt with some sort of monogram on the breast pocket. I had never seen such a thing. He wore gold-rimmed glasses that made it difficult to read his eyes. But he radiated energy. He got up from his desk, shook hands and grinned.

'Foley's been speaking well of you. Are you going to come aboard?'

'I hope so.'

'You'll be finished in UCD in September. What sort of degree will you get?'

'A good one, I hope. Politics and history.'

'It doesn't really matter, as long as you finish it. What are you interested in?'

I had submitted some freelance ideas to Donal O'Donovan, the features editor over the previous few weeks. 'Well, I've done some articles on the future development of the university at Belfield for Mr O'Donovan. And I'm doing a three-part series on discontent in the Guards.'

'Hah! Thank God you don't want to write about bloody politics. They all want to be political correspondent. Tell me, are you curious? I mean, if you were in my house and I went out to get you a cup of tea, would you read the letters on my mantlepiece?' 'Yes,' I replied unhesitatingly.

'Good,' he laughed heartily. 'Be here on the first of October.' And so I was.

Over the first year I generally worked a newsroom shift known as 'Evening Town: Coast'. Officially, one finished at 10.30 pm but it was usually later.

My duties included ringing the fire brigades at Tara Street and Dún Laoghaire and the Garda control at Dublin Castle every hour or so. I also checked at intervals with the lifeboat stations around the coast but since they were manned part-time by volunteers the call was often not answered. In between these exercises, the newsdesk plied me with a steady flow of press-releases, scripts from politicians and other items that might or might not make a paragraph in the morning's editions. It was tedious but I learned from it. Gerry Mulvey and his acolytes would coax me through errors of style or detail and always with the injunction: check it out; make the call; never assume.

I was regularly rostered for duty in Belfast. A core group of three or four reporters there had to be augmented from Dublin. The work was exciting but challenging. I found myself working alongside high-profile journalists from the UK, Europe and the US. *Irish Times* staffers generally stayed in the Central Hotel off Royal Avenue. We worked long hours out of a small office in Castle Street, covering the proceedings of the Stormont parliament during the day and the violence on the streets at night. The team kept going on a diet of high-carbohydrate food, alcohol and cigarettes—although I never smoked.

It was sometimes at least potentially dangerous. One night I was driving in an *Irish Press* staff car with Michael Keane, later editor of *The Sunday Press*. In the deeply loyalist Roden Street area, our car collided with a young man who sped through a traffic lights on a motor cycle. As he lay moaning on the ground, blood pouring from his head, a hostile crowd gathered. They recognised our Republic of Ireland number plate and southern accents and the situation threatened to get ugly. When two large RUC constables arrived to escort us from the scene we felt very relieved.

Two days later the young man arrived at the Central Hotel with his head bandaged, along with his father, to apologise to us. It was characteristic of the underlying decency and great courtesy that one so often encounters among the ordinary people of Belfast.

And it was a measure of the unhappy climate at *The Irish Press* that Michael Keane's biggest fear was that it would be discovered in Burgh Quay that an *Irish*

Times reporter had been travelling in one of their staff cars.

The most demanding assignment was covering the violence that followed the introduction of internment without trial in August 1971. Belfast erupted. Scores of dead and wounded filled the casualty departments. Whole streets and estates became battle-zones.

Journalists were rushed from Dublin, London and elsewhere. The skies over the city were filled with smoke. Once darkness fell, the flames from burning buildings and cars were red and yellow against the skyline. Beds were at a premium and we slept on floors and in armchairs. We were on the streets reporting the violence around the clock. We lost track of the killings and shootings.

At a junction near Flax Street Mill at 2 o'clock in the morning I found a platoon of British troops deployed in firing positions. I went over to the lieutenant to ask what was happening. There were two or three whirring noises in the air over my head, like a bird. The officer shouted at me, 'Get down! Get f xxxxxx down.' Although I had done a bit of shooting myself, I did not realise until then that bullets arrive before you hear the shots.

When something resembling order was restored in Belfast I was reassigned to normal duties in Dublin. In the Republic, there was a lot of focus on the condition of the Garda. The gardaí were badly paid, poorly provided for in matters of general welfare and subject to a disciplinary code that still owed much to the Royal Irish Constabulary (RIC) of the nineteenth century. Finally, the Government had set up a commission under Judge Charlie Conroy to recommend new arrangements for pay and operational conditions.

My three articles on the Garda in the summer of 1969 had gone down well. Nobody else in the newspaper was writing in the area and I developed my interest, making extensive contacts with gardaí, civil servants, prison staff, lawyers, judges and others engaged in the criminal justice system. I wrote a lot about crime, justice policy and the social dimensions of crime over this period. There was very little feedback. Ireland was scarcely at the forefront of new thinking in criminal justice.

Early in April 1971, Gageby called me into his office.

'How's your French?'

'Excellent,' I lied, sensing there was something in the air.

'Passport up to date?'

'Of course.'

'Seán MacBride is going to Vietnam, North and South, to inspect POW conditions. He can take a journalist with him.'

MacBride was a prominent Senior Counsel and a former Clann na Poblachta Minister for External Affairs. He was the son of Major John MacBride (executed in 1916) and Maud Gonne and he was a former chief of staff of the IRA. Among his many other *personae* MacBride was also a leading figure in Amnesty International.

It was to be the assignment of a lifetime. North and South Vietnam had mutual exclusion policies so if a traveller arrived in one jurisdiction with a stamp from the other in his passport he would be turned back. Very few journalists —and certainly no Irish ones—had been able to report from both sides. But MacBride had been assured by the Americans and the North Vietnamese that we would be allowed to travel through their respective jurisdictions.

Direct flights between the two capitals, Hanoi and Saigon, did not exist. So it would be necessary to go via Pnom Penh in Cambodia.

MacBride's first language was French and he spoke heavily-accented English. 'Zey bomb ze city szree nights a week,' he told me when I went to visit him at his home at Roebuck, in Clonskeagh. 'Zo, we will not zelay zere.'

I got my medical shots and bought some suitable, light clothing. Two weeks later, with $2,000 worth of travellers cheques and a communications pass authorising me to use either Cable and Wireless or Reuter wire systems, I set off for Paris with MacBride.

All seemed to go well at first. Fergus Pyle, *The Irish Times* correspondent in Paris, took a couple of days off his regular assignments to help with our visits to various embassies and legations. We spent a lot of time sitting on low chairs, drinking green tea with Indo-Chinese gentlemen. There was much shaking of hands and clucking of tongues. I understood little. Even when they spoke in French. 'Iz looking very good,' MacBride said after we had completed our visits. 'I am cerzain zis journey will now go ahead.'

The next day we bought our tickets at Thomas Cook's off the Champs Elysées. Air France from Paris to Moscow. From Moscow to Peking, as it was then known, by Aeroflot. Then—an exciting prospect—by train through Southern China to the North Vietnam border. From Hanoi we would fly to Pnom Penh and from Pnom Penh to Saigon. From Saigon it would be back to Paris.

I still have the tickets.

Two days after we bought them, the South Vietnam embassy said there would be no visas. MacBride and I flew back to Dublin. A controversy had broken out over the treatment of prisoners by the US and South Vietnamese forces. Reports emerged that captured Viet Cong were being confined in conditions of great cruelty in so-called 'tiger-cages'. Clearly it was the wrong time to have Amnesty International and *The Irish Times* come calling.

———

In September I made the most important decision of my life. I married Ann Byron who had been at UCD with me. In fact we had met at secondary school, through the Muintir na Tíre schools' debating league. I was knocked out in the first round. She won the individual speaker award at the finals in Dublin.

A little later I was assigned to the London office for a year to assist the London editor, Jim Downey. Anglo-Irish relations were plunging towards their nadir.

After British paratroopers shot 13 people dead in Derry on Bloody Sunday, 30 January 1972, mobs in Dublin stormed the British Embassy and burned it to the ground. The Irish Ambassador to Britain was withdrawn, down-grading but not breaking off diplomatic relations between Dublin and London.

It was a year of very hard work, long hours and little free time. But the experience was valuable. Jim Downey was an experienced journalist with an intuitive sense of *realpolitik*. He revelled in the Westminster experience and I enjoyed working with him. I became a member of the Westminster Press Gallery and got to know many of the MPs with an interest in Ireland. It was much easier to engage with Northern Ireland MPs like Ian Paisley or John Hume at Westminster than at home.

The Social Democratic and Labour Party (SDLP) abandoned the Stormont parliament and relations broke down completely between the SDLP and the Unionists. But back-channels were established. For a time, I found myself passing messages from the Unionists via Tory MP Norman St John Stevas (later Lord St John of Fawsley) to John Hume. I built good relationships with some of the Labour MPs who were then in opposition, notably Merlyn Rees who later became Secretary of State for Northern Ireland.

I got two good exclusives or 'scoops' while in London.

Responsibility in the British Cabinet for Northern Ireland rested with the Home Secretary. Through Tory contacts, I learned in late 1971 that the Heath government was planning to appoint a minister with sole responsibility for Northern Ireland. The name mentioned was Willie Whitelaw, then Leader of the House of Commons. When I wrote that a new minister was to be appointed it was, of course, denied. But in March, after the suspension of Stormont, Whitelaw's appointment was announced. The assignment of the charming and immensely capable Whitelaw to the Northern Ireland brief was to mark the beginning of *rapprochement* between Dublin and London.

In the latter months of 1971, reports were circulating that the British had deployed the Special Air Services (SAS) in the North. London denied that any SAS units were in Northern Ireland. But an individual close to 22 SAS Regiment advised Jim Downey and myself that SAS soldiers were operating on attachment to other military units. Thus while these 'special forces' were not officially assigned to Northern Ireland, they had members who were operational on the ground there. I succeeded in standing up the details of the claim and we ran with the story. It was not contradicted.

At Christmas Foley told me that he and Gageby wanted me to go to Belfast as Northern editor the following year, in succession to Henry Kelly. In the meantime, I was approached by Brendan MacLua, the successful publisher of *The Irish Post*, a weekly newspaper serving the Irish community in London. MacLua offered me a job as his assistant with the prospect of taking over the editorship. But I was looking forward to the challenge of Belfast.

However, when I returned to Ireland I was assigned instead to the newly-established 'EEC Desk'. I did not like it. I was deeply engaged in the Northern Ireland/Anglo-Irish relations area and I had no desire to be tied to a desk in Dublin.

I had heated words with Donal Foley who said he did not remember telling me I would be going to Belfast. But the tiff passed and we remained on good terms. I spent a few months grappling with the complexities of the coming Europeanisation of Ireland, mainly writing about how Irish industry and exporters would adapt to membership of the EEC.

I made good contacts with the people who staffed Córas Tráchtála (the Irish Export Board) and the IDA (Industrial Development Authority) and I travelled around Europe, meeting them. I developed a great respect for them, in particular Denis Pack-Beresford, their energetic and talented press director. They were true professionals and Ireland was well served by them.

———

Early in 1973 I was asked by Jack Marrinan, the general secretary of the Garda Representative Body, if I would be interested in reviving and editing the *Garda Review*, the force's monthly magazine. It had gone dormant for a couple of years so it would be a challenge to start it up again. I had got to know Jack when I was writing about the Garda in 1969.

It was an interesting offer, very different from what I had been doing. It would also allow me to return to university to take a post-graduate degree. There was no question of my being unhappy at *The Irish Times*. It was demanding but exhilarating. I enjoyed the company of lively colleagues and the sense of excitement that permeated the newsroom.

Some years later, I went to see the movie *All the President's Men*, the story of Watergate, the Nixon tapes and how the *Washington Post* brought down a dishonest president. In one scene, the *Post* editor, Ben Bradlee (played by Jason Robards) tells his two reporters, Bob Woodward and Carl Bernstein (played by Robert Redford and Dustin Hoffman) how fortunate they are to be working as journalists. 'It sure as hell beats honest work,' he assures them.

I empathised with that. I could scarcely conceive of journalism as work. It was fun. Nonetheless, I was disquieted about the notion of defining my career solely within *The Irish Times*. It had a world view—and a national view—that could institutionalise those who remained there too long or who had no other experience of life.

Most of my colleagues were puzzled at my decision to step out of the security and structure of the leading national newspaper. Most journalists worked their way upward to *The Irish Times* and once they got there they tended not to move out. It seemed a retrograde career move.

Editing the *Garda Review* was not an easy transition from *The Irish Times*. The Garda, by definition, was a conservative organisation and it was under great stress. It was trying to cope with a steep rise in armed crime, as the violence of Northern Ireland spilled over into the Republic. Serious problems of drugs and organised crime were emerging.

Meanwhile, the early generations of experienced gardaí from the 1920s and 1930s had come to retirement, leaving a deficit in management and leadership expertise. I was answerable to an editorial board that represented different ranks plus a nominee of the Commissioner. It was next to impossible to get agreement on anything and clashes were frequent.

But the experience of setting up, designing and editing what was effectively a new publication was valuable. One also learned a lot about how the bureaucracy works. That was to prove useful over the years. I made some good friends among a body that, by and large, was made up of honourable people with a sense of public service.

It was also great fun. The staff at Phibsboro Tower, where the Garda associations had their offices, were intelligent, unconventional people who took enormous delight in outwitting the bureaucracy of both Garda Headquarters and the Department of Justice.

There was Jim Cuffe, a self-declared cynic. But when he found himself in the middle of a bank raid one day, unarmed and alone, he tackled two armed bandits, subdued them and earned himself a Scott Medal for valour.

Johnny McEvoy was a former Dublin Castle detective. He liked to chuckle as he recalled an interview for promotion.

Interviewer: What steps would you take, Guard McEvoy, if you were to be confronted by an armed and dangerous man while on duty?
Johnny: Long ones, Sir. Very long ones.

He probably did not want the promotion anyway. He was one of the happiest men I ever met, cheerful and good-humoured. He had a long retirement and developed his considerable talent as a painter in water-colours.

I edited the *Garda Review* for two years, during which time I also completed *Guardians of the Peace*, a book on the early history of the force. I did my master's degree in politics at UCD and taught tutorial classes on the new campus at Belfield. All in all, I believed I had accomplished more than if I had stayed on at *The Irish Times*.

———

In May 1975 I had a call from Mike Burns who was editor of news features at RTÉ radio. I knew Mike through our mutual friend Maurice Manning. RTÉ was expanding the radio news service by adding news features programmes in the morning, in the evening and late at night. He wanted me to join a team that comprised some of the best news broadcasters in the country, including himself,

Seán Duignan, Gerald Barry and Kevin Healy. I accepted.

Burns was a superb editor and a joy to work for. I had an action-packed life with the news features team, learning the skills of broadcasting. We pushed out the limits of the new technologies that made radio a fast and flexible medium, such as satellite-based communications and lightweight, hand-held tape recorders that gave high quality sound.

But I found RTÉ a slow-moving organisation. The Garda moved with the speed of an ss Panzer division by comparison. The grip of government was tight and executives were cautious. They had to be.

Because of my experience with the *Garda Review* and my writing on crime and security in *The Irish Times*, I was often assigned to cover these areas for RTÉ. In October 1975, dissident IRA members Eddie Gallagher and Marian Coyle kidnapped Tiede Herrema, the Dutch general manager of the Ferenka plant outside Limerick. Ferenka employed 2,000 people and was something of a jewel in the crown of the Industrial Development Authority (IDA).

The kidnappers threatened to kill Herrema unless the Government met various demands. The Garda tracked the kidnappers and their prisoner to a council house at Monasterevin, 35 miles from Dublin and a siege situation developed which was to last for 17 days.

When the Garda located Herrema and his kidnappers at Monasterevin, Mike Burns got a call from a Garda contact. He telephoned me and I confirmed the details with a Garda source of my own in Naas. I jumped into my car and I was the first journalist on the scene.

But try as I might, I could not persuade the RTÉ newsdesk to run with the sensational news of the developing siege. I telephoned the newsdesk again, to no avail. When the BBC began to report the story later in the morning, RTÉ followed suit. I might as well have stayed at home in bed.

I covered 16 of the 17 days of the siege of Monasterevin. On the seventeenth day I was sent to Mayo to cover the west-Mayo by-election that took the young Enda Kenny into Dáil Éireann. That night the siege ended with the surrender of the kidnappers and Herrema being released.

I was bitterly disappointed not to have been there. Herrema did not speak to any media beyond a short few words when he was released and brought to the Dutch embassy in Dublin. But I wrote to him at his home in the Netherlands and he agreed to give me a lengthy interview—his first. I travelled to Arnhem to meet him and his wife, Elisabeth.

Ann and I subsequently struck up a warm friendship with Tiede and Elisabeth Herrema and we have seen each other frequently over the years. Their eldest son and I shared a birth date. Elisabeth referred to me as her 'Irish son' and there was always a card or a telephone call on my birthday.

My employment with RTÉ was on a yearly, renewable contract. But early in the new year I had a call from Fergus Pyle who had taken over as editor at *The Irish Times*. Fergus offered me the job of news features editor at the newspaper. It paid quite a bit more than my RTÉ contract and it offered the challenge of having my own page at the newspaper. I knew Fergus was having a difficult editorship for a variety of reasons and that the atmosphere at the newspaper was troubled. But it was where my heart lay and I accepted the offer.

5

IN AND OUT AT *THE IRISH TIMES*

Keep Up with the Changing Times
   —*Irish Times* advertising slogan, created by KATHY GILFILLAN

I rejoined *The Irish Times* in September 1976. But the days of Fergus Pyle's editorship were numbered and he knew it. 'You're the only rat I ever saw joining a sinking ship,' he remarked ruefully on my first day back in the office.

Fergus was a superb journalist. But his appointment in succession to Douglas Gageby, who had left after the establishment of the Trust, was ill-timed and had scarcely been prepared for by the organisation. And external circumstances could hardly have been less favourable.

The first oil crisis, following the Yom Kippur war in the Middle East, had plunged the economies of the west into recession. Advertising revenues at *The Irish Times* slowed to a trickle. Burdened with debt, through the Trust's acquisition of the ordinary shares, the company had to slash costs. Editorial budgets were cut back. The new editor was unable to maintain the pace of development and innovation that had been there in earlier years.

The newsprint budget was reduced so the newspaper had fewer pages. Fergus then took the disastrous step of reducing the typeface to squeeze more text into each page. An already sombre design now became impenetrable for many readers, especially older ones. After more than a decade of steady growth, circulation began to drop.

At the end of 1974, daily circulation was over 69,000. But in the first half of 1975 it dropped to 63,000. It rose again to 69,000 by December but fell steadily thereafter to a low of 61,800 by June 1977.

It was not just the type-size that was driving readers away. The new Managing Director, Peter O'Hara, believed that the paper could sustain a higher cover price. Three price hikes in 18 months had caused many daily buyers to reduce their frequency of purchase.

Some editorial policies did not help either. Sustained criticism of Ireland's designated EEC commissioner, Richard Burke, angered many readers. The criticism was persistent, sometimes personalised and there was a backlash.

When the newspaper ran a series of articles alleging brutality by Garda detectives investigating serious crime—the 'Heavy Gang'—there were allegations that it was dancing to Britain's tune. Faulty though such reasoning might be, it probably cost circulation too.

Pyle was courageous in running with the Heavy Gang reports. When they appeared in the newspaper there was a heated debate in the Dáil. Fine Gael's deputy for Galway South West, Fintan Coogan, came to the rescue of the Minister for Justice, Paddy Cooney: 'Is the Minister aware of the strongly held view throughout this country that *The Irish Times* is doing the dirty work for John Bull?'

Over and above these realities, Fergus was not the most organised of men and he was sometimes indecisive. He was the best of company, generous, widely-read and principled. But he had no training or conditioning that might have prepared him for the job of editor. He had joined the paper from Trinity and had always been a writing journalist. He had no experience of administration or management.

Worst of all for his editorship, there were two or three senior people each of whom felt he should have had the job rather than Fergus. Perhaps they were right. But it meant that the editorial department was a house divided. When he finally had to step down, it was after a delegation of journalists had gone to visit, first, Gageby and then McDowell, to say that he had lost the confidence of the staff.

Early in 1977, Douglas Gageby had his 'second coming' as editor and Fergus was transferred upstairs. Peter O'Hara left his job of Managing Director and Louis O'Neill became General Manager. Tom McDowell, as chairman and chief executive, declared that he would take responsibility for the profitability of the company.

There was—literally—dancing between the desks in the newsroom at the news of Gageby's return. He called a 'shout in'—an informal gathering of staff—and stood on a chair by the newsdesk. He told the journalists he would remain in the editorship for 'two years—maximum'. 'After that', he told them, 'you'll have a new editor and I hope it will be one of yourselves.' In the event, he stayed almost 10 years. And when he was succeeded in the job, it was indeed by one of those who had listened to him in the newsroom that day.

Douglas Gageby was perhaps a week back as editor when he sent for me. 'Your features page is the liveliest thing we have in this bloody newspaper. We're going to have to use it to get the circulation moving. Do me a plan and come over to the house around 11 tomorrow.'

I worked late into the night and hammered out a schedule of features and other initiatives that I believed would have a broad reader appeal. When I went to his house at Riversdale Avenue, off Bushy Park, the next day and went through them he seemed delighted. I also told him I proposed to change the typesize in the news features page to 9pt to improve its legibility. He agreed to give it a try. The results looked good. Gradually, other features pages followed suit.

Thereafter I would go around to Riversdale Avenue every couple of weeks.

Douglas's wife, Dorothy, would provide coffee and oatmeal biscuits while we planned features series and other editorial wheezes that would bring circulation forward. By Christmas the drop in sales had stopped. Then the figures began to move upward again.

We were lucky. The world was climbing back out of recession. EEC membership was bringing modest prosperity back to Ireland. Advertising picked up and Douglas was able to get additional resources for newsprint and editorial innovation.

A few months after his return he called me into his office one evening. 'We're going to start promoting the paper on radio,' he said. 'Louis O'Neill has put a budget together for us and I want you to take charge of it. By the way, I'm making you an assistant editor and I want you to supervise all the features departments.'

It was a big leap forward. I was 29 and my new appointment made me far and away the youngest journalist at executive level in the organisation. I got a pay rise and a nice Alfa Romeo company car.

But I was going to work for all this. I had to run the news features page, the promotional campaign on radio, a new television listings page and I had to keep a watching brief over the other features departments. These included the arts page, the Weekend supplement, the books pages and the special reports department which put out commercial supplements.

Douglas Gageby has been described as an intuitive editor. Of course he used his intuition and his judgment. But these were always well informed by careful research. A military man would not make the mistake of committing resources without the benefit of good intelligence. I was also given the task of co-ordinating the research and the promotional activity with Louis O'Neill and with the newspaper's advertising agency, Young's, based in Lower Leeson Street.

We were fortunate in having Jack Young, who had taken over the agency from his late father, as an *Irish Times* fan and supporter. He read the newspaper avidly each day and always had useful comments to make about it. He contributed to the newspaper's advancement in a far wider way than merely running the advertising campaign. His early death from cancer was a loss to us.

We were also fortunate in having a young woman from Northern Ireland called Kathy Gilfillan as our copy writer. She devised some simple but effective promotional lines that included 'Keep Up with the Changing Times'. Later, Kathy married Paul McGuinness, the manager of U2.

And we had a gifted effects and production executive, Brian Halford. He made our advertising sound different, authentic and arresting.

We met every week at Young's to plan strategy and tactics. In addition to myself, *The Irish Times* team comprised Dan O'Sullivan, circulation manager and Alan Moran, studio manager. Later, we had Donald Helme as our account executive. We worked well together.

After two years of immersion in the task of editorial development and building circulation, I had become uneasy that I was losing contact with writing journalism. I expressed that concern to Douglas. He asked me what I would like to do. I said I would like to go to Africa to report on Rhodesia. A couple of weeks later he told me to book a flight for Salisbury (now Harare) where the war of liberation against the illegal regime of Ian Smith was in full swing.

'If you want bloody writing, off you go,' he said. 'Send 1,000 words a day. You can come back in a month.' I renewed my immunisation shots and took off for Salisbury via London with several thousand pounds in travellers' cheques and cash. I was to come back with most of it because the exchange rate with the beleaguered Rhodesian dollar was so favourable.

The Rhodesian war was merciless. Before I left Dublin I had been briefed by Bishop Donal Lamont, an Irish Carmelite who had been based at Umtali (now Mutare) in the east of Rhodesia, close to the border with Mozambique. He had been expelled by the Smith government for publicly airing his critical views.

But Lamont's warning did not prepare me for some of the things I saw and the realities I encountered. I got a closer insight than many journalists into the reality of the bush war by using the networks of various Irish missionaries around the country. There were Jesuits and Carmelite priests and Marymount nuns. They were good people — brave, compassionate and committed.

In the tribal trust lands (TTLs) I found myself in villages where the dead lay unburied beside their huts. If they were killed by the Rhodesian forces they were left there as an example, *pour encourager les autres*. If they were killed by the Patriotic Front forces they were left there as 'witches'.

Many Irish people had emigrated to Rhodesia over the years, including quite a few since UDI (Ian Smith's 'Unilateral Declaration of Independence') in 1965. There was an exotically-named 'Mashonaland Irish Association'. People were very welcoming to me but hostile to the media and to world opinion in general. The tide of history was running against them and it was difficult not to feel sorry for them too.

I got a lot of help from Tim Horgan, a Kerryman who ran a fine restaurant in Salisbury. A young Irish couple, Ken and Eileen Ryan were hospitable, giving me important background and insights over dinner at their home. I also renewed acquaintances with a school friend from Roscrea days, Paul Robinson, who had qualified in science and gone to work with an engineering and manufacturing company.

In the northern trust-lands, near the Zambezi, I met white farmer families living on the last shreds of their nerves. Wives were fraught. Men were on the edge. Children went to school carrying SLR rifles. I particularly remember a family at Kariba Airport with a little boy, trailing a teddy-bear in one hand and clutching a semi-automatic rifle in the other. He can hardly have been more than 8 or 9 years old. It was a terrible way to live. Belfast was idyllic by comparison.

Getting around was difficult. Armed convoys travelled the roads between the main towns. But it was dangerous at night. Some journalists carried guns. A Rhodesian officer offered to sell me a Walther 9mm pistol but I refused it. I was very glad I did not have it when I was stopped at a PF roadblock near Umtali and searched. Five US dollars got me through.

I came home from Rhodesia stressed and very tired.

———

Later in the year Douglas Gageby decided on a reshuffle of senior editorial personnel. Gerry Mulvey had succeeded Donal Foley as news editor and now Gageby wanted to bring Gerry into his own office. Jim Downey had been appointed night editor on Gageby's return but he had also moved into Gageby's personal office.

Two jobs were advertised on the noticeboard—news editor and night editor. They were the key command jobs in the organisation. I did not intend to apply for either, preferring to remain as assistant editor with the brief I had.

At Riversdale one morning Douglas asked me why I had not applied. I told him. 'Well, you'd be advised to think of a change,' he said. 'I need a good night editor.'

The night editor role had become crucial. As the paper had grown in size and as the print run increased, the elderly Hoe & Crabtree press in the basement of the building laboured to complete its nightly task. Deadlines were pulled back time and again but the challenge of assembling the pages and getting the newspapers out of the building was mounting all the time.

'I think if I have to change I'd like to try the news editor job,' I replied, testing him. I knew that he wanted to give Conor O'Clery a run at the newsdesk. Conor had been a brilliant Northern editor and was proving himself a world-class correspondent.

Gageby grunted. 'Apply for the newsdesk then. Apply for them both. But I know which one you'll get.' Thus I found myself as night editor. Technically it was a promotion. I had complete authority over the final shape and content of the paper once the editor had departed the building.

It was intensive and demanding work. I came to the office at 4 o'clock and sat in on the afternoon conference. Then I stayed with the paper, without a break, until the first edition was printed, usually at around 1 am in the morning. After that I would go through the country or 'special' edition and instruct the sub-editors to make whatever changes I thought necessary for the city edition which would print around 3 am.

I generally took some sandwiches or a snack and got tea from the canteen. Sometimes I would cross Fleet Street, climbing the rickety stairs to the grandly-named Irish Times Club above the bookie's for a drink before going home. It was difficult to unwind and it was frequently 4 or 5 am before I would get to bed. It was a tough time for Ann as well. She was expecting our first child and the disrupted nights took a toll on her too.

The Irish Times Club was straight out of the eighteenth century. Officially, it did not exist at all. It occupied two scabrous rooms at the top of a house in Fleet Street, across from the newspaper. It opened once the first edition had 'gone to bed'—usually around midnight. There was no official closing time. The clientele comprised *Irish Times* men (no women were allowed) as well as the night shift from the *Independent*, detectives from Pearse Street and sometimes members of the Dublin Fire Brigade from Tara Street headquarters.

The routine as night editor was exhausting and it nearly led me to catastrophe. I was on duty on the night of 14 February 1981, St Valentine's night. When the country or 'special' edition was ready to go to press, I made the necessary changes for the city edition and decided to head for home.

The late night news reporter—'Night Town'—stayed until 4 am. Maev-Ann Wren was 'Night Town'. She was on the telephone as I passed the newsdesk and I waved a 'good night' as I went to the door. Later, I realised that there had been something, an alertness or tension, in her face as she spoke. But she waved back without taking the telephone from her ear.

She was hearing the first report that something seemed to be wrong at a night club on the north side of Dublin called The Stardust.

I went down to the street and sat into my car. It was before the era of the mobile telephone, but some *Irish Times* cars, including mine, were fitted with Motorola two-way radios. As I drove home, I realised I had not switched on the set. I would have had to pull over and stretch across to the footwell on the passenger side where the radio was mounted. But by now I was half way home and I decided to leave it.

Meanwhile, Maev-Ann had heard that there were multiple casualties at The Stardust. She asked the night switchboard operator to raise me in the car but, of course, he got no response. Then she acted with textbook professionalism. She notified Conor O'Clery, the news editor. She had the switchman turn out every reporter, photographer and sub-editor he could reach. And she told the production supervisor that the city edition would be late—very late. Then she went to the scene herself as quickly as the taxi could get her there.

More than 20 years later, Maev-Ann told me she was still affected by the scene and the sounds of the inferno.

In the morning I turned on the radio and learned of the tragedy that claimed 48 lives. I was stunned. My shock at the scale of death and injury was overlain with a sense of horror that *The Irish Times* had not known about it. I dashed out of the house to the nearest newsagent and saw that the front page had been transformed and carried the grim news of the night before.

Later in the day, I telephoned Maev-Ann to thank her for saving the night and to explain what had happened. Then I telephoned Gageby and told him too. He was sympathetic and supportive.

'A terrible, terrible night. Maev-Ann did a great job. So did everybody. Tremendous work all round. Don't worry.' He never mentioned it again. That was probably the most condign punishment.

Thereafter I became something of an obsessive about communications. The lesson of The Stardust was seared into my sub-conscious. In later years I carried a mobile phone *and* a pager—just in case.

The Stardust played on my mind. I think I had something of a crisis of confidence and I decided I wanted a break from pressure for a while. I was still only 30. But I had been working at a sustained pace since I was in my late 'teens.

I had got to know the US Ambassador to Ireland, Bill Shannon, himself a former journalist and senior editor at *The Boston Globe*. Bill had suggested that he would nominate me for the Nieman Fellowship at Harvard University. It was, and is, the most prestigious journalists' fellowship in the world. It would last a year and it was partly-funded.

I told Gageby what I wanted to do. He was a little taken aback but agreed to arrange unpaid leave of absence.

——

Then I had a telephone call from a man I had never met but whom everyone in Dublin media knew about—Hugh McLaughlin. Hugh was a self-made man from Donegal. He had a genius for publishing ideas and he had launched virtually all of the successful innovations in the Irish print market over the previous 20 years. His creations included *The Farmer's Journal*, *Woman's Way*, *Business and Finance* and *The Sunday World*.

A few months previously, in collaboration with John Mulcahy, publisher of *Hibernia*, Hugh had launched the *Sunday Tribune*, a serious, quality newspaper which aimed to fill the gap in the market left by the fact that *The Irish Times* published only six days a week, having no Sunday edition.

He told me that his partnership with Mulcahy was coming to an end and he was preparing to buy him out. In turn, he was going to sell a half share in the company to new partners, Smurfit Publications, a division of the Jefferson Smurfit corporation. Mulcahy had been editor of the *Tribune*. He and McLaughlin wanted to go their separate ways. Would I like to be the new editor of the *Sunday Tribune*, McLaughlin inquired?

It was not untypical, as I was to learn. He operated intuitively. He had never met me. But here he was offering me a full editorship. 'Are you sure I'm the man you want?' I asked. 'Oh yes,' he said. 'I know you've had a lot to do with building up the circulation at *The Irish Times*. You'd have an absolutely free hand in editorial policy.'

McLaughlin's proposal necessitated a reversal of plan. I thought long and hard about it. I had put in a demanding decade and I had been looking forward to a year in the academic groves of Cambridge, Mass. But the *Sunday Tribune* was only a weekly, I reasoned. If I took a good holiday first, it could be done. It was an offer one could hardly refuse: to edit one's own national newspaper at 31. Ann agreed, albeit with reservations.

I told Gageby that I would not actually need the leave of absence because I was going to edit the *Sunday Tribune*. He didn't like the idea and was sulky. 'Hmmph. I suppose you'll learn more there than in Harvard anyway.' He sent me to see Tom McDowell.

I had not really met McDowell before, other than in formal or large groups. I had never had anything like a conversation with him. I went down to his rather gloomy and old-fashioned office facing on to D'Olier Street. 'You have an offer from McLaughlin to edit the *Sunday Tribune*?'

'Yes. And I'm going to take it.'

'Why? You're doing very well here.'

I explained my reasons and I added a few more for McDowell's consumption. 'Well, Douglas said I'll learn a lot there and I think he's right. I've been stuck here too long doing things I don't especially want to do.'

McDowell smiled the enigmatic smile I was to come to know so very well in later years. He flew his fingers across his moustache in another gesture that indicated mirth. 'Hah! I thought so. Anyway, go if you must. But if it doesn't work out there'll always be a door open for you here. I take the view that all experience is valuable. Keep in touch with Douglas or myself.' It was a welcome reassurance and a generous, though also pragmatic, stance on McDowell's part.

My editorship at the *Sunday Tribune* was to last less than two years. Mulcahy had assembled a talented and eclectic team of journalists, many from the old *Hibernia* stable. I recruited a few more, including Cian Ó hÉigeartaigh from RTÉ who joined as assistant editor; Joe Carroll from *The Irish Press* and the versatile Kieran Fagan from *The Irish Times*. I inherited as deputy editor, Jim Farrelly, who had come from Independent Newspapers. He was to prove a strong and loyal colleague who went on to several senior executive jobs when he rejoined the Independent Group. Hugh McLaughlin understood the necessity of investing resources in publications in order to build circulation. We added a colour magazine, edited by Tom McGurk, to the paper.

Mulcahy had launched the newspaper in tabloid format. But tabloid still equated to down-market in the conservative Irish newspaper market. We had a brilliant design editor, Andy Barclay. I asked Andy how long it would take to change from tabloid to broadsheet. 'Would it be okay to start on Tuesday?' he asked nonchalantly.

And so he did. Circulation, which had been stuck at around 75,000, began to grow. It was eventually audited by the accountants, Coopers and Lybrand, at 117,000. That gave it a lead of more than 30,000 copies over *The Irish Times* and with a far higher concentration of ABC1 readers.

But I found working with Hugh trying. The company was under-capitalised. The Smurfit executives seem to have believed it would turn into profit more or less immediately—which I knew was impossible. Costs were high but there was a good managing director, Roger Bannon, who managed the cash-flow well.

With these circulation and readership figures, the company should have moved into steady profit within 12 to 18 months. Hugh had decided to launch a new morning tabloid newspaper in mid-1982, out of the same company, The Sunday Tribune Ltd.

The Daily News had virtually no capital and it quickly soaked up any cash there was. In October, the liquidator had to be called in and the company folded. The liquidator was John McStay. He said to me one day: 'The newspaper may have been a success. The company wasn't.' The newspaper was subsequently restarted under Vincent Browne who bought the title from the liquidator. Later, it was part-acquired by the Independent group.

——

After Christmas I telephoned Gageby and said I would like to talk about the offer of returning to the *Irish Times*. I met him and he sent me to see McDowell again. McDowell, in turn, told me to see Louis O'Neill who put me on the equivalent of an assistant editor's pay and assigned me to research and report on what was then emerging as 'new media'—teletext, interactive information retrieval systems and so on.

I enjoyed the assignment and learned a lot. I travelled to Europe and the UK with one of O'Neill's managers, Seamus Conaty, looking at innovative media projects. I was in no rush to go back to the editorial floor.

In retrospect, I realise that Gageby—and probably McDowell—was nervous about parachuting me back in at senior editorial level. Gageby was now in the sixth year of his 'second coming' and it was clear he could not go on for ever. There were quite a few people with their own ambitions around him who would see my return as a challenge to their prospects.

But by the summer I had had enough of looking at teletext systems and writing reports for Louis O'Neill. I think Louis had enough of it too. Then came another of those unexpected telephone calls that punctuated my career and changed everything.

John Meagher was chairman, principal shareholder and chief executive of a successful research company, Irish Marketing Surveys (IMS). He had learned about survey methods while working with Gallup in Canada, came back to Dublin and had built a fine business which had made him wealthy. When *The Irish Times* started using opinion polls to measure voter intentions, in the 1977 election, they went to IMS.

Jim Downey and I had worked closely with IMS and with John Meagher at that time. John and I had become friendly. We enjoyed each other's company. He was an expansive character and I particularly liked his sense of humour.

However, in 1979 John was invited by Tony O'Reilly to join the board of

Independent Newspapers and his working relationship with *The Irish Times* thus had to come to an end. He had become deputy chairman of the Independent Group and was close to O'Reilly. O'Reilly sometimes described John as his 'alter amigo'.

John called me at home over a weekend: 'O'Reilly wants you to edit the *Sunday Independent.*' It wasn't a message I particularly wanted to hear. I had met O'Reilly frequently over the years. He had invited us to parties at his country house, 'Castlemartin' in Co. Kildare. I had met him privately on a number of occasions when it seemed possible that the Independent organisation might invest in the *Sunday Tribune*—which it ultimately did. But I was happy back at *The Irish Times* and wanted to stay there.

'I don't think I want to do that,' I said. 'Please tell Tony I'm flattered and appreciative but I'm going to stay where I am.'

'He wants us to talk about it before you make your mind up,' John said. 'Will you come and have dinner with us and hear what he has to say?'

A couple of nights later I went to Independent Newspapers headquarters in Hatch Street for dinner. O'Reilly was not there. He was in China, I think. But John Meagher and I had dinner and at some point O'Reilly came through on a conference 'phone.

Meagher told him we were having a fine dinner but that I was adamant that I wanted to stay with *The Irish Times.* 'Have you told him about the terms, John?' He had. They were generous. A good salary, pension, car and expense allowance were to be topped off by an agreement for share options in Independent Newspapers. I later calculated that had I accepted, the share options would have been worth around €4 million in 2002.

'John and I understand that *The Irish Times* is where you feel comfortable,' O'Reilly said. 'It's a wonderful institution. It's Oxbridge. But we have huge resources and we'll be putting them into our titles over the next few years. You'd be able to do things with us that *The Irish Times* will only be able to dream about.'

There was a variety of reasons why I was resistant to O'Reilly's offer. I was not sure that he and I would want the same sort of *Sunday Independent.* And I felt that editorial considerations would generally take second place to commercial priorities. I explained these points over the conference line.

'How could we address your concerns on those?' O'Reilly asked.

'I don't know that you could,' I said. 'You don't have your editors on your board of directors. By definition, they stand behind the commercial executives in the organisation's pecking order.'

'I can't put you on the board. That's not how we do things,' he replied. 'But we might be able to look at some sort of group title.'

John Meagher interrupted. 'Maybe Conor might think about things overnight, Tony, and we can pick up again tomorrow.' O'Reilly chuckled down the line. 'Okay. Here's my best offer, Conor. This is the clincher. If you come and work with us, I promise I'll wear a monocle to work.' It was a quip at the eyeglass that

Tom McDowell wore as a constant accessory.

I went home and talked the offer over again with Ann. We agreed that *The Irish Times* had been good to me, bringing me back into the fold after the closure of the *Tribune*. But I had no security of tenure. I was being paid on a weekly basis as a 'consultant' to Louis O'Neill. Ann was in fulltime employment as a teacher and that was our financial anchor-point. We also had a little money left to me in my late mother's will when she died the previous April. But perhaps O'Reilly's offer was one we could not refuse.

O'Reilly asked me to come to lunch at 'Castlemartin'. We talked over the meal but I remained resolute. I drove him back to Dublin and we parted amicably as I dropped him at the Hatch Street offices of Independent Newspapers.

The next day I went to talk to Louis O'Neill and explained my dilemma. I never saw Louis move so fast. He jumped from his desk. 'I'm going to talk to McDowell and Gageby,' he said. Then he flew out the door and down the stairs to McDowell's office.

Less than an hour later, I was called to see McDowell. He sat in the office with Gageby on one side of his desk, O'Neill on the other. 'Louis has been telling us about O'Reilly's offer,' he said flatly. 'I'd like to make you a counter-offer.' I tried to keep a smirk off my face. 'We'd like you to come back to Douglas's staff as a deputy editor.'

Gageby now had four deputy editors: Bruce Williamson ran his personal office; Jim Downey looked after editorial content and policy; Ken Gray handled administration; Gerry Mulvey did general duty in the editor's office, writing leaders, chairing conferences and so on.

McDowell told me that Dennis Kennedy, who had been diplomatic editor and an assistant editor, was also going to be a deputy editor. I would be deputy editor number 5 or 6. But I would be on equal terms with the others. I asked for 24 hours to consider and went home.

That evening Tony O'Reilly telephoned the house and spoke to Ann. He urged her to persuade me to accept the Independent offer. But we agreed that I would stay with *The Irish Times*. The next day I went back to see McDowell and Gageby. Ken Gray, the deputy editor for administration, was there too.

'There's one difficulty,' McDowell said. I groaned silently. It seemed to be always a case of two-steps-forward-one-step-back. I inquired the nature of the problem.

'Douglas is concerned about getting other people's noses out of joint. So we'd like you to be an assistant editor for a couple of months. You'll have the deputy rank in three months. Now, we're both here to confirm that and Ken is a witness."

It was not worth arguing about. I accepted. I asked for one condition: an assurance that no grade would be created between deputy editor and editor. I did not want to have the appearance of authority without the substance.

McDowell turned to Gageby. 'Have you any plans to create some new grade, Douglas?' Gageby said no. We all shook hands on the deal. I was not unhappy to have turned my back on the Independent offer, although I knew that it would have been exciting working with the dynamic O'Reilly and with John Meagher. I was also turning down a lucrative share option.

Later, I telephoned John Meagher and told him my answer was definitely no. He expressed regret and wished me well. John had been very straight with me and I always held him in high regard. We remained friends. I last saw him with Tony O'Reilly in 'The Commons' restaurant at Newman House on Saint Stephen's Green at Christmas 2000. He looked poorly. Sadly, he died in 2001.

McDowell and Gageby held to their word. Shortly before Christmas 1985 I was promoted to deputy editor and to my surprise, shortly afterwards, appointed to the board of directors of The Irish Times Ltd.

———

In 1984, *The Irish Times* along with many other newspapers in Britain and Ireland had a windfall when the Reuters news agency was floated on the Stock market. The organisation had been held in common ownership and each newspaper received a cash sum in proportion to its shareholding. The Irish Times Ltd received almost £3 million. The question of what to do with it had to be decided at board level.

Louis O'Neill was clear in his mind about what should be done with the money. He believed that it should go into the purchase of a colour printing press to replace the 1950s Hoe & Crabtree which was near the end of its life and which could not print colour. Louis knew that the advertisers were demanding colour and that if *The Irish Times* could provide it, there would be a big revenue dividend for the paper.

Louis won the argument at the board and an order was placed for a small cold-set Uniman press with the firm of Man-Roland in Augsburg, Germany. It was not ideal for a national newspaper but it was all that the company could afford. The Uniman was in general use around Europe for smaller, weekly newspapers.

Eddie Shah, who revolutionised the production of British newspapers, before Rupert Murdoch moved his operations from Fleet Street to Wapping, had bought six of these machines for his plant at Poyle, outside London.

It was, in the scale of things at *The Irish Times*, a massive project. A number of working parties from across the organisation were established to complete the change. The old press had to be decommissioned and removed from the basement press hall that stretched from D'Olier Street to Fleet Street. *The Irish Times* would have to be printed under contract at the Independent plant in Middle Abbey Street for five months while the old press was being taken down and the new machine installed.

Jim Downey was given charge of the production of the newspaper over this crucial period. It was a key task and he discharged it well. The Independent machine (and the incoming Uniman) printed a page that was a full 4 inches shorter than *The Irish Times*. Ken Gray, who had done much of the existing design work on the newspaper in the 1950s, was given the task of redesigning *The Irish Times* in this smaller format. The readers scarcely noticed the change.

Jim Cooke, the production director and Freddie Snowe, the chief printer, were charged with commissioning the new machine and with training and adapting the staff. It was a big task, requiring both operational skills and diplomacy in dealing with the print unions. It was a leap forward in technical terms. The old Hoe & Crabtree was essentially a mechanical assemblage. The new Uniman was full of electronics.

I was tasked with planning new product and development once the machine would be installed. We knew that it would offer the facility to run new sections —Part 2s—each day and also to print in colour. We did some research to test readers' reactions to Part 2s and colour. Resoundingly they said no. They wanted no colour and they wanted no sections in their *Irish Times*. But we went ahead anyway.

When the new press was commissioned in 1985 we started a programme of innovation and development that brought *The Irish Times* ahead of its competitors in its appearance, its contemporary feel and its range of services. Parts 2s such as the Property, Weekend and Business supplements were very successful with the readership and the advertisers.

The company began to make significant profits for the first time and the foundations of a long phase of stability and prosperity were laid. It was probably Louis O'Neill's finest hour. Others directors had warned that if the gamble did not pay off the consequences could be catastrophic. 'It could drag the newspaper and the company to the bottom,' Douglas Gageby warned me one night in the office.

Louis was under sustained pressure over this time. But he stayed to his course.

6

| EDITOR

Beg, take a pedlar's pack, keep lodgers, take up a school, set up a mangle, take in washing . . . do anything rather than become a newspaper editor.
—ANDREW MARR, quoting *The Glasgow National*

On the fine sunny morning of 28 August 1986, I arrived at *The Irish Times* for work. I was duty editor for the early conference. But before I left the house I had a telephone call from Dermot James, later the company secretary, to say that the chairman would like me to come to a meeting at 11.30 am.

I had other things on my mind. Our second son, Conor, had been born 24 hours previously at the Rotunda Hospital. I needed to get over there as quickly as the day's business would allow.

I chaired the 11 o'clock conference and set up the planning for the newspaper for the working day. When I went down to Tom McDowell's office I found an unusually large gathering. McDowell sat behind his partners' desk as was customary. Grouped around on chairs were Douglas Gageby, Bruce Williamson, Ken Gray, Jim Downey and Dennis Kennedy. McDowell gestured me to a seat.

'Douglas has decided to retire,' he told us. 'It will be announced tomorrow. The process for selecting a new editor will begin immediately. It's an absolutely open contest, in spite of what any one of you might think about your being on an inside track, in spite of anything that may have been said to any of you.'

It could not have been more clear. A few days later the job was advertised in *The Irish Times, The Guardian* and *The UK Press Gazette*.

Initially I was not even sure I would apply. We had two young children and busy lives. We had had to deal with a lot of family ill-health, including that of my mother who had died in 1982 after some years of illness.

But I reasoned that if anybody else was appointed I would find myself with all of the losses and none of the gains. I would be worked very hard to somebody else's agenda. I put in my application.

A complex process for appointing an editor had been worked out between the company and the journalists' union in the newspaper, the National Union of Journalists (NUJ). The journalists were determined there would never again be a peremptory change of editors as had happened when Fergus Pyle was appointed in 1974—with troubled consequences for the newspaper, although it would be quite wrong to lay all or even most of the blame at Fergus's door.

It had been agreed that the job would be advertised and that there would be an interview process. When the short list had been reached, the company would give representatives of the NUJ sight of the names. The chapel would then have an effective right of veto—a 'negative sieve' as it was described. If the chapel felt that any candidate would not be acceptable to the journalists as editor, that person would be eliminated.

This process, of course, had to be advised to all candidates. I never knew if it caused any to withdraw or not to apply in the first place. But I would not be surprised if it did and some board members hinted as much to me later. Nonetheless, there were applications from outside the newspaper, from the UK. There was an application—or an inquiry—I learned subsequently, from a senior diplomat.

When the short list was advised to the chapel representatives it comprised just two names: Jim Downey and myself.

If it had come to a staff vote Jim would have got it there and then. Many of the journalists were left-of-centre politically and saw Jim as one of their own. He had been a Labour Party candidate in a general election some years previously. He was more gregarious than I and socialised a lot with his colleagues.

I was seen by some as politically doubtful. Insofar as I had any overt political affiliations I was seen as conservative, probably Fine Gael, although I have been a 'floating voter' all my life. But more than any of this, I was being characterised by some journalists as being too much of a development manager rather than an editor. It was an unfair and incomplete assessment, considering my wide experience as a reporter, features-writer and editor. The choice between Jim and myself was characterised by some wag as between the 'Yuppies and the Downeys'.

Other journalists, however, saw in me a more energetic spirit. I had a reputation and a track record as a good organiser. The more reflective staffers also realised that the newspaper was in need of a good shake-up and had to move forward. The last few years had, understandably, seen a slowing in the pace of change and an accumulation of tasks that needed to be done.

I prepared assiduously for the selection process, putting together a detailed, bound prospectus of my plans for the newspaper under various headings—news, features, the arts, sport, design, presentation and so on. I set out detailed policies on Irish and world issues and I described a circulation-building strategy that would bring us to a daily average sale of 100,000 copies in a decade. In the event, we beat the target by two years.

On 15 December Douglas Gageby stood on a chair in the newsroom and announced that I was to be the new editor. There was applause. But it was muted and I could see disbelief, not to say dismay, on some of the faces around me.

With exquisitely maladroit timing, the board had waited to a few days before Christmas to make its announcement. That night the newsroom's Christmas party was scheduled for a club called 'Hooray Henry's' in the Powerscourt Centre, off Grafton Street. McDowell advised me not to go but to 'have a glass of champagne at home'. It was just as well I did. Some of the more passionate spirits physically attacked Louis O'Neill in 'Hooray Henry's' for the terrible choice of editor to which he had been party.

The following morning Louis complained to me. One of my first tasks was to call in the miscreants and tell them to go and apologise to Louis. The two principal offenders swore they remembered nothing and I half believed them. But they did apologise to Louis and I told them the matter was now officially closed. Sixteen years later, on the day I left the building, one of them came to me to apologise again!

I must have had a somewhat fearful reputation. When I went to the office the next morning for my first day as editor, Eileen Lynam, Douglas's secretary, was in ahead of me. 'Congratulations,' she said somewhat nervously. She had a pot of coffee brewing and she offered me some. 'Well,' she said, 'do you want me to go . . . or stay?' 'Don't be daft,' I answered. 'Stay, of course.'

She stayed as personal assistant to myself and the other senior editors for 16 years. Later, she was joined by Rita Hughes and when Eileen left, Rita took her place.

We worked well and happily for all that time.

When the editors from the various sections trooped in for the 11 o'clock conference on the first morning of my editorship there were sheepish faces—and sore heads. Some had been openly declaring how their fortunes would soar in a Downey editorship. One or two others had already been identified to me, by their kind friends, as being among the more boisterous revellers of the night before. 'Never mind, lads,' I quipped with a malicious grin. 'It could be worse. It could be Vincent Browne.'

———

Taking over from Douglas Gageby was no small challenge. He had almost been deified by the journalists and by the Dublin media community in general. He had transformed the newspaper in the 1960s and then returned to save it when things went wrong in the 1970s. There were some who said that *The Irish Times* could not prosper under any editor other than Douglas Gageby. One senior public servant told a friend of mine that the paper would only last three months under me.

I saw myself with a three-stage programme ahead. First, I had to establish my authority and put in my own leadership structure. Second, I had to stabilise and consolidate the gains made over the recent years of Douglas Gageby's leadership. Third, I had to look forward with a new vision of what *The Irish Times* could be in the last decade and a half of the twentieth century.

Putting in an executive structure was a critical urgent matter. Virtually the entire senior staff had gone. Donal Foley had died unexpectedly in 1982. In the months preceding Gageby's retirement, Bruce Williamson and Gerry Mulvey had also retired. Dennis Kennedy had resigned his deputy editorship and gone to work as EEC representative in Belfast. Jim Downey had told Tom McDowell after my appointment that he would prefer to serve somewhere other than in Dublin. Ken Gray, the deputy editor for administration, was at retirement age and was due to go. I was without senior, experienced people upon whose support I could rely.

McDowell had put it to me that Ken Gray would be willing to stay on as deputy editor for a year or two to ease me in. Initially I resisted the idea. Ken was 60, I was 37. I had difficulty seeing how we would operate together. But McDowell urged me to give it a try. I did. It was wise and far-sighted advice. And I never made a better decision than to agree. Ken remained with me, and stayed on the board, for three more years. He was a tower of strength and wisdom.

I had inherited a strong Night Editor in Pat O'Hara and a first class Chief Sub in Gerry Smyth. But I still needed people to run the office, six days a week, for up to 18 or 20 hours a day. I also knew that I needed to appoint people who would be able to make up for my weaknesses and blind spots and to complement my strengths. Surrounding myself with individuals who simply reflected my own thinking would have been a serious mistake.

Seán Olson had been appointed as night production editor by Douglas Gageby. He was an experienced newspaperman whose family background was in Tipperary but who had been raised and educated in England. When the Uniman press was commissioned in 1985 he succeeded Jim Downey as night editor.

Seán could be mercurial. But he was talented and deeply committed to the newspaper, and I was fortunate to have him in position. He worked a four-night week so I had to roster other senior editors to cover the additional two nights. Later, I appointed Seán as a managing editor and he did valuable work on budgets, on new technology systems and on personnel. He was an all-rounder.

I formalised the position of duty editor which had been a *de facto* role under Gageby and I appointed two relatively inexperienced people to it.

Christina Murphy was education editor and the driving force behind the newspaper's wide range of educational services. She had been chairman of *Campus UCD News* while I was editor in 1967–1968 and we got on well together. I think she regarded me as her protégé.

She was energetic, fiercely loyal to *The Irish Times* and an absolute individualist. In spite of, or perhaps because of, her conservative upbringing in the west of Ireland, she had a liberated mind. But she chose not to be active in the women's movement, leaving it to other colleagues, as she went confidently about her own life. Christina accepted my invitation with enthusiasm and moved into the editor's office at once.

My other choice was Eoin McVey. He had started life as a trainee accountant but diverted to financial journalism instead. I had selected him to start the *Business Extra* section and at my urging Douglas Gageby had asked him to join the staff of the editor's office in 1985. Eoin had an eclectic mind. He was versatile, committed and knowledgeable in areas that I was not.

Between the three of us, I knew we could run the main daily business of the editor's office—writing leaders, running the conferences, taking the decisions on content that would be referred in from various departments each day as well as the telephone calls from readers or people who had some bone to pick or some project to promote.

I had financial authority from the board to appoint one other managing editor—a sort of reserve resource that I could apply wherever I felt the organisation might require reinforcement. I chose David Nowlan. His medical background and his sharply critical mind combined to create a useful manager and editor.

Ken Gray would deputise for me in my absences and in addition he would run the editorial budgets, the editorial personnel matters and the growing volume of legal business.

Bruce Williamson, still on the board of the company, would contribute an invaluable quota of leaders on international affairs each week. He had run Douglas's office for almost two decades. He had also been the letters editor, although there was no such official title at that time.

When Bruce retired, Douglas decided to appoint a fulltime letters editor. I was on the interview board and we selected Maeve Donelan. Maeve had been editor of *Awake*, the rival to *Campus UCD News*. She had strong views on a range of subjects and I reckoned that would make her a good letters editor.

With my duty editors in place, I started a one-by-one process of interviewing the other editors in the various departments. I offered each the opportunity of serving on and working with me, or, if they preferred, I offered to try to find some new place for them in the organisation. Without exception, they promised to work with me as best they could.

The only one who wanted to move was Jim Downey. I could understand his position. He did not want to work on in Dublin under a younger man who had once been his assistant. He said he would like to go back to writing and his chosen location would be London. The problem was we had an excellent London editor in Conor O'Clery.

An idea was formulating in my head, fostered by Bruce Williamson's advice to me, that a new world order was coming. The newspaper's finances were very tight. But I had some ideas regarding areas where savings could be achieved. I made initial inquiries about the costs that would be involved in opening a Moscow bureau and reckoned I could meet those by cutting back on a few other things.

I went to see Tom McDowell shortly after Christmas and said I wanted to put a proposal to the board: that *The Irish Times* would open a fulltime Moscow Bureau, the first such venture by any Irish news medium.

My proposal was that I would offer the job to Conor O'Clery (vacancies for existing jobs had to be advertised and competed for but a new post could be filled at the editor's pleasure). If O'Clery accepted, the way would be open for Jim Downey to go to London. I told McDowell that I could fund the initiative from other savings.

McDowell was enthusiastic. He waved aside the question of funding and told me he would 'get Louis to find the money'. Furthermore, the proposal would not have to be approved by the board. He could assure me there and then that it would happen.

The decision to send Conor O'Clery to Moscow was vindicated by events (see Chapter 7 for more detail on the Moscow assignment). But it also set a tone of innovation for my editorship and raised spirits and confidence across the newspaper.

————

The economic landscape in Ireland in late 1986 and early 1987 was grim. Within a few days of my appointment I had started the process of meeting individually with all the departmental editors. Without exception they were older than me, mostly with their families raised and educated. But in virtually every case, I discovered, their children had been obliged to leave Ireland to make a living. Many were working illegally in the US. Others were working on building sites in Europe. The lucky ones had found employment in the economic uplift that Margaret Thatcher's policies stimulated for a while in parts of Britain.

Louis O'Neill's decision to invest in the Uniman colour press would be justified in time. But when I became editor in 1986 it was far from clear that this would happen. Consumer spending was at a low ebb. Interest rates were high —mortgage rates were anything between 10 and 12 per cent. More than 250,000 people were unemployed. In many key areas, the black economy had subverted the legitimate economy.

The Irish Times was getting some of the new, colour advertising. But the economy was so flat that the company was trading just at break-even. The auguries for my editorship were hardly favourable.

7

A WIDER WORLD

*And worst of all, Mistaar Brady . . . too much, how do you say
. . . too much fooking democracy . . .*

—Soviet editor, explaining why his news organisation was in trouble

The editorial policies of *The Irish Times*, at the end of 1986, when I became editor, were a mixture of ideologies. The paper was economically conservative but socially somewhat radical. In certain respects it could be very pro-establishment. In others it could be almost subversive. Similarly, in operational matters, it was an amalgam of old and new in newspaper practices, systems, conventions and protocols.

It was the most innovative newspaper in the Irish market. Other newspapers had splendid journalists and gifted editors at various levels. But a newspaper's identity or soul is made up of more than that. Circulation at *The Irish Press* was dropping. The newspaper was into its long decline and staff morale was beginning to deteriorate. The *Irish Independent* was still largely caught in the value system of a conservative, religious Ireland that had not fully come to terms with change.

But I knew that although the newspaper was (generally) literate, thoughtful and open-minded, *The Irish Times* was trailing most of its contemporary European counterparts in the range and sometimes in the depth of its services.

I did not believe that there could be such a thing in the late twentieth century as a 'newspaper of record'. Too much happens in modern society to enable any medium to fill that prescription. I preferred the concept of *The Irish Times* as Ireland's 'newspaper of reference', the newspaper to which readers will look almost instinctively when important news develops, when significant issues arise in public life or when it is necessary to know what contending ideas are at play. The larger European countries generally have a number of such newspapers. Smaller countries tend to have one or two.

Comparable newspapers in other smaller European countries, such as Denmark or Finland, had moved on. Apart from general news, they made much more substantial commitments to the arts, to sociology, to the sciences, to international affairs than did *The Irish Times*. I believed that *The Irish Times* should not measure itself against indigenous competition but against similar newspapers operating in similar markets in Europe.

In particular, I felt that a newspaper occupying the role we did in Irish society had a responsibility to report the wider world beyond Ireland's shores in ways that were accessible to Irish readers and relevant to Irish interests. The great bulk of international news in Irish news media at this time was coming from syndicated or wire services. By contrast, newspapers of similar size in smaller European countries, such as *Berlingske Tiedende* in Denmark or central European newspapers such as *Neue Zurcher Zeitung* maintained their own correspondents abroad in key locations.

There were other aspects of the newspaper that I believed were calling out for attention and in some cases, if at all possible, for investment.

Design, layout and pagination were unchanged in many aspects since the 1950s. The fundamental design, largely the work of Ken Gray in 1958–1959, remained valid and relevant and much of it was still in place when I stood down in 2002. But at this stage many aspects required refurbishment and nobody was clearer about that necessity than Ken himself.

The sports pages were located immediately after the front page. It was a throw-back to the days when *The Irish Times* was the principal channel of news for rugby, golf, hockey and polo—the 'garrison games' as they were disparagingly referred to by Irish nationalists. In the 1980s it was a sequence in paging which I believe was unique among the newspapers of the western world.

'Ear-space' notices sat on both sides of the masthead on the front page, advertising shoes, hearing aids and umbrellas. They detracted, in my view, from the coherence and impact of the front page while lodging it firmly, in design and visual terms, in the 1950s.

The front page itself was filled with 'turns ins'. Few stories were fully reported there and the reader was invited to 'turn to Page ...' to complete most news items.

The newspaper had still not learned how to apply colour to its best advantage. The tones of editorial pictures and advertisements on the same pages often clashed terribly. Colour photographs were often simply run on black and white text, without any attempt to create a design context for them. This was not because editors were visually blind or over-cautious in their design approach. Often it was due to a lack of time within a pressured production process. To some extent it was also due to lack of training.

Most areas of content, apart from general news and photographs, were under-resourced and under-provided for in terms of paging. On many days, sport got just two pages. This was particularly counter-productive because the paper had a strong team of sports writers.

Features, the arts, books, popular entertainment, film and music all jostled for limited space that was little more than a page a day. There was no science or medical section (although Dr Roy Johnson of TCD wrote a lively science column once a week).

The Irish Times was often perceived as a bulky newspaper with a great deal of reading in it. That perception was sponsored in some part by its dense typography and classical design. In reality, it was often no more than a thin 16 pages on weekdays. In my first summer as editor I asked the board to permit me to expand it to 18 pages at my discretion. The board agreed but on many days, in practice, we did not get beyond 16 pages.

The newspaper's daily average circulation was hovering between 80,000 and 85,000. It had, in fact, dropped from a previous high in excess of 85,000. The poor state of the economy had depressed retail sales right across the board. *The Irish Times* had endeavoured to maintain its revenues by raising the cover price on a number of occasions in quick succession. As sales fell, we had learned that there were limits to the elasticity of the newspaper's cover-price.

The company was not making any significant profits. Results through the latter half of the 1980s showed either trading losses or modest surpluses—which in effect amounted to 'break even'. It was a problematic time.

I had thought long and hard about how I might bring the newspaper forward after what was seen as the high water mark of Douglas Gageby's editorship. Many critics believed and said there was very little that could be done and that *The Irish Times* for the future would do well to hold things as they were. Few seemed to think that circulation could be pushed forward without 'dumbing down' the newspaper.

In 1985, Seán Olson and I had prepared a position paper for Douglas Gageby and the board, setting out a range of issues that had to be addressed to enable the process of continuous editorial innovation and development to take place.

Douglas liked to compare a good newspaper to a good supermarket or delicatessen. It had to have all sorts of things on offer to tempt in the customer, he argued. Sometimes he likened it to a Christmas pudding. It had to have all sorts of things in it—differing tastes—to attract everyone.

I found the metaphor of a restaurant a useful one. In a successful restaurant, even the best menu, with the finest ingredients, has to be changed from time to time or boredom sets in with the clients. Tom McDowell and Louis O'Neill understood that well and always stretched themselves to ensure that the editor had at least some resources to enable him continually to refresh the editorial product, while maintaining core services and positions.

The position paper identified opportunities presented by the new Uniman press but also underlined an accumulation of problems that limited editorial initiative: restrictive work practices, outdated technologies (most European, UK and US newspapers had moved to computer-based editorial systems while we were still using manual typewriters); a worrying skew in the age profile of our journalists—too few young people, not many close to retirement age and a big rump of 45 to 60 year olds in the middle.

I asked Seán Olson to start a close examination of the editorial budget to see where we might make savings. The object was to build a small 'war chest' or 'fighting fund' which we could apply to a programme of development and innovation. Together we shaved a few thousand pounds here and there, effecting savings of around £200,000 a year. That would give us a cushion in the 1988 editorial budget.

Meanwhile, although things remained tight, the colour advertising, made possible by the advent of the Uniman Press, continued to trickle in, growing slowly in volume. The first significant commitment for a weekly colour advertising slot came from George McCullough, the managing director of the Brown Thomas department store on Grafton Street.

With the bit of extra funding, I began to look at ways in which I could give added value to the newspaper, refreshing the editorial mix.

We changed the pagination, switching sport to the back of the newspaper but giving it significantly extra pagination on a daily basis. The sports editor, Gerry Noone, was promoted to *The Irish Times'* racing paper, *The Irish Field*, thus enabling me to appoint a new, young and energetic sports editor, Malachy Logan.

We redesigned the front page, getting rid of the ear-spaces beside the masthead and the bizarrely–named 'semi-solus' advertisement on the bottom left-hand corner of the page. In its place, running the full length of the page, we now ran a daily digest, highlighting the main news of the day—domestic, international, finance and sport. At the same time, we moved BMD notices (births, marriages, deaths) off the outside back page to an inside page.

Simultaneously, we abandoned the practice of the 'turn in', reducing the numbers of completed stories on the front page to three or four maximum. But they were completed on page one.

There was resistance to all of this from among the more traditional and conservative journalists and in particular, from some of the advertising managers. But the board, to its credit, gave me a free hand. The regular reader research we undertook confirmed that the changes were generally satisfying to readers, although there was much clamour from older readers about transferring the deaths column from the outside back page to inside.

As soon as these changes were implemented, circulation began to rise quickly. The paper was certainly more accessible, more orderly, more contemporary in its appearance—and it was far easier for readers to find out what they needed to know.

I moved to strengthen important areas of coverage. Brian Fallon had singlehandedly looked after the books pages and much of the day-by-day features content. I appointed him to the new position of chief critic and put the novelist John Banville (who was a member of the sub-editing staff) in as literary editor. Karl Jones moved from property to become editor of the special reports section and I appointed Jack Fagan as property editor. Jack had spent many years as deputy news editor and was seeking a new challenge. He took to the property brief like a duck to water and was still in charge of property coverage when I stood down in 2002. I strengthened the financial department, the special reports department and the sub-editors department with additional staff.

The results began to show themselves in a newspaper that was livelier, more varied and more accurate. Between 1986 and 1993, the sales moved up from around 80,000 to well over 90,000.

But the single most significant area of editorial development was in the newspaper's foreign coverage.

——

Foreign coverage was important to *The Irish Times*. The newspaper had been an early and enthusiastic proponent of EEC membership. I resolved to continue that commitment and to expand the range of editorial services to support it. I also committed the newspaper to providing regular space for viewpoints on Europe that were contrary to our official line.

I believed that full European membership, in the long term, was incompatible with the absolute stance of military neutrality that had become an article of faith in Irish public life. Ireland would have to play its role, in concert with its European partners, in its own defence and, if necessary, in interventions elsewhere. Not everyone on the staff agreed with me.

Other foreign coverage issues were coming into focus. Ireland's international aid programme was beginning to grow. Important developments in military and strategic deployment were taking place in the US and in the Soviet Union. The SALT process for reducing nuclear arsenals was under way. The US had evolved the concept—if not the technology—of the 'Star Wars' defence system.

A few days after the 1986 Christmas holiday, I had a discussion with Paul Gillespie, the foreign editor, and asked him for his thoughts on the possibility of sending a staff journalist permanently to Moscow.

Paul was one of the most cerebral people on the staff. He put a lot of intellectual effort into his work—and it showed. His Achilles' heel was a certain lack of organisation from time to time. But his brilliance and enthusiasm more than compensated.

He was delighted with the Moscow idea and came back to me within a few days with approximate costings, a job description and a list of potential appointees. I was not surprised that he put Conor O'Clery at the top of the list.

O'Clery had joined the newspaper from the Northern Ireland civil service. He was a natural newsman and served as Northern editor and news editor. He had also covered the Soviet invasion of Afghanistan and had learned some Russian for that assignment. At this time he was London editor.

As mentioned in Chapter 6, I discussed the idea with Tom McDowell. It was a huge step for the newspaper but, as I pointed out to the chairman, *The Irish Times* was seriously out of line with other European newspapers in its cohort in not having its own *cadre* of world correspondents. McDowell was instantly supportive and enthusiastic.

Installing an *Irish Times* bureau in Moscow was not a straightforward matter.

We had to engage in a lot of palavering with the USSR Ambassador and his staff in Dublin, including at least one lavish lunch at the Coq Hardi restaurant for about ten people. The cost was so astronomical that I did not dare put it on my expenses claim for six months.

Finally, in March 1987, Conor took off for Moscow. Within days he was filing copy that became a talking point on radio programmes, in public houses, over dinner tables. He wrote lyrically of the lives of ordinary Russians as the USSR convulsed towards its final dissolution. He reported the political news, of course, but what seemed to strike a chord with readers were his accounts of everyday life —of shopping, of trying to buy a pair of shoes, of going to the cinema, of ordinary people's struggle to maintain hope and dignity in a collapsing social and economic order. He seemed to feature daily on RTÉ radio programmes which, of course, gave the newspaper good publicity and raised its profile.

The newspaper was fortunate to have him there at that extraordinary time. The initiative was a combination of the judgment of various people, confidence, events and, above all else, Conor's talents as a writer and correspondent. His tour in Moscow was to last three years—which saw the collapse of the USSR and the passing from public life of Mikhail Gorbachev, the architect of *Perestroika* and *Glasnost.*

—

By 1991, the fortunes of the newspaper had begun to improve somewhat. It was possible, over the next few years, to develop a small but highly productive network of correspondents around the world, giving *The Irish Times* a unique function among Irish news media as Ireland's window on the wider world. These were to be in addition to the newspaper's two permanent bureaux in London and Brussels.

Seán Cronin, the contract correspondent whom Douglas Gageby had appointed to Washington on a part-time basis, wanted to retire. Conor O'Clery had had a tough time in Moscow, covering the momentous events that saw the end of the Soviet empire and travelling extensively throughout eastern Europe and into Asia.

I proposed to Conor that he should transfer from Moscow to Washington, becoming the first fulltime, accredited, Irish correspondent in the US capital. Again, McDowell and the board were entirely supportive and the funding was built into the 1992 editorial budget, including a pension settlement for Seán Cronin.

Other international appointments followed. Séamus Martin followed Conor O'Clery as Moscow correspondent. Séamus was a good follow-up to Conor. A good linguist, he had a strong sense of history. He also had a quirky, sardonic sense of humour which was reflected in the many ironies of the Russian story as related in his copy.

In 1993 we appointed Jarlath Dolan as Africa correspondent and assigned him fulltime to South Africa to report on the transition from the apartheid regime. Just three months later, he was to die tragically in a motor accident. He was a considerable talent and a loss to the newspaper (see also Chapter 9). Later, Séamus Martin transferred from Moscow to become Africa correspondent. Again, Séamus's sense of history stood him in good stead. His reportage of the transition to majority rule was perhaps a high-water mark in his long writing career.

We strengthened our coverage around Europe as well. Paddy Agnew in Rome was put on a fulltime contract. Lara Marlowe, a young American reporter, with a background in *Time* magazine, was appointed to the staff as Paris correspondent and with a special responsibility for the *Maghreb* area of North Africa. Another talented reporter with a background in *Time*, Elaine Lafferty, was appointed to cover the west coast of the US on a contract basis. All three were fine writers and resourceful journalists.

Whilst the Soviet Union was crumbling, the eastern bloc went into upheaval and in November 1989 the Berlin Wall came down. It was clear that Germany was on its way to unification. Fergus Pyle, who had succeeded Douglas Gageby as editor from July 1974 to July 1977 had rejoined the writing staff and had served as Northern editor, for the second time, from 1987 to 1990. Fergus had good German and early in 1990 I asked him to go on a fulltime basis to Berlin. He wrote with historical and social insight about the emergence of the new, unified Germany.

Fergus later served as chief leader writer, working closely with me in the Dublin office. He was a gentle and learned man. He died after a short illness, aged 62, in April 1997.

As foreign editor, Paul Gillespie had stretched limited resources to retain the services of high-calibre correspondents in important news centres around the globe. He had contracted David Horowitz, a young Jewish reporter of English background, based in Jerusalem, to report for us from Israel. Horowitz came on stream just as the first *Intifada* got under way and gave us excellent service. Later, he was appointed as editor of *The Jerusalem Post*.

Paul balanced out Horowitz's coverage with additional material from Michael Jansen, an Englishwoman who had become something of an expert on the Palestinians' case. She was based in Cyprus and travelled extensively through the Arab countries in the middle eastern region. Through a combination of these two, *The Irish Times* got comprehensive coverage of the Middle East without incurring anything like the heavy costs of a fulltime bureau.

These appointments were sometimes described as mould-breaking in the context of Irish journalism at the time. In reality, *The Irish Times* was following the path of its counterpart newspapers elsewhere in Europe. It was, however, very different to the approach of our local competitors who preferred to rely on wire-copy.

But our policy was successful and our reader research confirmed that there was an appetite and an appreciation among our readers for accurate, balanced and Irish-mediated news from beyond our own shores. In relative terms, it was not as expensive as might have been imagined. We were careful to use resources as the news priorities altered. Thus, we closed Moscow even as we opened Johannesburg. And we closed Johannesburg once the transition to majority rule had taken place and the new government was seen to be working. We closed Berlin shortly after German unity had been secured.

In 2000 we opened Ireland's first fulltime Asia bureau when Conor O'Clery transferred from Washington to Beijing. The Beijing bureau was to be a victim of cost cutbacks in 2002 when advertising revenues collapsed, causing a funding crisis in the newspaper. The resident correspondent, Miriam Donohoe, who had succeeded Conor O'Clery, returned to Ireland to become a newsdesk editor. As a young western woman, a mother and homemaker (her family had relocated with her to Beijing), she had valuable insights into Chinese society and was able to translate these particularly well for an Irish readership.

The development of the newspaper's modest network of overseas bureaux continued through the 1990s. It never amounted to more than five or six correspondents working abroad at any one time. *Berlingske Tidende* or *Jyllandsposten* in Denmark each would have had three or four times that number. *Diario* in Lisbon would have had perhaps a dozen.

But *Irish Times* foreign coverage was distinctive among media on the island for having its own journalists in position on important foreign stories. It gave a valuable service to decision makers and key figures in politics, in the administration and in business.

I met Charles Haughey at a function one evening. The then Taoiseach complimented the paper on its international coverage, in terms I thought interesting. 'It's necessary for Ireland to engage on the world stage and it's important that Irish people understand why we're doing it so much. *The Irish Times* is always there whenever an Irish minister goes abroad. That's very good. It allows Irish people to see world events through Irish eyes.'

It also gave the general readership of *The Irish Times* a new, fresh dimension to their daily reading. *Irish Times* correspondents, as far back as John Edward Healy in the Great War, had always travelled abroad to cover big events. But 'parachute journalism' as it is now known, rarely generates the depth of insight and detail that will make its way into the copy of a resident correspondent.

Foreign assignments were tough ones for journalists. *The Irish Times* had no tradition of running far-flung bureaux and there was little by way of support structures. My own limited experience of working alone, far from base, made me aware that one needs as much back-up as possible. It is difficult to get an objective measure of how one is performing. It is easy to become apprehensive, perhaps even a little depressed.

I insisted that correspondents be provided with decent, safe housing, reliable banking arrangements and other facilities. But working on one's own, filing copy back to a newspaper one could not see, was not easy. This became less of a problem with the advent of the internet and the electronic edition of the *Irish Times*.

Where possible, I planned for either myself or the foreign editor, Paul Gillespie, to make a visit at least once during a foreign correspondent's tour or where we had a long-resident contract correspondent. Brief visits like this also enabled me get a good, first-hand feel for events on the ground in important news locations.

———

In June 1991, when Conor O'Clery was about to leave the crumbling USSR and Séamus Martin was about to take his place, I went to Moscow for a week. *The Irish Times* put on a reception to see off Conor and his wife, Zhanna, at the end of his three years and to launch Séamus and his wife, Anita, into his tour of duty.

Guests crowded into a wonderful old Russian restaurant that Conor and Zhanna had chosen. Tables groaned under the weight of Georgian champagne, varieties of caviar, trays of chilled vodka and delicious—unsurpassable—Russian ice-cream. All this in a country collapsing into political, economic, ideological and military failure.

We had perhaps 100 people at the reception—representatives from the USSR Foreign Affairs Ministry, diplomats, correspondents, members of the small Moscow-Irish community. We even had a KGB general. Toasts were proposed, speeches were made. Conor was thanked. Séamus was welcomed.

Because the restaurant was state-owned, the bill was calculated in roubles. But when it came to be paid, they wanted US dollars. The sum agreed was little more than the price of a good dinner for two in Dublin. It was a stark illustration of the penury of the once-mighty USSR.

Conor had organised a programme of visits for me which was enormously useful. I met government ministers, officials and other correspondents. On the night before we were due to come home, I had been invited to dinner by the editor-in-chief of an influential Moscow newspaper.

I learned during the afternoon that, unhappily, he was to be removed from office the next day. Nonetheless, the dinner was to go ahead. I arrived at the office shortly before 8 o'clock and I was escorted to the editor's magnificent, marble-walled suite. As seemed to be customary in the privileged enclaves of Moscow society, the table was laden with sumptuous food and a seemingly endless variety of vodkas, champagnes and wines.

The discussion started coherently enough. We spoke about the great changes in his country and about the troubles in mine. We agreed that most of the politicians were either fools or corrupt. His English was poor and we found it necessary to lapse into our equally inadequate French from time to time.

As the evening went by, the vodka began to take its toll and my host began to bring the conversation around to the subject of his imminent departure from the editor-in-chief's chair. He became understandably emotional as he began to recite the factors that he believed had contributed to his undoing.

Finally he spread his hands, palms upward in a gesture that indicated his willingness to accept his fate. He fixed me with a glassy, unfocused stare. 'Mistaar Brady . . . we are both *redacteurs-en-chef* . . . and we are comrades, *n'est-ce pas*?' I nodded in vodka-fuelled solidarity. 'Tomorrow,' he gazed around the marbelled walls, 'tomorrow, I leave all this. I tell you I am not sorry. This newspaper is . . . how do you say in English, gone to Hell?'

He poured more vodka for us both. 'Now, I will tell you why this newspaper has gone to Hell. There are three reasons.' He raised his glass. 'First, too much of this . . . too much vodka.' I could see his point but said nothing. 'Second . . . too many women in a man's business.' I shrugged my shoulders in a non-committal sort of way. 'And worst of all, Mistaar Brady . . . too much, how do you say . . . too much *fooking* Democracy . . .'

The next day I flew home. The by-now, ex editor-in-chief's vodka ensured that I slept for most of the flight.

———

In 1992 I took some time to see conditions at first hand in Israel and the Occupied Territories. The first *Intifada* had been under way for almost two years. We had invested a good deal of coverage in the region and I was impressed by the copy we were getting in particular from David Horowitz. I also wanted to see how the Israelis and Palestinians were handling their peace process. From today's perspective it may seem recklessly optimistic to even use that term. But this was before Camp David and the Oslo Accord and before the terrible polarisation and extremism that for so long has held Israeli and Palestinian in their grip.

I had a full programme of meetings with Israeli ministers and party representatives. The Labour government seemed to be genuinely hopeful of reaching an accommodation with the Palestinians and it was difficult not to be infected with the general air of optimism, notwithstanding the evident militarisation of the country.

It was also striking for an Irish person to contrast Israel's attitude towards its diaspora with that of our own country. Ireland's young people were being encouraged to flee, in order to find work in the US and elsewhere. Irish ministers and Irish-American politicians were hailed for seeking visas and work permits to enable young people to get away from Ireland. Meanwhile, Jewish men, women and children from Eastern Europe and elsewhere were pouring into Israel by the planeload, encouraged and subsidised by the Israeli government.

However, one's optimism faded when one got out of the cities and into the Occupied Territories. I had arranged a guide and translator through Palestinian contacts before I left Dublin. He was a young university graduate named Daoud

Kuttab, with excellent English, who lived close to Ramallah. He also worked as a journalist. I was to encounter him again in 2005, when we were both invited to serve on the board of UNESCO's international press freedom prize.

He picked me up at my hotel early in the morning and we set out for a series of visits and meetings, taking the road north from Jerusalem towards the Palestinian town of Nablus.

The first sight of the Jewish settlements on the West Bank could make the visitor think this is some sort of festive or recreational area. The new settlements (as they were then) protrude out into the Palestinian territory like probing fingers. They are marked out with dozens of blue and white Star of David banners. In the distance, they might be shopping centres or sports grounds. But when one drives closer, one sees that the perimeter fences are topped with watchtowers and razor wire and that the men walking in the fields have Uzi semi-automatic weapons slung over their shoulders.

The settlements, even then, were flagrant intrusions, land-grabs, backed by naked force and marked out with flags, just as loyalist or nationalist areas of Belfast are marked out with the Union Jack or the Irish tricolour. It was not difficult to anticipate that if the programme of building new settlements were to be continued, the Palestinian population would be enraged to the point that there could be no hope for future peace. And so it was.

Later in the visit we met members of the Hamas movement in Nablus. They were courteous and welcoming, offering us coffee and hummus. But in their sentiments they were a contrast with the affable Palestinian Liberation Organisation (PLO) supporters. Their threats of counter-attack against Israel were to be more than amply fulfilled in the years ahead.

———

In 1993, I paid a working visit to Southern Africa. I wanted to see again the beautiful country that had been Rhodesia and was now Zimbabwe. I planned to combine this with a visit to Lesotho to see at first hand the fruits of the Irish bilateral aid programme there.

In addition, I wanted to have discussions with newspaper executives in South Africa itself. I knew that there would be new challenges and opportunities for media companies in the post-apartheid phase. I thought it might be possible for *The Irish Times* to play a useful role in this and to bring the organisation to entirely new horizons, far beyond Ireland.

Zimbabwe was as beautiful as the Rhodesia I had worked in during the 1970s, although the signs of economic decay were everywhere. I had met President Robert Mugabe before and this time I paid a courtesy call on him at the Presidential Palace. He had become guarded and introverted, I thought, in contrast to the sparkling, open individual I had previously known.

I went to visit 'The Heroes' Acre', the memorial outside Harare, commemorating the dead of the Zimbabwe war of liberation. Mugabe's first wife, Sally, is also buried there. It was weedy and badly-maintained. A solitary soldier in a ragged uniform and broken boots attended as a guard-cum-guide. His expression of joy when I tipped him a few Zimbabwean dollars confirmed my suspicion that he saw few tourist visitors. It was quite sad.

The Irish bilateral aid programme in Lesotho had made an impact on the economy of the small mountain kingdom, landlocked on all sides by South Africa. I met many of the Irish professionals who were helping Lesotho with projects as diverse as running a stud for the local Basotho ponies and teaching local women how to knit Aran sweaters—which were especially useful in the cold, mountain regions of the kingdom.

It was heartening to see practical, on-the-ground results from Ireland's overseas aid programme. And the visit confirmed me in my view that *The Irish Times* had to maintain its window on the world. The big issues, increasingly, were not national but multinational ones. The visit to South Africa itself was fruitful in some respects and less so in others.

I visited our correspondent there, Patrick Lawrence, a fine writer and reporter who had excellent African National Congress (ANC) connections. We discussed the idea of sending a staff correspondent from Dublin, to be located in South Africa, but with a brief to cover the rest of the continent, with special emphasis on aid and development issues. In the immediate term, the new correspondent would work alongside Patrick, covering the transition from apartheid to majority rule.

Patrick was enthusiastic. When I got back to Dublin we advertised the job and, as already mentioned, Jarlath Dolan was appointed. Unfortunately, his life and a promising future were cut short when he was killed in a road accident near Bloemfontain, six months after his arrival. He was buried in his native Tuam, Co Galway, with a great many of his colleagues and friends from *The Irish Times* in attendance.

Jarlath had been travelling with Paddy Whelan, an *Irish Times* photographer, and two other journalist colleagues on a dirt road. They were working on a story about South African farming families and their attitudes towards the end of apartheid. The car skidded off the road and Jarlath, who had been sitting in the back seat, working on his laptop computer, was thrown out by the impact and died before help could be brought to the scene.

In Johannesburg, I visited various newspaper executives and editors, concentrating on the newspapers owned by the large corporations. It had been clearly signalled that the incoming ANC government would require them to be 'unbundled' from their corporate proprietors and that they would be looking for new owners, investors and professional management.

I canvassed the proposition that *The Irish Times*, as an independent newspaper with a fine tradition and a not-for-profit structure, might play a useful role in this process. I received enthusiastic responses. One senior executive set out a proposal in writing that *The Irish Times* might try to build a partnership of capital and management expertise with some other European newspapers, perhaps *The Guardian*, and that such a partnership might try to acquire the big Argus group.

It seemed to me to offer exciting new possibilities. *The Irish Times* had a unique structure and a unique role in Irish society. Would it not be a significant contribution on a much larger stage if its values could be replicated, even in part, in the media of the new, emerging South Africa?

I returned to Dublin and raised the idea with Tom McDowell. But it did not get anywhere. Realistically, in retrospect, I can see that our organisation simply did not possess the expertise or resources to undertake such a project. Three months later, the Independent group, led by Tony O'Reilly, moved in and bought the Argus group at a bargain-basement price.

8

THE NORTH WENT ON

'C' = 'Falls', or Catholic. 'P' = 'Shankill' or Protestant.
—Advice written on back of reporters' hands, 1969

*T*he *Irish Times* is the only daily newspaper on the island of Ireland with a significant readership both North and South. Its audited circulation in Northern Ireland is only a fraction of that in the Republic. Nonetheless, it sells up to 5,000 copies a day, almost exclusively among the senior political, administrative, clerical, educational and business cohorts.

It has always had a voice—and sometimes an influence—in Northern Ireland that is disproportionately greater than its circulation. Policy and decision makers regard it as important reading. Its coverage of the Troubles and the associated political processes has been widely acknowledged. Even in circles that are inimical towards Dublin and the Republic it is generally regarded with some respect. The reasons are partly historical.

The Irish Times was an all-Ireland newspaper long before the country was partitioned. The administrative, clerical, military and business classes that were its mainstay readership, knew Ireland as a unitary entity, albeit within the United Kingdom and the Empire. In the decades after partition, it often served as a link between clergymen, bank officials, senior constabulary officers and others and across the broad Protestant-unionist community. Standard features such as 'Constabulary News', 'Church of Ireland Notes' and the 'Court Gazette' were important links in a network of political and cultural relationships that had been violently disrupted in the period 1916–1922.

The Irish Times was the newspaper of Irish Protestants—if not always of Irish *Protestantism*. It carried the news of graduations from Trinity College, examination results from the Protestant boarding schools around the country, the doings of the Boys Brigade and so on. Bruce Williamson once described its role to me in the following terms:

> The vicar in Ballymena was probably in the same divinity class in Trinity as the vicar in Ballydehob. They're probably married to each other's cousins or sisters. Their sons and daughters are probably in the same boarding school. They're both hoping to retire to Bangor or Greystones. In the meantime, *The Irish Times* is their bush telegraph.

But history is only part of the explanation. More so than the other Dublin newspapers, *The Irish Times* had always maintained a substantial level of coverage out of Belfast, in particular. Resources were limited in the years after partition but the proceedings of the Stormont parliament and other political developments were covered by 'stringers'—local newsmen, usually working for *The News Letter*, who supplied copy on a contract basis. The standard of their reportage was high. They were reporters of the old school, usually with fast shorthand and good contacts.

When I joined the newspaper in 1969, the last of these, Bertie Sibbett, was still sending copy. It was always clean, crisp, accurate and fast. However, in 1965 Douglas Gageby decided to send an *Irish Times* staffer, full-time to Belfast. He chose Fergus Pyle, who was to succeed him as editor in 1974. Fergus was a good choice. He had joined the paper on graduation from Trinity where he had studied languages. He was enthusiastic and politically aware. He was also Protestant (his father had been a minister) and Gageby reckoned, correctly, that he would have good access to the political and business establishment in Belfast.

Was it prescience, good judgment or luck that persuaded Gageby to commit to the North at this time from the newspaper's limited resources? It was probably a little of each. For more than 40 years, the two parts of Ireland had glared at each other across the border with mutual suspicion and fear. But in 1965, with a Dublin meeting between Terence O'Neill, the Northern Prime Minister, and the Taoiseach, Seán Lemass, an apparent thaw in relations began. For a brief interlude, it appeared that something approaching normal relations might emerge between the two neighbouring jurisdictions.

Gageby's views on the North were different from those of his predecessors. John Edward Healy had been strongly unionist in his outlook and his *Irish Times*, once it had resigned itself to the existence of the new Free State, had defended partition. R.M. Smyllie broadly continued that policy, viewing partition as a necessary evil.

Unusually for a Belfast-raised Protestant, Gageby believed in the ideal of a united Ireland. His political heroes were Wolfe Tone and Thomas Davis but he insisted that his nationalism was of the constitutional variety and that violence should play no part in reconciling the two great traditions of the island.

In sending Fergus Pyle to Belfast, Gageby was in part responding to what seemed to be an opening up of attitudes. He was also looking towards the jubilee commemoration of the 1916 rising. This event was going to raise tensions in the North: Nationalists would undoubtedly celebrate while Loyalists would just as surely mount counter-demonstrations. Matters evolved as predicted. There was rioting as police tried to prevent the Irish tricolour being paraded on the Falls Road and, when Queen Elizabeth visited Belfast as a gesture of reassurance and solidarity with the unionists, a cement block was dropped on her car. The guns came out on the streets. A loyalist gang opened fire on a group of young Catholics at Malvern Street in Belfast and an 18-year-old barman, Peter Ward, was shot dead.

Fergus Pyle had moved to Belfast with his wife, Mary, and their young children. His reporting, whether from the parliament at Stormont or from the streets at night, was graphic and detailed. It set a new standard for the Dublin newspapers' coverage. It also gave *The Irish Times* a head-start when the Northern Ireland Civil Rights Movement took to the streets, 18 months later.

With the onset of violence and the crisis in civil authority in Northern Ireland, Fergus had to be supported with permanent staff and with reporters rotated through from Dublin. Henry Kelly and Renagh Holohan, both of whom had been at UCD with me, were dispatched to Belfast. In due course, Dermot Mullane, who had covered the 1968 Paris *evenments*, was sent on full-time assignment to Derry.

When Belfast and other urban areas erupted into full-scale sectarian confrontation in the summer of 1969, as many as 10 or 12 *Irish Times* staffers, including photographers, were working in shifts on the streets. The photographers were brave. Reporters might mingle anonymously with a crowd, but photographers' equipment identified them and made them ready targets for Loyalist thugs who detested the media. Some had narrow shaves and others were roughed up. But none, thankfully, was seriously injured.

In August 1970 I covered a march of the Royal Black Preceptory at Rathfriland in Co Down with an *Irish Times* photographer, Dermot O'Shea, who later went on to become photographic editor. One or two of the younger brethren spotted Dermot's cameras and identified us as being from the south. They threatened to throw us over a high wall into a field. (Rathfriland is a hilly place!) But a senior Blackman came through the crowd and ordered us to present ourselves before the Imperial Grand Master, Captain L.P.S. ('Willie') Orr, across the street. With much apprehension we were escorted into the presence of the head of the order. He greeted us cordially, took us to a nearby café and bought us tea and scones.

The concentration of editorial resources on the ground gave *The Irish Times* a lead in covering the news in the North. Gageby's strong editorial policy, grounded in his own intimate knowledge of society there, was also influential. Half a century of partition had created a condition of widespread ignorance in the Republic about the realities of life in the North. Few southerners ever ventured there. Business and cultural links were very limited. Few of us who went there as journalists had much prior knowledge of the place.

On my first reporting assignment in Belfast, Henry Kelly, by now a veteran of perhaps a year's experience, met me at the newspaper's office in Castle Street.

'Hold out your hand,' he ordered.

'For what?'

'Never mind. Just do it.'

I held out my left hand. He took my wrist and turned my palm upward. He wrote something on it in biro. I looked at it. It made no sense to me. It read: 'F = C' and 'S = P'.

'What's that for?' I asked.

'Important information. It might save your life. It stands for "Falls Road equals Catholics, Shankill equals Protestants."' It was typical of Henry's tomfoolery, but if it caricatured a situation it also told something of the truth.

Douglas Gageby's Northern editorial policy was grounded on a few principles. He detested Orangeism and never ceased to berate the Orange Order. He distrusted virtually all unionists but recognised that there were many moderates and genuine democrats in their ranks. He thought the setting up of the Social Democratic and Labour Party (SDLP) was the greatest thing ever to happen in Northern Ireland.

Simultaneously, he railed against the smugness and the sectarianism of the Republic. *The Irish Times* played an important role at this time in bringing liberal Catholics to a realisation that, in its own way, the Republic mirrored many aspects of the North's intolerance. The course of events through the 1970s and the 1980s brought Gageby along his own journey of discovery. His outlook changed as atrocity and counter atrocity pushed the boundaries of inhumanity ever further back. He understood the poverty, the deprivation and the lack of opportunity that drove people from both communities into the arms of the paramilitaries. But he did not hesitate to condemn any political activities that were not wholly peaceful.

By the time the Anglo-Irish Agreement of 1985 was signed at Hillsborough, I was a deputy editor and was working closely with Gageby and Jim Downey. We all shared the view that Hillsborough represented a significant step towards an eventual political settlement. The Agreement included a recognition for the first time by Britain that the Republic had a legitimate interest in the running of Northern Ireland. Dennis Kennedy, who was also a deputy editor at this time, dissented from the consensus in the editors' office. He saw the Agreement as an unwarranted encroachment on Northern Ireland's right to remain as a normal part of the United Kingdom.

By the time that I took over as editor at the end of 1986, the Northern political landscape was looking as grim as it ever had been. The sheen was coming off the Hillsborough Agreement. It had been constructed in such a way that it could not be boycotted or brought down, as had been the 1974 Sunningdale Agreement. Thus, it was hoped, that, even if the unionists did not like it, they would gradually accept its permanence and come to terms with it.

But unionist intransigence was greater than either London or Dublin had anticipated. Ulster (or at least Protestant/Unionist Ulster) continued to say 'no'. Nearly two years later, there had been no initiative or response from the unionists. The political process remained moribund, while the paramilitaries, and in particular the Provisional IRA, steadily ratcheted up their campaign of violence, becoming more proficient and more deadly.

In February 1987 the two main unionist parties—Ulster Unionists (UUP) and Democratic Unionists (DUP)—announced the setting up of a 'task force' to define a response to the Hillsborough Agreement. The 'task force' was led by Frank Millar, general secretary of the UUP and Peter Robinson, deputy leader of the DUP.

These were two of the younger generation of unionism, both energetic and intelligent men. A small flicker of hope was raised.

It was more than offset by the toll of violence. The feud between members of the extremist Irish National Liberation Army (INLA) and a breakaway group, the Irish People's Liberation Organisation (IPLO), took 13 lives. They included the wife of the INLA leader, Dominic McGlinchey, who was shot dead while she bathed her young children at their home in Drogheda.

In March the IRA murdered two detectives and a civilian prison worker in Derry. In April Lord Justice Maurice Gibson, the North's second most senior judge and his wife, Cecily, were killed by a 500-lb IRA bomb that destroyed their car on the Louth-Armagh border. They were returning to Belfast from a holiday.

In May, the security forces scored their largest single hit on the IRA at Loughgall. Eight IRA men—the core of its so-called East Tyrone Brigade—were shot dead by the SAS as they mounted an attack on the empty police station in the small Co Armagh village. An innocent civilian, driving through the village, was also shot dead.

It seemed that the cycle of violence could not be broken. There was a grim inevitability about the nightly headlines, reporting murder, intimidation and violence.

———

I was resolved to maintain our commitment to the Northern story, but I also believed that the paper had to be ready to move up a gear in its coverage. The situation post-Hillsborough was inherently unstable and events were going to move in one direction or another. Either the violence would descend into all-out war, or some new political phase would be opened.

Early in 1987 I set out on a round of meetings with party leaders and organisers in the North. The SDLP leader, John Hume, was frequently in Dublin and I met him regularly at Jury's Hotel, where he stayed. I travelled to Belfast and met Millar and Robinson and went to Stormont where I had discussions with Tom King, the Secretary of State and his press adviser, Andy Wood.

I thought long and hard about meeting the leadership of Sinn Féin and the small loyalist parties, each of which had links to one paramilitary organisation or another. I discussed the idea with Dick Walsh and with Mary Holland, whose weekly column was probably the most reliable *vade mecum* for anyone trying to ascertain what was going on in Northern Ireland over all those years. Dick and Mary both advised against it. It could be misrepresented. It was better to leave such contacts to on-the-ground reporters and commentators for the present.

The politicians were universally gloomy—with the exception of Hume. Millar and Robinson knew their unionist 'task force' report was a poisoned chalice. It was finally presented in July but it was politically stillborn. The two party leaders, Molyneux (UUP) and Paisley (DUP) repudiated its modest proposal that unionism should open 'discussions' with the British government on devising an alternative to the Hillsborough Agreement. In disgust, Robinson resigned—temporarily—as deputy leader of the DUP and Millar stepped down as general secretary at Glengall Street.

But Hume remained doggedly optimistic, against all the odds. I met him for breakfast at Jury's Hotel in September. He looked and sounded exhausted, as usual. He had good reason to be depressed, I reckoned. But, as so often with Hume, when everyone else was cursing the darkness, he claimed he could see a small light in the distance—the prospect of an IRA ceasefire. As outlined in Chapter 1, he held with this view and soon he was leading SDLP colleagues in secret discussions with the Sinn Féin leadership at the Redemptorist retreat house, St Gerard's, on the Antrim Road in Belfast. The first public echo of what Hume was telling me came about 14 months later, in November 1989, when the Secretary of State, Peter Brooke, said that the British government would talk to Sinn Féin if the IRA first renounced its violence.

Meanwhile, relations between Dublin and London were deteriorating. A series of confrontations had taken place over the failure of the Irish courts to allow the extradition of various paramilitary suspects to Britain. Relations between Haughey and Mrs Thatcher were brittle and there were tensions between the Irish Attorney General, John Murray, and his British counterpart, Patrick Mayhew.

P.J. Mara, the Government Press Secretary, called me to say that Haughey wanted to invite me to lunch at Government Buildings. Most of the discussion was about the impasse in the North. Haughey's hostility towards the British Prime Minister and her colleagues was not concealed. It sounded personal and was probably intended to be.

It was not at all clear that a newspaper—any newspaper—could do anything other than continue to report the dreary toll of violence and the stymied condition of the political process.

In September 1987 I was invited to attend the annual conference of the British Irish Association (BIA) at Ditchley Park, in Oxfordshire. The BIA had been established in 1970 with the aim of fostering relationships and understanding between the two countries, the moving spirit being David Astor, editor of *The Observer*. The BIA raised funds from British and Irish companies to maintain a small office and secretariat in London. Its principal activity was the holding of a conference each year, to which interested parties would be invited. The conference venue alternated between Oxford and Cambridge.

The conferences were held under the Chatham House Rule, nothing said at the meetings was attributable. They were attended by political leaders, army and police chiefs, community figures, churchmen and some journalists—from Britain, Northern Ireland and the Republic. I was to find the annual BIA conference an immensely useful resource and attended all but one conference during my 16 years as editor.

At Ditchley I found myself in a working group along with Frank Millar, now departed from his employment with the unionists and working with the Brian Walden current affairs programme on Independent Television. I was struck by Millar's combination of political acuity and fluency.

I had come to the view that *The Irish Times* had some ground to make up in its reportage of unionism and the politics of unionism. I felt that our policy towards the unionists was wanting in two ways. Gageby rarely gave them much sympathy in their political predicament and very seldom gave them any credit for attempting to come to terms with a situation that was probably beyond the boundaries of their own adaptability. And despite his detestation of Orangeism he had an inclination often to depict its demonstrations, its parades and other ceremonies as rather quaint and harmless family or community outings.

I thought the unionists needed someone to report and analyse their condition from the inside. At the same time we needed to call Orange extremism what it was—and to blow the whistle on its manifestations of bigotry and triumphalism. We had plenty of Protestants of various hues on the staff, including quite a few from Northern Ireland. But we did not have any committed unionists. I asked Frank Millar if he could turn out some comment columns for the newspaper. He agreed. They were widely remarked upon and so began a relationship between *The Irish Times* and the former general secretary of the Ulster Unionists (turned journalist) that was to prove important to both.

As the 1980s turned into the 1990s, I continued to meet regularly with Hume. I also developed good contacts on the official side in both governments. I met regularly with Dermot Gallagher, second secretary of the Department of Foreign Affairs, who was in charge of the Anglo-Irish section. On occasion I would meet him with his Number 2, Anne Anderson, who later went on to be Ireland's Ambassador to the EU. The daily reports from the Maryfield secretariat came straight to Gallagher's desk and while he was scrupulous about maintaining confidentiality on detail he was always willing to share his well-informed overview of events.

I also found that the British Ambassador, Nick Fenn, was a man with whom even brief conversations could be fruitful. He was a shrewd judge of where the game was at. He was subsequently appointed High Commissioner to India.

I knew that in spite of the terrible things that were happening on the ground, there were stirrings and signals of what might come to pass. Back channels and secret meetings took place right through the period 1987–1993. Hume was regularly meeting the Sinn Féin president, Gerry Adams, at least since the end of 1988.

————

November 1990 saw the first visible public signal from the British government that it would be willing to square up to an agenda that might, conceivably, meet republican objectives. The Secretary of State, Peter Brooke, told a meeting in his constituency that Britain had 'no selfish strategic or economic interest' in Northern and that if there was majority consent within Northern Ireland for unity with the Republic, Britain would not stand in its way.

Shortly afterwards, a Sinn Féin request came through Dick Grogan, our Northern editor, for me to meet Adams. I felt that things had moved on to the degree that the dangers signalled by Dick Walsh and Mary Holland in such a meeting had somewhat receded. I told Dick that I would travel to Belfast. A meeting was set up for the Sinn Féin office on the Falls Road and Dick dropped me off in his car. I spent about two hours with Adams and he confirmed that Sinn Féin was anxious to get into talks with the British and Irish governments. He also confirmed his belief that the IRA could be persuaded to call a ceasefire in certain conditions. There would have to be counter gestures from the British, although he did not specify what these would be.

After an hour or so, he invited me to go down the Falls Road with him to a Sinn Féin centre for lunch. It was only a few hundred yards but he was greeted every few steps of the way. 'Hiya, Jarry?' 'How's about ye, Jarry?'

Adams's replies were in Irish. 'Go maith . . . go maith.' 'Maith an cailín.'

When we got the centre, women were milling around with toddlers and babies in prams. We made our way to the cafeteria through a chorus of greetings and wisecracks — most of them unintelligible to me but which Adams appeared to be able to respond to with wit and humour. When we had chosen our food and found a table, however, it was quite different. Everyone knew that he was on business with this stranger. We were left alone to our conversation. I had the strongest sense of Adams's absolute authority and commanding position in this community.

I found it difficult to reconcile all this with the knowledge that the man sitting opposite me, picking at his beef stew and boiled rice, was the master strategist of the most ruthless and effective subversive network in Europe. And for all that he denied it, every journalist believed him to be a moving figure in the control and direction of the IRA's 'Army Council'.

It was the first of a number of meetings I was to have over these years with senior officers of Sinn Féin and other groups with paramilitary links. When it became public knowledge that Adams and Hume were meeting regularly in what became known as the *Hume-Adams Dialogue*, I felt *The Irish Times* was in a better position to understand what was going on and to take an editorial view on it.

The Irish Times came out strongly in support of the *Hume-Adams Dialogue* that formed the preliminary backdrop to the IRA ceasefire of 1994. I argued in editorials that while it was not right for either government to agree to talk to Sinn Féin at this time, it was acceptable for Hume to engage with Adams in order to persuade him and his senior colleagues to give peace a chance.

Other newspapers in Dublin did not take a similar view. The *Sunday Independent* was hostile to Hume and rallied most of its columnists in sustained criticism of him. He was deeply upset by the weekly tirades against him and told me so. The *Sunday Independent* later criticised President Mary Robinson when she met Adams and shook hands with him during a visit she made to the Falls Road. *The Irish Times* took a different view. I understood that a gradual process was under way to bring Sinn Féin, and Adams in particular, in from the cold in order to enable a dialogue for a settlement to get under way.

Through 1988 I made a number of other visits to Belfast. I met the mainstream unionist parties and I also met members of the smaller, fringe Loyalist parties. I was always treated with courtesy—although also with a degree of curiosity. One tattooed and ear-ringed gentleman in North Belfast was fascinated to meet someone who had been schooled by Trappist monks following the Order of Saint Benedict. He could not be persuaded that life at Roscrea was not defined by witchcraft, incantations and sorcery.

I was careful through all of this to keep the board of *The Irish Times* apprised of what was going on. I went to some lengths at the monthly meetings of the Trust and board to fill in the background to events. Some apprehension was voiced from time to time, especially that the newspaper might be unwittingly used to further a dangerous agenda. But in general the board and Trust were extremely supportive.

In 1989, I asked Frank Millar if he would be interested in joining the staff of *The Irish Times*. He had carved out a successful niche for himself in television, working with the Brian Walden programme. He had shown himself to have an aptitude for media work and he undoubtedly had an attractive career path ahead in TV. But I believed he might be persuaded to go the print route. Frank was living in London and our London editor, Ella Shanahan, was coming towards the end of her tour there. Ella was energetic, politically astute and had adapted well to the Westminster environment, but she did not wish to stay on in London. We would have to fill a vacancy when she returned to Dublin.

I was concerned that even though we were devoting considerable resources to our coverage of the North and to Anglo-Irish relations, we were still not getting the necessary depth of analysis in respect of unionism. This was no criticism of any of the journalists concerned. We had had a sequence of good Northern editors. They were invariably supported by good staff, usually two or three in addition to the Northern editor. But the assignment was tough. Hours were long and events, by definition, were unpredictable. All that the on-the-ground staff could manage to do was keep pace with news events as they unfolded.

I found that Northern editors generally began to fray at the edges after about two years and they were usually showing clear effects of strain after three. Their support staff worked hard too. We had a tragic loss in 1992 when a young reporter in the Belfast office, Anne Maguire, was killed at the wheel of her car as she drove back to work in Belfast. Ken Magennis, the Unionist MP for Fermanagh (later Lord Magennis) telephoned me to tell me that Anne had crashed her car not far from his home. She had died instantly. It appeared that she had either been taken ill or nodded off at the wheel.

Arrangements in London were little better. The London editor, Ella Shanahan, was fully stretched with coverage of politics at Westminster and she worked hard at maintaining contacts across the spectrum. We had an invaluable resource in Mary Holland who could move from the Falls Road to the Shankill to the office of the Secretary of State, writing with the same graceful fluidity and insight. But Mary was possibly at her least comfortable with unionist politicians.

I knew there was bound to be some apprehension about appointing a former general secretary of the unionist party as *The Irish Times's* London editor. There would be accusations of partisanship. For some, it would be confirmation of the paper's subliminal unionist or pro-British tendencies. Nevertheless, there was a long tradition of crossover between politics and journalism at *The Irish Times*. A number of staff had run for electoral office or worked as political organisers, usually on the left. If it was acceptable from the left, I reasoned, it should be acceptable from the right (if that was where one placed the Ulster Unionists). Moreover, Frank was gone more than three years from Glengall Street—a decent period of decontamination.

Eugene McEldowney was the news editor at this time. Eugene was a Belfast Catholic, born and reared in Ardoyne. An amiable but fiery colleague, full of passion and outspoken, he was at first aghast at the idea. I took him to meet Millar for lunch at the Westbury Hotel. There was some preliminary skirmishing as North Belfast Protestant and Ardoyne Catholic faced each other across the table, but after a couple of glasses of wine the conversation took off as between the best of friends. I went back to chair the afternoon conference, leaving the two of them at work on a second bottle of wine. Frank Millar joined *The Irish Times*.

Frank's addition to the coverage of the North significantly increased our editorial firepower, giving us a decided edge in reading the many minds of unionism. Before he had joined the staff, Frank came to me with a proposal for a series of in-depth, at-length interviews with the various political players, North and South, in London and Dublin. It was an idea that was both broad and deep. The interviewees would be asked to set out their stall as to their ambitions, their fears and the areas in which they believed they could contribute towards a settlement. We would give up to two full pages of *The Irish Times* to each interview.

'There's no visible political process right now,' Frank argued. 'This series can be something that takes the place of political dialogue or at least precedes it. It can be important.' The series started in January 1990 with an interview with Hume. Then, at intervals over subsequent weeks there were interviews with Peter Brooke, the Secretary of State; James Molyneaux, the Ulster Unionist leader; John Taylor, then viewed as a hardliner within the UUP; Peter Robinson, the deputy leader of the DUP and Cardinal Cahal Daly, the leader of the Catholic Church in Ireland.

The interviews were scrutinised in minute detail by the various players on all sides. Important indicators and possible concessions were identified. It was negotiation in advance of negotiation. We knew from our contacts within the

Department of Foreign Affairs and on the British side that they were regarded as an important first step towards opening real dialogue.

When the Belfast Agreement was signed and ratified by the people of all Ireland, North and South, in 1998 it reflected much of the thinking set out in Frank Millar's seminal series of interviews. It was a small contribution perhaps but one of which, I believe, the newspaper may be proud to this day.

——

Throughout the years in which I was editor the newspaper continued to devote considerable resources to coverage of the North. It was not merely a question of money. A great deal of intellectual energy went into it on a daily and weekly basis. The journalists on the ground were professional, committed and indeed often passionate about the story.

But *The Irish Times*'s contribution to covering Northern Ireland is not to be measured in any one series of articles or any particular editorial position or, indeed, in the labours of individual journalists. It should be measured in the consistent, day-in-day-out, year-on-year work on the ground by editors, reporters, photographers, columnists and contributors. It should be measured in the daily presentation of a composite picture that was as accurate, fair and balanced as human effort could make it.

The Irish Times aimed to ensure that an interested party, whether in Washington, London, Dublin or on the streets of Belfast, could always get a fair picture of what was happening. Feature writers or specialists for weekly magazines or Sunday newspapers can make a sometimes spectacular impact with one story or column. So can one-off TV programmes. The contribution required of daily journalism is different. It involves a demanding routine, it requires commitment, stamina and patience. It can make inordinate demands on its practitioners.

Gerry Moriarty stayed with the story in difficult years while he and his wife, Shelagh, watched over the failing health of their young daughter, Naoise, who died in February 2002. Déaglán de Bréadún was bi-locational during the years of Drumcree and the final negotiations of the Belfast Agreement, working long hours in the North and returning to his family in Dublin when circumstances permitted. He published a fine book, *The Far Side of Revenge*, at the end of his tour. It was critically acclaimed as one of the most accurate and insightful accounts of the peace process.

In later years, as the peace process dragged out and as the Sinn Féin/IRA axis dithered between the constitutional and the paramilitary pathways, some other media delighted in excoriating *The Irish Times* for its support for the process. Some of it, I believe, was sour grapes. Some of it came from convictions sincerely held.

The Irish Times adhered to the view that the only way forward was a

(Above, from left) Eileen O'Brien (*The Irish Times*), the author when editor of the *Garda Review*, Michael Heney (RTÉ) Jim Carney (*Irish Independent*), Ella Shanahan (*Cork Examiner*) and Pat Holmes (*The Irish Press*), on the first ever visit by journalists to Mountjoy Prison in 1973. (Below), the author on his first day in the editor's chair, 16 December 1986 under Willie Connor's portrait of R. M. Smyllie. Photos: *The Irish Times*.

R.M. 'Bertie' Smyllie, probably in The Palace, Fleet Street. In later years, there was a migration to The Pearl Bar, nearer the newspaper. Photo: *The Irish Times*.

Bruce Williamson on his retirement in the newsroom. Douglas Gageby looks on. Photo: *The Irish Times*.

The women writers of *The Irish Times* made a distinctive contribution to its development from the 1960s onwards. This group posed in the newsroom in the late 1970s for a promotional picture. Back row: (l-r) Gabrielle Williams, Maeve Donelan, Mary Cummins, Caroline Walsh. Front row: (l-r) Christina Murphy, Renagh Holohan, Mary Maher, Geraldine Kennedy. Photo: *The Irish Times.*

Douglas Gageby with a newsroom group in the early 1980s. At the desk: (l-r) Dennis Kennedy, Conor O'Clery (holding the poster). In the foreground: (l-r) Des Bury, Douglas Gageby. In the background: (l-r) Conor Brady, Pat Nolan, Paul Murray, Maeve Donelan, Pat Comerford, Clodagh Haugh. Photo: *The Irish Times.*

(Above) Tom McDowell toasts the old Hoe and Crabtree press at its decommissioning in 1986. Jim Cooke, production director, is fourth from left; the author second from right. (Below) Douglas Gageby, Tom McDowell and George Hetherington at the same event. Photos: *The Irish Times*.

Three of the major figures in *The Irish Times* in the years of change and development from the 1960s on. Christina Murphy, (right) led the newspaper's educational coverage and the development of its educational services. Fergus Pyle (below) was editor from 1974 to 1977. He was courageous and energetic, but circumstances combined to make his tenure difficult. Ken Gray (bottom right) pictured here on his retirement. He joined the newspaper in 1939 and served as deputy editor under Douglas Gageby and Conor Brady. His classic design, developed in the late 1950s, is still reflected in the pages of the newspaper and in the masthead. Photos: *The Irish Times*.

All friends together—for a night at least. At a NNI function, during the 1980s. (l-r) Éamon de Valera, *The Irish Press*; Brian Lenihan TD; Tom McDowell, *The Irish Times*; Louis O'Neill, *The Irish Times*; John Meagher, Independent Newspapers. Photo: *The Irish Times*.

Launching *The Irish Times*/ Aer Lingus awards for literature in 1988, at the Pierpoint Morgan Library in New York: (l-r) Conor Brady, editor, *The Irish Times*; David Kennedy, chief executive, Aer Lingus; Jacqueline Kennedy Onassis; Padraig McKernan, Department of Foreign Affairs. Photo: *The Irish Times*.

With the Taoisigh of the day. (Above) Charles Haughey, Michael Keane, editor of the *Sunday Press* and the author at the launch of Conor O'Clery's book *Phrases Make History Here*. Photo: *The Irish Times*. (Below) With Albert Reynolds at the presentation of a draft Defamation Bill prepared by the National Newspapers of Ireland. Louis O'Neill, chairman of NNI at the podium. Photo: Eric Luke/*The Irish Times*.

A rare photograph of *The Irish Times* Trust and Board together. This was on the occasion of a dinner to mark Douglas Gageby's retirement from the board (1988).
Back row: (l-r) Jim Cooke, Ken Gray, Louis O'Neill, Conor Brady, Derek McCullagh, Bruce Williamson.
Front row: (l-r) Don Reid, Matt Macken, Jacob Weingreen, Thekla Beere, Douglas Gageby, Tom McDowell (chairman), James Walmsley, Donal Nevin, Richard Wood, Colette Quigley, Desmond Neill. Photo: *The Irish Times.*

At the launch of Ivor Kenny's book, *Talking to Ourselves*, in 1994, a group of Ireland's editors, North and South. Back row: (l-r) Damien Kiberd, *Sunday Business Post*; Michael Brophy, *Star*; Vincent Browne, *Sunday Tribune*; Hugh Lambert, *The Irish Press*; Edmund Curran, *Belfast Telegraph*; Tom Collins, *Irish News*; Kieran Walsh, *Munster Express.* Front: (l-r) Vinnie Doyle, *Irish Independent*; Conor Brady, *The Irish Times*; Ivor Kenny; Michael Smurfit; Michael Keane, *Sunday Press*; Joe Mulholland, RTÉ; Fergus O'Callaghan, *Cork Examiner.* Absent: Keith Baker, BBC Northern Ireland; Aengus Fanning, *Sunday Independent*; Brian Looney, *The Kerryman*; Geoff Martin, *NewsLetter*; Colin McClelland, *Sunday World*; John Cunningham, *Connacht Tribune.* Photo: Lensmen.

negotiated settlement, supported across both communities, with full demilitarisation and an unqualified acceptance of constitutional means alone. I never saw any proposal for a better way.

We consistently demanded that Sinn Féin/IRA meet the full requirements of the Belfast Agreement in regard to decommissioning of weapons before they could be allowed fully to share in executive power. We took an editorial line that was strongly supportive of the Ulster Unionist leader, David Trimble, in these demands. For a period, the newspaper was referred to disparagingly in republican circles as 'The Decommissioning Times'.

And we insisted that Sinn Féin sign up for the Northern Ireland Policing Board, thus fully supporting and taking its place in the oversight of the new police. That caused some slight frissons with some of my contacts in Foreign Affairs. The Government had not yet come to that position. The Irish Times was seen from Iveagh House as pushing the pace and supporting a 'unionist' agenda.

In spite of—or possibly because of—the resources and energy that The Irish Times put into its Northern Ireland coverage over these years, the attitudes of Southern readers to our coverage remained something of a paradox. Our reader-research told us that very few readers in the Republic gave more than a cursory glance at our Northern coverage, apart from when there was violence to report. One piece of research told us that there were certain key words that simply turned readers off, immediately diverting them to some other item or to another page; the turn-off words included 'Paisley', 'unionist', 'nationalist', 'republican' and so on.

One word in particular—'extradition'—became a bugbear with readers. The extradition to the UK of persons accused of so-called 'political offences' was a bone of bitter contention between Dublin and London during most of the 1990s until the signing of the Belfast Agreement. In general, we took a line in support of such extradition applications by the British. But the arguments in each case were tortuous and often seemingly endless. I doubt if more than a handful of readers, beyond those individuals directly affected by the issue, read the acres of newsprint we committed to the issue.

But it was a central principle of policy—wholly endorsed by the board and the Trust—that we should not dilute or scale down our coverage. In times of important decision-making on the national question, sales of the newspaper always increased, and with them, the volume of relevant 'Letters to the Editor' —always a telling indicator.

When the time came to take the important constitutional steps—the removal of the 1937 claim to jurisdiction over Northern Ireland and the ratification of the Belfast Agreement—most of the other mainstream media had come to the same position as ourselves. That was gratifying, if also a little exasperating, having held the ground for so long, more or less on our own.

But even with the denouements of late 2004 and early 2005, confirming the continuing links between the 'republican family' and criminality, I believe the

Belfast Agreement has not been bested, at least as an ideal. It remains, in its essence, the preferred way forward to a society which can be inclusive, peaceful and based on the rule of law. Only time will tell if it can be sustained or whether it will have to be replaced by something that falls short of what the people of Ireland voted for.

9

THE ECONOMY, THE ECONOMY, THE ECONOMY

Editorials in The Irish Times *are like something written by an ould wan sitting in a bath with the cold water lapping around her fanny.*

— C.J. HAUGHEY

There was scarcely time to get my feet under the desk, before I had to position *The Irish Times* for one of the most crucial general election contests in the history of the State.

The election campaign of February 1987 was conducted in bitter weather. It reflected the national mood. The economy was in deep crisis. In late January a middle-ranking civil servant told me that at morning coffee break in the Department of Finance, the talk was of the International Monetary Fund arriving in Dublin to take over the running of the economy. Some economists spoke ominously of the banking system being under pressure. It was more a failure of the political system than of economics.

Through the 1970s and 1980s, the once monolithic party that had been Fianna Fáil had splintered and sundered. Fianna Fáil had its critics. But that its energy and singlemindedness had been important elements in driving the economic advances of earlier years could not be in doubt. Now those energies were dissipated.

The crisis of the North revealed deep fault lines in the party's understanding of what its nationalism should stand for in contemporary conditions. The bitterness of the arms trials and the split between moderates and extremists on the North accelerated the drift to faction that had followed the leadership contest between Charles Haughey and George Colley.

Overshadowing it all was the *persona* of Charles Haughey. Some within the party believed he was the devil incarnate. Others saw him as the Messiah. A great many in the centre-ground of the party were unsure of him but felt they should support the leader—if only because they were not going to be told what to do by anybody, least of all the Dublin media.

The net result was that Fianna Fáil had failed to get a grip on the economy in the early 1980s, notwithstanding a state-of-the-nation style address by Haughey, telling the public that Ireland was living beyond its means and that corrective measures would have to be taken. The struggle for power eclipsed every other task and diverted political energies.

The preoccupation of the political classes with Haughey extended to the media. Enormous energies and resources were invested by the newspapers and to a lesser extent by the broadcasters to reading the situation around him. Who was with him? Who was against him? Who was changing sides? Was he stronger or weaker in control at any given time?

Now the country seemed to be facing the possibility of economic meltdown. And the only prospect of rescue seemed to repose in Charles J. Haughey. He was antagonistic to many of the things *The Irish Times* stood for in its columns. To say that the newspaper faced something of a policy dilemma would be an understatement.

Somebody, it may have been John Healy, had once described Fianna Fáil as 'the natural party of government'. There was more than a little justification in that, although it was not a view taken by *Irish Times* leader-writers. Since 1932 the party had an almost unbroken majority support from the electorate. When it did go out of office, twice and briefly, the coalitions that replaced it lacked the coherence of a single-party government.

So it was in the period 1982-1987. The coalition of Fine Gael and Labour was relatively successful in certain areas of policy, notably in regard to consolidating Ireland's new relationship with the European Economic Community and in redefining the relationship between Ireland and the UK over Northern Ireland, through the 1985 Hillsborough Agreement. But the ideologies of the two parties were very different and their respective solutions to the State's economic woes were poles apart.

Fianna Fáil has always proclaimed a grievance against *The Irish Times*: that it has been inimical to the party and that it is inherently biased against it. That certainly was not so in the general election campaign of February 1987.

A critical stance towards government—whoever happens to be in power—is deeply engrained in the culture of *The Irish Times*. It goes back to the founding editors whose excoriations of the Dublin Castle administration were framed within broad, pro-establishment principles.

Since Fianna Fáil had been in office for most of the time since 1932, it was therefore natural that the party and its leadership should have come in for a greater share of criticism. John Edward Healy and R.M. Smyllie set the newspaper's tone towards Fianna Fáil in the 1930s and 1940s.

I resolved from the beginning that whenever possible I would write my own editorials on key national issues and at key times. Douglas Gageby had not always done do, often delegating the task to others, usually Jim Downey or myself. I opened a round of discussions about the coming election with the political staff.

Opinions were divided. Bruce Williamson offered the view that since Haughey and Fianna Fáil had got the country into the jam it was in, we should be in favour of obliging them to get it out.

In a succession of editorials which I wrote in the three weeks leading up to Polling day, I placed *The Irish Times* clearly, but cautiously, as favouring a change of government. There were health and safety warnings about Mr Haughey. But the editorial stance of the newspaper was clear. If the economy were to be turned around, it was not going to be done by the present government.

It was difficult to put aside one's fears about Haughey on the Northern issue. The arms trials were long past but he had all but scuttled the New Ireland Forum and he had railed against the 1985 Hillsborough Agreement.

I judged Haughey's stance on The North to be largely pragmatic. He attacked the Forum and the Hillsborough Agreement, in my view, simply because they were the achievements not of Fianna Fáil and himself but of his political opponents. I had many fierce arguments with John Healy about this. Healy reasoned that Haughey was simply doing what the Leader of the Opposition had to do. I disagreed. The national interest had to come before party advancement.

At the same time, I reckoned that once in office, Haughey would work the Hillsborough Agreement as assiduously as if he had been its architect himself. I discussed it with John Hume, who took the same view.

But the over-riding issue was the economy. On 10 January, the editorial ran:

Could Garret FitzGerald or Dick Spring, embarking on their enterprise of government a little over four years ago, have thought it would come to this? Hardly. An administration that came to office with so much promise, in which so much hope and goodwill were reposed, stands battered, humiliated almost.

It has been clear for some time that the business of government has all but ceased . . . Is there anything this Government can profitably do for the people who elected it, by hanging on in office for one more day? Even its once-ardent admirers are saying no. The business community which welcomed Garret FitzGerald as the Taoiseach of economic expertise wants change. The Labour movement which gave the young Dick Spring the chance to prove himself, sees its members' living standards eroded, their jobs vanishing. It is not merely a question, at this stage, of material loss. National morale is on the slide.

On 21 January, I wrote a second leader castigating the Government.

The economic crisis which it promised to confront is more acute than when it came to office just a little over four years ago. Unemployment has reached levels unimagined at that time. National morale has steadily dropped . . . the Government's failures outweigh its successes.

These editorials displeased many who could not conceive of *The Irish Times*, implicitly, if not yet explicitly, urging readers to put Garret FitzGerald out and to put Charlie Haughey in. Quite a few readers wrote in or telephoned their sentiments of disgust. It did not please all of my colleagues either. Dick Walsh, political correspondent, was angry and said so. Dick's position was that Fine Gael and Labour had inherited the mess left behind after Haughey's first disastrous term as Taoiseach and they had done as good a job as possible in the circumstances.

But though *The Irish Times* called for change, I was not prepared to have Charles Haughey painted as a blameless saviour either. In particular, there were reasons to be concerned about his position on the Anglo-Irish Agreement. Fianna Fáil had refused to be bound by the conclusions of the New Ireland Forum and Haughey had castigated the Agreement, sending Brian Lenihan to the US to condemn it there.

On 18 January Haughey went on RTÉ radio to detail his economic policies, or rather not to detail them. He spoke in vague, general terms about 'going for growth' and 'creating more resources'.

The following day *The Irish Times* editorial described his performance as 'vague and generalised', adding, 'Mr Haughey must tell a lot more.'

> . . . The big question mark over Mr Haughey stems from the fact that he funked tough decisions on the economy before—at a time when the problems were considerably less complex than they are today. Even more harsh decisions will have to be taken if the next government is to discharge its primary task of restoring the economic health of this State. What grounds are there for believing that Mr Haughey, if he becomes Taoiseach, will have the strength and resolution to act accordingly?

At editorial conferences, some journalists and section editors now began to argue in support of a possible coalition between Fine Gael and Des O'Malley's Progressive Democrats. If another FitzGerald-Spring government were to be an impossibility, there might yet be an alternative to Haughey in the form of a FitzGerald-O'Malley coalition.

Many in Fine Gael supported this notion, regarding the PDs as more natural allies than the Labour Party. Had there been a pre-election pact between the two, it is possible that the result of the 1987 election would have been quite different —and also the history of Ireland over the next 15 years. But O'Malley was not for throwing in his lot with Fine Gael. After the election, Fine Gael members complained bitterly about what they described as Des O'Malley's loss of nerve.

———

Haughey became Taoiseach for the second time on 10 March 1987 on the casting vote of the *Ceann Comhairle*. Brian Lenihan became Tánaiste. P.J. Mara was appointed as Government Press Secretary. Ray MacSharry, as expected, became Minister for Finance. MacSharry's brief was to get to grips with State spending and to slash the cost of running the country. He was to undertake his task with a single-mindedness that earned for him the soubriquet 'Mac the Knife'.

When the results of the election confirmed that Fianna Fáil would form the next government (albeit as a minority administration), the outgoing Taoiseach and leader of Fine Gael, Garret FitzGerald, announced that he was stepping down as party leader.

Garret had been a man of many parts. One significant part of him was a journalist. For some years he had written an 'Economic Comment' column each Saturday in *The Irish Times*. I spoke to him on the telephone at home and asked if he was planning to go back to journalism. He said he would be interested in doing a weekly column for the newspaper once he had got some other matters out of the way. We agreed on terms and, thankfully, on a moratorium of a few weeks before he would start. I had no money in the budget to take on new contributors.

Garret's column is still running in *The Irish Times*. It rarely constitutes light reading and sometimes it is penetrable only to readers of singular determination. But it has been a bellwether for many important trends and developments in Irish society. Political realities prevented Garret FitzGerald from doing what needed to be done for the Irish economy in the 1980s. But as an analyst he has been second to none.

The new leader of Fine Gael and of the Opposition in the Dáil was the Kildare deputy Alan Dukes. He defeated the deputy leader of the party and former Minister for Foreign Affairs, Peter Barry, as well as John Bruton, who had been Minister for Finance.

Dukes was FitzGerald's *protégé* and, importantly, was highly regarded by Garret's wife, Joan, who was a powerful influence in party circles. He had a reputation for being short-tempered and was often perceived as arrogant. He had a brilliant academic record and he could certainly be argumentative and pedantic. But as I got to know him around this time, I found that he had a quick sense of humour and went to some lengths to make himself amenable. I think he knew he had the reputation for arrogance and sought hard to counter it. He was not always wholly successful.

Fine Gael was in poor shape after losing the election. Labour's leader, Dick Spring, went off to lick his own wounds and began the process of reinventing the party which he was to bring back to power in the 1990s. But Fine Gael's road and Alan Dukes's options were much less clear.

On a chilly night in March, Dukes went to a joint Fine Gael-Chamber of Commerce meeting in the Dublin suburb of Tallaght and announced one of the most radical initiatives in the history of Irish public life. He committed Fine Gael to supporting the Haughey government in its economic policies so long as, in the judgment of the Fine Gael party, they were in the national interest.

It was a remarkable initiative. In the previous November, Garret FitzGerald

had called on Fianna Fáil to join in all-party support for the harsh budget that
would have to be framed for 1987. The suggestion had been greeted with derision
in Fianna Fáil circles. Later, in the course of the election campaign, a call from
FitzGerald to Fianna Fáil, demanding that they specify the cuts they would make
in public spending, was similarly rejected.

Dukes was taking the high ground. A cynical view was that he had no choice.
No responsible party leader could obstruct the work of rescue that now had to be
undertaken. And there was no prospect of any immediate resumption of the Fine
Gael-Labour alliance. So he was not going to be in power. He might as well be
seen to do the generous thing. Moreover, Dukes needed time to re-build a
demoralised party.

So John Healy argued, both to me personally and in his column. Dick Walsh
and our own political staff were enthusiastically in support of Dukes's initiative.
I was sure the newspaper should support Dukes and we came out strongly in
favour of what became known as 'The Tallaght Strategy'.

The steadying effect of the 'Tallaght Strategy' in reconciling public opinion to
the harsh medicine that MacSharry had to administer was considerable. What
was to come by way of cutbacks across the public services was to be deeply
painful. Dukes effectively closed off the possibility of political backlash for the
crucial early months of MacSharry's *blitzkrieg*.

Dukes got some public acknowledgment for his patriotism—but not a lot.
Some of the most influential of the Fine Gael party backroom strategists were
resentful and doubtful about the 'Tallaght Strategy'. Almost from the moment of
his election as leader—and certainly from the date of the Tallaght speech
—Dukes had people working against him within his own camp. Six months later,
leading figures in the party were in open defiance of their leader's stance.

One evening in March I was having a drink with a friend, David Molony, one
of the brightest young Fine Gael figures at this time. He had held the Fine Gael
seat in North Tipperary that was later won by Michael Lowry. 'Dukes will never
bring the party back to the high-water mark of Garret's time,' he told me. 'And
when they see that he can't do it, he'll be ditched. They won't stop to ask if
anybody else is more likely to do it than Alan.'

In fact, Garret FitzGerald had largely set the scene for Dukes's 'Tallaght
strategy' in a number of statements after the election. On 8 February he had
proposed that the parties should form an 'economic forum' to agree on national,
shared economic policies, in the fashion of the 'New Ireland Forum' which had
sought to create a pan-nationalist consensus—and did so with some effect.

In later times I was struck by the accuracy of David Molony's prediction.
David left politics in his forties to concentrate on his law practice in Thurles, Co
Tipperary. He was a big loss to public life. He was disappointed that Garret
FitzGerald had not given him some promotion, even as a junior minister. He died
unexpectedly in 2002, aged just 50.

Shortly before he resigned the leadership, in November 1990, Dukes invited me to lunch at the Grey Door restaurant and asked me to bring one or two *Irish Times* colleagues with me. We had a lengthy, and bibulous, lunch that stretched into the afternoon. That was very much a rarity for me as I always made it an article of faith to be present for the main afternoon editorial conference.

But I was struck by Dukes's downcast spirits and his anxiety to talk. Indeed, he seemed to be unwinding and opening himself up as if he was in the presence of friends. In the sense that we were not out to take his job, I suppose, he was. His resignation was finally hung on the poor showing of the Fine Gael candidate, Austin Currie, in the 1990 presidential election. But in reality, the knives had long been out for him. Looking back, it is perhaps remarkable that he survived as leader for almost four years.

———

As soon as Haughey's Government took office, Ray MacSharry set about his campaign to rein in the public finances. *The Irish Times* was in a dilemma. On the one hand, we had argued that the new Government had to give priority to solving the crisis of the economy. On the other hand, the newspaper had always urged high investment in State services like health, education and social welfare.

Now there were to be swingeing cuts across the public services. Recruitment was frozen. Public servants, including teachers, local authority workers and health workers were offered 'career breaks' of up to five years. It was a clever initiative. Many were happy to step out of the workforce with the security of knowing they could be guaranteed re-entry when they wished. The State's wage bill began to drop.

Later, a full-blown scheme for voluntary severance was introduced, the first such scheme for the public service in the history of the State. MacSharry announced that the State would pay up to £130 million in compensation for 10,000 redundancies in the public sector.

On 22 February Haughey had indicated that he wanted to prioritise the restoration of some form of national agreement on pay. If government, unions and employers could agree on a programme that controlled wage claims, it would go a long way towards restoring some confidence in the economy.

Haughey had appointed a young North Dublin TD, Bertie Ahern, as his Minister for Labour and to him fell the task of advancing negotiations with the social partners. Ahern was the ideal choice. He was emerging with a reputation as a natural-born negotiator.

Talks between Government and the Irish Congress of Trade Unions opened in May. It would be some months before the programme involving government and social partners could be agreed, but the opening of talks sent important signals. At the same time, minds were concentrated by the possibility of closure of the giant Packard plant in Dublin and by the loss of hundreds of jobs at the Baxter Travenol plant at Castlebar, Co Mayo.

Another important initiative of Haughey's—although somewhat later in his administration—was the establishment of the National Treasury Management Agency. Some very senior figures in the civil service, notably the Department of Finance, were opposed to the idea. I had telephone calls from a number of these, describing it as a first step towards picking off the 'plum jobs' for Fianna Fáil favourites. But *The Irish Times* applauded the move. The strategy behind the creation of the Agency was to take the management of the national debt away from the Department of Finance and place it in the hands of skilled fund managers.

The Agency was placed under the charge of a particularly able civil servant, Michael Somers, who had been second secretary of the Department of Finance. Over the coming years, Somers and a small, hand-picked team managed the debt in a way that saved billions for the taxpayer. As borrowings matured, the Agency would relocate loans in markets where interest rates were lower. In time, the Agency was to be given additional tasks. But its contribution to stabilising the economy was significant.

The country held its breath in the first few months of Haughey's new government. From the perspective of today's levels of economic success, it is difficult to imagine how uncertain things appeared at this time. It was far from clear that the precipitous decline in the national finances could be halted. The news each week brought contradictory signals.

The absence of any collective agreement on pay meant that workers in every sector felt they had to assert their own claims and look after their own interests. Work stoppages and threats of stoppages—often unofficial in the sense that they were not approved by union leaders—were frequent.

There were strikes, at the ESB, at RTÉ, at the Shelbourne Hotel, in the radiography departments at the hospitals. In June, non-consultant hospital doctors went on strike. In May there were power blackouts as a result of the dispute at the ESB. In August the provincial bus services were shut down when drivers went on strike. The leading industrial stocks on the Irish Stock Exchange were dropping in value, wiping millions off savings and investments by corporations and individuals alike.

Unemployment remained around the 250,000 mark and continued to rise through April. Blue chip companies continued to shed jobs. Guinness announced they would cut 800 from the workforce. Irish Distillers dropped 200. Hanlon's ambulance factory in Longford was shut with a loss of 250 jobs. 750 went at Waterford Crystal. 360 went at the Galtee bacon plant at Mitchelstown, Co Cork. Irish Steel laid off 200. Even Trinity College dropped 150 general workers off its payroll.

In reality, many companies were restructuring and shedding payroll costs in anticipation of recovery. In the prevailing conditions of depression it was easier to sell the notion of smaller workforces and new, more efficient technologies. Many companies were, in effect, using the recession to shake out their workforces and to re-equip for the future.

But international conditions were improving and interest rates began to come down. First, the banks took 1 per cent off interest rates for business borrowers. Then home loan rates began to come down. In March, a trade surplus of £46 million was recorded. In June it had reached £181 million. A drop in the US dollar in April somewhat eased the pressure of the national debt.

In June the Goodman International company announced it was investing £250 million in meat plants around the country and in August it announced that it had signed a contract worth £37.5 million to supply beef to Iran. The Government put an export-guarantee scheme in place, effectively undertaking to compensate Irish beef processors if their overseas customers defaulted on payment.

In June the rate of inflation was down to 2.8 per cent, the lowest for nearly 20 years. In July the IDA said it had 76 new overseas industrial investments in the pipeline and that up to 5,000 jobs would be created. These were small straws of hope blowing in a still chilly economic wind.

In November the Central Bank estimated that the economy would grow by 2 per cent in the current year. Two per cent would scarcely transform the country's fortunes. But it would be movement in the right direction. And it would match Haughey's pre-election promise of securing modest growth.

In November the three-year agreement between Government, unions, employers and farm organisations was finalised. The National Programme for Economic Recovery was acclaimed as a triumph for the Government and in particular for Haughey and Ahern. Workers were to have modest percentage raises over the three-year period while the Government pledged itself to modest concessions on taxation. Above all, the pact was to give Irish business and Irish enterprise a stable framework within which to plan and develop for the future.

On 13 November the Government announced that State expenditure for the year ahead would be reduced by £485 million. The next day in the Dáil, the proposed cuts were supported by Fine Gael and the Progressive Democrats. This was a radical experience in Irish politics.

The largest single area of State expenditure, by far, was health. A complex and notoriously inefficient system of health boards and committees covered the country. Money poured into the health services, apparently without end. Health was to be MacSharry's first target.

As the scale of the MacSharry cuts became apparent, health workers began to protest. In May the Minister for Health, Dr Rory O'Hanlon, was booed and jostled by health employees when he visited Waterford. Two western health boards bluntly refused to keep within the budget allocation set by the Department of Health. Mass protests were organised at the Dáil. On 24 June a national day of stoppage was called and marchers took to the streets in cities and towns.

Across the country, hospitals were shutting services and in some cases closing their doors for good. St James's in Dublin shed 300 beds. Dr Steevens', the Royal Hospital on Dublin's Upper Baggot Street and Monkstown Hospital all closed.

MacSharry's second target was education. It was fortunate for Irish education that the Minister for Finance had first concentrated his firepower on the larger target represented by the health system. The price of restoring economic stability became starkly apparent as health facilities shut their doors and as health workers took to the streets in protest. Teachers, parents and others involved in education took one look at what was happening in health and resolved not to let it happen to their schools and colleges.

The Irish Times found itself playing a role in defence of the educational infrastructure that was, in the long term, significant. Christina Murphy, whom I had appointed as a duty editor, had been writing about education right through her career in journalism. She remained deeply committed to the advancement of Irish educational standards. She, in turn, had been instrumental in appointing Michael Foley as education correspondent. Michael could scarcely have hoped to compete in breaking news stories with the *Independent's* John Walshe, but he brought a considerable intelligence and a sense of social purpose to his coverage of education.

They both had good connections to the Minister for Education, Mary O'Rourke. They also had excellent connections with the various lobby groups in the educational sector—the teachers' unions, the parents' representative-associations and so on.

In May, Christina asked to talk to me confidentially about what she was hearing in regard to proposed cuts in the education budgets. 'They're going to destroy the primary schools sector if they go ahead,' she said. 'Mary O'Rourke is caught between a rock and a hard place. As a member of the Cabinet she has to support the cutbacks but as a teacher she knows that damage on this scale can't be undone.' We agreed that *The Irish Times* would do all it could to mobilise opinion in defence of the primary schools' budgets. But we would do so within a general, continuing support for the Government's economic stringency measures.

Teachers sought ICTU backing to block the educational cuts in August. Mary O'Rourke announced cuts of £80 million, which the teachers claimed would translate into 2,500 fewer teachers and bigger classes.

From September, *The Irish Times* sustained an almost daily campaign of coverage on the looming cuts in education—especially the primary sector. Columnists, reporters and feature writers focused on the issue. The letters page became a noticeboard of protest from educationalists, parents and others. When the Dáil reassembled in October, the Opposition—and not a few of Fianna Fáil's own backbenchers—took up the case. A wall of opposition to the cuts in primary education was being constructed.

On 23 November *The Irish Times's* editorial ran:

It is the very arbitrariness of the teacher cutbacks which has provoked the strongest public reaction . . . the parents' organisations have mobilised themselves very effectively—and rightly so—against the teacher cutbacks. But, in the longer run, they must also consider what alternative measures would be acceptable to them. If the government does back away from national school cuts, the equivalent funding—£20 million—must be found in some other direction: higher taxes, additional charges for some educational services. Cuts in the secondary school budget?

On 24 November the Government was defeated in the Dáil. It had asked the House to endorse a motion recognising that the 'National Programme for Economic Recovery represents an equitable sharing of the burden by the different sections of the community'. The defeat was, effectively, a rejection of the proposed cuts in primary education.

The Irish Times editorial the following day observed:

There are apparently some mutterings of discontent in the Fianna Fáil party over Mrs O'Rourke's personal performance. This is unfair: it was the Government which decided on the package of cuts and making a scapegoat out of the Minister for Education is no solution to the wider problem of finding alternative means of saving the £20 million represented by the primary education cuts.

The next day the Government promised to review its proposals for primary schools. A few days later, O'Rouke suspended Circular 10/87 which would have given effect to increasing class sizes. On 11 December Haughey promised to maintain the quality of Irish primary schools and a joint review group of Government and the Irish National Teachers' Organisation (INTO) was established.

Haughey, clearly irritated by what he saw as obstruction of Government policy, warned of an election and there was talk of a pre-Christmas dissolution of the Dáil. On 2 December the Government suffered its second Dáil defeat in little more than a week on its proposal to abolish the National Social Services Board.

The Irish Times had played a supporting, but not insignificant, role in preventing the reduction of a fine system of primary education. I do not claim we were alone among the media in urging caution. It was a combined effort. The *Irish Independent* took a similar line led by their well-informed Education Correspondent, John Walshe. But we were singular in the consistency of our focus and the scale on which we allocated resources and space.

I often wish that we had done the same in regard to the health services. It might have been possible to prevent at least some of the damage inflicted which has not been put right to this day. On the other hand, the health sector did not have the strong, united lobby in its defence that the education sector had.

The Government's health estimates went through the Dáil on the same day that the motion of confidence was defeated, again enabled by Fine Gael's and the

Progressive Democrats' decision to abstain.

By September the annual trade surplus was £1bn and Haughey announced on 18 September that the economy was on the way to recovery. On 16 December the Economic and Social Research Institute (ESRI) said that the national debt could be 'stabilised' by 1990 without the need for further cuts.

The next day IDA committed itself to creating 40,000 new jobs a year up to 1990. Mortgage rates fell a further 0.5 per cent. Two days before Christmas, Bertie Ahern, the Minister for Labour, announced there had been no unofficial strikes in the previous three-month period.

It was clear that the State was beginning to break out of the economic stasis that had hung over it through much of the 1980s. The Government's policy of harsh medicine was essential if the economy were to be turned around. But at the same time it was clear that a terrible price was being paid across the range of state services—hospitals, schools, social welfare, policing and so on.

The newspaper remained firmly supportive of the Government's broad policies of economic stringency and reconstruction. But it could not be indifferent or remain silent as state services were slashed, hurting ordinary people and perhaps inflicting irreversible damage on the community.

Internal tensions at the newspaper rose steadily as these issues became more acute. John Healy and I spoke on the telephone daily and sometimes more often. I listened to Healy though I did not always, or even often, take his advice. But it was important to hear his perspective as the clamour and protest rose against the Government's harsh cost-cutting policies.

On the other hand, the political staff, led by Dick Walsh, was more harshly critical of Haughey in particular and of his government in general. Dick's political voyage had been complex. He was originally close to Sinn Féin, during its Marxist years. He was a man of extraordinary acuity and intelligence as well as great personal charm.

He was not the only journalist with Sinn Féin associations within the newspaper. A cohort of five or six, none at senior level but nevertheless influential, were either members or had been members of the so-called 'Stickies'.

Some individuals who were involved in left-wing politics were also active in the NUJ chapel. I knew they were watching their new editor with interest, especially to ensure that the newspaper did not veer too far to the right at this time of real social tension. I was aware of them. And they were aware that I was aware of them. But there never was any real trouble between us. There was a healthy and cautious respect for each other's positions.

The Irish Times did not deviate from its position of support for the Government's broad economic objectives. But we deepened and extended our coverage of the areas most directly affected by cutbacks.

John Healy felt we were being over-critical of the Government and we fell out. He resigned his column and we did not speak for a year. Later, when he had been appointed by Haughey as a special press counsellor in Brussels (during Ireland's presidency of the EC) we resumed cordial relations. He stood me a fine dinner in Brussels. Healy was an idealist and a visionary, but he and I rarely talked without temperatures rising.

The news editor, Eugene McEldowney, constructed a loosely-grouped *corps* of reporters and commentators with interests and expertise in social, medical, economic and educational issues. They came together in conferences and often worked in collaboration. Among the group were Pádraig Ó Móráin, social services correspondent, a former social welfare official; Mary Cummins, formerly a nurse, who wrote about women's affairs; David Nowlan, medical correspondent and Christina Murphy, who was one of my two duty editors but who never relinquished her interest in the educational field.

Everything we began to learn as the year went by convinced us that the health and education cuts were biting too deeply. Christina continued to lead and direct coverage of the spending reductions within the education sector. We sent reporters all over the country, under David Nowlan's general guidance, to report on the deterioration of the health services.

As the year closed, it was becoming apparent that the once seemingly doomed vessel of the Irish economy might at least have halted its course on to the rocks, even if it had not quite turned around. MacSharry did the business. But it was tough work. I admired him, even though we were critical of much of what happened under his hand. I know he found his mission stressful and sometimes distasteful. Later, when he was Ireland's European Commissioner, he told me as much.

Other aspects of life in Ireland during the year had been grim. It had been the year of the Loughgall ambush, of the mass-murders at Enniskillen and of the kidnapping and mutilation of Dublin dentist John O'Grady. In my end-of-year editorial, I wrote:

It was a year to raise hopes rather then one in which to mark great achievement. Ireland did not climb out of the economic rut into which it had dug itself, but at least we stopped digging. Nor will 1987 be remembered as the year that Irishmen stopped murdering fellow-Irishmen in the name of politics or religion. Yet it may be remembered, in time, as the year in which the seeds of a new political settlement began to grow, pushing through the stony soil of the North.

GROWING THE *TIMES*

*If the circulation goes up you'll get a modest share of the credit.
But by God, if it goes down, they'll know whose head to come
looking for.*

—*Irish Times* Governor, PROFESSOR JAMES MEENAN

At the board of *The Irish Times* it was frequently emphasised by Trust members, in particular, that the newspaper was not 'about circulation'. That was true, in the sense that the editor was never in my experience called to review content or policy, on the grounds that either might antagonise or alienate readers.

But, of course, in the more general sense, no newspaper can be indifferent about circulation—or more precisely, about readership. I frequently argued at the board and at meetings of executives that readership is 'the engine that pulls the whole train'. If readership is moving forward or is at least steady, everything else should fall in behind it—sales revenue, advertising and the newspaper's fundamental, financial viability.

Maintaining or advancing readership is firstly the task of the editor. A famous editor of *The Times* of London once said that his first responsibility was to ensure that he was not to be the last editor of *The Times*.

In the first six months of my editorship I was asked on a number of occasions to set out my projections for circulation. I usually referred to the presentation I had put up when applying for the job. I was optimistic about circulation growth, although not as optimistic as later performance would have justified.

After one meeting, a member of the Trust, James Meenan, who had been Professor of Economics at UCD, came over to me at lunch. Board lunches were always buffet-style, with one course on a single plate. Meenan balanced his plate in one hand along with a wine glass and puffed at his pipe with the other.

'It's all guess work, isn't it . . . that circulation thing earlier?' he suggested. 'Informed guesswork,' I responded warily.

'Well, don't worry about it,' he laughed. 'If the circulation goes up you'll get a modest share of the credit. But by God, if it goes down, they'll know whose head to come looking for.'

Circulation did increase through 1987, right up to 1991. But it was not going to be sufficient, I knew, merely to add to the audited circulation of the newspaper. *The Irish Times* had to grow in its outlook and in what it stood for. Its policies had to evolve, as the society it served also changed and evolved.

Almost since its foundation in 1859, the newspaper had been a curious blend of conservative and liberal values. In the early years of the Irish Free State, it railed against the climate of censorship and repression that was being sponsored by the Cumann na nGaedheal Government. Yet it supported that Government in its economic policies and in its firm law-and-order stance against those who remained unreconciled to the Treaty.

The Irish Times attacked Cosgrave's 'Committee on Evil Literature' and the Censorship of Publications Act 1929 that followed. It opposed legislation that prohibited divorce and that added heavy penalties for anyone supplying contraceptives. Yet, the editor at this time, John Edward Healy, was scarcely a man of radical outlook.

The newspaper's combination of economic and political conservatism and social liberalism continued in Bertie Smyllie's editorship. Smyllie's *Irish Times* hammered away at the censorship of books, of cinema and of theatre through the 1940s and 1950s.

Inevitably, *The Irish Times*'s stance was to bring it into confrontation with a Catholic Church that was growing in strength and influence in the new State. In 1950, a controversy blew up in the newspaper's letters column under the heading 'The Liberal Ethic'. It crystallised into an argument over the role and special position of the Church, as provided for in Article 44 of the 1937 Constitution. The debate was vigorous and sometimes bitter. It was sustained for many months, with literally hundreds of letters pouring into the office each week.

When I became editor in 1986, the arguments over contraception, divorce, abortion and gay rights were still going on. *The Irish Times* had consistently argued that personal conscience and freedom of choice ought to be the principal determinants in these issues. It was alone among the national newspapers in most of this.

By the time I stepped down from the editorship in 2003, these arguments had all been resolved. The 'liberal agenda', with which *The Irish Times* had been synonymous, had been effectively attained. And *The Irish Times* had been joined on the liberal ground by all the other national media, although I believe we were still the only newspaper that argued explicitly in favour of a law permitting abortion in Ireland in limited circumstances.

It was perhaps flattering for us to find our traditional positions now taken up in this way. But it also meant that *The Irish Times*'s distinctiveness would henceforth have to be defined in different ways. I believed that *The Irish Times* had to broaden its view towards a world that was increasingly connected through travel, technology and the globalisation of economies. I also believed it had to broaden its appeal within Ireland. The urban-rural divide was disappearing.

There was no reason why *The Irish Times* of the future should remain largely a Dublin-focused newspaper.

'Policy at *The Irish Times* grows out of the walls,' Tom McDowell often quipped. In many ways he was right. I had no desire to alter the inheritance of liberal, progressive policies that had come to me through a line of editors going back to Dr Shaw. But I had to add to it. And that would take resources.

On the important political principles, *The Irish Times* would remain constant. The paper was in favour of the extension and deepening of the European Communities. It was in favour of a united Ireland but through strictly constitutional methods. It believed that the 1937 Constitutional claim to authority over Northern Ireland was not sustainable and should be replaced, in the context of a negotiated settlement, with an aspiration to unity.

On the great East-West divide, the paper was firmly on the side of western democracy, although it could be sharply critical of US foreign policy. It supported Ireland's stance of military neutrality, although it questioned the long-term sustainability of absolute neutrality in a more integrated Europe.

I believed we had to sustain these positions while developing the newspaper's perspective on the important influences that were shaping the world as we came towards the end of the twentieth century. I wanted to extend coverage of the sciences, of the new technologies and of the global issues that were emerging—AIDS, world income distribution, the future of Africa, the emergence of China as a big economic power. We needed to build up the newspaper's resources by appointing journalists to specialise in these areas and, where necessary, to work and report from abroad.

In time, I wanted to build up a greater presence for the newspaper across Ireland outside of Dublin. But in the meantime, I wanted to put a special emphasis on reporting change and development in the regional cities, the towns and villages.

Tom McDowell and Louis O'Neill could hardly have been more supportive. If I had an idea that required resources, Louis scoured and juggled the budgets to make it happen. If it was a smaller project, Seán Olson used his not infertile imagination to garner some savings within the overall editorial budget figures.

We developed the foreign news network and strengthened coverage across most areas of the paper. The new Part 2 sections came on stream—Weekend, Property, Business, Sport (initially on Mondays only). Christina Murphy developed an imaginative Part 2 called *Working and Living*. It was a blend of educational, vocational and careers news and information. It was immensely successful in bringing in new and, in particular, young readers.

I believed strongly in an integrated approach that co-ordinated editorial content, promotion, circulation and research activity. It was a more developed form of Douglas Gageby's 'Christmas Pudding' theory. Editorial provided the material to meet the range of tastes, promotion notified its availability to the readers, circulation efficiency ensured that the paper was available where it was wanted and in the numbers required, research confirmed—or otherwise—that the reader was satisfied.

Much of the circulation advance of the 1980s had been achieved through this methodology. Editorial instinct would be tested by research. For example, Gageby was convinced that a full TV listings, taking a whole page, would draw many additional readers to the newspaper. We made a variety of mock-up pages, tested them with readers, using the research company. The results were clear and positive.

When the page was launched, we put on a sustained promotions programme using radio, posters and our own in-paper spaces. The circulation staff canvassed newsagents and added additional copies as sales picked up. Then we used research to test readers' reactions again. If there were aspects of the page the readers found attractive, we generally enhanced these. If there were aspects they disliked, we would consider if they had to be modified. Frequently we set aside the research and went with our instincts, calculating that readers' tastes would adapt. It wasn't exactly rocket-science. But it helped to bring the paper to an ever-widening and increasing cohort of readers.

This approach was used across much of the content. But it was resolutely eschewed in relation to hard news or editorial policy. It was recognised that these were areas in which the paper had to lead—rather than respond to latent or expressed desires.

During Douglas Gageby's editorship, promotional activity was a joint editorial-commercial operation. But it was content-led, directed by myself and later, for a time, by Paul Tansey who was appointed to succeed me when I went to edit the *Sunday Tribune*. But in the early 1980s it migrated from editorial to the commercial side of the organisation.

In spite of my best endeavours, I never succeeded in getting it transferred back. It was guarded jealously by the sales and marketing executives. They took the view that this was more a commercial than an editorial area of activity. I reasoned that since the process was driven by the newspaper's content, the people who created that content and were closest to it—editors and journalists—should direct it.

I lost that argument. My way was unorthodox in terms of traditional newspaper structures. But in latter times, many other successful newspapers in Europe and the US have put the promotional function under editorial direction, with positive results.

The circulation figures strengthened more or less consistently through 1987–1993. But the company finances were problematic. The board agreed on a series of price rises which made the paper relatively expensive, in a period when cash was tight. The commercial executives argued that since we were offering a richer and more varied editorial menu than our rivals, we could charge a good deal more. We tried it, but the result was a slump in sales. In 1989 we had passed through the 90,000 barrier. In 1993 the prospect arose that we might fall down through it again.

Fortunately, the economy was beginning to strengthen. Unemployment was still well in excess of 200,000 but it had fallen back from the peak of 250,000 recorded in early 1987. Profits remained low but there was enough each year to maintain a sense of innovation in the newspaper.

We strengthened the news area, adding staff to the politics team and creating new specialist roles. This meant that reporters like Frank McDonald, for example, who had built a reputation in the planning and development area, could be freed from routine newsroom tasks in order to concentrate fulltime on their specialties.

Extra paging and resources were provided for sport which was thriving under the leadership of Malachy Logan. Patsey Murphy, who had come to the newspaper from New York, via the *Education Times*, started an innovative weekly section titled *Shopfront*. Kieran Fagan edited a TV page that was informative, eclectic and, above all, accurate. Caroline Walsh, who later became literary editor, ran a lively features page,

The 1990s saw a great surge in activity in Irish arts, entertainment and culture. In part, this may have been due to the shortage of conventional career opportunities for young people. Everywhere there seemed to be new bands, new artists, new writers, new film-makers. And for the first time, Irish artists and entertainers began to make their mark in significant numbers outside of Ireland.

The Irish Times was ahead of other Irish newspapers in its coverage of arts and culture. *The Irish Press* challenged us for the high-ground with its *New Irish Writing* feature, edited by David Marcus. But I believed we had to consolidate our lead in the general area of arts and culture and that the newspaper should engage directly with these areas, encouraging talent and not merely reporting it.

I discussed the idea of an *Irish Times* literary prize with John Banville. He was all for it. I was of the view however that it should be an international prize, reflecting the international standing and outward vision of *The Irish Times* and not merely confined to Ireland. Banville, with Gerry Smyth, the chief sub-editor who was also a published poet, refined the idea and we devised the concept of a series of prizes for literature from the English-speaking world but with a special prize also for Irish writing.

Louis O'Neill and I had already talked about doing something in this area. He was enthusiastic. Unfortunately, we did not have the funds to do it on our own and we knew we had to find a partner. Louis suggested Aer Lingus. So we went to meet David Kennedy and Bill Maxwell, chief executive and corporate affairs director respectively at the airline. They were as enthusiastic as we were and a happy, if brief, alliance was formed.

The scheme of the prizes would involve travel for judges, critics and contestants, principally from North America and Britain. The airline took care of that. We appointed an administrator from our own staff, initially Seán Hogan and later Gerard Cavanagh, and undertook to provide coverage of the prizes each year, including a presentation ceremony to be held in Dublin. David Kennedy asked the President of Ireland, Dr Patrick Hillery, if he would agree to present the prizes and he responded positively. Every two years thereafter, the President of Ireland did the honours.

Early in 1988, David Kennedy and I, along with some *Irish Times* and Aer Lingus staff, travelled to New York and London to formally launch the literary prizes. In New York we were hosted by the prestigious Pierpoint Morgan Library. In London, the Irish Ambassador kindly allowed us to use the Irish Embassy at Grosvenor Place for the launch.

The acceptances among the New York guest list were a reassuring affirmation of the newspaper's reach. Jacqueline Kennedy Onassis and Governor Mario Cuomo were present. Curiously, the Dublin TD Liam Lawlor, later jailed for obstructing the corruption in planning tribunal at home, also turned up. To this day I have no idea how or why he happened to be there. He was not on any invitation list I saw, although had he been, he would have been welcome.

Aer Lingus had to pull out of the prize in 1990 due to trading difficulties at the airline. By then *The Irish Times* had improved its finances to the point at which we could take it on ourselves. Over the years, the prize became a recognised and coveted award in international literature. Unhappily, it was discontinued after I stepped down in 2002.

Tom McDowell, Louis and I shared the notion of establishing a series of events or activities that would link *The Irish Times* to areas of activity across Irish society. Thus the literary prize was followed in time by the Boyle Medal for Science (in association with the RDS). Professor Dervilla Donnelly, a Trust member, was instrumental in this initiative. Later, we set up *The Irish Times* Theatre Awards, in association with the ESB. Gerry Smyth, by now managing editor with responsibility for all the features areas of the newspaper, was the driving force behind this.

We already had a number of important educational events running, established by Christina Murphy. And we had for years run *The Irish Times*/PA Management awards for successful Irish businesses. This was Tom McDowell's particular favourite. The awards were always presented by the Taoiseach of the day and Tom very much enjoyed acting as Master of Ceremonies and joint host with the Managing Director of PA Management (Ireland).

These were important linkages that helped to broaden thinking within the newspaper and that challenged the instinctive tendency of journalists to talk mainly, sometimes exclusively, with other journalists.

––––

One of the most significant developments over this period was the establishment of *www.Ireland.com*, the website of *The Irish Times*. The website developed out of a shared vision between the business side of the organisation and the editorial side. In the early 1980s, Louis O'Neill had tasked one of his managers, Seamus

Conaty, with researching and putting up proposals for the development of an electronic publishing subsidiary. Seamus was a former Co Cavan footballer who had spent almost 20 years working in the Fleet Street newspaper milieu. He was gruff, determined and focused. I liked him enormously and although I did not always agree with him I developed a great respect for his judgment.

I had worked with Seamus in 1983 when I returned to *The Irish Times* after editing the *Sunday Tribune* and through him I had some feel for the exciting developments that were beginning to emerge around the internet. But my involvement and knowledge were peripheral by the early 1990s.

The Irish Times Ltd had a subsidiary company, Itronics Ltd, which had already set up a number of small but commercially successful operations, including a legal data base, Lexis, which was operated as a joint venture. Seamus Conaty was managing director of Itronics, reporting to Louis O'Neill.

In 1992 Seamus came up with the idea of publishing a daily summary of *The Irish Times* in electronic form, to be transmitted to customers overseas either by facsimile or by a newly-emerging communications system called e-mail. Louis asked me to assign an editor for the project. I chose Joe Breen, previously chief sub-editor. Joe was a dynamic, imaginative editor with a passion for the new technologies.

The combination of Seamus Conaty and Joe Breen was mercurial but productive. The electronic summary was not a great success. It proved extremely difficult to sell. But it was an important learning step on the way to the later development of the full electronic version of *The Irish Times* on *www.ireland.com*.

It was Seamus Conaty's inspired idea to register the domain-name *Ireland.com* to The Irish Times Ltd. When the full portal website got under way in 1995–1996, *The Irish Times* was among the first half dozen newspapers in the world to have a web edition. Joe Breen built a small staff of enthusiastic young journalists and designers around him and they ran an innovative and exciting operation from across Westmoreland Street with an electronic newsroom in Ballast House.

Later, on his return from Africa, Séamus Martin took over as editor in succession to Joe Breen. Deirdre Veldon became editor of *www.ireland.com* and an assistant editor of *The Irish Times* in 1999.

As editor of *The Irish Times* I had final editorial responsibility for the content of the website. I insisted that *www.ireland.com* editors and journalists attend the regular conferences. I wanted to ensure a high degree of cross-fertilisation between electronic and print journalists.

But I had no input into the commercial management or structure of Itronics Ltd. Louis O'Neill and Seamus Conaty were firmly of the view that the web edition journalists and designers should be kept separate from the newspaper's journalists. This argument was largely based on cost. They argued that if the website were to be asked to carry the high costs of newspaper salaries, it would lose money and be a drain on the company.

I argued the opposite view. I believed that an integrated newsroom, with print and electronic journalists working side by side, would create an exciting new dynamic. I also had a feeling that it might actually be less expensive. I lost that argument too. But in time, many newspapers began to come to my view. And the integrated newsroom is now commonplace.

The advent of www.Ireland.com gave the newspaper a great boost in prestige and profile. It also gave it a sizeable boost in circulation, in my view. In June 1996 we passed the 100,000 daily ABC mark and the circulation continued to climb right up to my last six months as editor, in June 2002, when it peaked at 120,397.

At least some of this circulation growth came from the young, returning graduates and others who had begun to flock back to Ireland as the economy grew. More than 100,000 came back in the period 1995–1998 and thousands of these became buyers and readers of the daily *Irish Times*. They had been linked to Ireland by *www.ireland.com* and had the habit of reading *The Irish Times* on screen during the years of their absence. When they came back they translated into print-readers.

By the mid-1990s the newspaper had the ideal circulation and readership profile. Circulation rose slowly but steadily. The ABC1 profile firmed up as educational standards were raised, as the skilled and professional classes expanded in numbers and as the economy grew. We had the readers. The advertisers followed. There were nights when we had to turn away tens of thousands of pounds worth of advertising because we did not have the pages to print it.

Audited circulation figures: *The Irish Times, The Irish Independent and The Irish Press*, 1956 to 2003

Year	Times	Independent	Press
1956	36,267	182,650	132,318
1960	35,033	171,502	119,658
1962	33,300	174,005	116,552
1964	35,642	169,996	122,844
1966	44,563	174,342	110,688
1968	53,850	171,335	102,578
1970	55,150	165,970	99,080
1973	67,976	166,890	94,115
1975	69,304	174,981	87,934
1977	62,325	175,336	92,064
1979	77,316	189,794	102,424
1982	87 433	173,838	101,393
1985	86,911	173,707	83,205
1987	87,352	151,733	75,912

Year	Times	Independent	Press
1990	94,929	154,234	60,287
1992	92,797	149,065	50,443
1994	93,678	145,452	38,889*
1996	102,460	160,032	
1998	111,729	163,367	
2000	116,280	168,184	
2001	120,397	170,075	
2002	114,537	169,533	
2003	117,565	162,463	

*The Irish Press ceases publication.

Note: In each case the figures given above are the second half-year ABC

11

WORKING WITH THE TRUST

. . . To publish The Irish Times *as an independent newspaper primarily concerned with serious issues for the benefit of the community throughout the whole of Ireland, free from any form of personal or party political, commercial, religious or other sectional control.*
—First Objective; Memorandum and Articles of The Irish Times Trust

When it was announced on 5 April 1974 that *The Irish Times* was to become a trust, the news was greeted by the media community with a degree of puzzlement. There were no acclamations. But journalists recall that there was a general sense of approval. Favourable comparisons were drawn with the Scott Trust that runs *The Guardian* in Britain. The newspaper's own business editor raised some questions in an article the next day. But they were not taken up elsewhere by other business journalists.

Between 1963 and 1974 *The Irish Times* had come back from the brink of extinction, through a period of remarkable resurgence, to a state of modest prosperity, led by editorial and circulation success. The Trust, it was announced, would protect *The Irish Times* from takeover. The ordinary shareholders had sold their interests to the new body, which would be composed of respected individuals, drawn from various walks of Irish life, north and south.

The newspaper would operate to a set of written principles. Future editors would be obliged to support these principles. By and large they reflected what had been *de facto* the newspaper's policies of recent years.

In an editorial headed 'New Every Morning', the newspaper itself expressed a breezy optimism about the new dispensation:

The setting up of a trust to maintain *The Irish Times*—as announced yesterday —is a reaffirmation of the independence of *The Irish Times*: it is a guarantee to those who produce *The Irish Times*, to those who read *The Irish Times* and to those who are otherwise associated with *The Irish Times* that it will continue as before. Moreover, it is an assurance that an Irish institution is completely protected from outside takeover or control . . .

. . . The Irish Times apologises to no-one. It prints its news and it sets out its views . . . Today is a very big day, not only for *The Irish Times*, but also for journalism and the newspaper business in Ireland. The full ramifications of yesterday's annoucement may not become clear for some time. Journalism benefits. The newspaper-reading public benefits. All those who work in this newspaper will submit, humbly, that the people in general benefit.

No dividends would be payable to those who would hold the shares in trust. Shares might not be bought or sold. Profits would be put back into building the newspaper. If the Trust failed to discharge its obligations (publishing the newspaper on the stated principles), its directors would have to petition the High Court to wind up its affairs. Any proceeds thus arising would be passed to charity. 'A charitable foundation has been established', the newspaper announced, 'which will ultimately benefit from the profits of the newspaper.'

In this sense, *The Irish Times* was to become a charity. Contrary to a misconception that later became widespread, this did not enable the organisation to avoid or reduce any taxation liability. However, the newspaper's respected business editor, Andrew Whittaker, observed that the timing of the deal was significant—given the imminence of important changes in Irish taxation law:

The announcement yesterday . . . was timed so that the holders of the two classes of preference shares (quoted on the Stock Exchange) could benefit from a substantial mark-up of their share-prices today, so diminishing the capital gains tax they would pay upon realisation of the sale of their shares . . . in some six weeks' time.

Whittaker went on to observe that 'the question of reduction of capital gains tax liability, which might seem to arise because of the imminence of the new tax's valuation date, in the sale of the ordinary controlling (unquoted) shares, seems irrelevant.'

Whittaker's sharp analysis went into some detail in regard to the valuation that had been placed on the ordinary shares. He observed that their price was lower than that given by the market to certain Independent Newspaper shares that had been traded the previous September.

However, he stated: 'The sale price by the (Irish Times) directors would seem to have been at the high end of the arguable price range. Against which it might be said (though no party to the arrangement has said so) that the company passing in this sale was unique.'

'No financial argument', he concluded, 'could be final in this circumstance.'

Notwithstanding the business editor's pointed questioning, there was a general welcome for the creation of the Trust from the staff of the newspaper. It was announced that the chairman and chief executive of the Trust would be Major Thomas Bleakley McDowell. He would also continue to serve as chairman and chief executive of The Irish Times Ltd—which would continue as the operating company.

Newspaper trusts are not rare. The best-known example in these islands has been the Scott Trust, mentioned above, that runs *The Guardian* on a not-for-profit basis in the UK. There are many newspaper trusts in the Nordic countries. In the United States, the best-known is the Poynter Trust that operates the *Times* of St Petersburgh, Florida. In Ireland, *The Irish Farmers' Journal* is operated by a trust.

Gageby's editorial had stressed that an 'Irish institution' was now completely protected against 'outside takeover or control'. This was one very good reason for converting *The Irish Times* to a trust. There can be little doubt that the company would have become a target for acquisition, sooner or later. The Canadian tycoon Roy Thomson (Lord Thomson of Fleet) may have had such an interest at one point, although later correspondence between Tom McDowell and the Taoiseach's office would seem to suggest that Thomson's enthusiasm waned in the early 1960s.

The setting up of the Trust now made such a move impossible. That it served the valuable purpose of guaranteeing Ireland's newspaper of reference against outside takeover, then and since, is indisputable.

The Trust was Tom McDowell's brainchild from start to finish although he took a good deal of professional advice. His principal advisers in Dublin were Don Reid, a taxation specialist at the firm of Stokes Kennedy Crowley (formerly Stokes Brothers and Pim); Robin Lewis-Crosbie and George Overend, senior partner at the solicitors firm of A & L Goodbody. In London, he consulted Arnold Goodman (later Lord Goodman), a leading lawyer and chairman of the Observer newspaper which was also, at that time, controlled by a trust. Don Reid was to succeed Tom McDowell as chairman of The Irish Times Ltd in 1999.

Working with these—but above all drawing on his own imaginative capacities —McDowell fashioned a novel construction that simultaneously achieved a number of objectives.

It secured the continuing independence of *The Irish Times* from external takeover. It provided the newspaper with a valuable charter of aims and objectives —an editorial *vade mecum*—that has stood the test of time.

It also allowed the directors to take their profit from the success and effort of the previous decade. Significantly, it enabled Tom McDowell to remain in charge of the newly-defined institutions—the company, the Trust and a charitable 'Foundation' which in reality operated only on paper.

It was provided for that Tom McDowell should remain as chairman and chief executive for as long as he so wished, on terms and conditions no less advantageous than those put in place on his appointment to run the new structures.

It was a remarkable construction. The statement of editorial principles, in many ways, simply expressed the outlook, heritage and character of *The Irish Times*. But it gave it permanence and a solid foundation in an Ireland that was changing rapidly. It also enabled Tom McDowell effectively to have his cake and eat it. He had sold his shares and yet he remained in charge of the organisation. And it placed him in a position of singular power at the apex of the new institutions.

The membership of the Trust (the members were styled as 'Governors') was a cross-section of the great and good of Irish society. They were drawn from North and South, from differing religious backgrounds and from a variety of professional and institutional experiences.

In addition to Major Thomas Bleakley McDowell, the founding membership was announced as comprising the following people: William Blease (later Lord Blease), was Northern Ireland's leading trade unionist. From southern trade unionism there was Donal Nevin, assistant general secretary of the Irish Congress of Trade Unions. The presence of Jacob Weingreen, Professor of Hebrew at Trinity College, ensured that there could be no charge of anti-Semitism. There was James Meenan, the Professor of Economics from UCD and chairman of the Royal Dublin Society. Thekla Beere was the retired Secretary of the Department of Transport and Power and chairman of the Commission on the Status of Women; she had held a higher post than any woman in the Irish civil service. Peter O'Hara was a businessman who later was to become Managing Director of The Irish Times Ltd. James Walmsley was a distinguished former official of the Colonial Service and chairman of Eason and Sons Ltd. Richard Wood was a well-known Cork businessman and was involved in many civic causes.

Initially, the columnist John Healy was a 'Governor' of the Trust. He remained so for a year until he decided to become involved in his own newspaper in the west of Ireland. No other journalist was ever subsequently appointed. This was in contrast to newspaper trusts elsewhere, notably the Scott Trust that operated 'The Guardian' in the UK. No employee of The Irish Times Ltd (save 'the said Thomas Bleakley McDowell') could serve on the Trust. Again, unlike the Scott Trust, this excluded the editor of *The Irish Times*.

This set of interlinked institutions was topped off by the uniquely secure and entrenched position of the 'said Thomas Bleakley McDowell'. The 'A' share provision of the Trust secured him from any attempt to remove him by other directors. In any motion to remove him, his personal vote would outweigh any combination of votes among the other directors.

He also had the power to remove or appoint directors and Governors. The Governors of the Trust—who were also members of the board of the company— had a permanent majority. And no decision of the board was valid unless it was supported by at least two Governors.

Only one authority stood clear of McDowell's. That was the power of the editor, to order and prescribe the content of the newspaper, on a day-to-day basis, subject to the authority of the board. In the ultimate, of course, the editor could be removed. But he was 'solely responsible' to the board for the content of *The Irish Times* (including the content of advertising). There is no doubt that this construction came into existence specifically to accommodate Gageby and to meet his vision of an independent editorship.

The Trust took its work seriously, in my experience. It met once a month, August excepted, in McDowell's gloomy office, around a couple of extended tables. After a private meeting that might last perhaps an hour, the Governors would be joined by the editor and, later, by the General Manager (later styled successively as 'Managing Director' and 'Chief Executive'). This procedure enabled the editor and the Governors to discuss editorial matters privately.

When the Trust meeting 'closed', the meeting of the board of The Irish Times Ltd would 'open'. The executive directors—the editor's senior deputies and the manager's senior executives—would troop in. The board meeting might last another hour. The company accounts would be reviewed. Circulation and advertising figures would be presented by the manager. Production and printing problems, if any, would be aired. There might be further discussion of editorial matters, although McDowell kept these to a minimum at the board, preferring to deal with them at the Trust meeting.

I always disagreed with him on this. The editor was responsible for implementing the *directors'* policy, not the *Governors'*. McDowell argued that the editor should not be obliged to discuss his decisions in the presence of his subordinates. It was never a problem as far as I was concerned. On the contrary, I was often glad to have the support of executive directors like Bruce Williamson, Ken Gray, Pat O'Hara or Eoin McVey when issues of detail might arise.

After the board meeting there would be a buffet lunch and a glass or two of wine. McDowell disliked sit-down lunches and preferred to have people circulate. It was useful. Governors spoke much more freely over the informality of the lunch than sitting around the table.

Trust and board meetings were quite formal encounters. Discussion of editorial content was often detailed and sometimes tensions arose around the table. But the Governors and board were universally supportive in my period as editor. I was never given anything that came remotely close to a directive or a reprimand.

The Governors were all assiduous readers of the paper and one had to be *au fait* with content across every section in order to maintain one's position in what could sometimes be an extended dialogue.

Once a year all Governors and directors had to affirm, on oath, their commitment to the principles of the Trust. A solicitor came with his bible and 'swore' each of us individually as well as witnessing our signatures.

Once a year, also, my contract of employment had to be renewed. Tom would sign the single sheet of paper to a ripple of 'hear-hears'. I think very few people in the organisation—or outside—realised that the editor of *The Irish Times* had to go on the hazard, as it were, of having his employment renewed every 12 months.

In the overall, the Trust worked well. In 16 years as editor, I never once came under any untoward pressure in regard to editorial content or policy. There were times, however, when some of the Governors disagreed with me and issues would have to be thrashed out at the meetings.

Differences of opinion often centred on coverage of Northern Ireland. There were vigorous arguments on the extradition question in the early 1990s. Sometimes there were issues over the reporting of sex abuse cases in the courts. Foreign coverage came up from time to time. Some Governors would argue that the newspaper was being too harsh on Israel. Others felt we were too easy.

The columnists often came in for fire. I frequently found myself having to defend opinions that I did not share—or at least defending the right of someone to express those opinions.

But in the end I was always told to 'carry on' as I thought best. Tom McDowell was unfailingly protective. He frequently reminded Governors that whereas they might have had a month to think about an issue, the editor often had to make a decision in a few minutes.

As the years went by, however, I felt that McDowell came increasingly to dominate the Trust. In the early years of my editorship, he would sound me out about possible candidates for the Trust. But in later years he came up with some names that worried me. In one instance I expressed my views very strongly. That individual never joined the Trust. But McDowell did not ask me for my views again.

And as difficulties grew within the organisation from the mid-1990s onward, I recognised a growing tendency for issues to be delayed as they were dissected by the Trust. Executive directors became aware that important developments were moving too slowly. The advantages that we held over our main competitors—the Independent group—would be eroded.

The Trust discharged its principal duties of ensuring the publication of *The Irish Times*, on the basis of the principles set down, faithfully and conscientiously. This was, and is, no small thing in a media environment that is increasingly driven by profits and in which the traditional values of quality journalism are under assault.

The members, in my experience, were without exception people with a genuine sense of public service. They saw themselves as contributing to something valuable—which they were. They received a small annual honorarium. In my last year as editor, I believe it was around €4,000.

But the institution undermined much of its credibility, not least with its own staff, through failing to evolve in accordance with contemporary principles of good governance.

The Trust was inextricably bound up with the persona of Tom McDowell. It had been tailored to meet McDowell's criteria, and to a lesser extent, Douglas Gageby's. Adapting it to the post-McDowell era would prove difficult.

Tom McDowell was—is—a man of great complexity. He could be considerate to a fault. In our years of working together, his gestures of kindness to me and to my family were innumerable. So it was with other members of the extended *Irish Times* organisation. The spouse of a staff member who was ill would have flowers sent to the house, with a solicitous telephone call, perhaps offering financial or other assistance, if it were needed. If a reporter were to be in trouble—perhaps over some gaffe—there would be a query to know if the Chairman could help in any way. Rules and regulations could always be flexed to help someone in difficulties. Tom's pleasure in giving help to those in need of it was palpable and genuine.

His respect for the editor's independence in regard to the content of the newspaper was absolute. Over 16 years I never once had the slightest attempt at an encroachment. And I have no doubt there were many occasions when the editorial line, the treatment of a particular story or the advancement of a particular journalist were gall and vinegar to him.

His Achilles' heel was his absolutism. He believed he had the responsibility to decide on virtually everything, in the ultimate. Whether it was the menu at a board lunch, the brand and model of motor-car to be driven by certain employees or the choice of new equipment for some department, he immersed himself in the detail. Staff at all levels knew he had the final say, and that he frequently invoked it. He exercised the right to second-guess or over-rule anything—apart from the day-to-day content of the newspaper.

The problem with this approach was that while it worked in the early days, with a small company, operating a relatively simple business-model, it was not sustainable as the organisation grew and as he got older.

Tom sometimes displayed a singular capacity for appearing not to dwell on things that displeased him. On a number of occasions, as the climate of public thinking changed, I asked him to reappraise some of the ways in which the Trust operated.

From an early stage, he took the view that it should operate out of sight. After the early years, neither the appointment nor the departure of governors was recorded in the newspaper. There was no mechanism through which the members of the Trust might meet staff of the company. It issued no documentation. It made no public utterances.

A journalist searching in the cuttings library of *The Irish Times* for information on the Trust would find only three or four relevant clippings. These included the announcement of its foundation in April 1974, the accompanying editorial written by Gageby and the analysis of the deal done with the ordinary shareholders, written by Andrew Whittaker.

In 1996 a sombre panel was published in *The Irish Times*, setting out the aims and objectives and the current membership. This came about after a series of critical articles had appeared in *The Phoenix* magazine and after calls for clarification had been made by the editorial committee.

Yet the Trust constituted the ultimate authority behind the country's leading journal of news and opinion. Because it held the balance of power on the board, it had the authority to make editorial policy, to influence the editor, indeed to fire him, if it came to that.

It was perhaps remarkable that it received so little attention in other media.

The Phoenix magazine regularly excoriated the Trust for its failure to deliver on the understanding that it would endow hospitals, schools and scientific research. In all the years, *Phoenix* would point out, not a penny had been diverted from the organisation to any charitable cause.

This was not quite the full picture. Modest sums were allocated each year from The Irish Times Ltd to sponsoring good causes. Smaller sums, on occasion, were donated to certain charities. But in general, the charge was accurate.

Although I was not a member of the Trust, I believed the institution was being damaged and I raised the issue with Tom on several occasions. He was defensive and argued that the critics misunderstood the status of *The Irish Times* as a 'charity'. It did not exist to fund *charities*. It *was* a 'charity'—in the same way that the Lifeboats Institution or the Red Cross is a charity.

The legal definition was, no doubt, fulfilled. But it was impossible to escape from the expectation that good causes would 'ultimately' benefit from the profits of *The Irish Times*.

In conversation, Tom would sometimes defend the Trust against criticism on this count by pointing out that the Scott Trust did not provide any benefits to charity either. It was a fair point. But there was one significant difference between the circumstances in which the Scott Trust came into being and those in which The Irish Times Trust was born.

In 1934 the Scotts divested themselves of their newspaper with no profit to themselves. They simply handed over the controlling stock to the trust. The Irish Times shareholders took their profit on their shares in 1974. Thereafter, it was up to the *The Irish Times* to pay off the money borrowed from the Bank of Ireland.

In the restructuring of 2001–2002, the Trust was disempowered in considerable measure, so that while it controls the shares, its operational authority is now *de facto* secondary to that of the board.

It deserved better because it did—and does—represent a noble aspiration in a business not generally noted for its altruism. And I believe that Tom McDowell's contribution to Irish newspapers will rise above the bad press that came his way in 2001–2002. That he brought much of it upon himself by his unwillingness to adapt to necessary change and by his conviction that things had to go in certain ways, is beyond doubt. But he secured the autonomy of the newspaper. He ensured it had the wherewithal to bring it to contemporary levels of excellence. And he confirmed a tradition of editorial independence that will endure.

The deal done with the ordinary shareholders to establish the Trust in 1974 was posited on the assumption that the company would continue to make profits to pay off the borrowings. Andrew Whittaker had questioned the wisdom of this and his cautionary instincts were borne out. Later in the year, the western economies went into recession as a result of the Arab oil embargo that followed the Middle-East war. Revenues at *The Irish Times* were slashed and the company faced into a lean period in which its solvency was far from assured.

| ON MATURE RECOLLECTION

The odds must heavily favour Mr Lenihan . . .
—*Irish Times* editorial before Fianna Fáil's selection of Brian
Lenihan as its presidential candidate

Influential news media are sometimes accused of over-stepping a line that should supposedly exist between *reporting* the news and *making* the news. Often the accusation is levelled by those who dislike its policies, or sometimes by rival media.

The proposition that such a line can exist at all is something of a *reductio ad absurdum*. Modern media scholars, as far back as Marshall McLuhan in the 1960s, have recognised that the news media are not merely a mirror of events.

Their presence frequently alters the course of events. They become, in effect, part of the story. This has been true since the London *Times* altered the conduct of the Crimean war by reporting leadership blunders from the battlefield and a crisis of supplies in the army.

Editors and journalists are uncomfortable with the idea. They cherish myths about their detachment. So they struggle against it—and rightly—for the most part. Yet there are occasions when it will happen. And there may be little that they can do to prevent it. One such occasion for *The Irish Times* occurred in the course of the 1990 presidential election campaign.

Early in 1990, there were stirrings in the political undergrowth about the upcoming election for the President of Ireland. In 1983 Dr Patrick Hillery had been returned unopposed for a second term as President. He had taken up the role as Head of State more than six years previously when President Cearbhall Ó Dálaigh had resigned after a stand-off with the Cosgrave government.

But now, after 13 years in Áras an Uachtaráin, he was about to return to private life. Dr Hillery's presidency had been low-key and had provided a stabilising influence during years that were often politically turbulent and divisive.

After his apparently tranquil tenure, the presidency had come to be seen by many as something anodyne, a backwater, an institution that was largely isolated from the cut and thrust of public life. The President had adhered scrupulously to the constitutional and behavioural requirements of his office. He was seen but rarely heard. His presence at functions was wholly ceremonial and he could be relied upon to cause no controversy by word or deed.

In reality, as it came to be realised, Dr Hillery had been robust and courageous in discharging his constitutional responsibilities. He also worked extremely hard, visiting a huge number of institutions and communities and participating in many public events.

He had been a vigorous Minister, a tough European commissioner and a fierce political campaigner. But in the presidency he gave an initial impression of shyness, reticence almost. Yet he was warm on a one-to-one basis.

I was once on a flight to Germany when he was travelling on a state visit. He worked the entire length of the cabin, delighting the passengers with his easy charm. 'Your president is so *simpatico!*' a German woman sitting beside me exclaimed delightedly, after he had spent a full quarter of an hour talking to her about her holiday in Clare.

As 1990 went by, speculation began as to who would follow Hillery as the seventh President of Ireland. And by the early autumn the outlines of a coming contest were becoming clear. It was to be a contest in which *The Irish Times* was to play an unexpected and unorthodox role that was not of its own choosing.

After the long Hillery years, there was something of an acceptance, at least in Fianna Fáil circles, that the presidency 'belonged' to Fianna Fáil. Since Douglas Hyde, the first President, every incumbent had had a Fianna Fáil pedigree of one form or another.

Two candidates emerged within Fianna Fáil. John Wilson, a 15-year veteran of various Cabinet posts from Education to Defence and TD for Cavan-Monaghan, let it be known that he was interested. A former teacher and later a university lecturer in Latin, he had a stentorian mode of address that might have fitted the role. The other candidate was Haughey's Tánaiste and long-time political ally, Brian Lenihan. Early indications of possible interest by Gerry Collins, the long-serving TD and Minister from West Limerick, did not materialise into open contention.

Lenihan's health was poor. He had for years suffered with a liver complaint that was ultimately to end his life. It was recognised that he was coming towards the end of a long and demanding career in the Dáil during which he had held a succession of ministries. He had also been a key figure in the Fianna Fáil party and in the rehabilitation of Charles Haughey in the aftermath of the arms crisis of 1970. The presidency was seen by many within the party, and beyond, as a fitting honour for a popular man who had faithfully served party and country.

The day before the Fianna Fáil TDs made their choice between Lenihan and Wilson, I wrote an editorial in the following terms:

The odds must heavily favour Mr Lenihan. It is difficult to envisage his colleagues denying what he has so clearly indicated as his goal: to be Head of State, after decades of service to public life, to his party and to the democratic process. In other circumstances Brian Lenihan might have been Taoiseach.

Fine Gael and Labour had already made their selections for the presidency. Both Garret FitzGerald and Fine Gael's deputy leader, Peter Barry, had let it be known that they did not wish to be nominated. Either would have been a strong contender and FitzGerald would have been the bookies' favourite. Their unwillingness to go forward created serious problems for the party and for the leader, Alan Dukes. On Dukes's urging, the party had nominated Austin Currie, the former SDLP politician and civil rights leader from Northern Ireland, who had won a Dáil seat for Fine Gael in west Dublin.

Currie had been a popular and attractive figure in the context of the Northern civil rights campaign. He had been a leading light in the early years of the SDLP. But Fine Gael members had mixed views about his suitability in Dublin politics. He put great effort into his presidential campaign but it did not appeal to the popular imagination. His unsuccessful candidacy was to prove the final nail in Dukes's political coffin.

It was the Labour leader, Dick Spring, who defined how the 1990 presidential election was to be fought. In doing so, he dramatically changed the nature of the presidency and altered the course of Irish public life.

In April Spring announced that Labour was proposing Mary Robinson (neé Bourke), a 46-year-old member of the Senate, elected by the Trinity College constituency. Robinson was well-known in legal circles, having also held the Reid professorship in law at Trinity. She was from a comfortably well-off Mayo family. She had a good track record of involvement in personal rights issues and the women's movement. She was a Catholic, married to a Protestant, Nick Robinson, at one time the resident cartoonist at *The Irish Times*.

The announcement took the political establishment and the media utterly by surprise. Robinson had actually left the Labour Party some years previously and had run for the Senate as an independent. She had split from Labour because she disagreed with the 1985 Anglo-Irish Agreement which had been negotiated by the government in which the party was a coalition partner. But if her dissent cut her adrift for a while from Labour it may well have helped her with her Trinity College constituency.

It appeared at first a curious, almost a daring, choice. Robinson had little public profile outside of the Dublin, professional middle classes. She was intelligent and ambitious. But she was regarded as a dull speaker with a somewhat ponderous air about her and a rather old-fashioned sense of dress and presentation. At the Dublin bar she was regarded as rather forbidding and over-serious.

What few outside of the Labour Party knew was that a group of advisers that Dick Spring had built up around him had devised a sophisticated strategy to bring Labour into a pivotal position in Irish politics come the next election. Capturing the presidency, with a new, fresh message, was a step on the road to that end.

By nominating Mary Robinson in April, Labour, supported by the Democratic

Left—which had sprung from Official Sinn Féin—and some independents, got a significant head-start in the campaign. At an early stage, it became clear that all the conventions and the received wisdom about presidential campaigning had gone out the window. Robinson kicked off her programme by addressing a women's meeting in Allihies, at the extremity of the beautiful but remote Beara peninsula in West Cork.

The campaign team achieved a complete makeover on the rather dowdy Robinson image. Smarter clothes, a more flattering hairstyle and the assistance of a cosmetics expert transformed her into a figure of some style. Her speeches were carefully modulated and infused with a language of inclusiveness, of care and of respect for the rights of the individual, especially women. Spring, meanwhile, expressed parallel sentiments, arguing that a newly-defined presidency should serve to highlight social injustice, wealth imbalance and failures and inadequacies on the part of the administration.

Lenihan was the clear favourite to win the election right through the summer. In predicting that he, rather than John Wilson, would secure the Fianna Fáil nomination, *The Irish Times* editorial observed on 17 September:

> ... Where Brian Lenihan would have to be considered almost certain to secure the prize against Austin Currie and Mary Robinson, it would be a much more evenly matched contest with John Wilson as the Fianna Fáil candidate.

The capacity of the Robinson campaign to appeal across a wide spectrum of different interest groups was remarkable. Her appeal to the Dublin middle classes was perhaps predictable. But she struck a ready note with women of all classes and circumstances and with younger people, right across the country.

The Irish Times had always tried to have an even-handed approach among contending candidates or parties at election time. It was standard procedure for the news editor to assign one of his deputies to maintain a strict, daily tally of the column inches and the numbers of photographs that were allocated to each side. If one side or another appeared to be getting a disproportionate share of the exposure, that would be remedied in the days ahead.

The coverage of the Robinson-Lenihan-Currie contest in the 1990 presidential election, however, presented particular problems in seeking to achieve this balance.

Generally, in the case of the big parties, we endeavoured to give more or less equal billing. The equation became more complex when one began to deal with smaller parties. Clearly, a smaller party with a proportionate share of the vote could not aspire to the same levels of coverage as a big, national party.

On the other hand, I was enjoined by the requirement of The Irish Times Trust that 'special consideration shall be given to the reasonable representations of minority interests and divergent views'. So the underdog or the gadfly interest had to get a bit of extra showing, often to the intense irritation of the big battalions.

The daily running total of column inches was further refined to show a breakdown between news, features and other material. The photograph count was broken down by location and size. A front page picture would obviously have more impact than one on an inside page. So too a picture above the page fold was thought to be worth more than one under the fold.

I began to realise that pictures of Brian Lenihan might actually be counter-productive to his campaign. His illness was taking a toll on him. He looked gaunt and stressed. Dark rings formed under his eyes. His ready smile began to look contorted. Bad as the photographs were, when the newspaper's ascerbic cartoonist, Martyn Turner, got to work on the Lenihan caricature, the results were frightening. I raised this with Martyn and suggested he might ease up a bit on Lenihan. And I asked the picture desk to refer all photographs of Brian Lenihan to me for clearance.

There was also an issue with the newspaper's columnists. The stable of columnists had been created in order to achieve a good spread of views, backgrounds and preoccupations across Irish society. Generally it worked well. But it became apparent as the campaign went on that every commentator on the newspaper favoured Robinson. Two or three of the women journalists, indeed, had participated in an early think-tank that she held at her home to plan media strategy.

An editor has difficult choices in this situation. By definition, columnists are paid to give their opinions and editors should be slow to suppress or seek to modify those opinions. I sought to alleviate the pro-Robinson thrust of the columnists by ensuring that the news coverage for Currie and Lenihan was generous. I imposed a moratorium and told the columnists that they must avoid the subject of the presidency in the final week of campaigning. Mary Holland, in particular, was very annoyed with me about this.

By October, support for Robinson had grown and she was closing the gap with Lenihan. Nonetheless, an *Irish Times*/MRBI poll taken in the first week of October showed Lenihan leading Robinson by a comfortable 17 per cent of intended first preferences. Fine Gael's Austin Currie was trailing behind the field. Robinson, perhaps sensing that she was not going to overtake Lenihan, said that a transfer arrangement between herself and Currie 'would be sensible'.

———

It was shortly after this that a remarkable sequence of events began and that a little-known student of politics at UCD, Jim Duffy, appeared on the scene.

Many politicians, journalists and others had heard reports over the years about an attempt by Fianna Fáil front-bench figures to pressurise President Hillery in the discharge of his presidential functions.

According to these reports, telephone calls had been made to persuade him to refuse to dissolve the Dáil in December 1982 after Garret FitzGerald's administration had lost a Dáil vote on the Budget. If FitzGerald were unable to secure the confidence of the House, it would be open to Charles Haughey, as leader of the opposition, to seek to do so. The callers were reputed to be Lenihan and Clare TD Sylvester Barrett, a former constituency colleague and friend of President Hillery.

However, the issue had never come to a head in the media or elsewhere and it faded from general consciousness, even in political circles.

The Constitution gives the President of Ireland few real powers. But one substantive function it does confer is the power, at the President's absolute discretion, to refuse a request to dissolve the Dáil. Clearly, if there had been such an attempt to influence Hillery it would have been wrong. But equally, since there had been no such action by Hillery in 1982 or at any other time, any attempt, if there had been one, had been rebuffed.

In retrospect, it is clear that elements in Fine Gael sprang a carefully-laid ambush for Brian Lenihan.

When Austin Currie's campaign was launched in October, Fine Gael went on the offensive against Lenihan, raising questions about his ability to act independently of Haughey. As President, he would be in thrall to Haughey, Fine Gael argued. An early statement from Currie referred to Lenihan's 'habits of loyalty to Mr Haughey for half a lifetime' and suggested it would be difficult to see how these 'might be abandoned' if he became President.

The issue of the 1982 telephone calls to Áras an Uachtaráin was raised when Brian Lenihan appeared on RTÉ's *Questions and Answers* programme on 22 October. Garret FitzGerald was also on the panel and Brian Murphy, a former chairman of Young Fine Gael and a member of the Currie campaign team, was in the audience.

When a question was asked, from the audience, about the role of the President in the dissolution of the Dáil, FitzGerald immediately raised the issue of the alleged telephone calls to the Áras in 1982, claiming that no fewer than seven calls were made to try to pressurise President Hillery to refuse to dissolve the Dáil, effectively giving Haughey the opportunity to attempt to form a government.

Brian Lenihan, who seemed flustered, said that FitzGerald's information was 'fictional'. FitzGerald retorted that it was not. He said he had been at the Áras that evening and knew what had happened. When Lenihan was asked if he had made the calls he said: 'No, I didn't at all. That never happened. I want to assure you that it never happened.'

It was a fateful statement from Lenihan, over the national airwaves. It probably cost him the presidency and his ministry. Because just five months previously he had stated in a taped interview with Jim Duffy that he had, in fact, called President Hillery and spoken to him on that night.

Duffy was researching his MA thesis on the subject of the presidency. He had visited Brian Lenihan at the Tánaiste's office on 30 May and taped more than an hour of conversation with him about different aspects of the office.

In his book *Lenihan His Life and Loyalties*, James Downey recalls that when Duffy saw Lenihan for the interview he was 'shocked by his deathly appearance'. Downey wrote:

> Lenihan had undergone a 'rejection crisis' which had very nearly killed him, and the medication prescribed to prevent the rejection accounted for much more than his dreadful appearance, it gravely affected his memory and judgment and caused him to make statements that were both inaccurate and imprudent. He should not have been at work, much less acceding to requests like Duffy's. It was one more example of his inability to say no. This time his good nature would have ruinous effects.

Brian Lenihan told Jim Duffy that he had telephoned Hillery and had 'got through' to him. But the President was angry and told Lenihan to 'lay off', according to the version of events taped by Jim Duffy.

Jim Duffy had called *The Irish Times* a few weeks previously, offering to write some articles on the institution of the presidency in the run-up to the election. I arrived at the office one afternoon and found him talking with Dick Walsh who introduced us. Later, Dick showed me some of the articles in draft. They were interesting, well-written and informative. One of them did, however, purport to throw light on the events of 1982. It said that calls had been made by Haughey, Lenihan and Barrett and that the President had responded angrily.

Jim Duffy's original article made no mention of his taped interview with Brian Lenihan. But on the morning after the *Questions and Answers* programme, he called Dick Walsh and told him about the tape. His initial concern, Dick told me, was to vindicate himself and to confirm the content of the article that he had written some days previously.

Dick acted as any newsman would in these circumstances. He urged Jim Duffy to publish the contents of the tape or, alternatively, to give an 'interview' to *The Irish Times* setting out what he knew from his research. Jim Duffy was apparently very nervous and went back to UCD where he asked a number of academics about the propriety of releasing a tape that had been acquired for academic purposes into the news media. Senior faculty in the Politics Department apparently advised him against it on the grounds that it would constitute a breach of academic ethics.

I had a meeting over lunch with the Moderator of the Presbyterian Church in Ireland, Finlay Holmes, and arrived at the office around 2.30 pm to find the place in a state of high excitement. Jim Duffy had played his tape to Dick Walsh. Then he played it again with Dick, Denis Coghlan (political correspondent) and myself listening in the quiet of my office. The voice was clearly that of Brian Lenihan. The details were specific. There was no doubt that Lenihan on Jim Duffy's tape was saying things that were flatly at variance with what he had said on television the previous night.

To say that we had an explosive story was putting it mildly. The course of action followed by *The Irish Times* over the subsequent 48 hours created something of a controversy in other media and led to accusations that the newspaper had crossed the line from *reporting* the news to *participating* in the news. The reality was that we took the only course of action we could, if we were to discharge our function as a newspaper, while at the same time trying to be fair both to Brian Lenihan and to Jim Duffy.

I realised that the contradiction between the Duffy tape and what Lenihan had said on *Questions and Answers* would probably blast his hopes of the presidency. I did not welcome the task of bringing that contradiction into the public domain. But our duty as a newspaper demanded that it be done.

I did not know Brian Lenihan well but I had met him on a number of occasions and, as with most people, liked his combination of affable charm and sense of humour. I knew that he had been unwell and that he was very anxious to secure the presidency at the end of a long and arduous political career. His wife, Ann Devine, was the daughter of a close colleague of my late father. I had no desire to be the vehicle of destruction for her husband's hopes and aims. Nonetheless, the story had to run.

There was also the problem of Jim Duffy's status *vis-à-vis* his academic superiors at UCD. He felt that if he were to commit a breach of academic ethics, he could be in serious trouble with the college authorities. I spoke to one academic contact on a confidential basis. He was not clear about what 'academic ethics' might mean in this context. But he ventured the view that it could cost Duffy his degree if he caused a major incident, bringing the university into conflict with the political establishment. (I never established whether these 'academic ethics' derived from any written code or whether they were simply based on what was assumed as custom and practice.)

Dick Walsh, Denis Coghlan and I discussed the issues. Later in the afternoon I sought the advice of Ken Gray and Eoin McVey. In the end I reckoned that the best way of dealing with the issue would be for us to run a relatively low-key report in the morning, stating that *The Irish Times* had 'corroborative evidence' that Haughey, Lenihan and Barrett had made the disputed telephone calls to President Hillery in 1982. However, we would not give any sources.

One subsequent account of the episode quotes *The Irish Times* as claiming it had 'conclusive evidence' that the telephone calls had been made. We never used that phrase.

As I saw it, our report would bring the story into the public domain by giving Brian Lenihan and his campaign advisers the opportunity to clarify what had happened. It would also, crucially, protect Duffy from any sanctions or punishment at the university.

Other media were later to express bafflement at this course of action. *The Irish Times* had exclusive possession of a major scoop, they reasoned. Why did we not simply go ahead and publish it? There were two parts in the answer to that.

First, Jim Duffy and not *The Irish Times* held possession of the tape. He made it clear that he was not prepared to hand it over to us. Of course, we had heard the content of the tape but Jim Duffy had made it clear, in allowing us to listen to it, that he simply wanted to confirm the correctness of his article, published some days previously. I did not feel free to use publicly what had been revealed under privilege, especially if it was going to cause him perhaps to lose his degree.

Second, I wanted to be as humane as possible towards Brian Lenihan. If he were willing to come forward, even at this late stage, he might rescue himself from the jam he was in.

I asked Jim Duffy if he would be happy with this. He seemed relieved and left to go back to UCD.

The report appeared on the front page the following morning. I gave instructions that it was to be low-key but visible. It contended for space against the murder of a Belfast taxi-driver, an offer from President Saddam Hussein to engage in direct talks with President Bush and the news that 45,000 people had turned out to see Charles Haughey perform the official opening of the Tallaght Shopping Centre.

But if the report was low-key, the reaction was not.

The Government Press Secretary, P.J. Mara, was on the telephone to me at home before breakfast.

'What's all this "corroborative evidence" stuff?'

'You know I can't tell you, P.J. But I think Brian Lenihan probably knows himself at this stage. Why don't you give him a call and ask him?'

'I have. He says there's no evidence of anything.'

I was dumbfounded. I could not understand how Brian Lenihan was still denying things. 'Well, you'd better call him again, P.J., because what we have is pretty strong.'

There was a pause for a moment. Then he asked: 'How strong?'

'Well, let me put it this way. If it was evidence being put to a jury, you'd be looking at a conviction.'

I went to the office. Maev-Ann Wren, the duty editor, was anxious and worried. 'There's something terribly wrong here,' she said. 'Lenihan is denying everything. He must be delusional or else the medication has wiped out his memory.' Lenihan's denial was being carried on all the radio news bulletins.

Meanwhile, Jim Duffy had been on the telephone from UCD to Maev-Ann. He was in trouble, not from the college authorities but from some Fianna Fáil-supporting students who were searching the campus for him—to an end perhaps better imagined than described. He had taken refuge in the college chaplaincy building.

I telephoned him there and asked him what he wanted to do. He was agitated, not surprisingly, and said he needed legal advice. I suggested that he should go to see *The Irish Times*'s solicitors, Hayes and Sons on St Stephen's Green, and I sent Maev-Ann in an 'Irish Times' car to collect him, undertaking to go and see him myself once he had safely arrived.

Then I telephoned P.J. Mara. I repeated that our information was solid and asked that he convey that information directly to Brian Lenihan.

'We know all about Jim Duffy and his tape,' P.J. Mara said.

'Well, how does Lenihan see it?' I asked.

'He still denies it ever happened. He says "let them publish what they have". He doesn't care.'

'P.J., that's crazy,' I said. 'He can save himself from a lot of grief if he deals with it up front.'

'Well, I know, but he's in denial. You have to do what you have to do.'

I went to see Jim Duffy at Hayes and Sons' offices. He was with Adrian Glover, the principal of the firm, who had just taken him to lunch at the Friendly Sons of St Patrick Club a few doors away. Maev-Ann had told Jim Duffy that he could see Adrian, or any other solicitor, privately for advice and that we would meet the costs.

Jim Duffy had spoken privately with Adrian but was happy to speak with me also, in Adrian's presence, at this stage. I asked him what he wanted to do. He said he wanted to publish the tape but he would like it to be broadcast so that there could be no dispute as to its authenticity. I could understand that but I pointed out to him that this way *The Irish Times* would lose its 'exclusivity' on the contents of the tape. But he was sure of what he wanted to do. I got him to agree to leave most of the content to be reproduced in the following morning's *Irish Times* but he wanted the key exchanges and statements by Brian Lenihan to go out on RTÉ.

I telephoned Ken Gray and asked him to arrange a room at the Westbury Hotel if possible for later that afternoon. Word was put out through the political correspondents and at around 4 pm Jim Duffy, accompanied by Ken Gray and Eoin McVey, played the tape to a packed room of journalists and broadcasters.

The rest is history. Brian Lenihan went on RTÉ television at 6 o'clock and gave his famous 'mature recollection' interview to Seán Duignan. It was a disastrous performance. He stared into the camera. His presentation appeared laboured, contrived and painful. Within days, under pressure from the Progressive Democrats, Haughey had sacked him from his position as Tánaiste and as a member of the Cabinet. It was a painful and ignominious process for a man who deserved better.

On election day, 7 November, Brian Lenihan did well, coming in at the head of the poll with 44.1 per cent of the first preferences. Robinson got 38.9 and Currie trailed in at a poor 17 per cent. However, when Currie's second preferences were allocated, Robinson took the lion's share, almost 77 per cent. Robinson was elected—but only with Currie's transfers—a fact that was rarely mentioned subsequently when she reached extraordinary heights of popularity as President.

In the editorial of 6 November 1990, the day before polling, I tried to summarise the issues:

A fortnight ago, any outcome other than victory for Mr Brian Lenihan appeared improbable . . . if votes were to be cast on the basis of candidates' straightforwardness and honest, unambiguous self-presentation, Mr Austin Currie would have to head the field . . . for the great majority of voters . . . it is a choice between Mr Lenihan and Mrs Robinson.

On 1 November 1995 Brian Lenihan died of the liver disease that he had fought for many years.

If he had a grievance against me or *The Irish Times* I think it was put aside and buried. Six months after the presidential débâcle he published a hurried book in which he said that 'some journalists' at *The Irish Times* lacked integrity and that the newspaper had betrayed its 'liberal ethos'. In the context of what had happened the previous November this was self-exculpatory but understandable.

I was asked to respond but did not do so directly. I felt that the last thing either Brian Lenihan or *The Irish Times* needed was a round-two confrontation. Instead, I agreed to a request from Sam Smyth of the *Sunday Independent* and put all the facts, correspondence and notes before him to enable him to adjudicate on what had happened. Sam Smyth and the *Sunday Independent* were scarcely sympathetic to *The Irish Times*. But I had considerable respect for his integrity and professionalism.

He examined all the facts and the following week (2 July 1992) he wrote as follows:

After speaking to two of the principal *Irish Times* people involved in the Duffy tapes story—and Duffy—it would be difficult to fault the paper's handling of a delicate, if sensational, story. They have a plausible, valid answer to every accusation. The old dowager's shoes are clean.

About a year before he died, Brian Lenihan wrote to me in conciliatory terms, assuring me that there were no 'hard feelings' and suggesting that we meet for lunch. I responded positively and I am happy to say that cordial relations were restored.

It was a little more difficult to deal with Brian's sister, Mary O'Rourke, who by now was Minister for Education. She asked Christina Murphy to arrange a lunch for the three of us at the Westbury. She paid for the lunch in advance and when I arrived she gave me the most fearful tongue-lashing about what *The Irish Times* had done to her brother.

I explained that *The Irish Times* had taken all the steps it reasonably could to save Brian from the worst impact of the revelations. I reminded her that we initially ran a low-key report, merely saying we had 'corroborative evidence' about the 1982 telephone calls. I related my conversations with P.J. Mara and Mara's resigned air when he realised that nothing was going to deflect the candidate from his position of absolute denial.

She took it on board and then said, 'Well, I wanted to clear the air on this. We'll have contact in the future and I didn't want any misunderstanding about where I stood.' We did, indeed, have subsequent contact on many occasions while she was in Cabinet and later as Leader of the Seanad. We got on well and I believe we respected each other.

A few months after he stepped down from the presidency, I telephoned Dr Hillery and asked him to meet me for a meal one evening. We went to the Stephen's Green Club where we had the dining room to ourselves. I asked him what really happened in 1982 when he was President and when the telephone calls started coming into Áras an Uachtaráin.

Hillery was genial, as ever, but guarded. He answered my questions hesitantly and economically. But he told me enough to confirm that he had not taken any telephone calls on the evening the FitzGerald government fell. Nonetheless, it was clear that calls had been made. Later I learned that the calls had been made but were fielded at the Áras switch by the President's *Aide de Camp*, an Army captain.

Brian Lenihan had attempted to get through to the President but he had not succeeded. Whether it was the passage of time, the effects of his medication, or perhaps wishful thinking, he clearly told Jim Duffy that he had done something that he had merely attempted to do.

It was not the only time in my experience as editor that I encountered a conflict of evidence that grew out of an individual's inability to differentiate between an action that had merely been planned and one that was actually accomplished.

Normally reliable, honest people can approach the same issue with flatly contradictory versions of an event—and yet may be telling the truth as they understand and believe it to be.

And sometimes a newspaper can get caught in the middle.

13

PRESENTS COME AND
PRESIDENTS GO

It wasn't Independent Newspapers, however, but the well-disposed Irish Times *and* RTÉ *who were responsible for the lowest point in Mary's relationship with the media.*
—from *Mary Robinson: The Authorised Biography*

When President Mary Robinson was inaugurated in St Patrick's Hall at Dublin Castle on 3 December 1990, there was a sense that something wonderfully new, hopeful and fresh had happened in Irish public life. What had been a rather pedestrian inauguration ceremony on previous occasions was transformed by the glamour and elegance of the new President in her purple and gold. The delivery and theme of her inauguration address sent frissons around the great hall. She quoted from the poetry of Séamus Heaney and Eavan Boland and spoke of reaching out to Ireland's 'fifth province'—the Irish *diaspora* scattered around the world.

There was electricity in the air and then there was sustained applause when she concluded: 'May it be a Presidency where I, the President, can sing to you, citizens of Ireland, the joyous refrain of the fourteenth-century poet as recalled by W.B. Yeats, "I am of Ireland . . . come dance with me in Ireland."'

I was at the back of the hall, with Vinnie Doyle, the editor of the *Irish Independent*. With no sign of the applause dying down, we caught each other glancing at our watches. We had newspapers to get out.

Later that evening, I caught the end of the State reception. There was an air of *fiesta*. Labour Party workers and veterans of the women's movement toasted each other at the taxpayers' expense. Some were literally weeping with joy. The President, nodding and smiling, moved among the crowd that pressed around to clutch her hand or merely to catch a glimpse.

That Mary Robinson is one of the most remarkable Irish people of her generation is not in question. But in retrospect, it is difficult to measure the extent to which she was an initiator of change, as distinct from a personification of new values and priorities that were in the ascendant in Irish society. In many ways, her most far-reaching contribution to the process of change in Irish society was *behind* her. She had been an important figure in pushing through reforms in personal rights and freedoms, such as contraception, the care of children and so on.

Did she *cause* change or did she merely *reflect* the change that was happening anyway? Did her presidency continue the process of change or was it simply an affirmation of change which she herself had played a major role in bringing about? These were questions with which I found myself having to grapple at frequent intervals, as we formulated editorial policy on this quite new style of presidency.

There was an impression, sometimes fostered by other media, that President Mary Robinson and *The Irish Times* were bound together in some sort of shared ideological agenda or mutual understanding. In reality, relations between the newspaper and her presidency were never more than polite and functional. And at times they were positively hostile.

In the early stages of her campaign a number of women journalists at the newspaper attended one or possibly two of her strategy meetings. They included Mary Maher, Mary Cummins and Mary Holland. In addition, Donal Nevin, formerly general secretary of the Irish Congress of Trade Unions and a member of The Irish Times Trust, was initially listed as one of her campaign supporters.

I called the Chairman, Tom McDowell, when I saw Donal Nevin's name on some of Mary Robinson's literature. Any party political support or affiliation was clearly incompatible with membership of the Trust. McDowell called Donal Nevin and told him he had to choose. Donal, realising the difficulty he had created for himself, did so. He stayed with the Trust and in time became Vice-Chairman.

It was also likely that a majority of the journalists at the newspaper would have been Robinson voters. And virtually all of the opinion columnists had endorsed her in one degree or another. But most journalists are naturally cynical and generally inimical to anyone in power. The revolutionary hero they lionise today can be tomorrow's establishment target. After a period of euphoria and novelty, a somewhat more level perspective emerged on the Robinson presidency.

I met Mary Maher in the newsroom the day after the election. She seemed dazed. 'This feels all wrong,' she said wryly. 'We've never been on the winning side of anything before!'

My editorial on the day before the presidential election was hardly a ringing endorsement for the would-be President Robinson:

Part of Fianna Fáil's counter-attack on Ms Mary Robinson is that she is not what she would wish to appear: and that she is, in reality, certain things that she pretends not to be. That argument, in some respects, is not difficult to sustain. Ms Robinson has been, in some measure, reconstructed. Her marketing team has adjusted her very appearance, softened her political stance and occluded certain of her views . . . if votes were to be cast on the basis of candidates' straightforwardness and honest, unambiguous self-presentation, Mr Austin Currie would have to head the field . . . regrettably he has not succeeded in making sufficient impact with the voters.

A few days later, perhaps infected with the euphoria that followed the election result, I had abandoned my nit-picking approach:

Mary Robinson's success . . . is phenomenal . . . it marks the point at which a narrow and often cruel road, journeyed by a society often narrow and cruel, gives the first sign of broadening out; widening into a more tolerant and accommodating carriageway, offering its users the choice of travelling at their own pace and in whatever company they wish.

The voters—the women in particular—came out to make a statement for the rights of the individual; for the right of a woman to break out of the stereotype which Church and State have tacitly enforced for decades; for a candidate who represented personal independence, confidence and self-respect; for a woman whose own circumstances affirmed that it is possible to be a successful mother and wife, an active Catholic and yet to represent a platform which has been characterised as repugnant to mainstream Irish opinion.

Over her first year in office, in particular, *The Irish Times* was taunted by other media about the extent of its presidential coverage. I decided to spend an evening in the cuttings library upstairs, immersing myself in the archives, comparing our coverage of Mary Robinson with that accorded to her predecessor, Patrick Hillery, when he had taken office in 1983.

The story-count and picture-count on Robinson were far higher. But it was clear that she was saying and doing more newsworthy things than the low-profile President Hillery. She was, simply, a more interesting story. That was borne out by the extent of foreign coverage she received. A woman president was unusual and interesting. The European media liked her. UK critics of their royal family pointed to her as an example of what a democratically-elected head of state could be—as distinct from a hereditary monarch. She was also extremely photogenic.

At one point, someone on the news desk team argued that we should appoint a 'presidential correspondent' who would build an expertise about the story. It would have been justified on the grounds of manpower, or womanpower, as there were few days when Mary Robinson was *not* doing something that warranted coverage. I turned down the idea, partly on the grounds that it might be too like the British media's 'court' correspondents, assigned to report on the doings of the royal family. As time went by, I gradually reduced the scale of presidential coverage, shortening routine news reports, using smaller photographs and putting more of them on inside pages.

But the reality was that Mary Robinson used the presidency to highlight many issues and to further many causes that were traditionally part of the editorial platform of *The Irish Times*. Nothing could have been more natural than that it should laud her when she took initiatives to reach out to the marginalised and disaffected, when she spoke out against intolerance and discrimination or, indeed, when she controversially shook Gerry Adams's hand in Belfast, before there was a visible peace process.

The supposed common agenda between the newspaper and the Robinson presidency did not go beyond that. There were no cosy chats around the Áras fireside or dinners with the Trust. There was no tick-tacking with her press aide, Bride Rosney, beyond working out the logistics of covering public occasions.

We maintained the practice, begun with Patrick Hillery in 1988, of inviting the President of Ireland to present the annual *Irish Times* Prizes for Literature. Initially, Mary Robinson accepted, following the precedent set by Hillery and invariably spoke well, charming the audiences and mingling with the writers, judges and others involved in the event. The following year we were told she was 'unavailable'. But Gerard Cavanagh, the administrator of the prizes, had some sort of a family contact to Mary Robinson and, on appeal, the presidential mind was changed.

In March 1994 we invited her to give the key address at the bi-annual *Irish Times-Harvard University Colloquium*. This event, initiated by Christina Murphy, was staged alternately at the Institute of Politics at Harvard or at one of the Dublin universities. The President was visiting the UN at New York and we managed to date the Colloquium to coincide with her presence in the United States.

I invariably found myself puzzled in Mary Robinson's company at the contrast between her public and her private manner. She could dazzle a hall and charm a room filled with people. But she seemed to freeze in a one-to-one situation. At least she did with me. Perhaps she did not feel secure or comfortable in the company of journalists or editors.

At the *Irish Times-Harvard University Colloquium* she gave a bravura speech about the role of the UN in resolving world tensions. Afterwards the president of the university hosted a dinner for those involved, with President Robinson as the guest of honour.

Our host sat on Robinson's left while I sat on her right. After she had taken her seat she stared straight ahead as if in a trance. I heard the university president make some complimentary remarks to her about the speech. I heard no answer and saw just a slight nod of the head. After a minute or two of stony silence, I added my compliments. Another nod.

Desperately, I tried another tack. As a girl, my late mother had been at boarding school at Muckross Park in Dublin. In her old photo albums I had come across some photographs showing groups of young girls together in the grounds of the school, happily laughing and posing for the camera. My mother, Amy MacCarthy, stood at one side. Beside her was Tess O'Donnell, Mary Robinson's mother. I mentioned the coincidence, my finding of the photographs and described the happy scene of long-ago school days. Not even a nod this time. I gave up and concentrated on the guest to my right.

A few months later I was at an opening night at the Gate theatre with Ann. A couple of minutes before curtain up, the director, Michael Colgan, rushed over to where we were having a drink. He seemed flustered and concerned. '*La Robinson* is here with her son at short notice,' he explained. 'Will you sit beside her and bring them down to the hospitality room at the interval?' 'Sure,' I agreed. Colgan and I were friends and he was under all the pressures of a first night.

A member of the theatre staff brought us to a row of seats that had been partially cleared for the President and her son, Aubrey. Ann and I took our seats and a few minutes later the President and Aubrey arrived. Michael Colgan, unnecessarily, introduced us and moved off. We had a few minutes before the performance was to begin.

Ann leaned forward and engaged young Aubrey in conversation about school and such matters. He was about the same age as our older son, Neil. It was a pleasant, informal encounter and it held promise of being an enjoyable evening of entertainment.

I had not met the President since we had been at Harvard. I said that I thought the visit had gone well and thanked her again for her participation. She stared at the stage and nodded.

Reckoning that perhaps she was 'off duty', and anxious to put work out of her mind, I expressed my admiration for Michael Colgan and his achievements as director at the Gate. She continued to stare at the stage. I gave up again and read my programme until the lights dimmed and the performance started.

Mary Robinson's official biographers have used the adjective 'shy' more than once in describing her. If that is what I encountered, they understated the case. I have always felt that there was more to it. Perhaps there was a wariness, a nervousness, about the media. Or perhaps, in spite of everything, she regarded *The Irish Times* as less supportive and less helpful than it might have been.

———

We had two disturbing encounters with Mary Robinson. The first was while she was President, the other when she had taken up her job as United Nations High Commissioner for Human Rights. Both involved the newspaper's most experienced foreign correspondent, Conor O'Clery.

In March and April 1995 President Robinson made a tour of South American states. Conor O'Clery, then based in Washington, was assigned to cover her visits to Argentina, Brazil and Chile. The tour was marked by a series of mishaps and failures of planning and communication. Mrs Robinson's authorised biography, co-written by Olivia O'Leary and Helen Burke, says 'judging from the media coverage (the trip) seemed to lurch from one embarrassment to another'.

Things first went wrong in Argentina. The authorised biography says, 'It wasn't independent Newspapers, however, but the well-disposed *Irish Times* and RTÉ who were responsible for the lowest point in Mary's relationship with the media.'

Elsewhere in the biography, Mrs Robinson appears to blame the Department of Foreign Affairs press office and the then Irish Ambassador to Argentina for part of the problem. 'I think the Ambassador wasn't very sympathetic to what we were about,' she says.

The biography goes on: 'These were state visits so the host country called the shots. Bride (Rosney, Mary Robinson's special adviser) did not do her usual preparatory visit, so advance arrangements were left to ambassadors on the ground who would not, understandably, want any hassle with the host government.'

The President was invited to visit a poor *barrio* district at San Moreno outside Buenos Aires served by Irish Dominican sisters. Initially it was understood that she would do so. But it appears that the trip was blocked by Argentine President Menem. The nuns and local people had put on a welcome party out of their meagre resources and when the President did not arrive they were understandably distressed. A group of them then set out in a bus to attend a wreath-laying ceremony, at which the President was to honour the Irish-born founder of the Argentine navy, Admiral William Brown.

The bus got stuck in mud on the highway and by the time they got into the city the wreath-laying ceremony was over. But Conor O'Clery had delayed at the scene and met them there. When he was told what had happened, he telephoned the hotel in central Buenos Aires where the presidential party was staying. Bride Rosney, the President's adviser, then arranged for the nuns and their friends to come and meet the President there.

This series of mishaps led to a great deal of unfavourable commentary in the Irish media. The general thrust of it was that Mary Robinson had let down her own people in order to avoid antagonising those in political power in her host country.

Later in the tour, when she was in Chile, she found herself at a state banquet and was asked to shake hands with the former dictator General Pinochet. The RTÉ camera crew was ordered by the Chilean authorities to leave the room before the handshake—at her request. No doubt it made the encounter somewhat less embarrassing for her. But many journalists were shocked at this rather crude attempt at media-manipulation. The picture that emerged was not just one of disorganisation and lack of preparation but of a desperate attempt to 'spin' the accompanying media.

The somewhat ramshackle organisation of the tour and the President's apparent willingness to accommodate her hosts' political agenda gave rise to speculation that she was preparing the way for a United Nations appointment for herself. O'Clery asked her if she was interested in being Secretary-General when the incumbent, Boutros Boutros-Ghali, stepped down. She said she was not 'qualified' for it but that she would welcome a woman in the post.

I knocked out a fairly vinegary editorial:

The President's reply was suitably bashful. No one would take it as a denial ... Those who say she is interested (in the post) claim to discern careful calculation in her international schedule, spreading her visits strategically in order to secure international support when the time comes ...

... the South American tour has been characterised by a sequence of sour moments and rather transparent attempts at buck-passing as one embarrassment succeeded another. Sympathisers of the President speak with concern of attempts to cramp her style and her vision of the office. Others in contact with her activities speak of her sense of restlessness and recognise a growing tendency to hauteur and stiffness about her.

The episode left a bad taste in many mouths and tarnished the President's hitherto more or less unblemished image.

Mary Robinson's second, and perhaps more serious, clash with *The Irish Times* was in September 1998 when she made a visit to Tibet as UN High Commissioner for Human Rights.

Conor O'Clery had moved to Beijing to open *The Irish Times*'s first Asia bureau in 1996. He travelled extensively throughout China, reporting from many far-flung and remote parts of the country. But like other western media representatives, he was forbidden open access to Tibet.

When it became known that the UN High Commissioner was planning to visit Tibet, he applied to the Chinese Foreign Ministry for permission to accompany her. To our surprise, he was granted permission, along with Charlie Bird of RTÉ.

But five days before the visit was to take place, the Foreign Ministry advised O'Clery that it had withdrawn his permission to travel at the request of the High Commissioner in Geneva. To me, this had resonances of President Robinson requesting the ejection of the RTÉ camera crew in Chile three years previously.

When O'Clery met her in Beijing at the Irish Embassy she told him that having an Irish-only media entourage would 'send the wrong message'. She appeared to be anxious that her visit would not be seen as an Irish one but as a UN one.

This seemed untenable to me, since she did not block the travel arrangements for Charlie Bird and the RTÉ camera unit. I sent an urgent fax to Robinson protesting her action and urging her to reconsider. But she held firm. There was a further exchange of faxes with her press secretary. But it was clear that *The Irish Times* was not going to Tibet.

We published a story detailing what had happened and describing how she had vetoed Conor O'Clery's visit. A few days later she wrote a 'Letter to the Editor' in which she claimed that she was 'deeply disappointed' at the outcome of her endeavours to assemble a 'pool' of journalists for the visit, which would have included Conor O'Clery. No matter how I read it, it made little sense.

I felt that in blocking Conor's visit to Tibet, Mary Robinson was in effect striking a blow against much of what she was seen to stand for. Conor O'Clery was well-known in international media circles. Here was an opportunity for a respected and experienced Irish journalist to report at first hand from a country where human rights had been denied and where victimised people were begging for the outside world to keep its focus upon them. It was, I felt, an irony that an Irish-born High Commissioner for Human Rights should effectively silence an eloquent commentary on conditions in Tibet. Charlie Bird's documentary was transmitted in time. But there is no printed record of what happened, and did not happen, in those days of Mary Robinson's Tibetan visit.

——

Dealing with Mary Robinson's successor, Mary McAleese, was a good deal easier, although the 1997 presidential election campaign threw up its own difficulties for the newspaper.

I had known Mary McAleese since the early 1980s when we worked together as co-presenters of an RTÉ current affairs programme called *Europa*, which looked as aspects of society around the various states of the European Union. I found her personally warm, down-to-earth and easy to work with although she could be prickly if crossed. She was a devout Catholic, conservative in her beliefs but intellectually well able to defend them.

When she was nominated as a Fianna Fáil candidate for the presidency in 1997, she found herself on the receiving end of a smear-campaign that sought to portray her as an IRA fellow-traveller, as well as an individual whose personal beliefs and convictions were the antithesis of Mary Robinson's.

It was a contentious election, marked by dirty tricks and nasty smears. It started with Albert Reynolds, the former Taoiseach, declaring his hand and seeking the Fianna Fáil nomination. For a time, it appeared that he was allowed to believe he would get it. In the end, he was effectively shafted by his former colleagues.

When Mary Robinson stepped down in September 1997, two months short of her full seven-year term, to become UN High Commissioner for Refugees, there was initial speculation that John Hume would step forward and become President of Ireland. Had he shown a willingness to do so, it is probable that he would have been acclaimed without a contest.

Some senior SDLP figures made contact with *The Irish Times* to make the case for Hume stepping out of Northern political life at this time. Their organisation was in need of revitalisation. Other senior figures were concerned that the SDLP was in electoral decline. Certainly, their concerns were to be borne out by subsequent election results. I wrote one editorial setting out the logic of their concerns:

It has been said, against his (John Hume's) candidacy, that he is needed more than ever for the multi-party talks which resume next week at Stormont and that if he were President it would mark a further dividing line between nationalist and unionist Ireland.

But there are many—including very senior SDLP figures—who believe that the time is right for the party to stand on its own feet, without Mr Hume. Were the party fronted by Mr Séamus Mallon at the talks it would be very well led indeed. There is even an argument that if Mr Hume were out of the talks many unionists would be more encouraged to view them as a real and welcome opportunity for a fresh beginning.

Hume telephoned me at the office after that and made it clear that he was not going to disengage from the talks process. I put it to him that he had done himself no good by appearing to dither, considering the possibility of going for the presidency and then finally turning it down. 'I won't walk away from the process now at this stage,' he said. 'We can have an agreement with the unionists and that's a much bigger prize than being President of Ireland.' He was right, of course, however elusive a prize that agreement was to be.

Mary Robinson was going to be a difficult act to follow. Fine Gael nominated Mary Banotti, a grand niece of Michael Collins and a member of the European Parliament. She was well known and well liked but she was to be outshone by McAleese's campaigning abilities and people-skills.

The Labour party nominated Adi Roche, the Cork woman who had committed herself to a courageous and dangerous project, bringing aid and hope to the children suffering as a result of the nuclear disaster at Chernobyl in 1985.

Derek Nally, one of the early founders of Irish Victim Support and a former general secretary of the Association of Garda Sergeants and Inspectors, ran as an independent. I knew Derek since my time as editor of *Garda Review* when he was a member of my editorial board. He was a principled and honourable man and a good candidate, standing clear of party affiliations.

Dana Rosemary Scallon, the Derry-born MEP and former winner of the Eurovision Song Contest, ran as an independent candidate, representing a range of traditionally conservative views on family life and the law.

In October, a leaked memorandum from within the Department of Foreign Affairs described Mary McAleese as having Sinn Féin sympathies. At around the same time, the Sinn Féin President, Gerry Adams, said that he did not have a vote in the election but if he had one he would cast it for McAleese.

Derek Nally took up the cudgels against McAleese over her supposed Sinn Féin sympathies. His background in the Gardaí would have made him naturally hostile to a movement whose associates had murdered and injured many of his fellow-officers. But his remarks were uncharacteristically caustic. This was not the Derek Nally that I knew.

When he announced his candidacy in October 1997, I wrote a supportive editorial:

> He is a remarkable composition of radical and conservative, of simplicity and sophistication, of innovative thinking and plain-speaking. He believes in essential virtues—patriotism, justice, honesty, compassion—and at the same time declares himself firmly committed to the rule of law. He is passionate in his concern for victims but he does not run with the hang-'em-and-flog-'em brigade. He sees the roots of crime in poverty and inequality. And he believes in speaking out when someone has to put a name on corruption and the abuse of power.

But a week later, he had dug himself into a political hole and seemed to be unable to climb out of it.

Seizing on the leaked department of Foreign Affairs document, he described Mary McAleese as 'working to a different moral agenda than most people in the Republic'. She was not 'a proper person' to be President of Ireland, he asserted. When these statements drew fire upon himself from media commentators and others, he refused to withdraw them, arguing that if the claims in the leaked memo were untrue, Mary McAleese should sue the official who wrote them.

Derek Nally did his political prospects untold damage and effectively sabotaged his own campaign. I wrote more in sorrow than anger:

> The most charitable interpretation of Mr Nally's attack is that his tongue ran away with him. But his allegations were serious and while he has ceded a little ground he has not withdrawn them . . . it may be that he was ill-advised. He was certainly ill-informed . . . Derek Nally has entered the presidential race as a straight talker. He is also a gentleman and it would be a gentlemanly thing to do even at this stage if he were to apologise to Prof McAleese for seeking to label her as a fellow-traveller of the Provisionals.

There was also a subliminal hostitlity to Mary McAleese among some journalists at *The Irish Times*. Some of the women journalists, in particular, were wary of her conventional Catholicism and what they saw as her social conservatism. It crept into coverage here and there. But in credit to those who disliked her or what she stood for, the coverage was generally fair and restrained and required no editorial intervention.

Later in the campaign, The Labour Party candidate, Adi Roche, became the victim of an attempted smearing-by-association.

Adi Roche's brother had been an officer in the Irish defence forces. In the 1970s he had been obliged to resign his commission during a period when any possible breach of security was regarded as a sacking offence.

Late in September, newspapers and other media began to receive anonymous communications, detailing this long-forgotten matter. At the same time, some individuals close to the Chernobyl Children's Project began to circulate stories alleging that she was autocratic and capricious in her style of management and leadership.

As with the leaking of the DFA document in the case of Mary McAleese, the smears probably benefited Adi Roche in the long term. There was a great deal of admiration for her and a great deal of sympathy, especially in relation to the dragging up of her brother's unhappy Army record.

We defended Adi Roche vigorously against these smear-attempts. Later, we secured and published, across two full pages, a set of documents that strongly suggested her brother had been victimised in the defence forces. It was claimed that this was because he had insisted on acting honourably and honestly in a controversy that arose from a drink-driving case.

On 25 September, my editorial concluded as follows:

Such tactics are utterly reprehensible: Ms Roche or her family cannot be held accountable in any way for whatever happened to her brother when she was a child, scarcely into her teens. Happily, the smear attempts have been seen for what they are. Indeed, if one is to judge by listener and reader reaction in the media, they have, if anything, brought a volume of support and sympathy for Ms Roche's candidacy. There may be other reasons why she should not be President of Ireland. She lacks some of the heavyweight experience of Mary Banotti, the parliamentarian and Mary McAleese, the trained lawyer. And she has difficulty confining herself to using just a few words where she sees an opportunity to squeeze six dozen into a sentence. But she carries no penalty points from what has emerged after her enemies have done their worst this week.

Bizarrely, when the election results were in, and when it became clear that Adi Roche had done badly, I was attacked on radio by the Labour Party's media adviser, Fergus Finlay.

Fergus Finlay had put a lot of his personal support behind Adi Roche's campaign and he was deeply disappointed when the qualities he saw in her candidacy were not similarly acknowledged in the media. In particular, I suspect, he was irritated when *The Irish Times* did not agree, as many in the party felt it ought, with whatever Labour decided to do.

He went on radio, alleging that Adi Roche had not had fair coverage in *The Irish Times*. He said that the high standards and integrity that were once to found at the top of the newspaper seemed to operate no longer. Later, when he published his book *Snakes and Ladders* he referred to his 'feud' with *The Irish*

Times. 'It may not cause champagne corks to pop in the editor's office,' he wrote, 'but I hereby declare it over.'

I had been scrupulous to maintain balance in coverage between the candidates. Indeed, when I checked the final figures with the newsdesk it turned out that Adi Roche had received slightly more print coverage than Mary Banotti and a higher picture count than either Banotti or McAleese.

I called the radio station and asked for a head-to-head with Fergus Finlay. When he came back on air I confronted him with the hard, factual statistics of our coverage. He made a half-hearted attempt to maintain his argument and then finally went silent.

Later Dick Walsh, a good friend of Finlay's, berated me for being so hard on him. 'I'm like any other animal, Dick,' I replied. 'I defend myself when I'm attacked.'

14

| A TALE OF THREE BISHOPS

If you're wrong . . . the Church will destroy The Irish Times.
—Catholic Canon lawyer on hearing of the Bishop Casey inquiry.

My period as editor at *The Irish Times* coincided with the years of the great levelling of the hierarchical Catholic church, as it had operated in Ireland, more or less since the immediate post-Famine era. A great deal of its power and influence was dissipated through social change and a series of revelations that shook the confidence and belief of a traditionally-loyal flock.

Much of this process was played out in the media, not least in *The Irish Times*. It presented us with particular problems and choices. As it went on, I had the overwhelming sense of the church as an authority institution that was unable to square up to awkward facts even when they were staring it in the face. Inevitably, that put it on collision course with the news media.

I was saddened by what I saw happening in front of my eyes. I had been brought up and educated within the Catholic faith. I had, and have, many friends in the religious life. It was an area of my editorship that I found difficult, as I watched people, generally of good intention, dig themselves ever deeper into holes of their own making.

One afternoon in January 1992, a duty news editor at *The Irish Times* took a telephone call from a man with an American accent who said he wanted to talk about a young boy whose father was a senior figure in the church in Ireland. According to one, probably apocryphal account of the conversation that circulated later in the newspaper, the deskman quipped that some of his own immediate colleagues had fathers who were church figures too. It was true. Sons and daughters of the manse or the rectory were always numbered among the editorial staff.

This, of course, was different. The duty news editor referred the call to the news editor, John Armstrong. An hour later, when John came into my room, having telephoned to say he needed a few minutes in private with me, it had become no joking matter.

John and I had joined the newspaper together in 1969, he coming from *Trinity News* and I from *Campus UCD News*. We worked well together and I could instantly see trouble written across his face. He sat down opposite.

'We've had a call from a man who says he wants to tell us about a boy in

America who's the son of Bishop Eamonn Casey,' he said quietly. The quieter he was, the more serious usually was John's intelligence. It may have been his grim manner, but for some reason, I sensed that this was not going to prove another of the inventions or hoaxes that are regularly phoned in to newspaper offices.

John read from his notes. 'This man's name is Arthur Pennell. He's the partner of a woman called Annie Murphy. She claims she had an affair of several years with the Bishop of Galway, Eamonn Casey, and that he's the father of her child, Peter, who's now 17 years old. She wants to tell us the whole story.'

'Did you talk to him?' I asked.

'Yes. He seemed genuine. I had the impression that he wanted to get all this out into the open. He seemed under pressure himself.'

I had considerable respect for John's judgment. He was a thoughtful and painstaking editor.

After his conversation with Arthur Pennell he had spoken with Annie Murphy, who gave him the address of her home in the town of Ridgefield, Connecticut. He had asked if she had any evidence to support her claims, such as documents or letters.

John suggested that the best course of action was to pass these details to Conor O'Clery, lately arrived in Washington as our new North America correspondent. Conor was the most experienced foreign correspondent we had. It would be best if he went to meet these people who were about two hours drive from him.

John left to brief Conor by telephone. I sent for the biographical file on Eamonn Casey from the library and took it home with me that evening.

Casey was by now 65 years of age. He was one of the most flamboyant members of the Irish hierarchy and one of the 'strong men' of the Catholic church. Born in Kerry, he had originally come to prominence for his work among Irish emigrants in Britain. His first episcopal appointment was as Bishop of Kerry, later transferring to the more prestigious Galway diocese.

He had become something of a charismatic figure, fronting the Third World aid organisation Trócaire, and had often spoken out against the actions of western financial and political interests, especially the United States. In 1986 he had been convicted of drink-driving in Britain and his frank acknowledgment of his crime, his contrition and a declared purpose of amendment, earned him some points with public opinion in Ireland.

When Pope John Paul II visited Ireland in 1979, Bishop Casey was one of the prominent faces on platforms and in the Pontiff's company. A special Mass for the youth of Ireland was held at Ballybrit racecourse, outside Galway, celebrated by Pope John Paul. Casey was a sort of master-of-ceremonies, accompanied by the Dublin priest Fr Michael Cleary. It was an ironic combination, given that both churchmen were to be exposed as having violated their vows of celibacy and to have fathered children with dependent, vulnerable women who had come under their influence.

It is frequently the case, when a news organisation is given a lead into an apparently dramatic story like this, that the sources turn out to be unreliable or untruthful or both. But three days later, when Conor O'Clery reported back from Ridgefield, Connecticut, where he had travelled to meet Arthur Pennell, Annie Murphy and her son, Peter, it was clear that none of these applied.

Conor telephoned me to say he had met the sources. He said he thought they were telling the truth, although he guessed that Annie was highly strung and that the household was under a lot of emotional strain.

I had asked him to tape a formal interview with Annie Murphy and Arthur Pennell and to forward a copy to me in Dublin so that we could form a second judgment on what he was being told. When I got the tape and listened to it, I found myself in agreement. This was a coherent narrative with the ring of truth about it. When John Armstrong listened to the tape he came to the same conclusion.

I called a conference of some senior editors and John and I went through what we knew. The problem was that we had no corroborative evidence of Annie Murphy's story. There were no incriminating letters from the Bishop or anything such. If we published what we had been told, he might simply deny it and we would have nothing to fall back on. All we had was an allegation and our own sense that Annie, Arthur and Peter were telling the truth.

Annie Murphy's narrative detailed locations and dates in which she had spent time with Casey. She also mentioned some friends and former work colleagues in Ireland who, she said, were aware at the time of her relationship with the Bishop. We reckoned that we needed to put a couple of experienced reporters on the case to check out these details before we went any further.

The possibility of simply walking up to Bishop Casey's house in Galway and confronting him with the allegations was also considered. But we had reason to believe that he himself was under severe emotional pressure. I had no desire to cause him a cardiac seizure or to be the instrument of his deciding to do something foolish to himself. In any event, if we confronted him without any corroborative evidence, we would still be leaving the way open to a simple denial, without any fallback position for ourselves.

One or two newsroom reporters, apprised of the story, initially refused to have anything to do with it—to the irritation of Armstrong and myself. I could have ordered them to take the assignment, but what would have been the point? Eventually we got a small group of three, divided up the tasks and gave them 48 hours to complete them. Meanwhile, O'Clery went back to Ridgefield, Connecticut, to explore a range of supplementary questions which we thought might lead us to concrete evidence.

There were big issues for *The Irish Times* in the unfolding story. And there were serious ethical questions. If we ran with the story and it proved to be untrue, or incapable of being proven, it would be catastrophic for the newspaper. *The Irish Times* was still seen by many as a newspaper that was hostile to the Catholic church and this would be construed as an attempt to damage the church and one of its leading prelates in Ireland.

We discussed the possibility that the whole thing might be a ruse, set up to trap the newspaper. Clever and unscrupulous elements were at work on the far-right wing of Irish Catholicism. The destruction of *The Irish Times*'s credibility and reputation would be no small prize for such people. There was also the possibility, I feared, that running with the story might force Casey to a private reconciliation with Annie and Peter, after which they might retract or deny what they had told us, thereby leaving us exposed.

There were ethical issues too about invading the private lives of individuals. Irish media have generally been more reticent in this area than their British counterparts, especially where there is no demonstrable linkage between a person's private life and the manner in which that person discharges his/her public or professional functions.

But as a Catholic bishop, Eamonn Casey publicly espoused virtues of continence and chastity which, it now appeared, he did not practise in his own life. His prominent place at the side of a Pope, whose own stance on issues of private morality was so stern and uncompromising, seemed especially invidious. On the other hand, when one read back through his pastorals and other public statements, Bishop Casey's record was compassionate and moderate. He was never of the hellfire and brimstone school.

There was also the possibility, I realised, that Bishop Casey's offence —assuming that Annie Murphy's story was true—might well be known to the higher church authorities, either in Ireland or in Rome. He was not the first senior churchman to find himself in this situation. Was it possible, I asked myself, that somehow he might have regularised the whole situation *vis-à-vis* his ecclesiastical superiors?

I needed advice. I sought out an expert in Canon Law, himself a well-known churchman, and asked him to meet me. I said I needed an evaluation of a sensitive situation. I needed to know what church law might have to say about it and to ascertain how the church authorities would generally deal with this sort of issue. Without revealing the identity of the bishop in question, I outlined the circumstances of the case.

The unfortunate man appeared to be shocked. His first reaction was 'It's —— —, I assume,' naming another senior churchman. I told him I would neither deny nor confirm any name he put to me. He accepted that.

Then he outlined the relevant sections of Canon Law. It was not impossible, it seemed, that the bishop might have 'regularised' his situation by confessing, 'shunning' the woman and providing for the material welfare of the child. It might be achievable under Canon Law, he told me, but he doubted if it would have been possible 'politically' at the Vatican.

'You may have difficulty proving this, you know,' he told me as we parted. 'And if you're wrong or if you can't prove it, the church will destroy *The Irish Times*.

That's got to be part of the moral calculus too. In the long term, wouldn't this society be much worse off without it?'

The bit about providing for the material welfare of the child set a thought running in my head. If Bishop Casey had, indeed, 'provided for' Peter Murphy, that might be the best, provable confirmation we could get of Annie Murphy's story.

And so it turned out to be. One by one the reporters came back to John Armstrong with nothing more than additional circumstantial detail. Annie Murphy's best source, a friend now living in Galway, was not willing to go on the record although she told a reporter that she believed Eamonn Casey to be the father of Peter Murphy.

Conor O'Clery explained the situation to Annie Murphy and Arthur Pennell. They had begun to become irritated at what they saw as excessive caution on the part of *The Irish Times* and told him they were thinking of bringing the story 'elsewhere'. I remember after Conor called me to tell me this, I went to bed that night thinking how nice it would be!

But the following day he was back with the break in the story. Annie Murphy had directed him to a New York priest who had been the conduit of payments from Bishop Casey to her over the years.

Conor went to visit the priest and found him to be disarmingly frank about the money. He provided Conor with details of payments made over a period of years and gave him the name of a firm of solicitors in Kerry which had forwarded the funds from Ireland. When he showed Conor some of the documentation it became apparent that more than IR£70,000 had been paid out of a reserve account operated by the Diocese of Galway.

It was the only incontrovertible evidence upon which we could run a report. Conor put an official request through to the Bishop's residence in Galway, asking for a meeting to discuss certain financial payments to Annie Murphy. It turned out that Casey was on holidays in Malta. But a message came back to say that he would meet *The Irish Times* on his return in two days time.

The meeting was set for the Skylon Hotel, close to Dublin airport. But Eamonn Casey never showed. The same evening the Vatican announced that he had tendered his resignation to the Pope. Later, he flew out of Ireland to New York on an Aer Lingus flight and went to a secret destination in South America.

There was consternation in the church and bewilderment in the media. We alone knew the full story but I insisted that we hold to a minimal stance, simply reporting the following day that *The Irish Times* had been seeking to interview the Bishop about money that he had paid to an American woman in Connecticut. In time, of course, the entire story came into the public domain.

The fall of Bishop Casey was a monumental event in Ireland. By comparison with what was later to emerge during the 1990s about clerical sex abuse of children, his offence was perhaps a venial one, and came to be regarded as such. But in its time and circumstances it was seen as a shocking revelation of the gap between what the Catholic church preached and what some of its leading figures practised.

The dramatic fall-off in religious practice, the steep decline in vocations to the religious life and the near total loss of authority by the institutional church that took place during the 1990s, can be said to have begun with the fall of Bishop Casey.

One of the most revealing and perhaps saddest aspects of the Casey saga was the way in which he was effectively isolated by the rest of the Catholic church in Ireland. In the final days before our inquiries concluded, I learned that some of the bishops had picked up straws in the wind and had knowledge that something was afoot.

I made attempts to reach a number of those whom I understood to have been alerted. With the matter reaching its *denouement* I thought Eamonn Casey should have the support of his peers when the news broke. I had no idea, of course, that he was going to flee the country. I telephoned two Episcopal offices and left messages for the bishops in question. I never got a call back.

———

Later, I had a further insight into the poor ability of the church to cope with a challenge or crisis in my contacts with another bishop, Brendan Comiskey of Ferns.

In 2002 Bishop Comiskey resigned as Bishop of Ferns after it became apparent that he had failed to respond adequately to problems of sexual abuse within his diocese. A priest of the diocese, Fr Seán Fortune, took his own life before he could be brought through the courts to answer for a saga of abuse, conducted in a number of parishes over more than a decade.

Bishop Comiskey's lack of action, when parents initially complained about Fortune, was indefensible. He evaded the issue, moving Fortune to another parish. When the Garda finally investigated the allegations, an important file mysteriously went missing.

I had got to know Bishop Comiskey in the early 1990s. He had invited me to dinner one evening to meet the English religious affairs writer Peter Hebblethwaite. But he did not turn up, leaving Hebblethwaite and myself to get acquainted as best we could.

He was interested in the media and we would meet occasionally over a meal or sometimes we would talk on the telephone. I liked him. I found him thoughtful and essentially a humble man. I became aware that he felt very isolated in his responsibilities. He had turned to alcohol to try to cope with the situation in which he found himself.

He never detailed any of the scandals that had taken place in his diocese. But I knew that he was under immense pressure and stress. On a number of occasions I asked him if there was anyone else in the hierarchy to whom he could turn for advice or support. But from what he said it seemed they were the last people he felt he could turn to.

His resignation in April 2002 perhaps overshadowed his earlier, courageous but doomed effort to initiate a debate within the Catholic church on the issue of priestly celibacy. Some of his brother-bishops, so reticent at the time of Bishop Casey's fall, suddenly found their tongues and turned on him. In September 1996, he announced that he was taking a three-month 'sabbatical' because of stress. In reality he was going to the United States for treatment. There were many who believed he would not return. On the announcement of his 'sabbatical' I wrote an editorial acknowledging his stance:

> For an Irish bishop to challenge his Cardinal and his Pope to a public argument is effectively to make the clerical ground shake underfoot. Few outside the Catholic church's clergy and hierarchy could appreciate the courage of Bishop Comiskey's *demarche* in calling for a debate on celibacy . . .
>
> But in taking the stand he did, Bishop Comiskey also restored a much-needed sense of hope among many of the Catholic faithful who were in despair of ever hearing a questioning voice from among the bishops on the great, divisive practical issues facing a church in crisis . . .
>
> Bishop Comiskey's contribution to the debate in his church has helped to restore for many Irish Catholics their sense of participation in shaping its future after it has gone through a particularly difficult period.

Whatever alleviation his American visit may have afforded Bishop Comiskey, it did not last long. The following February, when a friend and diocesan adviser of the Bishop's was found dead in a Wexford apartment, the corruption and mismanagement of his diocese became headline news.

Bishop Comiskey had not returned from the us. There was a widespread view that his fellow members of the hierarchy did not want him to return either. On 17 February the editorial ran:

> There are some who want to see no more of Bishop Comiskey. But there are many others who await his return with an open-minded preparedness to hear his side of the story. Should there not be room for at least one man among the Hierarchy who has the courage to acknowledge that he has met with demons, that he has fallen, that he has picked himself up again and that he has the will to fight on? Is Christ's church not, after all, a church of sinners? Are there not enough plaster saints on parade?

One could hardly argue that Bishop Comiskey should not have resigned. He had lost the confidence of too many of his flock and too many of his priests. Yet I always felt that he was a man with more to offer, had circumstances been different. Christ's church, after all, was founded as a church of sinners. If the world were populated only by saints there would be no need for it.

Undoubtedly the most unpleasant series of encounters between *The Irish Times* and the Catholic hierarchy over these years concerned the then Archbishop of Dublin (later Cardinal) Desmond Connell.

Archbishop Connell was at once both a predictable and unexpected appointment as archbishop. He had spent most of his religious life as an academic at University College Dublin. As such, he was not the choice of the priests of the archdiocese. He was regarded as a man of markedly conservative views and this, presumably, commended him to the like-minded authorities in Rome.

In time, he built a reputation among his priests for considerable personal kindness, coupled with a certain gaucheness that may well have been the product of years of academic isolation. I encountered him from time to time at official functions and found him generally affable. But his relationship with the media and with *The Irish Times* in particular was not a happy one.

Archbishop Connell inherited a can of worms in the form of unresolved cases of child sexual abuse by clerics in Dublin. His critics alleged that his responses to the problem had the effect, primarily, of protecting the church. His public credibility was damaged after he denied making payments in regard to the sexual abuse perpetrated by a priest of the archdiocese, Fr Ivan Payne. When it was revealed that the archbishop had, in fact, made such payments, he fell into a miasma of contradictions and verbal formulae that caused even some of his closest supporters to cringe.

There were several instances in which Dr Connell, having made some public statement that led to trouble, attempted to put out some different gloss or interpretation. Unfortunately, in at least one instance—when President McAleese took Anglican Communion at Christ Church Cathedral in Dublin—he attempted to put the blame on the media and particularly on journalists in *The Irish Times*.

The newspaper had always had first-class religious affairs correspondents. John Horgan had covered Vatican ii. John Cooney succeeded him. Pat Nolan had held the brief during the late 1980s. In the years of my editorship, the newspaper was served exceptionally well by a number of religious affairs correspondents. Joe Carroll, later Washington Correspondent, held the role until 1994. He was succeeded by Andy Pollak and Andy, in turn, was succeeded by Patsy McGarry. If I were to choose journalists from the ranks of *The Irish Times* for their qualities of integrity, conscientiousness and competence, all of these would be high on the list.

The newspaper's most public clash with the archbishop came about, however, not over the issue of child sex abuse but over the above-mentioned taking of Anglican Communion by President McAleese shortly after she came to office in 1997.

On Sunday, 7 December 1997, the newly-elected President attended service at the Church of Ireland cathedral of Christ Church in Dublin. It was a notable weekend. Newspapers marked the seventy-fifth anniversary of the foundation of the State with editorials and special commemorative features. At Christ Church, the new President, a practising Roman Catholic, caused something of a sensation by electing to take Anglican communion. It was a bold and daring gesture, spanning ancient theological, political and racial divides.

The President's gesture seemed to be in defiance of Canon Law. Even the most recent Roman Catholic Catechism (1994) made it clear that Catholics could not take Anglican Communion because Protestant churches 'have not preserved the proper reality of the Eucharistic mystery in its fullness, especially because of the absence of the sacrament of Holy Orders'.

When I heard the news, I felt affirmed. Mary McAleese had been characterised as inflexible and zealously orthodox. But now she was showing herself in different colours. Catholic Irish people of my generation had recollections of their parents being prohibited from attending Protestant services. A memorable photograph from 1949 in some of the history books showed Catholic members of the Cabinet sitting in their motor cars outside the doors of the church, while the obsequies were taking place inside of the (Protestant) President of Ireland, Douglas Hyde. My editorial the following day lauded her action:

> If she has done nothing else she has thrown some sand in the eyes of those who wish to characterise her as ultra-orthodox or a hard line, traditional Catholic. Rather has she confirmed that she is indeed a woman of complex and at times contradictory impulses. She is for gay rights but against divorce. She is for women priests but against integrated education . . . she is a devout and practising Catholic but she is prepared to bypass a solemn prohibition of her Church's law in order to make a statement of reconciliation.
>
> Mrs McAleese declared that her presidency would be about building bridges . . . At Christ Church on Sunday she made a measurable start in building a bridge from her own tradition to that of the Church of Ireland.

But Dr Connell took a very different view of the President's action. More than a week after the event, the archbishop was a guest on Eamon Dunphy's radio programme. In the course of his interview he said, *inter alia*, that the President's taking of Anglican Communion was 'a sham'.

The following day, 17 December, *The Irish Times* reported the details of his interview with Dunphy under the headline 'Taking C of I Communion a sham, says archbishop'. There was an immediate, and predictable, reaction from outraged Protestants and from many Catholics who felt that the use of the word 'sham' was insulting and hurtful.

The letters columns of the newspaper were bombarded. Dozens of telephone calls came into my office and many more to the news desk. Radio discussion programmes took up the issue. The vast majority of those who expressed themselves were angry at the archbishop.

There were others who defended the substance of his statement but who were upset at the way in which he had expressed himself. One priest from the Meath diocese went on RTÉ radio making the point that 'this was what the Reformation was about, after all'.

Archbishop Connell began to back-pedal, explaining that he had not intended to use the word 'sham' in a pejorative way. Then on 22 December he gave another interview to journalist Mebh Ruane and attempted to put the blame on *The Irish Times*.

It was certainly true that in picking up his remarks from Eamon Dunphy's radio programme, *The Irish Times* had given them much more prominence. And the newspaper's editorial stance was critical of the archbishop. But it was baseless to blame us. He was sorry 'for the offence', he told Mebh Ruane, but blamed it 'very much on the way *The Irish Times* put its headline'. It was 'very bad', he added.

We had been scrupulous to give full, direct quotes and to ensure that headline, introduction and context were fair. I was concerned for the sake of the sub-editor involved. She was among the most painstaking members of the department and entitled to her professional reputation, even if her name was not on the article.

The following day, we reproduced the original report with the controversial headline and I took up the cudgels with Dr Connell in the editorial:

> The headline and the accompanying report from page 9 of our editions . . . are reproduced today in page 7, enabling readers to judge for themselves whether the headline was a fair and accurate reflection of what Dr Connell said. Perhaps indeed, from the Archbishop's point of view, it may have been 'very bad' for it took his remarks . . . into the mainstream of public awareness. But it was not 'very bad' in the way the headline was drafted. As an exercise in sub-editing, it was in fact, exemplary of that rather exacting craft . . .
>
> Dr Connell may not be the most adroit media performer. And he may feel that the media's need to compact and condense arguments does a disservice on occasion to the complex and nuanced issues with which he is concerned as a spiritual leader. But it might be pointed out that he has twice had the facility of these columns in recent days, without restriction as to length or presentation, in which to make his case . . .
>
> Headlines, by definition, are a *précis* of a following report. Had this one said 'C of I Communion a sham, says Archbishop,' Dr Connell might have a legitimate complaint. But the headline was specific to his point. It said that the taking of Communion was a sham. Since these reports of recent days were in the context of President McAleese's taking Communion at Christ Church, it is impossible to see how the headline could be faulted or misinterpreted. Moreover, the full context of the Archbishop's remarks was quoted in the report. Dr Connell is a man of considerable intellect and reputed humanity. It

is therefore all the more surprising to see him fall back on the hardly sustainable position of blaming the messenger. And one wonders whether he paused to consider the journalists whose work . . . he called into question.

. . . the journalists . . . are entitled to their reputations. They should not have anyone's finger pointed at them when they have done their jobs with competence and professionalism.

We heard nothing more from Dr Connell on the issue. I knew he had the reputation of being a kind man and I had, perhaps, expected some word of affirmation for the sub-editor whose work had been described in such negative terms.

When he retired as archbishop he was succeeded by Diarmuid Martin, a Vatican diplomat whose brother, Séamus, had been on the staff of *The Irish Times* and who also had an accomplished career as a journalist and writer elsewhere.

The new archbishop proved himself very quickly as a communicator. He went on TV and radio shows and displayed an ability to put out the church's message in terms that were accessible to ordinary Catholics.

Perhaps, after all, somebody, somewhere in the church, was learning lessons.

15

'A VERY DEEP CRISIS IN OURSELVES'

With what are we now to compare ourselves—Ceaucescu's Romania? the Ayatollah's Iran? Algeria?—there are similarities . . .
— Irish Times editorial on the 'X' case decision in the High Court

On occasion, a newspaper will be presented with a challenge that goes to the fundamentals of what it should be about in society.

'The press lives by disclosure', Francis Williams, the English editor and biographer once said. But there are times when disclosure can bring a newspaper into outright defiance of the law. When that happens, it can be a very unequal contest.

The gloomy days of January 1992 had been enlivened by yet another crisis in Fianna Fáil. This time, it was the end for Charles Haughey. His former Minister for Justice, Seán Doherty, had gone on a late-night television chat-show to confirm that he had brought transcripts of illegally tapped telephone conversations to the then Taoiseach in 1982.

Fianna Fáil's dark night of the soul was to be resolved—or so it seemed for a while—when Haughey was replaced as Taoiseach and party leader by Albert Reynolds.

But even as Reynolds was settling into the Taoiseach's suite at Government Buildings in Merrion Street, a crisis that was to touch on the deepest human and moral issues was evolving not far away.

The Law Library at the Four Courts is one of the great sources of leaked information in Dublin. Little remains confidential once it has been put into the system where lawyers and their support staffs engage with each other, bargaining, swapping information and perhaps sometimes seeking each other's advice. Unusual cases, or unusual litigants, are noted. Information passes by word of mouth, in the cafeteria or in the adjacent pubs and restaurants. Sooner or later it will be picked up by journalists.

Towards the end of the first week of February 1992, rumours began to reach the ears of *Irish Times* journalists that something unusual involving an abortion case was afoot in the Attorney General's office.

I met a senior judge at the theatre. We were speaking during the interval and as the bell rang to call the patrons back to their seats he remarked that one of his colleagues was facing a terrible dilemma. I had no idea what he was talking about. I went back to *The Irish Times* office and checked the court reports for the following day. I found nothing to enlighten me.

Next day Niall Kiely, from the newsdesk, told me he had picked up something too. He thought that through some of his legal contacts it might be possible to get to the bottom of whatever was going on. He asked two or three reporters to check the story.

Forty-eight hours later, newsroom reporter Carol Coulter, who in time was to become the newspaper's legal affairs correspondent, told the newsdesk that she had stood up the details of an extraordinary and tragic story. The events that unfolded were to be known as the 'X' case. The news editor and his deputy came hotfoot to my office to brief me.

Carol's information was that the Attorney General, Harry Whelehan, had been granted an interim injunction by the High Court, preventing a 14-year-old girl, a rape victim, from leaving Ireland to have an abortion. Whelehan had cited Article 40.3.3 of the Constitution in seeking the injunction. This was the 8th Amendment —the so-called 'pro-life' measure, aimed at preventing abortion in Ireland—that had been ratified by referendum in September 1983 after a bitter and divisive campaign.

Other details were sketchy. Carol understood that this was a case of 'statutory rape'—unlawful 'carnal knowledge' of a minor. The sequence of events appeared to be that the girl's parents had made a complaint to the Garda, alleging that their pregnant child had been violated by an adult neighbour. In time, the neighbour was to be convicted and sentenced.

The distraught parents told the Gardaí at their local station that they intended to take their daughter to London for an abortion. But they wanted to secure DNA evidence to enable them to prove charges against the man who was responsible for her pregnancy. They wanted DNA material to be taken from the foetus in London once it had been aborted and they wished to know if this would be admissible as evidence in court.

The Gardaí did not know the answer immediately. The Garda investigation was headed by Detective Inspector Tony Sourke, a widely experienced officer with a track-record in successful investigation of serious crime. He had sought legal advice from the office of the Director of Public Prosecutions (DPP). The DPP's office, in turn, notified the Attorney General's department. There, the matter was brought to the attention of Harry Whelehan.

Whelehan decided that there were inescapable constitutional implications in what had been put before him. He instructed counsel to seek an *in camera* hearing at the High Court, requesting that the girl be restrained from leaving the jurisdiction. The interim injunction had been granted by Mr Justice Declan Costello.

The newsdesk was satisfied that Carol Coulter's story was well-sourced. I asked for details of the source and I too was satisfied that it was reliable and that it was an adequate basis upon which to proceed to publication. *The Irish Times* did not subscribe to the principle, widely applied in the US, that a report always had to have two independent sources. One good source, I believed, is infinitely better than two or three bad ones. And in my experience, sources that sometimes appear to be independent of each other often turn out to have a common origin.

But the implications of deliberately defying an *in camera* order of the High Court were serious. To publish details of a case heard *in camera* would be a contempt of court for which the penalty might range from a heavy fine to imprisonment or both. It might even threaten the publication of the newspaper.

I faced many motions alleging contempt of court in my years as editor. Virtually all of these arose out of some inadvertent publication or presentation of material. They were invariably disposed of through an apology proffered in court by learned (and expensive) counsel and in some cases by a contribution towards costs. But if we were to defy this order, it would be impossible to plead error or inadvertence.

Moreover, Declan Costello had the reputation of being a meticulous and stern judge. A son of former Attorney General and Taoiseach John A Costello, he had been active in Fine Gael and tried to draw the party in a new social-democratic direction in the 1960s with a series of policy platforms entitled 'Towards a Just Society'. As a member of the Young Fine Gael branch in UCD I had responded to the stimulus of this new message, along with others that included John Bruton, Henry Kelly and Vincent Browne. I had attended meetings where Costello had been presented as the new, radical face of the party.

I had also got to know his father, John A. Costello, on foot of interviews I had conducted with him and other previous Attorneys General while preparing my postgraduate thesis at UCD. Costello *père* was a garrulous and entertaining man, in some contrast to the reserved and rather remote figure that Declan Costello seemed to present.

But Fine Gael had rejected Costello and he re-entered the cloistered world of the Bar. Appointed to the High Court, he was now aged 66. He was not a man, I knew, who would take lightly to having his orders ignored by a newspaper.

As on many occasions before and after, I knew it was time to talk to our excellent legal advisers, Hayes and Sons. I called Andrew O'Rorke, the second most senior partner in Hayes and arranged an immediate meeting. Not entirely to my surprise, Andrew seemed to have picked up something of the story as well. But he groaned when he learned that we had fairly full details.

'And you're going to go ahead and publish all this?' he asked resignedly.

'If we can. What are the implications?'

'I think you know pretty well what the implications could be. If you breach an *in camera* order, that's contempt. If Declan Costello gets nasty about it you could go to jail, plus landing the newspaper with a hefty fine.'

'Yes, I know that. But what's your gut feeling about it?'

Andrew thought for a moment. Then he said, 'You'd obviously have to plead the public interest. It's a hugely explosive issue. The courts would have to consider that argument. But there's no way of knowing with any certainty what might happen. It's an editorial decision ultimately.'

There was also the possibility that, even if Mr Justice Costello were prepared to allow a contempt to pass, the Attorney General, Harry Whelehan, might take a different view. Whelehan was a popular and gracious man. I had met him socially on occasion and found him good company. He was known to be of conservative views and he had a reputation as a stickler for procedure.

I returned to *The Irish Times* office. The story had by now been written and was ready to run. It told all the salient facts but it had been carefully scrutinised to ensure that it contained nothing that could identify the girl, her family, the accused man or even the area of the city in which the rape had happened.

It was one of the very rare occasions on which I went to the board and the Trust with an issue prior to publication. I arranged to speak to the chairman, Tom McDowell, and set out what happened, rehearsing also my conversation with Andrew O'Rorke. McDowell listened carefully, asking occasional questions.

'So what do you think you should do?' he inquired.

'I think we have to publish and face whatever consequences may follow,' I said.

'I agree completely,' he replied. 'I'll ring around the members of the Trust to advise them. I'm sure they'll see it the same way. If they don't, I'll come back to you.'

'This is the sort of thing *The Irish Times* is for,' McDowell said finally. 'We'll back you in whatever happens, be assured of that. If we have to go beyond Costello to the Supreme Court we will.'

I was greatly fortified by the chairman's reaction. He was by nature cautious. But when it came to an issue like this, Tom McDowell always displayed the instincts of a true newspaperman.

I had thought that he would suggest we seek senior counsel's opinion. But there would have been little point in this. Counsel would confirm Andrew O'Rorke's advice and tell us that we ourselves had to decide what risk we were prepared to carry. Going that route would simply have delayed things.

I saw the story into the paper, placing it on the front page, under a report and picture of Albert Reynolds receiving his seal of office as Taoiseach from President Mary Robinson. Then I went home and had a deeply anxious night. *Irish Times* delivery vans always dropped off early copies of the newspaper in the small hours, along with early editions of the *Irish Independent* and *The Irish Press*. I went down to the doorstep to retrieve the first bundle of newspapers at 4 am.

None of the others was carrying the story. When I got the later editions of the *Irish Independent*, I saw with sinking heart that they had not 'lifted' it from our early edition, as was their frequent practice. If I was in trouble, I was in it on my own.

But by mid-morning, the storm had broken. RTÉ news ran a short item, well down the bulletin at 9 o'clock. Other radio programmes picked up the report and sent their own staff hurrying to quiz their legal contacts. Then the evening papers seized on the story and gave it headline treatment. Our reporters in the Four Courts were alerted to watch for any motion to cite *The Irish Times* for contempt. But nothing happened. I breathed a little more easily at the end of the first day.

The initial order secured by Harry Whelehan from Mr Justice Costello was an *interim* injunction. It had the effect of freezing matters pending a full High Court hearing of the Attorney General's application to prevent the 14-year-old girl from travelling out of the jurisdiction for an abortion.

When the case came to hearing before Costello a few days later, it was again *in camera*. But by now, the public controversy had engulfed the airwaves, the print media and even the Dáil. The Labour leader, Dick Spring, and the chairman of the Progressive Democrats, Michael McDowell, himself a senior member of the Bar, were demanding information about the circumstances of the case and, in particular, about the Attorney General's actions.

Any attempt by the courts to enforce the original *in camera* order would have been futile at this stage. The jails would be filled with hundreds of reporters, broadcasters and public representatives.

Harry Whelehan pleaded publicly that 'the publicity and public controversy so far given to the matter . . . should cease forthwith'. It was a measure of his distress but also of his unrealistic understanding of the dynamics of the media and of the force of public opinion.

On 15 February, while the public was awaiting the outcome of the full hearing before Declan Costello, *The Irish Times* endeavoured to put a reality-check in place around Harry Whelehan's plea:

The court has an inherent right to rule that its proceedings be held in camera. That was done, in the words of the Attorney General, 'in order to protect the interests of the parties and to ensure that the highest standards of justice were adhered to'. But this is a small society. By the middle of last week, the details of the case were the talk of the Law Library, the gardaí, the welfare services, the solicitors' offices and ultimately the dining tables and living rooms of the capital. Colleagues told colleagues who told their spouses. Word spread in offices, by telephone, in bars. The wonder is, perhaps, that it took so long to reach the newsrooms of the national media.

The Attorney General's plea that the 'publicity and public controversy so far given to the matter . . . should cease forthwith' is thus somewhat unrealistic. Every person in this State who has reached the age of reason is confronted with the profound implications of the case and has a legitimate—indeed a compelling—interest in its outcome. The concern and apprehension which are now widespread cannot be ruled to disappear. Meanwhile, the general public is informed, at worst, by rumour and at best by TV, radio and newspaper from outside the jurisdiction . . .

I have no idea whether Mr Justice Costello considered taking action when his *in camera* order was first breached by *The Irish Times*. We had taken a calculated gamble in order to fulfil our 'duty of disclosure'. We would have responded vigorously to any attempt to silence us and there is little doubt that other media would have followed suit. Perhaps there was still as much of the politician in Declan Costello's instincts as there was of the jurist.

But two days later, when he delivered his judgment on the case, there was a dam-burst of public anger. In the case of *The State v. Miss 'X'*, Mr Justice Costello upheld the Attorney General's application that the girl be compelled to remain in the State for 10 months. The implications were horrendous. She was going to have to carry the foetus to full term and then be delivered, at 14 years of age, of her rapist's baby.

Mr Justice Costello's judgment confirmed many of the details of the case that had been in circulation. He outlined how the girl had been violated by the father of a school friend during visits to his house. Describing the friend's father as 'depraved and evil', the judge went on to describe how the abuse had begun when the victim was 13 years old. In a later section of his judgment, he set out how the girl had threatened suicide and cited the evidence of a clinical psychologist who believed that she was capable of taking her own life.

Political representatives and others went into uproar. There were calls for the resignation of the Attorney General. I believed these were misplaced and unfair. Harry Whelehan was acting conscientiously as he saw it. He was not responsible for the insertion of Article 40:3:3 into the Constitution. There were demonstrations and torch-lit processions in Dublin, along O'Connell Street and outside the Dáil.

One Fianna Fáil deputy telephoned me, apparently with drink taken, and abused me for 'causing the whole thing'. Then he suggested that *The Irish Times* should call for Whelehan's head and for Costello to step down from the bench. Harry Whelehan 'should have dropped the f****** file behind a cupboard,' he mumbled. I listened for a few minutes and then hung up.

We did not call for Harry Whelehan's or Declan Costello's heads. That would have been quite wrong. But we did have the advantage, through reporter Mary Maher, of a 'back-channel' line of communication to Ms 'X' and her family. Through Mary we knew that the family was taking courage and comfort from the media coverage.

The next day we reflected the sense of outrage across the community. Martyn Turner's cartoon articulated a searing commentary. He depicted a pregnant school girl in pigtails, a teddy bear trailing from one hand, standing on a map of the island of Ireland, with barbed wire entanglements piled high, all around the coastline. The caption read: '*17th February 1992: The introduction of internment in Ireland—for 14 year old girls*'. Turner's cartoon was widely reproduced elsewhere and the image of the schoolgirl was to become symbolic of the 'X' case.

Under the heading 'DESCENT INTO CRUELTY', I wrote in the leader of the following morning:

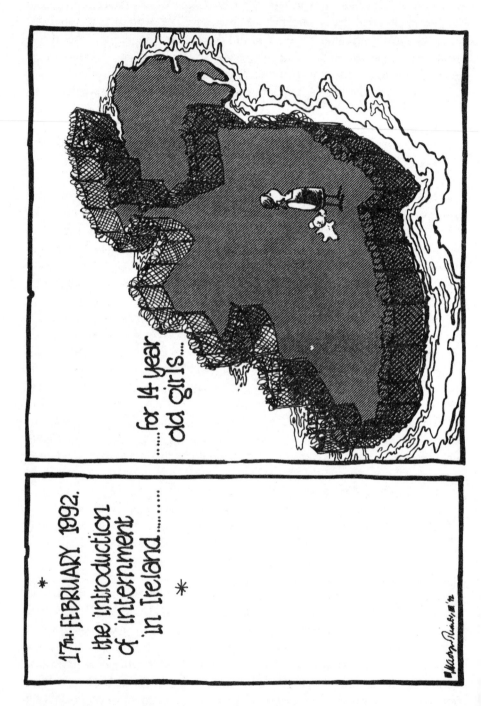

Martyn Turner's cartoon depicting Ireland of 17 February 1992

What has been done to this Irish Republic, what sort of state has it become that, in 1992, its full panoply of authority, its police, its law officers, its courts, are mobilised to condemn a 14-year-old child to the ordeal of pregnancy and childbirth after rape at the hands of 'a depraved and evil man'? With what are we now to compare ourselves?—Ceaucescu's Romania? The Ayatollah's Iran? Algeria?—There are similarities . . .

It is difficult to envisage a more bitter paradox for this unfortunate family. They turn to the Garda Síochána, as would any outraged parents when their daughter is violated. They co-operate in the criminal investigation which is undertaken—no doubt in good faith—by the local detectives. But instead of seeing the alleged perpetrator of the crime charged, they find themselves and their daughter subject to injunction under the ultimate threat of imprisonment.

. . . We have landed in the nightmare, a nightmare brought on by a combination of political cowardliness and sectarian triumphalism, together with some genuine but profoundly ill-informed idealism. There was no demand here for abortion in 1982–83. But SPUC and the other pressure groups wanted their way; the politicians had not the foresight or the courage to stand up to them: and we opted for the Eighth Amendment to the Constitution.

Mr Justice Costello's judgment must not go unchallenged. The grounds for possible appeal are varied and obvious. He has effectively set aside the threat to the child's life . . . he has restrained the personal liberty of the child and her parents . . . he has held that there is a derogation from the Treaty of Rome, where many eminent jurists believe that Irish law has to stand subservient to that of the (European) Community.

Time is of the essence. Thus the legal channel of appeal must be utilised immediately. But only slightly less urgent is the political agenda which is now presented. It must be presumed that the politicians who sponsored and supported the 1983 Amendment did not envisage the use of crime branch detectives, judges and injunctions to enforce the completion of pregnancies by child rape victims. It was certainly not in the minds of many of those who went out in good conscience and voted for the Amendment eight years ago.

Over the ensuing days, however, the full extent of bewilderment and apprehension among the political establishment became apparent. There were calls for legislation to give an extra weighting in law to the life of the mother *vis-à-vis* a foetus. There were calls for an immediate, new referendum. But nobody could put down any wording that could keep abortion out of Ireland and at the same time solve the immediate crisis surrounding Miss 'X' and her family.

The electorate, encouraged by politicians that included Charles Haughey and Garret FitzGerald, had bought a nonsense in the referendum. It supposed that it could somehow cut itself off from the moral issues that the rest of the world had to square up to, while exporting its unwanted pregnancies to Britain. Now the fatuity of that proposition had been challenged and nailed. No matter what way the politicians, the churchmen and the lawyers twisted or turned, the problem would not go away.

President Mary Robinson, with calming understatement, declared two days later, 'We are experiencing as a people a very deep crisis in ourselves. I hope we have the courage which we have not always had, to face up to and to look squarely and to say, . . . "this is a problem we have got to resolve."' It was an unprecedented intervention by a President in a current public controversy.

In a sense, that controversy has still not been resolved. The immediate issue of the 'X' case was dealt with by way of appeal to the Supreme Court. Declan Costello's judgment was set aside and the girl was allowed to travel to England where she had her abortion.

But the Supreme Court decision left the situation in regard to abortion confused and uncertain. It determined that far from preventing abortion in Ireland, the so-called 'pro-life' amendment had, theoretically at least, opened the possibility of abortion more or less on demand.

Almost a decade later, after much hand-wringing by the politicians and after lengthy deliberations by the Oireachtas Committee on the Constitution, a new legal framework was put in place. Abortion may be possible in Ireland in certain limited circumstances now. But in practice, Irish women still take the plane to London. Little, if anything, has changed, beyond the fact that they are no longer at risk of being arrested for doing so.

———

Following within a year of the Bishop Casey controversy, the case of Miss 'X' cast a deep shadow over Irish society. Both events fed into a process of more honest self-assessment. But it was painful. Comfortable and self-serving illusions were shattered. Successive hypocrisies were shown up. Then one horror of exploitation and abuse after another was uncovered. Eamonn Casey's offence came to be seen almost as venial by comparison.

The 'X' case was followed by the revelations from Wexford, Bishop Comiskey's Diocese of Ferns. Then came a flood of child rape cases and allegations of abuse against priests and religious across the country. Revelations of abuse at orphanages and other institutions began to emerge.

For many Irish men and women it was a loss of innocence. Many did not know, and refused to believe, that such things were happening. But parents, in particular, empathised with the circumstances of the 'X' case and were shocked by the abuse that had been taking place in an apparently safe and normal suburban setting.

It was neither easy nor pleasant to report these matters. But we reported them in full. For that—especially for our court reporting of the sexual abuse cases—we drew a lot of hostility. *The Irish Times* was frequently accused of seeking to destroy the moral fabric of society. Abusive telephone calls and threatening letters were not infrequent. Envelopes containing excrement were posted to me. On two occasions members of extremist pressure groups picketed the offices. One group threatened to picket my home but that never materialised.

But if I had any doubts that we had done the right thing in the 'X' case, they were dispelled by a letter I received, two years later. It was marked *private and confidential* and it was hand-written in a large, looping style, indicating that it had been penned by a young person, perhaps a teenager. It was from Miss 'X' whose identity, by now, I knew.

It was a 'thank you' note. 'I am fine now and getting on with my life,' she said. 'I wanted to say "thank you" to you and the other journalists who told the truth about what had happened to me.' It was probably the most valuable and affirming letter I ever received in 16 years in that office.

16

LEARNED FRIENDS, LIBEL
AND CONTEMPT

The most vile example of yellow-press journalism.
— REX MACKEY SC on *The Irish Times*

In 1986 the National Newspapers of Ireland launched a special project aimed at having the Irish law of libel reformed. NNI is the umbrella body of Irish national newspapers, representing their common interests in dealings with government and with international media organisations. Its director for almost 20 years has been Frank Cullen.

Two years of research and preparation went into the project initially. In 1988, I was asked to lead a delegation of NNI editors to meet the Taoiseach, Charles Haughey. The purpose of the meeting was to present Haughey with a researched report, setting out the gap between Irish libel law and that in comparable jurisdictions, and seeking new legislation. The report had been compiled by two respected academics, Kevin Boyle, Professor of Law at Essex University and a colleague from the Law Faculty of University College Galway, Marie McGonagle.

It was the first of many such delegations and submissions. The encounter with Haughey was replicated with Albert Reynolds and John Bruton. There were meetings with Ministers for Justice, Attorneys General, the Law Reform Commission (LRC) and the Bar Council. The LRC produced two reports in 1991, urging reform in both the law of contempt and the law of defamation, including libel.

In 1996 the Report of the Commission on the Newspaper Industry, chaired by former Chief Justice Tom Finlay, recommended to the Government that 'extensive changes in the law of libel . . . be introduced as a matter of urgency'.

When I ceased to be editor in 2002, not a single sub-section of either the law of libel or the law on contempt had been altered. At this writing, Ireland still operates a law of defamation that is more than 40 years old—the Defamation Act 1961—and that bears little relationship to the realities of the twenty-first century. There is promise of a new defamation act and the establishment of a press council. I have no doubt these will come. A great deal of preparatory work has taken place in the Department of Justice. But the promise has been on the table from successive Ministers for many years.

Libel suits against newspapers were relatively rare until the 1970s. But as that decade went by they became more frequent. The litigants were often politicians or public officials. As the Irish news media became more assertive and more probing, people in public life found themselves coming more frequently under scrutiny and under criticism. When they consulted their lawyers, they often found that they not only had a good case but one which was likely to give them—and their lawyers—sizeable cash damages and costs.

The newspapers were slow and un-businesslike in responding to this new situation. They found themselves increasingly on the receiving end of costly litigation. But they did little to put their own houses in order.

Writing in 1995, Boyle and McGonagle recalled, with considerable understatement that in the late 1980s, when they were first retained by NNI, there was 'a certain lack of responsiveness on the part of Irish newspapers towards their readers'. They noted:

> There was no formal complaints system. Readers who telephoned or called in person to newspaper offices were often given the run-around and little satisfaction. What began as mild annoyance, sometimes became anger or resentment as a result of the newspaper's insensitivity . . . for the ordinary reader with a grievance, it was difficult to make their voice heard . . . the overall picture . . . was one of haphazard treatment of, or regard for, the readership. Newspaper personnel continued to be defensive in the face of criticism; the concept of the newspaper consumer had not yet taken root.*

> * Report on Libel, NNI, 1996.

Irish defamation law weighted the odds heavily against the publisher-defendant. The newspapers were often hapless in dealing with the issue. They invested little or nothing in training journalists to avoid libel. They operated for a long time on the basis that it was better to pay plaintiffs some 'nuisance money' to make them go away. Over and above this, public servants who chose to sue had the advantage that the State picked up their costs—win, lose or draw. But if they did win, they got to keep the damages awarded. It was a win-win situation for the plaintiffs and very bad for the newspapers.

Exceptionally, one of the early high-profile cases taken by a civil servant did not succeed. Peter Berry was Secretary of the Department of Justice. He was effectively the State's senior security official, with the Garda, the prisons and the intelligence network answerable to him *de facto* on a daily basis.

An *Irish Times* photograph was published showing a group of Sinn Féin protesters in Dublin, carrying a placard with the words 'PETER BERIA—FELON SETTER'. Berry sued *The Irish Times*. Berry claimed he was libelled by the play on the spelling of his name—suggesting comparisons with Stalin's notorious secret police chief. The term 'felon setter' also had derogatory resonances, evoking the persecution of Irish patriots under the *ancien régime*.

To the astonishment and delight of *The Irish Times*, the jury found against Mr Berry. It seemed, from what was picked up informally later from the jury room, the feeling was that the newspaper had simply been doing its job. The notion of making the newspaper suffer for reporting what was happening seemed unfair.

Years later, when I met Peter Berry, he was still angry about what had happened. He saw it as part of a campaign against him by the newspaper. In truth, he got a fairly hard time from *The Irish Times* whose ethos in many respects would have been distasteful to him. The subsequent revelations of his role in the Arms Crisis of 1969–1970 showed him to be a man of integrity and some courage, albeit moved by professional impulses that were sometimes close to obsessive.

But *The Irish Times*'s victory in the Berry case was very much the exception. Right through the 1970s and 1980s, the newspapers took a hammering in the courts, or on the way into them. Some of these cases derived from the publication of statements or claims that were alleged to be injurious and which could not then be proven in the courts. But the greater number was due to simple error or to mistakes made in good faith, during the editing process.

The law on libel was set out in the 1961 Defamation Act. It was weighted heavily against the publication and in favour of any plaintiff who took an action. In contrast with other alleged torts, a claim for libel was assumed to be valid. It was up to the publisher to prove that the words or material complained of were not libellous.

An apology tendered by a publication did nothing to mitigate guilt. It was tantamount to an invitation to the plaintiff to write his own cheque. An apology might diminish damages, but it was taken as an admission of culpability and, as such, newspapers rarely offered it—even though it might have served to defuse a complainant's anger.

Time and again I encountered complainants who told me that all they had ever sought was an apology. When that was not forthcoming, they felt they had no option but to sue. What might have been dealt with in a paragraph became inflated into a full-scale High Court case with serious implications in terms of money and stress for all concerned.

A bizarre system operated of making lodgements in court. This meant that a defendant could effectively own up to an alleged libel, put a value on the claim and lodge an appropriate sum in court to meet that claim. The case would then go to a jury. If the jury 'beat' the sum lodged in court, the defendant would face all costs and full damages.

Mens Rea did not apply in libel cases. The fact that a libel might have been inadvertent counted for nothing. Most difficult of all, the courts required high levels of proof—often *de facto* the burden of criminal proof—that was 'beyond a reasonable doubt' in accepting a defendant's evidence. It was rarely possible for a newspaper to produce evidence in support of its stories that could measure up to that standard.

In short, once a newspaper got into the courtroom it could rarely hope to win.

So the imperative for the newspaper companies was to stay out of court—to settle in advance, however painful it might be.

It was frequently claimed by editors and journalists over these years that the libel laws constrained them from publishing the truth about people and institutions that were subsequently shown to be corrupt or venal.

I was never sure that it was as simple as that. In my experience it was the inability to get hard-and-fast information, rather than fear of legal consequences, that hindered publication. I do not have in mind here information that would necessarily stand up to courtroom scrutiny. I refer to information that would satisfy an ordinary reader of the newspaper that there was a case to answer. The real difficulty was that reporters often could not get beyond rumour. And that was rarely if ever sufficient, nor should it have been.

When we got reasonably accurate and reliable information on matters of legitimate public interest at *The Irish Times* we generally proceeded to publication, in one form or another, having made as good a calculation as possible about the likelihood of legal action. I cannot recall an instance in which we did otherwise.

——

A high-profile case in point was the newspaper's investigations in 1977 into the activities of the Garda's so-called 'Heavy Gang'.

Through the mid-1970s, the Garda became engaged in many serious criminal investigations as the IRA's campaign of violence spilled over into the Republic. Although they had little experience of organised crime, nonetheless they began to have considerable success and a series of convictions was secured, often on the basis of incriminating statements alleged to have been made by the accused persons.

Late in 1976 I was approached separately by two members of the Garda, a detective and a uniformed officer, expressing concern about what they saw as an emerging pattern. Suspects were being arrested, statements were being elicited, convictions were being secured. But there was a consistent pattern of allegations of brutality, threats and psychological pressure from persons in custody.

After one serious crime, I was told, a detective (who later went on to the most senior ranks) had threatened to use his baton against his colleagues to protect prisoners who were being brutalised during interrogation.

On another occasion, during a murder investigation, a senior officer briefed investigators with the words 'You have the right men. They'll allege you mistreated them anyway. So if we're going to take the losses, we'll take the gains too.' That was interpreted as urging the investigators to get statements out of the suspects, whatever happened.

'Sooner or later someone is going to be maimed for life—or killed,' the detective told me. 'The situation is getting out of control.'

The following week, I spent a couple of days in the *Irish Times* library, reading through some of the cases mentioned by the two Gardaí. The patterns of which they spoke were clear enough.

I was in a difficult position. Two years previously, I had been the editor of *The Garda Review* and as such I had semi-privileged access to many Garda sources. I did not wish to abuse that privilege and therefore I could not be directly involved in any investigation by the newspaper.

Instead I briefed the editor, Fergus Pyle, and the news editor, Donal Foley. Fergus's response was to assign Jack Fagan, a deputy news editor, to review the files and to give an independent *prima facie* report to him.

Jack's report, delivered before Christmas 1976, was detached and clinical. But it confirmed that a pattern was discernible and that there appeared to be a serious problem of mistreatment of persons in custody. A small team was put together in the newsroom, including Joe Joyce, Don Buckley and Renagh Holohan, and they set about tracking down and interviewing witnesses in the relevant cases.

The inquiries went into the New Year and lasted about six weeks. When all the interviews had been concluded, the reporters had a sizeable file of information. Much of it could not be substantiated to courtroom standard. But there was enough. Medical evidence supported claims of ill-treatment. Relatives and other witnesses confirmed details. Here and there, concerned Gardaí quietly advised reporters that they were on the right tracks.

There was no way in which the investigation by *The Irish Times* would withstand courtroom scrutiny. It was a mixture of direct evidence, hearsay and supposition. But it told the truth about a bad situation. When the articles were published, there was a huge public and political reaction. The brakes were put on the activities of the 'Heavy Gang' and there were long-term reverberations throughout the criminal justice system.

I was present at the final conference at which Fergus Pyle gave the go-ahead to run the series of articles. He had read through the material and he was apprehensive. 'Shouldn't we have all this on affidavit?' he asked, looking at the sheets of copy paper around the desk.

'There isn't a chance,' Donal Foley told him. 'It was hard enough to get most of these people to talk in a pub. They're not going to sit down with a solicitor and swear to it.'

I remember Fergus looking glum. 'Well, there's no point in asking the lawyers about all this,' he said. 'They'll just tell us what we know. That we're putting our heads in a noose.'

'The story is right,' Foley said. 'This stuff has the ring of truth about it.'

The reality was that Fergus would carry the can, not Foley or anybody else, if the story blew up in our faces. But Fergus gave the go-ahead, knowing that he, and the newspaper, were largely defenceless. It was a brave decision, for which he was subsequently not given sufficient credit.

There were no libel suits against us over the 'Heavy Gang' investigation, or indeed over the newspaper's subsequent *exposé* of serious irregularities within the Fingerprint Section of the Garda's Technical Bureau.

I have always pointed to these as instances of a newspaper being enabled to publish, provided it took its time, researched its facts properly and was careful —as we were—to shield sources and, where necessary, to hold back on naming identifiable individuals. There were also, of course, many instances in which it was not possible to go to publication because allegations or supposed facts could not be stood up.

Above all, the 'Heavy Gang' was also a classic case in which the newspaper had the assistance of 'whistle-blowers'—insiders whose information was accurate and trustworthy. It was not so easy to get whistle-blowers in other contentious areas, such as the corruption of the planning process, the bribing of politicians or indeed in the area of sexual abuse of minors.

————

But the bulk of libel business was much more prosaic. It arose out of errors, misunderstandings and glitches by reporters, sub-editors or production staff. Some examples:

A man accused of a crime—let us call him 'Pat Murphy'—gave the wrong name in court, calling himself 'Jack Murphy'. Unhappily for the newspaper, there was also a real 'Jack Murphy', living in the same area. The real 'Jack Murphy' sued for libel and recovered costs and damages, along with an apology.

A public servant was severely criticised in judicial proceedings. A photograph of another public servant was inadvertently placed beside the report. The latter gentleman, claiming that he had been libelled, sued and recovered costs and damages.

A professional man, charged with an offence, was brought before the court. The reporter who covered the case was given incorrect details of the charge by the court clerk. The man claimed that he had been libelled because he had not been charged with the offence reported in the newspaper. He too recovered costs and damages, plus an apology.

A government functionary was criticised by a committee investigating public spending decisions. The young reporter mixed him up with another functionary of similar name. The latter claimed he had been libelled and sought damages and costs, which he got.

Other cases derived from articles or letters submitted by people outside the staff of the newspaper. A 'Letter to the Editor' about planning and development issues in Dublin made a jocose reference to the work of a well-known architect. To my surprise, he sued the newspaper and collected significant damages for his troubles. He was, of course, within his rights to do so. But I had not anticipated an action from a man of his accomplishment.

By the early 1990s, libel actions and threats of libel action against us were running at the rate of one every two weeks. It was not much different anywhere else. We knew that things were just as bad at Independent House and on Burgh Quay at the Irish Press group.

NNI pressed ahead doggedly with its lobbying of successive governments. Following the Boyle McGonagle report of 1988, it was decided to establish a system of readers' representatives within the newspapers—a sort of Ombudsman's department. The initiative was launched in 1989 with a lot of publicity and, it should be said, with a lot of goodwill from among the newspapers themselves.

In reality, there was more appearance than substance to the scheme in some newspapers. The term 'readers' representative' was self explanatory. The idea was to offer readers an identifiable channel and a named individual through whom a grievance or a complaint might be pursued. But in at least one instance the readers' representative was the editor's secretary. In another case it was a junior staff member from the personnel department. Few of the readers' representatives had the influence or access from top to bottom within the newspaper that were essential if the scheme were to succeed.

Some newspapers did make a real effort. At the *Cork Examiner*, a former editor of the newspaper, Fergus O'Callaghan, was appointed. At *The Irish Times* we appointed David Nowlan, who was one of four 'managing editors' and who had, as such, the seniority and authority to go about his business in such a way that he had to be taken seriously. He was assisted by Mary O'Brien who had transferred to the newspaper from an Irish Times subsidiary, Irish Times Training Ltd. Mary had the right combination of organisational insight and an approach that could be tough or conciliatory as the situation demanded.

I introduced a 'Corrections and Clarifications' column at the same time. In the late 1990s, the readers' representative office and the column system were handling in excess of 700 items a year and this did have the effect of siphoning off many complaints and grievances that might otherwise have brought us into court.

But by the late 1990s the system had effectively ceased to function in any newspaper apart from *The Irish Times*. When David Nowlan retired he was succeeded as readers' representative by a former news editor, Niall Kiely. I encouraged Niall to join the Association of Newspaper Ombudsmen, which he did. Through this connection, we realised that Ireland and Irish newspapers were seriously out of line with international best practice.

In 1995, Boyle and McGonagle reported, again with sombre understatement: 'it must be acknowledged that not all the newspapers have shown themselves as committed to the Readers' Representative Scheme . . .' The epidemic of libel actions probably reached its peak in the mid-1990s.

Successive attempts were made by the NNI to force the hands of those in power to reform the legislation. At one point, a former parliamentary draughtsman, Marcus Bourke, was hired to draft a libel bill which was then presented to the Taoiseach, Albert Reynolds, in the hope that it might be brought as a proposal before Cabinet.

At *The Irish Times* we had pretty well got on top of the libel issue by this time. We had set up a system of regular training seminars on libel, led by Marie McGonagle and relying heavily on the input of Andrew O'Rorke from Hayes and Sons and, occasionally, on the expertise of barristers whom Hayes and Sons had briefed for us in various cases. Later, Karen Erwin became involved and played a very useful role in the training process.

We were fortunate in having Hayes and Sons as our advisers on libel. Initially, our business was handled by Adrian Glover, the firm's senior partner. A quiet-spoken, understated practitioner of the old school, Adrian had a keenly developed sense of judgment and a feel, in particular, for how certain judges were likely to react in given situations.

When Adrian retired, he was succeeded by Andrew O'Rorke. Andrew had all of Adrian's qualities allied to a keen sense of politics. He was widely-connected throughout public life and had strong links to the Fianna Fáil organisation. He also had an excellent feel for cases. His practical, down-to-earth wisdom and his encouragement saw us through many a crisis.

I had reinforced the editing system within the newspaper by the addition of two more layers of scrutiny as material made its way forward for publication.

This was facilitated by the installation in 1990 of the *Atex* publishing system. Journalists and editors now worked on computer screens rather than typewriters, and copy was passed from one individual to another not on paper but on the screen.

I extended the system of duty editors in my personal office so that at any time, day or night, while the editing process was in train, at least one senior editor was constantly checking the copy for libel and other problems. This function was separate from those of the sub-editors engaged in the actual processing of copy and the preparation of pages.

In addition, I created a new backbench of sub-editors known as 'Revise'. These were three senior, skilled sub-editors whose task it was to trawl through the copy and the finished pages, last thing before publication. The training programmes, the new system of duty-editors and the revise sub-editors, all contributed to getting libel down to a fraction of what it had been.

There were down-sides to this. The addition of new layers of control caused resentment among journalists—generally among the less careful and conscientious, because they were the ones who were more likely to be caught out in some failure of procedure and brought to book. It also added to costs. The more journalists tied up in editing and supervision, the fewer were available to go out on the ground reporting.

Some other Irish newspapers solved the libel issue in different ways and paid the price in a different coin. For many, libel became the only test of material presented for publication. If a story was cleared for libel, other considerations such as fairness, taste or invasion of privacy were simply put aside.

The length of time I spent preparing files, in consultation with lawyers and generally hanging around the Four Courts was a terrible drain on my time and my energies.

The Irish Times had a tradition of showing absolute respect for the legal process and for the courts. If the newspaper's presence was required in court, even at district level, the gravity of the situation would always be recognised by the editor's personal attendance.

I suppose it was a form of flattery. Usually it worked. I realised that the presence of the editor of *The Irish Times* in court represented an entertaining diversion from the humdrum of minor civil actions and petty crime. Judges and lawyers were on their toes, knowing that the business in which they were engaged would be reported with more than usual care and detail.

Bewigged barristers with idle time on their hands would often drop into whatever courtroom the case involving *The Irish Times* was being heard. They would mill about the court, enjoying themselves hugely. Many were contemporaries and friends from UCD days and there was usually much winking and hooting at my discomfiture.

One day Dermot Gleeson, later a distinguished senior counsel and, for a time, Attorney General, stood grinning as a judge weighed the issues involving some case that had been misreported in his court. Joining his wrists together and nodding in my direction, Dermot mimed a handcuffing. We both burst out laughing.

———

Dragging the editor into court did not always have the desired effect. It backfired on one occasion in 1993, through the clever tactics of an elderly barrister called Rex Mackey. This came to be known as 'The Case of All the Kellys'.

The defendant, a Mr Eamonn Kelly, was accused of a serious offence under the Misuse of Drugs Act, namely being in possession of IR£500,000 worth of cocaine.

The Garda Drugs Squad had been investigating Mr Kelly's activities for a long time and they regarded his arraignment as a significant achievement. When he was convicted, on 15 May 1993, in Court NO 14 of the Dublin Circuit Criminal Court, presided over by Judge Cyril Kelly, the Gardaí missed no opportunity of letting the media know how pleased they were.

The *sub judice* requirements in the coverage of a criminal trial were clear and simple and *The Irish Times* always honoured them scrupulously. The evidence given in court was reported straight and without adornment or embellishment. Sometimes, in high-profile cases, there might be an accompanying colour piece, describing the atmosphere around the courtroom or something such. But anything touching on the evidence before the court was off limits.

However, there was one grey area. As judges increasingly sought victim impact reports and the testimony of expert witnesses, in order to aid them in determining sentence, it had become more common to have a convicted person put back for sentencing. Thus there could be a gap of days, weeks or even months between conviction and sentence.

The media had operated on the basis that *sub judice* restrictions ended once the jury's verdict had been brought in. The hearing of the case was over. It had been determined by the Supreme Court as a matter of law and a matter of fact that a judge, sitting alone, could not be influenced by anything other than the evidence that had been put before the court.

Thus, on the morning after Mr Kelly's conviction, but before he had been sentenced by Judge Kelly, *The Irish Times* published a considerable volume of detail about the Garda investigation, about Mr Kelly's career and about the extent to which he had come to be regarded as a big fish in the Dublin crime scene.

I had chaired the 11 am conference at *The Irish Times* when the duty news editor came to my office, ashen-faced, to announce that an application had been made in the Circuit Criminal Court, by counsel acting on behalf of the convicted Mr Kelly, to have me arraigned for contempt.

Mr Kelly's counsel was Rex Mackey SC, a practitioner of many years' experience in criminal proceedings. Now in his seventies, he was regarded with a mixture of affection, awe and good humour by barristers, judges, reporters and others who worked in the courts. A former actor with the Abbey Theatre, he always gave an animated performance and was regarded as one of the very colourful characters at the Bar.

A few minutes later, the court reporter came on the line and gave me further details of what had happened when Mr Kelly had appeared before his namesake, Judge Cyril Kelly, an hour previously.

Mackey, realising that his client was facing a stiff sentence, had addressed the court in shocked and outraged tones, waving a copy of *The Irish Times* under the judge's nose. His client's reputation had been blackened by the newspaper, he argued. It was, he said, a clear and flagrant contempt of the court.

It was now impossible for his client to be viewed as anything other than a serious figure in the criminal underworld, he declared. It was therefore only right that he should have a new trial. In the meantime, he was applying to the court to have the editor of *The Irish Times* and the reporter who had written much of the material, Paul O'Neill, cited for contempt.

Judge Kelly had apparently asked to see the newspaper. He considered it for a while and then agreed to consider Mackey's application. He instructed the clerk to communicate with the newspaper, ordering us to respond.

At *The Irish Times* we were dumbstruck. Every publication in Dublin had followed these ground rules for as long as we could remember. We felt we had done nothing wrong. I called Andrew O'Rorke at Hayes and Sons. He felt the same way. 'Well, you've got to admit Rex is doing whatever he can for his client,' Andrew laughed. 'His client has been convicted, he's got no case to defend so he's going to go for you.'

Andrew arranged a consultation with Peter Kelly sc, who later became a High Court judge. Here was the third Kelly on the scene—hence 'the case of all the Kellys.'

Peter Kelly had represented *The Irish Times* on a number of occasions. A cheerful, ruddy-faced man, with Reubenesque dimples, he started his law career as a civil servant in the Central Office at the Four Courts and had progressed to the Inner Bar. He perfectly fitted the requirements for a good libel lawyer, once outlined to me by Andrew O'Rorke. 'Sometimes,' Andrew had said, 'what you need is not just a good advocate but also a good apologiser.' Peter was a superb apologiser.

The lawyers' advice, having read the published material and having heard what had transpired in court, was that we should respond the following day by appearing in the Circuit Criminal Court to make a full apology.

Judge Cyril Kelly was relatively inexperienced. Unusually, for a Circuit Court judge, he had come directly to the bench from the junior bar. He was popular, regarded as easy-going and in both Peter Kelly's and Andrew O'Rorke's opinion, would be very happy to have this chalice pass from him.

I would attend the court, along with Paul O'Neill, who had written the contentious article. We would be accompanied by Andrew and a note-taker from the our chairman's office. The appearance of Peter Kelly, a respected senior counsel, would have the effect of mollifying the court, it was hoped. It would be earnest of the respect in which Judge Kelly and his court were held.

The presence of the editor, it was reckoned, would be further evidence of the newspaper's contrition and the seriousness with which Mr Mackay's application was being considered.

We assembled in the courtroom the next morning. We stood respectfully when Judge Kelly took his place on the bench. Rex Mackey rose to address the court. He reiterated his plea of the previous hearing. His client had been vilified by the newspaper. The court itself had been treated with contempt. He repeated his call for a retrial.

The judge inclined his head and looked interrogatively towards Peter Kelly. Kelly too rose to his feet. 'Your Lordship, I represent *The Irish Times*, its editor, Mr Conor Brady and Mr Paul O'Neill, the reporter in question.'

'And what have you got to say on behalf of your clients?' the judge inquired. Kelly rehearsed our agreed apology. There had been no intention of interfering with the proceedings of the court. There had been no intended contempt. Nor could there have been a contempt, he explained, citing the Supreme Court judgment that a judge could not be influenced by anything other than what he heard in evidence before him in court.

'I believe my learned friend, Mr Mackey, to be mistaken in his contention,

Your Lordship,' Kelly went on. 'Nonetheless, I am asked by my clients to apologise to the court and to express the seriousness with which they view these matters—a fact evidenced by the presence here in court of the reporter in question, Mr O'Neill, and indeed by the presence of the editor, Mr Conor Brady.'

'Mr Mackey?' Judge Kelly raised an interrogative eyebrow towards the other side of the room. Mackey rose, slowly, as if weighed down by a heavy burden. He adjusted his wig, cleared his throat and embarked on his address to the court.

'Your Lordship,' he began. 'I am unable to believe the hearing of my ears. The most appalling contempt has been visited upon Your Lordship's court—while the gravest wrong has been done to my client, Mr Kelly.'

He waved his, by now, well-battered copy of *The Irish Times*. 'This is the most vile example of yellow-press journalism. Not from the worst of England's tabloid rags could we expect the mischievous allegations that have been put together here. This is nothing less than a calculated and pernicious attempt to break the golden thread of justice than runs through Your Lordship's court and that is so well recognised by all who have business here.'

The court clerk was staring open-mouthed at this. The room was electrified. I saw Judge Kelly gasp in disbelief. This performance was straight off the Abbey stage.

Mackey whirled around to point a finger accusingly at Paul O'Neill and myself. 'But not merely are these people willing to seek to subvert the work of this court, my Lord. They have sought to convey an impression of regret, of contrition by appearing here before you this morning. There appears to be some view, held by this Mr Brady, the editor of this newspaper, that merely by appearing here this morning, surrounded by his legal advisers, he can somehow undo the harm he has done and the affront he has offered to this court.'

I could sense a stirring in the courtroom around me. Adrian Glover, our solicitor, glanced nervously in my direction. Peter Kelly smiled but without any mirth. The judge began to look distinctly worried and shifted uneasily in his seat.

I suddenly began to feel angry. I was sitting helplessly on the bench, while this actor laid out his stall. *The Irish Times* did not deserve to be treated in these terms and I did not deserve to be described in this language.

'I call upon Your Lordship, to show in the strongest terms your stern disapproval of what has been done by this newspaper,' Mackey continued. 'I ask that your utter disapproval be demonstrated in the most clear manner.'

It was a classic theatrical performance. The judge was visibly taken aback and decided, wisely, to adjourn the court to consider Mackey's plea. During the recess, I grew angrier at this attack, as I saw it, on the integrity of the newspaper and on me personally.

When the judge came back, he announced that he was disallowing the pleas for a retrial but he was going to fine the editor of the newspaper and the journalist IR£5,000 each.

To this day, I am not sure what we were fined for. In time we appealed the case to the High Court and in turn to the Supreme Court. The Supreme Court found that it might indeed be possible to be in contempt of court on the basis of what we had done.

I must confess I lost track of the issue after that. Rex Mackey may not have got his client off. But he had succeeded in pushing back the legal boundaries that bit further against the media.

It was an instructive episode for me. I found myself on the receiving end of unwarranted abuse and accusations against which I could not defend myself. I understood from it, just how searing an experience it can be for people to go through the courts and to be subject to vilification and attack. For me it was a relatively painless affair. I had my own counsel and my support team. But it was still a salutary passage.

For those involved in the 'case of all the Kellys' there were some notable sequels. Judge Cyril Kelly subsequently resigned, along with a Supreme Court judge, Hugh O'Flaherty, over the handling of a case involving a Dublin architect, Philip Sheedy, charged with manslaughter. Peter Kelly became a High Court judge and subsequently threatened proceedings against *The Irish Times* himself in an unrelated matter. Eamonn Kelly, the defendant, served six years in prison. Rex Mackey died in 2000, aged 78 years, still practising at the bar.

17

'A VERY BAD PLAN'

I've solved the problem about Louis's succession
—TOM MCDOWELL, appointing his daughter as deputy MD of
The Irish Times

As the 1980s turned into the 1990s, with my editorship in its fourth year, *The Irish Times* was advancing in terms of circulation and readership growth. The ABC figure was rising. The range of editorial services had widened. Our research services, operated through Des Byrne's *Behaviour and Attitudes* company, told us that the readers' belief and confidence in the newspaper were strong.

These were significant achievements in the context of the newspaper's recent history. There had been a sense among some of the staff that the modern *Irish Times* could not thrive without Douglas Gageby. It was seen so much as his creation, there was a sense that it would not work without him.

The circumstances of Fergus Pyle's editorship had been unhappy and Douglas was seen as the returning saviour. But at 70-plus he was unlikely, even if required, to make a third coming.

I was fortunate in my timing. I also had strong support from Tom McDowell, Louis O'Neill and the Trust and board members. They knew that the organisation could not afford another editorial crisis and that success could not be taken for granted. I worked extraordinarily hard and the lives of those close to me were bound up inextricably with my work. I was also, it seemed, reasonably good at what I was doing. And I had a strong team of journalists.

With the editorship stable for the foreseeable future, *The Irish Times* had to start planning for succession at the top of the business side of the organisation.

Tom McDowell held the positions of chairman of the Trust and of the board, as well as being chief executive of both. He was now 68 and while he might go on as chairman, it was clear that he could not indefinitely carry the burden of an expanding executive role.

Louis O'Neill was managing director. As such, he effectively ran the business on a day-to-day basis. He was coming to his retirement age of 60. He was a fit and energetic man. But some provision would have to be made for his succession or, if he were to stay on into his sixties, for some significant support.

The company and the newspaper were doing well. Louis's crowning achievement had been the purchase and commissioning of the Uniman colour press which continued to give the newspaper a lead over its commercial rivals. Revenues climbed steadily as advertisers saw the attractions of fast, flexible colour.

We were building the circulation and, more importantly, strengthening the newspaper's profile of ABC1 readers. It was a good combination and though Louis and I had our differences, sometimes vigorously expressed, generally we worked as two people who recognised the interdependency of what they did.

But we also knew, as did McDowell, that tremendous challenges lay ahead. In time, our rivals would build their own colour presses. There was a constant threat of a predatory attack on the Irish market by the UK dailies. Profit margins were still tight. We had struggled to pay off the debts incurred in the establishment of the Trust in 1974. Our survival would depend on constant innovation, improved efficiency and, above all else, putting out the best newspaper in the country.

McDowell and I discussed the commercial succession on a number of occasions through 1988 and 1989. When I was appointed editor he had declared that our working relationship would be open and consultative in all important matters.

We took a full day away from the office at a hotel in Dún Laoghaire and went through every aspect of what would be required in succession to Louis if and when he decided to step down. I knew that Tom and Louis were also discussing these issues.

Tom threw out a few names as possible candidates for managing director to see what I thought. At one stage he pitched in the suggestion that I might go to the Harvard Business School or to some management college in Europe and that I might take on the combined positions of editor and managing director.

It did not seem a wise idea, we both agreed eventually. I was a reasonably good editor, I knew. I had no reason to believe I could be a good business manager. However, Tom did not let go of the idea immediately. If I had a strong financial director, he reasoned, it could be done.

In retrospect, I have sometimes regretted that I did not do it. Had I done so, I believe the company might have been spared some of the difficulties it was to encounter in 2001–2002. Ironically, I was to be blamed for many of these anyway. Why the editor should have been held accountable for commercial difficulties outside of his area of responsibility, I remain puzzled. I remain even more puzzled as to how certain people succeeded in putting this proposition into circulation.

As we neared the end of the 1980s, however, there was no clarity about Louis's plans. Or if there was, it was not vouchsafed to me. But I was also growing concerned at our slow pace of change.

A successful newspaper requires leadership at two levels. There has to be vision, both editorial and commercial. The big issues and the fundamental values have to be identified, kept in clear focus and firmly pursued. The big initiatives, the visionary plans and objectives have to be attained and affirmed.

But at another level, a newspaper's success depends on the daily, indeed hourly, attention to a myriad of routine, often low-level tasks. They are often humdrum, repetitive and time-consuming. And they almost invariably require minute co-ordination and collaboration between different departments and sections of the organisation.

It is not unlike a ship. The captain and navigator on the bridge must plot the course. The deck officers and others ensure that the routines are taken care of around the vessel. If either function is slowed or diminished, trouble lies ahead.

By the end of the 1980s I had a sense that the organisation was not always functioning as it should at 'deck level'. The great vision and the grand plans were there. But on a day-to-day basis we were not getting things done as quickly or as efficiently as we ought. The organisation, and the tasks it sought to discharge, had grown too large and too complex for our existing resources and structures.

The structure of the organisation, with two separate authorities, editor and managing director, was complex. This meant that many projects required a joint approach from within editorial and business departments.

In Irish newspapers this was unique. But it was not unknown elsewhere. The model worked well at *The Guardian*, for example. At *The Times* of London, a strong but controversial editor, Geoffrey Dawson, had written 70 years earlier about the necessity for 'the closest co-operation' and 'daily compromises' between the editor and 'the manager'.

Some important projects that required 'the closest co-operation' between editorial and other departments did not go as well as they might have or at the right pace.

An example: By the late 1980s, *The Irish Times* was one of a small minority of European newspapers where journalists still used manual typewriters. Elsewhere, journalists used computer-based systems to write their copy and often to design their pages. This eliminated what was known as 'double key-stroking'—the process in which everything written by a journalist had to be, in effect, typed out again by a compositor.

The switch from a manual to an electronic publishing system had been costly for newspapers in the UK and elsewhere. It meant job losses in traditional print unions. But it added hugely to the operational efficiency of newspapers and over time it brought costs down significantly.

The Irish Times moved slowly to this transition, even though it had led Irish national newspapers in adapting from hot-metal composition of type to electronic photo-composition systems. It moved far too slowly. Joint working parties from editorial, production, finance, personnel and other departments pondered and chewed over the project from 1986 onward. When eventually a decision was reached, the chosen system—*Atex*—was reaching the end of its life-cycle. I believe we were the last newspaper in Europe to purchase *Atex* before it was discontinued.

It was good system. But it dated from the 1970s ('sunset technology', as an American colleague described it to me). Yet it was expected to carry us into the twenty-first century. The choice of *Atex* was undoubtedly safe. But it was ultra cautious and it left us behind international best practices.

On top of that we inflicted further disabilities on ourselves in applying the system. For all its limitations, *Atex* was capable of further development. It was technically capable of being used for the partial make-up of pages, thus speeding production and giving editors and journalists, and indeed advertising staff, far greater control and accuracy over content.

However, these were areas that were traditionally the preserve of the print unions. The company decided not to take the print unions on but to leave them in control of page make-up and layout. I could understand that there was a reluctance to get into possible conflict at this point. These were changes that would wipe out much of the printers' craft. Independent Newspapers had been obliged to concede extremely generous terms to its staff in order to make this transition.

But it was a decision that left us short of where we might have been operationally. Seán Olson, the managing editor who handled the project and who recognised the potential of utilising *Atex* to its fullest, was bitterly disappointed. And it obliged us to retain numbers of production staff that might otherwise have been offered the opportunity to leave on agreed terms.

Our transition to *Atex* was a compromise. The opportunity was missed to execute a strategy that should have been confident and bold.

Louis O'Neill had built a good team of executives around him. But they required to be reinforced and expanded in certain areas. If Louis were going to serve on, I argued, he needed stronger structures to enable him drive things on a day-to-day basis. He also needed to expand and redefine his lines of managerial control.

For example, the single largest cost area in the organisation, by far, was salaries and wages. But the company had limited resources and mechanisms in place to manage its human assets. There was a good 'personnel department'. It was well-run and efficient within its brief. It did the formalities as staff moved in and out and around the organisation. But there was no fully-fledged human-resources function as it would be defined today. There was a clear need for performance reviews, professional intervention programmes, formal career development structures and so on. Louis and I had discussed this and we both recognised the requirement.

The Irish Times Ltd had operated in the past on a benign, almost indulgent basis. Its culture was tolerant and generally supportive. But as the organisation grew in size and complexity this was no longer enough.

What happened, in reality, was that individual human problems kept on landing on Louis's desk and, when they arose within the editorial departments, on my desk. Increasingly, much of the working day became a succession of crises, personal issues and local difficulties around various departments. It was grinding me down.

———

One morning late in 1989, Tom McDowell asked me to come to his office for coffee. It was something we did regularly, certainly once a week. This morning he told me that Louis had agreed to stay on after his 60th birthday, 'on a short-term contract basis'. 'I know that we have to do things about the structure around him and we still have to provide for his succession,' McDowell said. 'But this takes the pressure off us.'

It would have been a great loss had Louis departed peremptorily on his 60th birthday. Even had he stood down as MD I assumed he would remain available on a consultancy basis and that he would stay on the board. I was heartened by Tom's affirmation that something would be done about the structures around Louis. In particular, I was anxious that we provide him with good backup in the human resources/personnel area.

As it turned out, it was probably the last time I felt any real optimism that the issue of the company's commercial leadership would be fully addressed as I believed it needed to be. It was to be a full nine years before a successor was to be appointed to Louis O'Neill. And when it happened, it was under conditions of acrimony and recrimination.

In January 1990, Tom McDowell's wife, Margaret, died. She had been ill for some time but she was a private woman and few people outside of her immediate family circle knew that her condition was so serious. They were an extremely united couple and her death was a heavy blow to Tom.

There was no further discussion of strengthening the structures around Louis or of providing for his successor. It was as if Louis was to continue, on a basis of three months' notice, more or less indefinitely. It was not good for anybody concerned and it meant that the future development of the organisation was unclear.

By 1994, I began to wonder if I would be better out of the editorship. I would have completed eight years by the end of that year. They had been years of extremely intensive work. My predecessor, Douglas Gageby, had held the chair for 10 years in his first editorship but with a much smaller newspaper and for nine in his second. I spoke with my family about stepping down. I was 45. I would have plenty of time to re-establish myself in something less pressurised.

But in November 1994, Tom McDowell dropped the metaphoric bombshell, which none of us could have anticipated.

I had returned from a week's leave—my one and only miserable attempt at skiing—in Austria. Shortly after 1 o'clock Iain Pratt, the company secretary, telephoned me at my office. Could I come to see the chairman at 2 o'clock? I agreed and went down stairs at the appointed time.

Tom was walking up and down his office in an agitated mood. He offered me coffee and then sat down behind his desk. 'I've solved the problem about Louis's succession,' he said solemnly. 'I've appointed Karen as deputy managing director, with the intention that she succeed Louis when the time comes. Of course that will depend on Louis's opinion of her. And she's going on the board.'

Karen Erwin was Tom's younger daughter. A solicitor with Goodbody's, I had met her with Tom on a number of occasions over the previous decade. A lively, likeable woman, I had found her socially pleasant and engaging. But the idea that she should take control of the commercial future of *The Irish Times* made no sense to me. She had no experience of the business. She could not have a developed knowledge of the issues we faced.

My mind scrambled to find a response that might equal my sense of shock. It failed.

'What does Louis say about this?' was all I could muster.

'I told him at my house the other night. It's a great relief to him.'

'And the Trust . . . the board?' I asked weakly.

'It's not a matter for either the Trust or the board. The appointment of a deputy managing director is an executive function. It's completely within my authority.'

It was true that no formal structures existed for the appointment of a new managing director—in contrast with the editorship, where a detailed, precise process had been laid down by agreement with the NUJ. But there was a universal awareness throughout the company that sooner, rather than later, the issue of Louis O'Neill's replacement would have to be addressed. The company might have likely candidates in mind. But it was widely assumed that when the time came, a notice would go in the newspaper and on the notice-boards internally inviting applications.

There were at least three people on Louis's own senior staff who would have been considered as possible successors. One or two editorial executives would also have been mentioned. But above all, it was assumed that any number of bright, ambitious and experienced people from outside the company would apply for this blue-chip job. Moreover, a number of Louis's senior team felt they were overdue their places on the board as executive directors. Here was the chairman's daughter leap-frogging ahead of them, as they saw it.

The Irish Times's editorial values proclaimed openness, transparency, accountability, equality of opportunity and fair play. It seemed to me that what Tom McDowell was proposing ran counter to all of this. A great chasm would open up between what the newspaper stood for editorially and how it went about its own business.

There was a sense across the organisation that in setting up the Trust, taking his profit in 1974 and then having been installed as chairman and chief executive, Tom had the best of both worlds. Now it seemed that he wanted to have the *Irish Times* baton pass on to the next generation of his family.

I picked my words carefully. But I was blunt. 'Chairman,' I said, 'you've stunned me. I had no idea that your mind was going in this direction.' The formal appellation was reserved for very solemn moments. And this was one. 'You have no idea of what's going to happen. There'll be uproar across the organisation. Can you just put this on hold and let's talk about it?'

'It's too late,' he said calmly. 'Karen has handed in her resignation at Goodbody's and she's on her way here at this minute. She's in the car. I want you to meet her. She'll be counting on your support.'

I felt as if I was being carried along on an avalanche. It was the only time in more than six years dealing with Tom as chairman that he had not consulted me on a matter of such proportions. I was baffled, angry and alarmed. But I managed to keep a cool head.

'You're going to damage yourself, Chairman,' I said. 'You've spent a lifetime building this institution on fine principles. You're going to be accused of nepotism. Above all else, you're going to place an intolerable and unfair burden on Karen.'

He looked at me quizzically. 'Come now, Conor Brady, you know that nepotism is the advancement of a family member who is *unworthy* of it. That can't apply in this case. Karen has got what this job needs.' When Tom addressed me as 'Conor Brady' it was always a sign of his gathering exasperation.

I had no doubt that Karen was a skilled and accomplished lawyer. One did not achieve a partnership in Goodbody's without a lot of hard work and achievement. But the idea of parachuting her into a business she knew nothing about, over the heads of all of Louis's senior team, horrified me.

I tried another tack. 'I recognise Karen's talents, of course. And the job requires considerable talents. But this is a very bad plan. Would you not consider doing what Tony O'Reilly did with his children? Bring her in at a lower level, perhaps, to set up a proper legal department. And defer her board membership.' (Tony O'Reilly, the chairman of Independent Newspapers, had brought two of his sons into the company. But he had started them at lower level functions, enabling them to learn the business from the ground up. Apart from that, there was the fact that O'Reilly was the largest single shareholder in Independent Newspapers. Tom McDowell, by contrast, was not a shareholder any longer in *The Irish Times*, other than through holding the 'A' share that secured him in office.)

'It's not a valid comparison,' McDowell replied. 'She's extremely highly qualified. And she'll be making a considerable career sacrifice in coming here. It's not easy to turn your back on a partnership in one of the country's leading law firms, you know.'

And thus the die was cast. Karen arrived. I wished her well and left. I remember that when I went into my own office, Eileen Lynam brought me a strong cup of tea, left it tactfully on my desk and went out without saying a word. Later, she told me she had never seen me look so shocked and she reckoned I needed sustenance.

I went to see Louis O'Neill. He was deeply upset. I telephoned one or two members of the Trust. They were cautious. The next day, the place was in the uproar that I had predicted. Louis O'Neill's senior managers were furious. It was a slap in the face to people who believed they were being told, in effect, to forget about going any further. The editorial committee of the journalists asked for an immediate meeting with me. The committee was led by Dick Walsh and Mary Maher. They were angry, as was every other member of the delegation. They had also asked for a meeting with the chairman but were told that he had gone home sick.

The company secretary, Iain Pratt, telephoned to tell me that Donal Nevin, a member of the Trust and former general secretary of the Irish Congress of Trade Unions, had been appointed as vice-chairman and was acting for Major McDowell. I was puzzled by this. I had always understood that in the event of his being incapacitated, the functions of the chairman would be taken over by Don Reid, who had been appointed to the Trust in 1988.

I met the editorial committee. I explained that I had no foreknowledge of what had happened. But I argued that Karen should be given a chance to prove herself. The editorial committee was not mollified. The committee saw it as a re-run of what had happened in 1974 when an untested editor had been put in place without any consultation and with unwelcome consequences.

Some days later, Tom called a meeting of the board of Irish Times Publications Ltd. This was not the main board of the company but an extended board that included the senior executives from the commercial and editorial departments. Because of his illness, the meeting was to be held at his house.

It was a surreal experience. The entire senior executive cohort of the organisation sat around the dining room table with Tom at the top, flanked by Donal Nevin and Karen. Louis O'Neill and I sat opposite each other.

Tom spoke of the necessity for change. He said that Louis needed back-up and that he had persuaded Karen to make the sacrifice of leaving Goodbody's to join the company.

He said that Karen was extremely highly qualified and that her appointment had been greeted with enthusiasm by the members of the Trust, many of whom had met her over the years.

When he had finished there was a stony silence around the table. It endured for perhaps 30 seconds but it felt like an hour. We trooped out, mesmerised.

———

Two days later, with the anger showing no sign of abating around the organisation, I succeeded in gaining what seemed like a small victory. But in the long term, it was significant.

The coalition government between Fianna Fáil and Labour was not going well. The Labour leader and Tánaiste, Dick Spring, was bringing a lot of criticism on his head for appointing party hacks and friends to public positions. I wrote an editorial accusing him of 'Caribbean-style nepotism'.

Later, I was credited with great Machiavellianism in laying this charge against Spring. Some people purported to see in the editorial a commentary or parable about internal events at the newspaper, rather than about Dick Spring and the Labour Party.

In reality, I had no such grand scheme in my head at all. But I saw later how a political mind might have made such a connection The editorial was swiftly answered by a 'Letter to the Editor' from Labour Party TD Joe Costello. How dare *The Irish Times* make such an allegation against the Labour Party, he demanded, given what was happening on its own doorstep?

I telephoned Donal Nevin to apprise him of the Costello letter. One of my duties under my contract was to advise the chairman when anything was due to appear in the newspaper that concerned the newspaper itself or the company.

'What will you do with the letter?' he asked.

'I'm publishing it tomorrow.'

'Do we have to?'

'Yes. And if we don't Costello will read it into the record of the Dáil and it will appear everywhere.'

I heard Donal Nevin sigh. 'Well, we'll have to publish a rebuttal along with it.'

There would be no difficulty in principle with that. The editor often appended a note to a letter by way of explanation or response to some issue raised. But I wasn't going to do it in this instance. 'Sure, Donal. You draft the response as acting chairman and let me have it by 7 o'clock. I'll make sure it runs along with the letter.'

'What will I say?' Nevin inquired after a moment.

'Why don't you say that the appointment of the next managing director will be publicly advertised and filled on merit and by competition?' I ventured.

'Could I say that?' he inquired. 'I don't see why not,' I answered. 'It's what's in place for the appointment of an editor—more or less.'

Half an hour later he telephoned his response to Costello's letter. I jumped with delight. Here was the acting chairman committing the company to a formal process for filling the company's top commercial position.

If the company was committed to advertising the job that meant there would have to be some sort of assessment and selection process. I authorised the letter, along with Nevin's response, for publication and they both appeared the next day.

It was the thin end of the wedge. Within weeks, with Tom McDowell's return to work, the editorial committee had presented a demand that they be given a role in defining the process for the appointment of a managing director. A working party was established, comprising two nominees of the board and two nominees of the committee. Donal Nevin and Ken Gray, my former deputy editor and a former member of the board, represented the company. Dick Walsh and Mary Maher represented the committee.

Three months later, a formula was agreed and was ratified by vote of the board. It effectively mirrored the arrangements for the appointment of an editor. When either vacancy arose, it would be advertised both internally and externally. An interview panel would be assembled. It would include a suitably qualified, independent outside assessor. In the event of a vacancy for managing director, it would include the editor. In the event of a vacancy for editor, it would include the managing director. Any person with any family connection to any candidate could not participate.

At one level I was elated. It meant that everybody had an open chance of getting the top commercial job. But at another level it locked me into a process for which I had no stomach. I would be placed in the position of having to adjudicate on my chairman's daughter, as I thought. (In the event, when Louis O'Neill stepped down in 1999, Karen did not put herself forward as a candidate.)

I also feared that it might bind me into the newspaper for an indeterminate period of time. When Tom first announced that he was bringing Karen in, I had thought seriously about relinquishing the editorship.

But now I felt, in a real sense, locked in by what had happened. It was crucially important, I felt, that *The Irish Times* should not fall *de facto* under the hegemony of a family dynasty. Its independence had been bought and paid for by the sweat and the efforts of its staff, including me, over almost 20 years. I was going to have to be there when the process of replacing Louis formally kicked in—whenever that would be.

In the meantime, I began to make the first moves to prepare for my succession by identifying possible future editors among my own staff and giving them as much developmental experience as possible.

At the end of 1995, with the agreement between the board and the unions in place, the company moved into a period of unease and tension. I had a sense of foreboding. Karen Erwin took up position as deputy to an evidently unwilling and unhappy Louis O'Neill. Many of the commercial staff went into a state of ill-concealed resentment and apprehension.

My task was to get on with producing the very best *Irish Times* that our resources and talents could make possible. When the crisis *did* come, it was going to be the quality of the newspaper that would bring us through.

18

REPORTING *EL DIABLO*

No leader since the foundation of the State, with the exception of Éamon de Valera, has raised such passions of loyalty and suspicion, of adulation and excoriation . . .
—*Irish Times* editorial on the resignation of Charles Haughey
as Taoiseach

One of the questions most frequently asked of Irish journalists when they talk about their work is 'Why did you not tell us about Haughey over all those years?' It is a fair question. It is rarely answered fully, because few editors or journalists know the answer themselves.

There is little tradition of self-examination or self-inquiry in Irish journalism. I do not believe any media organisation has a formal audit system to measure its performance, other than readership and circulation figures. The only process that approximates to any such assessment is perhaps that undertaken by the Broadcasting Complaints Commission. By definition, that does not include material in print.

I imagine that somebody, somewhere, will choose the question about Charles Haughey and the media as a thesis subject. Perhaps it is being done already. A complete picture may, in time, emerge. Meanwhile, editors will have varied responses to it.

Some will blame the libel laws. Or they may cite the culture of secrecy in Irish public life in which information that is readily available in other jurisdictions is denied to the media. Others will indict the entire political-administrative-business establishment. A few will probably argue that the Haughey story was, in effect, told by the media, time and again, but that few people wanted to know the truth.

The truth lies somewhere between all of these propositions and encompasses elements of each one.

In 1992, weary of assault from some Fianna Fáil elements and from some among the business community who alleged that *The Irish Times* was making a crusade against Haughey—and jeopardising the process of national recovery in the process—I set about making my own inquiries to see how the newspaper might write the definitive Haughey story.

I armed myself with every file that might be relevant from *The Irish Times* cuttings library. I took the files on Haughey, his family, his friends, his cabinet colleagues, any company that he had been associated with. When I had exhausted the files, I organised searches at the Companies Office to seek out any possible connections or pseudonyms that might lead me back to him.

Then I arranged for searches at the Registry of Deeds to track his known real estate interests. I organised an inquiry into the funding and construction of his holiday home on Inishvicillaun. I traced the acquisition and refurbishment of his yacht, the *Celtic Mist*. Dick Walsh, the political editor, snorted derisively when I told him what I was at. 'A complete waste of time,' he declared. 'The "hoor" has covered his tracks too damned well to turn up anything.' He was right. The exercise yielded precisely zero.

The only insight I had ever got into Haughey's finances had been in 1981 when I was editor of the *Sunday Tribune*. Somebody sent me an anonymous package in the post. It was a photocopied set of what appeared to be his personal bank statements from the Allied Irish Bank in Dame Street, Dublin. It showed an overdraft of around IR£200,000, but beyond that it told me little. The serial numbers for cheques drawn could have meant anything. There were no lodgements. All I could glean from it was that the Fianna Fáil leader was running a heavy overdraft.

Wrongly, in the light of subsequent revelations, I gave Haughey the benefit of the doubt. This was one bank account. How could we know what might be in others? Perhaps he had cash deposits or other collateral. It seemed unlikely that the bank would allow an exposure of this magnitude without having proper securities in place.

I undertook some informal probing at a high level in the bank. If we were to put questions to them what response would we get? The bank would refuse to discuss the affairs of any client with a third party, I was told.

I took the view that in themselves the statements told us nothing conclusive. They showed, at most, part of a picture. I hoped that there might be more packages, showing us the lodgements side of Haughey's finances. But nothing came.

And it could also be argued that it was a private matter. Haughey was a wealthy man and a public figure. But he was entitled to the privacy of his bank account unless there was evidence of some wrong-doing. I held off publication. The business editor, Des Crowley, was unhappy with my decision but abided by it. Later, when he had moved to *The Irish Press*, he ran with the story.

If one asks why the media did not publish what is now known about Charles Haughey, the following has first to borne in mind. It took three sworn tribunals, invested with the powers of the High Court, six judges, 20 senior counsel, approximately 40 other lawyers and any number of court-authorised officials, working over 5 years, to find out what we now know about Haughey, his money and the circle of people who bankrolled him.

And none of these tribunals would have got off the starting blocks were it not for the supermarket heir, Ben Dunne and the events of a certain night in Miami, Florida, in 1992.

Even the parliamentarians, protected by absolute privilege, had been unable to crack the security screen around Haughey and his cronies.

By the end of my editorship the Dublin Castle tribunals had uncovered much that revealed at least three distinct strands of corruption that had run through Irish public life for perhaps 20 years. The reality is that the Irish media had succeeded in learning very little of substance about any of these over this time.

First, there was the network of 'donations' from prominent business figures, orchestrated by Haughey's financial fixer, Des Traynor. Year on year, Haughey's lifestyle was funded through Traynor's shakedowns, putting the politician ever deeper in thrall to developers, business figures and others.

Second, there was the web of connections between politicians, developers and officials that deeply corrupted the planning process, especially in Dublin County. Among these politicians were men who had come to positions of influence on Haughey's political coat-tails.

The third strand of corruption was the creation of elaborate, off-shore tax-evasion schemes, principally through what became known as the Ansbacher accounts. The chief architect of these was, again, Des Traynor. When the report of the judicial tribunal into Ansbacher was released in July 2002 it showed that many of the country's most respected public figures had availed of the opportunity created by Traynor to cheat on their taxes and to transfer wealth, generated in Ireland, to supposedly secure and invisible accounts in the Cayman Islands.

But these three strands did not operate in isolation. They cross-fertilised and reinforced each other. There were common factors, notably the *eminence grise* that was Des Traynor and, behind him, the powerful, ambitious figure of Charles Haughey. An ever-growing circle of people became aware that those on the inside-track were on the make and asked themselves, why not me too? A veritable culture of sleaze grew within sections of the political-business elite.

It trickled down and spread outward. The model and standards set from the top were willingly embraced down along the political food-chain. Only mugs seemed to play by the rules, paying taxes at punitive levels, working for a living without inside connections or the benefit of favours from people with their hands on the levers of power, at whatever level.

When a loophole in taxation law was identified, enabling depositors residing outside the State to avoid tax, bank accounts with addresses in the UK and elsewhere began to be opened all over Ireland. Tens of thousands of otherwise decent people saw no difficulty in lying about their residential status to their local bank officials. And many local bank officials saw no difficulty in accepting this at face value.

Corruption in the form of working the system, usually with inside knowledge and co-operation, came easily enough to some Irish people in the 1970s and

1980s. It was fuelled by a widespread sense of injustice in regard to the taxation system. Until the mid-1970s farmers paid no income tax at all. Business and industry paid little. The weight of taxation rested on wage and salary earners who were governed by the PAYE (Pay As You Earn) system, often referred to bitterly as 'Pay *All* You Earn'.

And since it seemed that everyone 'at the top' was 'at it', those at lower levels found it much easier to justify their own actions.

Why was so little of this reported in the media? Crime investigators will acknowledge that the most difficult offence to investigate—in which it is hardest to secure evidence—is so-called 'victimless crime'. Where criminal and victim are engaged in some common purpose, the victim cannot testify against the perpetrator without incriminating himself.

So it is with journalism. The great majority of *exposés* in the media come about because somebody, somewhere wants to get somebody else into trouble. They tell their story to a willing reporter or programme-maker and thus it makes its way into the public domain.

Even now, with freedom of information legislation and with the immense power of web-based search systems, there is often little that journalists can do to advance an inquiry without the co-operation of willing, inside sources. In the 1970s and 1980s they had even less leverage.

The people who were involved in bankrolling Haughey, who were doing deals for the rezoning of land, who were setting up Ansbacher accounts with Des Traynor, who were enriching themselves through one illicit scheme or another, were not going to shop their collaborators—or each other.

A further factor was that Irish journalists did not move very much in moneyed or business circles. Outside of the small cadre of journalists who wrote about business, the vast majority of them had no connections with people in banking, property development, business or commerce. Journalists tended to mix with other journalists or with people of similar backgrounds—people in education, the arts, politics, the civil service, the law, academics, publishers and so on. Thus, while many journalists, probably most, had a general sense that there were insider-circles and beneficial networks in operation, they did not have access to them.

Even business journalists did not have access. Some made the transition from journalism to business themselves. But business editors and writers generally remained outsiders, viewed with suspicion and wariness by the people who were the subjects of their professional attentions. Similarly, political journalists formed their own cohort and generally remained at a distance from their subjects. But apart from a small few who crossed over to become political advisers, or in some cases to take seats themselves, they had no personal connectivity to what might have been going on.

Journalists and media organisations have no powers of search or right of access over and above those available to the ordinary citizen. They have no authority to sequester documents. Nobody is obliged to answer any questions they may ask.

Thus, the Irish media was confined, for the most part, to asking questions about Haughey. They were simply not in a position to secure answers. But they did ask the questions, repeatedly and with vigour.

We also did it in *The Irish Times*. Dick Walsh in particular was like a dog with a bone about Haughey's unexplained money. Week after week in his column he posited the key questions about Haughey and his wealth. How could he afford the lifestyle he lived on a politician's official income? How could he fund the mansion, the island, the yacht and apparently endless entertainment in Dublin, London, Paris and elsewhere? This presented inordinate difficulties for a newspaper that prided itself on its factual accuracy and whose charter committed it to ensuring that comment and opinion is 'informed and responsible and identifiable from fact'.

The questions repeatedly laid before the bar of public opinion by Dick Walsh —and other journalists, notably Vincent Browne, both as editor of *Magill* and as editor, after me, of the *Sunday Tribune*—were not easily dismissed. But Haughey made it clear time and again that he would not, in any circumstances, offer any explanations about his lifestyle or his wealth.

Within *The Irish Times*, John Healy was the counterpoint to Dick Walsh's probing. 'How much more of this piss-and-vinegar stuff are you going to run from Walsh and his socialist pals?' he bawled down the telephone at me one morning after a particularly vituperative assault in Dick's column. He warmed to his topic. 'This is the crowd that want to nationalise the banks, collectivise the farms, tax everyone out of existence. Charlie has more brains in his little toe than the whole lot of them. That's why he's rich and most of them haven't the arse in their britches.'

If the newspaper was not to lose its credibility and its reputation for fair-dealing there had to be limits to what could be said about Haughey—and the frequency with which it was said—without some evidence.

When all was boiled down, *The Irish Times* and every other news medium had failed to lay a glove on him. That Haughey was living well beyond the means of a Dáil TD or even a Taoiseach was as clear as daylight. But it was entirely possible that he had built up private wealth through astute investment over the years. There was no documentary trace of any impropriety, of any conflict of interest, of any beneficial involvement in anything shady or improper.

It became necessary to view Haughey through two different prisms—and to report him and write about him at two different levels. He was Taoiseach, a Taoiseach with energy and a certain style. He had to be reported fully. And where appropriate, it was necessary to praise him. He contributed significantly, if belatedly, to the Northern Ireland peace processs. Not everybody in the Dublin establishment was willing to recognise that. To many, including some *Irish Times* journalists, he could do no good. His every action was suspect.

An illustration of this mindset occurred during the Irish EU presidency in the latter half of 1990. Haughey had to host the heads of government at a dinner during the June summit in Dublin. It became known that he planned to put the Derrynaflan treasures on display at the dinner. The Derrynaflan hoard comprised an ancient jewelled chalice and other precious artefacts that had been recovered from a field in Co Tipperary some years previously. The artefacts had been restored to their former glory and were due to be displayed at the National Museum of Ireland.

There was an immediate outcry. There were letters to the paper comparing the hoard to the Book of Kells. Callers to the radio programmes argued that these were sacred objects and not suitable for exhibit in the setting of a State dinner. Most of the academic establishment were quite at ease with the proposal but a vociferous minority accused Haughey of philistinism, opportunism and exploitation of a national treasure.

I took the view that this was much ado about nothing. A lot of it, I felt, was grounded in snobbery, stimulated by antipathy to the notion of Haughey strutting around Dublin Castle, glad-handing the leaders of Europe. *The Irish Times* came out firmly in his support. My editorial of 6 June took up his case:

> The Derrynaflan hoard is a marvellous representation of those skills and abilities which flourished in Ireland centuries ago. It is surely not inappropriate that an opportunity be taken to allow the men and women who represent our European partners to view, to appreciate and to admire this wonderful collection of ancient Irish craftsmanship . . .
>
> Some of the objections raised would suggest that the Taoiseach is going on some sort of a jamboree, with the Derrynaflan Chalice being passed around like the Sam Maguire cup. The banquet for the heads of government is not some sort of dinner dance with spotprizes . . . the Taoiseach's and the Government's task is to make it a memorable occasion here, reflecting our modern capacities and the best of our heritage and traditions. There is no reason why the Derrynaflan treasures should not be shown with pride.

I also weighed in the balance that at no time at *The Irish Times* had I come under any pressure from Haughey to moderate the newspaper's stance or to back off the story.

When I was editor of the *Sunday Tribune* in 1982, I was approached by the former head of a semi-state body who said he was representing the view of 'concerned businessmen' and asked that I curb the activities of Geraldine Kennedy, the newspaper's political correspondent. I told him that she had her job to do and that as long as her facts were right I would support her. He did not seem surprised at my answer and gave me the distinct impression that he felt he had to go through the motions with me.

Around the same time, the *Tribune's* publisher, Hugh McLaughlin, told me he had a similar approach from 'some people around Haughey'. Hugh made a great show of instructing the telephonist at the *Tribune* to keep a note of what Fianna Fáil figures telephoned the office. He knew perfectly well that she would do no such thing. Instead she came straight to my office and warned me. I sent her to the newsroom to pass on the same warning to Geraldine.

I had regular telephone calls at *The Irish Times* from P.J. Mara, Haughey's press adviser and later Government Press Secretary. Usually they were to protest some alleged 'lack of generosity' in our coverage of Haughey's speeches or doings. Occasionally there might be a throwaway remark about 'that poisonous f****r Walsh' or 'the bitter champion of the plain people of Ireland, O'Toole'.

Sometimes Mara would call in advance of a significant speech and suggest in a friendly and bantering way that it might merit a leader. 'Maybe a subject for a "thunderer", do you think?' he would ask, half seriously. Sometimes I obliged. In private, Mara could be hilariously funny, describing his working relationship with Haughey, whom he referred to sometimes as *El Diablo*.

In all the blizzards of criticism and innuendo, Haughey only once threatened legal action. It arose out of a column written by Fintan O'Toole after Haughey had stood down as Taoiseach, in which his offences were catalogued but with the addition of a new one. He had arranged for his son, Seán, to have a seat in the Seanad, Fintan wrote. Haughey telephoned the office around 7 o'clock in the evening and asked to speak to me.

'Yes, Deputy Haughey,' I greeted him with the formality he liked, while desperately racking my brains to think what he might want.

'I'm afraid this is a bit unpleasant,' he said reasonably. 'There's a very nasty piece in this morning's *Irish Times*.'

I still hadn't quite made the connection. 'Which piece is that, Deputy Haughey?'

'It's Fintan O'Toole. He says that I arranged for my son, Seán, to have a seat in the Seanad.' Instantly I understood.

'Now, Mr Editor,' he said evenly, 'I've taken a fair amount of abuse from your newspaper over the years, most of it actionable and most of it untrue. And I've never made this threat before. But if that isn't retracted—withdrawn absolutely and immediately—I'm suing and so is my son. He secured the seat through his own hard work and he's entitled to the credit for that.'

I did not have a difficulty with what he was saying. Neither did Fintan when I called him at home. We drafted a retraction and published it the following morning in the 'Corrections and Clarifications' column. Nothing more was subsequently heard about it.

Haughey's grip on power was weakening by the end of 1991. He had attempted —and failed again—in 1989 to secure an overall Fianna Fáil majority in a snap election. Instead he was forced into an unprecedented and humiliating coalition with the hated Progressive Democrats. In 1990, he delivered the head of his lifelong confidant and political associate, Brian Lenihan, to the same PDS, in the aftermath of the presidential election débâcle.

Then in 1991, revelations of a 'golden circle' began to emerge, seriously damaging his credibility. Details of controversial deals were leaked by business associates of some of those involved. Some details came to *The Irish Times*, others went to Sunday newspapers. One set of allegations which we were unable to verify appeared a week later in a Sunday newspaper.

These reports were swiftly followed by Seán Doherty's revelations that he had ordered illegal telephone taps for Haughey and had delivered him transcripts of telephone conversations that had been illegally monitored. In 1992, Haughey stepped down as Taoiseach. But even yet, no more was known about the foundations of his wealth than when he had started rising in public life. The truth did not begin to emerge until 1996, when somebody with an inside track on the golden circle decided to give reporter Sam Smyth perhaps the most devastating exclusive in Irish media history.

Ironically, Smyth's story did not focus on Haughey at all. Its principal characters were Ben Dunne, part-heir to the Dunnes Stores supermarket empire, and a relatively junior but ambitious Fine Gael cabinet minister, Michael Lowry.

Dunne had been ousted two years previously from his senior executive positions within the supermarket group after bitter differences developed between him and other members of the family. Ben Dunne had been kidnapped and held for ransom by the IRA in 1981. Then in 1992 he had been arrested on drugs charges in Miami, Florida. Not surprisingly, a great deal of lurid publicity had followed.

Smyth's story appeared in November 1996. It revealed that Dunne had paid IR£300,000 for renovation and an extension at Lowry's home in Co Tipperary. The work was paid for by Dunnes Stores and invoiced to a construction company that was engaged in work at the ILAC Centre in Dublin where Dunnes were an anchor tenant.

Lowry operated a refrigeration company which provided services to Dunnes. It became clear that what was involved was a dodge, enabling Lowry to be paid his fees without incurring any taxation liability.

But what was perhaps more significant than the information about Lowry and Dunne, was its source. It emerged quickly that it was coming from a supposedly confidential report by Price Waterhouse into the affairs of the Dunnes group. It had been commissioned by Mrs Margaret Heffernan, Ben Dunne's sister and also part-heir to the empire, when the family split over the company's past performance and future direction.

The Price Waterhouse report detailed a series of irregular payments that had been made by Ben Dunne during his period in charge of the supermarket group. Once the Lowry story broke, reports swiftly began to circulate that the Price Waterhouse document also detailed a number of substantial payments to Haughey.

Cliff Taylor, the business editor, told me he wanted to work on the story for a few days. He said he believed he had contacts that could bring it further. Lowry was sacked from his ministry by the Taoiseach, John Bruton on 2 December. That afternoon, Cliff came into my office and told me he could confirm from his sources that the sum involved was in excess of IR£1 million. But this information was not contained in the Price Waterhouse report *per se* since Dunne's payments to Haughey had not come through the Dunnes Trust but from companies offshore.

Cliff was a calm, methodical journalist. But he was extremely nervous about the story. Nonetheless he was confident about its accuracy and in time he was vindicated by the McCracken Tribunal. He felt it was better not to name Haughey but to report that a 'senior Fianna Fáil figure' had received the money. I did not ask Cliff to tell me his sources. I had confidence in him and I was happy to go with his judgment. The story ran the next day.

By now the political establishment was in an uproar. The Dáil Committee on Procedures and Privileges appointed a former Circuit Court judge, Gerard Buchanan, to investigate. Dunnes Stores agreed to hand over the Price Waterhouse report to him on a confidential basis. His report, as had been expected, was inconclusive in many key aspects. The Oireachtas then moved to establish a tribunal of inquiry, with full High Court powers of compellability, under the chairmanship of Mr Justice Brian McCracken.

The whole story of Haughey's money had started to tumble out. Within months, the McCracken tribunal had elicited the truth about donations to Haughey by Ben Dunne. Other donors' names were uncovered one by one. Finally, even more unpalatable revelations emerged concerning the handling of the fund raised among business donors for Brian Lenihan's medical care in the United States.

Des Traynor was central to the entire business. He had set up an invisible bank within a bank that became the Ansbacher accounts. When the report of the inspectors in the Ansbacher accounts was published in July 2002 it revealed the full extent to which Traynor had effectively run a tax avoidance scheme for scores of people prominent in Irish public and business life.

––––

The case of Des Traynor illustrates the impossible task faced by Irish journalists in trying to penetrate the wall of secrecy that surrounded the Haughey court.

Traynor was not known to many journalists. Business reporters knew about him, of course, but he did not give interviews or make himself available for journalistic contacts of any kind. He was, however, an extremely well-connected and widely-respected figure in the Dublin business scene. He was well-known as a man who gave excellent financial advice and he was able to put clients in contact with services that appeared to meet their financial needs. For a great many of these, of course, he was providing illegal, tax-avoidance routes to the Ansbacher accounts.

Many of his clients were referred to him through the Dublin accountancy firm of KPMG, formerly Stokes, Kennedy, Crowley (SKC). This conveyed an additional cachet. SKC was a highly-respected firm that provided accountancy and taxation services to many of the great and good in Irish public life. The Ansbacher report identified Don Reid, an SKC partner, as one of the tax-advisers who referred a great many clients to Traynor. Reid had been part-architect of The Irish Times Trust and had been appointed to the Trust by Tom McDowell in 1988. In early 1999 he succeeded Tom McDowell as chairman of The Irish Times Ltd. He stepped down as chairman in April 2002, three months before the publication of the Ansbacher report.

Des Traynor had come under close scrutiny from time to time in *The Irish Times*, mainly in articles written by Frank McDonald, the newspaper's environment correspondent. Traynor's name continued to appear on Frank's radar screen as he treaded his way through deals and arrangements on the Dublin property scene. If any journalist could have put the finger on Des Traynor it was Frank McDonald. But in spite of the closest scrutiny and much investigative work over many years, neither Frank nor any of his colleagues got even a fraction of the information about Des Traynor that the Buchanan and McCracken inquiries, armed with their powers of discovery and compellability, elicited in a matter of weeks.

When Traynor died of a heart attack in May 1994, Frank was given the task by the news editor of compiling his obituary. It was hard-hitting and it emphasised Traynor's links with the developer John Byrne (with whom Haughey was frequently linked in speculation) and with the disgraced Australian politician Brian Burke.

For some reason, I did not see the item before it was published. Had I read it, I think I would have held out some of the more pungent elements until a later date, certainly until after the funeral. There is a long and honourable tradition in Ireland of allowing a family to bury its dead in peace, regardless of the character of the deceased.

It was, of course, entirely accurate, as events were to prove. But we know that with the wisdom of hindsight.

The morning the obituary appeared, a storm of anger was launched against the newspaper. All day the telephones rang as one senior business figure after another berated me for the *post mortem* assassination of their friend's character. The wife of one friend of mine, himself a prominent figure in the semi-state business sector, called the house to say that she was angry beyond words with me and *The Irish Times* and never wanted to have anything to do with me again.

We gave a right of reply, in a sense. A Dublin solicitor wrote a 'Letter to the Editor' saying the report 'grossly misrepresented the real character and talent' of Des Traynor. We published the letter, along with an appreciation by JPC who wrote of Traynor's 'natural talents, financial acumen and shrewd judgment'. The writer added: 'Des was the person you went to if you were in trouble and he took great pride in helping you resolve your difficulties.' Indeed. When Haughey finally stepped down in January 1992, I tried to summarise events in a leader, 'The Haughey Years':

> For almost 30 years Charles Haughey has been in or around the active centre of Irish public life . . . he has influenced the very agenda of Irish politics, almost continuously, since he first attained ministerial rank. No leader since the foundation of the State, with the exception of Éamon de Valera, has raised such passions or loyalty and suspicion, of adulation and excoriation . . .
>
> There have been the inspirational periods: his galvanising of the economy on his return to office in 1987, his commitment to the vision of a new and united Europe, his proud and insistent nationalism, his thoughtful amelioration of the entitlements of the elderly and handicapped, his imaginative support for the arts. Yet, so much of what passed for considered policy was little more than pragmatic adaptation to political opportunity. So much of what he did was actuated in the most transparent fashion for electoral advantage. There were periods of great statecraft. There were occasions of the most graceless opportunism.
>
> It is easier to comment on his style that to judge his substance. The mansion, the island, the yacht, the paintings and all the rest—take them together with his contemptuous refusal ever to make any explanation as to how he acquired this great wealth—and it is clear that one is dealing with an extraordinarily complex character. That he was capable of the most profound misjudgments about the people he placed around him is certain. That he encouraged the cult of the adventurer and then failed to control those who took adventurism to its ultimate and unacceptable limits is also now clear.
>
> That he worked like a Trojan for Ireland is unquestionable. But it is no longer his Ireland: nor that of his generation or outlook. Ireland has come of age in a way that Fianna Fáil now knows about but has not yet come to terms with or responded to. As surely as de Valera's hour of departure was clearly marked in 1959, so too is Charles Haughey's at this time . . . it is now the hour to see in the new.

The contest between Haughey and the media that had sought over more than 30 years to penetrate his curtain of secrecy could be said finally to have ended in 1997. The McCracken tribunal was presented with the details of Ben Dunne's donations.

Much more was to emerge in the subsequent tribunal, presided over by Mr Justice Moriarty. But the reality is that none of the information would ever have come to light through the efforts of the media alone. It took the tribunals, with their extraordinary powers, to get to the truth. And they, in turn, would not have come into existence were it not for the bitter dispute that had divided the Dunnes Stores empire.

Fundamentally it was about money. It was money too that had finally opened the first cracks in the scandal of the Dublin planning process. *The Irish Times* and in particular, Frank McDonald, had been highlighting for years the bizarre processes and voting procedures at Dublin County Council. The linkages between planners, elected councillors and developers had been spelled out many times.

In the summer of 1993 Frank and Mark Brennock had worked on a detailed series of reports alleging that members of Dublin County Council had received money in brown envelopes in public places from lobbyists and representatives of development companies. They had received specific information in relation to one councillor who was now deceased. His will had shown him to be possessed of a very large cash balance at the time of his death—a sum that was wholly out of proportion to his income as an unskilled worker.

There was an immediate political uproar. *The Irish Times* was castigated for dishonouring the reputation of a dead man. Fianna Fáil Minister John Wilson called me 'a disgrace'. Fianna Fáil TD Charlie McCreevy telephoned me and expressed his contempt and disgust. I subsequently had lunch with him and went into the detailed evidence behind the allegations.

A Garda inquiry was launched. Naturally, it got absolutely nowhere. I knew one senior Garda assigned to the task. He was an utterly honest and fearless police officer. After a couple of months of his inquiry I asked him to come for a cup of coffee in Bewley's one morning. I asked him how the inquiry was going. He laughed heartily.

'I set up interviews,' he said. 'The subjects come along with their solicitors. I ask questions. They ask their solicitors should they answer. Usually the lawyer says no. So I ask the question again. Then they just pick a spot on the wall over my head and stare at it. It's a joke.'

It was only when two Dublin barristers offered a cash reward for hard evidence of corruption in the planning process, placing notices in the newspapers and lodging the reward fund in a bank in Northern Ireland, that things began to happen.

It has always been an absolute tenet of *Irish Times* editorial policy that we never paid for information, other than the normal payments to journalists and contributors. I often wondered subsequently if we were right to hold that position so rigidly. It was a stance that was taken for all the right reasons. But in eschewing what we saw as one evil, we may have allowed a greater one to proliferate.

19

LÁ I SAOL EAGARTHÓRA

If all you had to do was edit the newspaper . . . this would be the best job in Ireland.

—DOUGLAS GAGEBY on the editorship of *The Irish Times*

What does the editor of a newspaper do in a working day? What are the priorities? A newspaper is unique in that it has to be fashioned anew each morning. It lives for the day. It is, literally, tomorrow's fish and chips wrapper or padding for the cat's basket. It changes its content and its statement each morning. And yet a good newspaper must do this against a set of constant standards and principles.

It is, by definition, imperfect. It is never what it should be. It is a daily or nightly compromise between a desired perfection and the constraints of time, space and resources.

It is a target-of-choice for the fantasist, the serial-litigant, the crank, the obsessive and the hoaxer. Its listening ear is sought by heads of government, ministers, ambassadors, lobbyists and public figures of every kind. Its best days are often the worst days for somebody else. Disaster, crisis and the spectacle of someone having to eat humble pie in public are grist to its mills.

A fall of snow or a night of storm can disrupt its distribution. But perversely, a spell of bright sunny weather can also see its sales pattern wither. It is a whimsical, ephemeral thing that seeks to persuade its readers, and sometimes itself, that it can present a quotidian measure of the human condition.

Being in charge of something like this is not a part-time commitment. You eat, sleep, drink and breathe its daily and nightly rhythms. You have to be able to think simultaneously in different time-frames. And you have to be able to switch your focus from the present to the future very quickly.

You take decisions on the content of a page, a report or a headline. Meanwhile another part of your brain has to be working on long-term issues. What is the lead picture for tomorrow? Will we launch a new supplement next year? How big is the story tonight from Washington? Where is the Middle East peace process going to be six months from now?

There are as many different ways of doing an editor's job as there are editors. What works for one may not be appropriate for another. But whatever the variations, the daily and nightly process rolls on. Whether it is edited badly or well, the newspaper will still come out—probably.

For me, the working day normally began sometime after 7 o'clock. The morning newspapers came in an *Irish Times* van, usually sometime after 4 am. The thump of the diesel engine and the wallop of the parcel hitting the front step outside the house were always sufficient to wake me.

By 9 am or so I would have gone through the newspapers, noting where things might have been done better, identifying items for follow-up, checking where the *Independent* or the *Press* might seem to have an edge over us. Then there would be a round of telephone calls to various editors and desk-heads. Usually too at that stage I would make my 'briefing calls'—to my own sources in politics, the public service and so on.

The day at *The Irish Times* revolved around three conferences. Some journalists found this burdensome and I was often pressed to adopt a more *laisser faire* approach. But I could not, and still cannot, see any alternative to detailed, minute planning and constant assessment and review of content, across all sections.

We had our meetings at 11 am, at 3 pm and at 6.15 pm. These were held in a conference room off the editor's office. Generally I chaired the 3 pm conference and sometimes the 11 am. Often I chaired both. The 6.15 pm conference, a 'standing' conference, was held in the newsroom and was always chaired by the night editor.

At the 11 am conference, editors from the various departments attended with their outline schedules of content for the following day. At 3 pm there were full schedules and we fixed the page planning and the allocation of space. After the conference a small group of senior editors would decide on and discuss the editorials for the following day. At the 6.15 pm conference we shaped the front page, decided on photographs and sometimes had a first run at headlines and captions.

On Tuesdays we had, in addition, a features and ideas conference. This was an 'open house' at which any staff member or regular contributor might attend. At this meeting the editors of the features sections would set out their planning for the week ahead. There would be a preview of known news engagements. This was where editors, columnists and others could throw in ideas, comment on the paper or simply sound off about things.

Some of the better-known writers attended frequently. Mary Cummins, Mary Holland, Fintan O'Toole, Déaglán de Breadún, Nuala O'Faolain, Dick Walsh, were regular attendees. Others like Kevin Myers, John Waters or Vincent Browne rarely, if ever, attended.

A serious newspaper can be described as an information partnership. It is a cohort of people engaged in a common enterprise, constantly sharing views, information and opinions. And they take, literally, hundreds of decisions each day and night on the results of this process. They choose headlines, pictures, page-designs; they assign reporters, photographers and feature writers; they decide which events to report and which to ignore. Ninety-nine per cent of the time, the editor knows to let them get on with it.

An editor must keep firmly fixed in the forefront of his mind that he, and the newspaper, work for the readers. I always devoted as much time as I could each day to going through readers' letters, answering their telephone calls and sometimes asking readers to meet me in order to talk through issues they had with the newspaper. It was invariably time well spent.

On most days I would have arrangements to meet one or more editors or journalists from among the staff. We would work over a coffee or a cup of tea in my office, reviewing editorial plans, budgets or personnel issues.

Three or four times a week I would take 'MBWA' time—management by walking about. The editorial departments were spread over three floors. I went from desk to desk, often perching myself on the edge among press-releases, reference books and other paraphernalia, asking people about their work and about the paper. That way I kept in touch with what was happening in the newsroom, in business, in features, in photography and so on.

Lunch was usually at the desk with a sandwich from the canteen. Over lunchtime, RTÉ's *News at One* was invaluable as was the BBC's *World at One*. I would usually utilise the lunchtime interval to run through the UK newspapers and to glance at *Le Monde*, *El Pais* and the *Herald-Tribune*.

Frequently there were visitors to be met. Many ambassadors paid a 'courtesy call'. We had a standard routine for that—tea or coffee and biscuits and a 45-minute conversation. Usually the foreign editor, Paul Gillespie, would sit in. Sometimes he seemed to know more about events in their country than visiting dignitaries.

Staff issues arose frequently. I made it a point of being available immediately or as soon as practicable to any journalist who said he/she wanted to see me. On most days I would have two or three due to come to talk to me in my office about matters of concern to them. Sometimes the issue was professional. Or it might be personal. I worked very much on the principle that if one could eliminate or alleviate issues of stress for journalists they would give of their best. That approach was generally vindicated—but not always.

Legal business took up an inordinate amount of time. Broadly, it fell into two categories.

Pre-publication legal work involved liaison and consultation with our solicitors, and sometimes with counsel. An item for publication might be *prima facie* libellous. But it was usually possible to find a way around the legal pitfalls. We were never once successfully sued for anything we published that had been previously 'legalled'. That was a tribute to our own journalists and editors and also to our legal advisers, Hayes and Sons.

Post-publication legal work could be even more demanding of time. When we received a solicitor's letter, a writ or some other notification of intention to start proceedings against us, we had to respond smartly.

A speedy response could sometimes solve the problem. But if it did not, there was a detailed drill to be followed. Reporters' notes had to be preserved and written statements had to be secured from the journalists and possibly from the sources involved. I did little of this myself. But I had to maintain an overview. And if the proceedings went ahead, I had to become fully involved. We did not often actually end up in court. But we spent many long days and weeks in the Four Courts, sometimes settling an issue with just minutes to go before a hearing. It was tedious, boring and it frayed at the nerves.

Dublin editors, in my experience, did not much frequent the 'cocktail circuit'. There are 40 embassies and consulates in Dublin and the editor of *The Irish Times* will be invited to the national day celebrations of each one and to a great many formal dinners. And there are immense numbers of organisations offering 'hospitality' for one reason or another on every evening of the week.

Only a few of the diplomatic missions impinged on policy for the newspaper and I generally confined myself to these. The British and the Americans were, of course, involved in the Northern Ireland issue and I developed working links with their successive ambassadors. Insofar as time permitted I would respond to invitations from others and, of course, any ambassador who wished to visit the newspaper was made welcome.

Perhaps once a week on average, I would have a working lunch with a political figure, a senior civil servant, a diplomat, or some useful source. If the lunch were at my invitation I would usually take them to the Stephen's Green Club. *The Irish Times*, unlike the *Independent*, did not have in-house dining facilities.

As I moved through a succession of editorial positions, I had come to understand the importance of developing international linkages with other newspapers and media. For all its supposed open-mindedness, journalism can have an inherent tendency towards parochialism. Journalists who are curious about so many things can be oddly uninterested in how their counterparts elsewhere do their jobs.

I was often struck by the fact that colleagues who had travelled abroad would visit parliaments, galleries, cathedrals, museums and other places of interest. But few if any seemed to take the time to make contact with the local newspaper.

An excellent exchange system, *Journalistes en Europe*, had operated since the 1970s, for young journalists who wished to work abroad for a year. A number of *Irish Times* staffers had participated and benefited greatly. But each year, when the announcement went on the noticeboards, there would be a maximum of one or two applications. In many years there were none.

In 1985 I was asked to join the board of the European Journalism Centre (EJC) at Maastricht in the Netherlands. It was a new institution, set up with EEC funding, to provide training at all levels for journalists across the Community. I served as chair of the Board of Counsellors at Maastricht and over the years arranged for many *Irish Times* journalists to take training courses there, ranging from basic newsroom skills to advanced management.

It gave a lot of our people the opportunity to meet fellow-journalists from other European countries and to learn about differing approaches to their work. In many instances, they came back to say how much they had been affirmed when they discovered that we did many things better than in some organisations that were much bigger and sometimes better-resourced. That helped to build pride and confidence.

Some years later, in 1995, I became the chairman of the World Editors Forum (WEF), based in Paris. WEF represents about 200 editors in more than 30 countries. I held the chair for five years and used the networking and professional services to develop aspects of the *Irish Times* in accordance with best international practices. As chair of WEF, I also sat on the main board of the World Association of Newspapers and as a member of its International Press Freedom Committee.

Involvement in EJC and WEF was stimulating. It made extra demands on my time, naturally. But I always felt that the newspaper benefited from the importation of new ideas.

The working day at *The Irish Times* was busiest between 3 pm and perhaps 8 pm. By 5 pm I would have been through the proofs of the early features pages. By 8 o'clock I would have read the leaders, the *Irishman's Diary*, the opinion columnist of the day, the features pages and the principal news of politics, business, international affairs, sport and so on.

I would generally visit the newsroom and the caseroom where pages were made up by the printing and graphical staff. I tried to make it home for the RTÉ News at 9 o'clock. Through the latter part of the evening I would monitor RTÉ's current affairs programmes and, invariably, *Newsnight* on BBC2.

I would keep in touch with the night editor on a dedicated 'hotline' that ran from the Irish Times switchboard to my home. It was old technology, dating from the 1950s. But it was wonderfully efficient.

Three or four times each month I would drive back in, sometime before midnight. It was important to see how matters progressed both in editorial and production departments as the night went by. I was always confident that the physical production of the newspaper was in good hands with Jim Cooke, Derek McCullagh or any of their lieutenants. I always made a point of telephoning in advance to let the night editor know I was coming in. There was nothing of a surprise inspection about these visits.

When Jim Cooke retired, Derek McCullagh was appointed as production supremo. A quietly-efficient, rugby-playing man, Derek was an accountant and had been deputy managing director. He brought all of these disciplines to bear on his task of getting the newspaper out in adverse conditions.

In the busy round of a newspaper's daily cycle there is little room for reflection or relaxed conversation. In 1984, when I was a deputy editor, I was one of a group of friends that formed a once-a-month dinner and discussion group. It was agreed that we would fix the first Tuesday of the month for our meetings. Not surprisingly, perhaps, and not very imaginatively, we became known as the 'First Tuesday Club'.

At first our meetings were held at the Grey Door restaurant on Pembroke Street. Later we varied our locations, sometimes taking advantage of dining facilities that might be at the disposal of one or other of our members.

We were an eclectic group and good friendships grew within it. For the most part, we comprised men and women in busy jobs. Most people felt the need to connect and converse with other individuals whose lives and work were wholly different from their own. Sometimes we would have a guest speaker join us. At the end of the meal everyone gave their contribution to cover costs to the honorary treasurer.

The First Tuesday Club still meets and I still attend. Membership is more a state of mind than anything more formal. But people have come into the group by invitation. It includes or has included journalists, politicians, theatre people, churchmen, university staff, artists, gardaí, lawyers, bankers, business people, public servants *et al.*

Normally, between 10 and 20 members would be present. Some diplomats became members. Jean Kennedy-Smith, appointed by Bill Clinton as US Ambassador to Ireland, was a member. So too was her successor, Mike Sullivan. Ivor Roberts, British Ambassador in Dublin from 1998 to 2002, was a member. I found the group both a useful sounding board and a listening post. I cannot say I ever got an exclusive or a scoop from it. But I learned a lot about what was going on in Irish society.

There were, and are, many such groups that now meet in Dublin. There was a myth that my predecessor, Douglas Gageby, did not mingle with people in positions of political, financial or administrative power. But he was for many years a leading member of the 'Murphy Club' which operated in much the same way as the 'First Tuesday'. The 'Murphy Club' included at least two former Taoisigh, the chairmen of the leading banks, several bishops and many business people from supermarket chiefs to the heads of the big semi-state enterprises.

Much of my time as editor was spent working with the directors of the other departments, across the Irish Times organisation. Maintaining this relationship was delicate and sometimes problematic. But in general it worked well.

The Irish Times's model of management had gone through many changes since its foundation. But under Gageby and McDowell in the 1960s it broadly reflected the 'Dawson' formula that came into existence in the London *Times* in 1922. Under the formula agreed between Geoffrey Dawson, editor of *The Times* and the proprietor, Lord Northcliffe, the editor and the 'manager' were separate authorities, each with his own responsibilities and reporting separately to the board on these.

The essence of this was expressed in The Irish Times's Memorandum and Articles of Association, as amended in 1974 with the setting up of the Trust. It stated that the editor was solely responsible for the content of the newspaper. It also stated that the editor had to be a member of the board of directors and that the policy of the newspaper was the 'policy of the directors'.

Thus a system of twin authorities developed in the organisation. It worked well, although it required much painstaking collaboration and co-operation across the editorial-commercial divide. It irked some people on the commercial side. They saw it as an aberration from what they had been taught in business school to think of as a 'normal' business structure. It functioned well elsewhere, for example at *The Guardian* in London. But it sat somewhat uneasily with many of the commercial executives who worked under Louis O'Neill and later under Nick Chapman.

The system guarded the editor's independence. For example, the editor had his own small unit of IT specialists. This meant that editorial computers and databases were securely held in editorial hands and were not accessible to anyone else. If an *Irish Times* journalist told a source his information would remain confidential and within the editorial system, we had the technology to guarantee that. Editorial department administered its own budgets, agreed in advance with the board. We also ran our own recruitment and promotion procedures, but always within policy and budgetary terms agreed by the board.

These arrangements secured the independence of the journalism of *The Irish Times* within the organisation. I believe that was valuable. But it certainly meant that the editor, in Douglas Gageby's phrase, had a lot more to do than just edit the paper.

An editor is a leader—and physical presence is important for that. But the people one leads are generally highly individualistic, with a developed sense of their own independence. One cannot be too interventionist. On the other hand, an editor is paid to take difficult decisions. Getting the balance right between these two is problematic. It is one of the most difficult aspects of an editor's role.

Very often, I felt, the most important thing in my daily round was simply to stop by a journalist's or an editor's desk and say: 'good story', or 'great picture', or 'good call'. I worked on the basis that one should keep criticism to a minimum. Generally, if one has the right people in position, they will take the right decisions. But preparation and training are necessary. So is the existence of clear procedures. I rarely took issue with a journalist over a wrong judgment call—we all made many of them. But I was slow to forgive any failure to adhere to procedure. That, I felt, reflected either arrogance or laziness.

The famous Confederate cavalry General of the American Civil War, Nathan Bedford Forrest, was once asked the key to victory in a military engagement. 'Who gets there firstest with the mostest,' he replied.

Many things have contributed to the development of *The Irish Times* as a fine newspaper. Tradition, commitment and a sense of pride in what it does have all been important. But the availability of plentiful resources to enable editors to do the job has been key. Even in the leanest days of the 1940s and the 1950s, the management of the newspaper ensured that R.M. Smyllie got whatever could be pared off the profit-and-loss account to produce the best possible newspaper.

Thus, at its best, *The Irish Times* could usually get to the story quickly, and with 'the mostest' in terms of journalistic firepower and expertise.

What is an editor's job about? Above all else it is about making judgment calls —dozens of them—every 24 hours.

20

THE COMING—AND THE GOING—OF SPRING

... it is impossible to see how anyone could support them in the future without seeing them first undergo the most radical transformation. We will not support any government with the track record of this one.

—DICK SPRING on Fianna Fáil just before he entered
government with that party

D ick Spring was probably the most influential figure to have crossed the Irish political landscape during the years in which I was editor of *The Irish Times.*

His impact and legacy have possibly been under-stated for a number of reasons. He stood down from the leadership of the Labour Party at a relatively early age. In power, he took deeply unpopular decisions that dissipated much of the aura of idealism that surrounded him in opposition. He was—is—a man who can come across as gruff, although he can also be immensely charming when he wishes. He tends to give out an air of being grumpy and aggressive.

But in the years that he was in Government—and in particular in the period 1992 to 1997—Spring effected a profoundly progressive and modernising influence on Irish public life.

The Fianna Fáil-Labour Programme for A Partnership Government, 1993–1997 was the blueprint from which many of the most progressive aspects of modern Irish society were formed. Many of its objectives, then only at conceptual stage, now form the bedrock of today's social and civil rights and entitlements. It proposed, for the first time, a coherent set of measures for the accountability of those in office and it sought to enshrine important public values to which mere lip-service had heretofore been paid.

Some of it came to nothing, including one objective that was close to the heart of the news media: the updating of the laws on contempt and defamation. Other elements were delayed. The Fianna Fáil-Labour government did not last its course. But many key proposals of what had been agreed were then incorporated into the programme of government of the 'Rainbow Coalition' that followed, holding office until 1997.

Equality measures affecting women, the disabled, Travellers; legislation on ethics in government; registration of the interests of Oireachtas members; freedom of information legislation; legislation on divorce and family rights—all of these have grown from the 1993 document.

The provenance of the 'Programme' was something of a paradox. The first draft was substantially drawn up by Albert Reynolds's adviser, Martin Mansergh, who spent days and long nights trawling through Spring's policy positions. Then he built a Fianna Fáil response to these, effectively defining common ground between the two parties, in anticipation of a post-election, Fianna Fáil-Labour dialogue.

It was then negotiated in detail by teams delegated by Albert Reynolds and Dick Spring. There were major concessions on both sides. Fianna Fáil persuaded the Labour side to abandon its opposition to the fiscal and budgetary guidelines that were set down by the EU in the run-up to the Maastricht Treaty. As a *quid pro quo*, Fianna Fáil bought into Labour's proposals for the creation of a 'third banking force' to break the duopoly of the large Bank of Ireland and AIB groups. In the event, EU deregulatory developments brought competition to Irish banking beyond the imagining of Labour Party activists at the time.

There were many hands stirring the pot in which the 'programme' was boiled. But it was, in a very personal sense, Dick Spring's view of how Ireland should develop as a state and as a society. And even though many of its key components were proposed by Fianna Fáil, they were promulgated by a pragmatic Fianna Fáil in order to lure Labour into coalition.

Spring caught a tide of new values and priorities that have helped to shape much of what is good about modern Ireland. He was central in the Northern Ireland peace process. He played a key role in exposing the first identified problems of ethics in public life—the irregularities surrounding the beef-processing industry. And he mobilised Irish altruism to focus on global issues such as AIDS, hunger and economic imbalance. He boosted Ireland's efforts through the bi-lateral aid programme, assisting poorer countries in Africa.

Much of this he did directly as Tánaiste and Minister. Much of it was effected indirectly. It was Spring who invented the Mary Robinson presidency, although it quickly passed out of his control and assumed an influence and a powerful dynamic of its own.

I knew Dick Spring from schooldays at Mount Saint Joseph Abbey, Roscrea, in the late 1960s. We were neither friendly nor unfriendly. He was a year behind me but we sat in adjoining desks in the Old Oratory study for a year. There was a rule of absolute silence in study so there was little dialogue. He was 'Richard' Spring then. He was a quiet, private boy, almost taciturn. But he became animated in the debating society and, of course, on the sports field. I am sure he was the only Roscrea man to have played Gaelic football for his county and international rugby for Ireland.

Roscrea had a strong tradition as the *alma mater* of politicians. That tradition went back to the early years of the state. The Mulcahy family gave a distinguished son to the Cistercian order. As Dom Columban Mulcahy he went on to be abbot of the daughter-house at Tarrawarra in Australia. The Fianna Fáil Ryans sent their sons there—their grandsons were there in my time. Quite a few past pupils sat in the Dáil or Seanad. It was also a popular choice for the education of politicians' sons. But 'Richard' Spring was, I think, the only one whose father was a Labour TD. It came across occasionally in debating.

I was, nonetheless, somewhat surprised when I heard that he was going to contest his father's seat in 1981. I was doubly surprised, but delighted and proud as a Roscrea man, when he was elected as leader of the Labour Party on the resignation of Michael O'Leary in 1982. The impressions of schooldays were clearly wrong or had been overtaken. The reticent schoolboy of the 1960s had been transformed—by university, by success in sport, by a strongly competitive instinct.

Our paths rarely crossed in those years when he was starting in politics and I was building a career in journalism. Although I covered both Westminster and Stormont and reported on politics in London and Belfast, I had never been assigned to political coverage in Dublin. That was my own choice. Leinster House had a pernicious attraction for many journalists. I had seen too many of my colleagues become detached from reality in the Leinster House swallow-hole or bored to distraction in the press gallery.

But I watched with admiration, Spring's maturing into a strong, astute and target-driven leader.

His first experience of government (apart from a brief period as a junior minister at Justice) seemed to be a poisoned chalice. He became Tánaiste and Minister for the Environment when the Fine Gael-Labour coalition was formed in December 1982. A year later he transferred to become Minister for Energy.

It was a bad time to be in government. The economic policies of the 1977 Fianna Fáil government led by Jack Lynch had proven disastrous, driving the country deep into debt. These problems were compounded when Lynch was succeeded by Charles Haughey.

When Garret FitzGerald and Dick Spring stepped into the posts of Taoiseach and Tánaiste respectively in 1982, the economy was steeply over-borrowed, overtaxed and underperforming. But it deteriorated very much further as the decade went by, with the Government divided between the ideologies of Fine Gael and Labour. At the end of 1986, it became clear that it would be difficult even to frame an agreed budget for the coming year.

The FitzGerald-Spring government of 1982–1986 did not solve the country's economic problems. But its role in helping to advance the peace process in Northern Ireland was crucial and Spring was centrally involved in it. He led the Labour Party delegation to the New Ireland Forum that laid the basis for a pan-nationalist front, in time facilitating the dialogue that led on to the process.

The high point of that Government's role in the Northern saga was the signing of the Anglo-Irish Agreement at Hillsborough in 1985. Hillsborough created a set of structures that gave the Republic—and by extension, nationalist Ireland—a role, as of right, in the affairs of Northern Ireland. It also created institutions and procedures that were incapable of being boycotted. The process of levering unionism to the point at which it had to engage in dialogue, sooner or later, was now irreversible.

Two other things impressed me about my former schoolmate and made me realise the steel that was behind the understated exterior.

Labour had long been plagued by the manipulations of its extreme left-wing, known as 'Militant Tendency'. They made life intolerable for Labour ministers, persistently seeking to subvert any policies that they saw as compromises with the centrist parties. Spring took them on with his own cabal of tough men (and one or two women) and effectively broke their power. He used his period in opposition, from 1987 to 1992, to bring Labour into a set of policy positions that left open a range of coalition possibilities.

The other thing that made me admire Dick Spring was the way he dealt with the aftermath of a bad car smash that left him with serious spinal injuries. I had two encounters with him that fore-shadowed the accident.

We had met for a pot of tea in the Mont Clare Hotel. He was on his way to Kerry. He stood, glanced at his watch and said, 'I've got to go. I'm due in Tralee for 8 o'clock.' It was just after 5 pm.

'You'll need at least four hours to get there,' I said.

'We don't have four hours,' he grinned as he trotted down the steps into his State car.

A year later, on a winter's evening, I was driving south from Dublin. On the straight stretch of the old N7 road between Kildare and Monasterevin, I saw a dark saloon with blazing lights sweep into my rear-view mirror. I was driving fast, perhaps 60 mph. The ministerial Mercedes zoomed past me. I recognised Spring's profile through the passenger window.

He was in constant pain for many years after a driving accident. I believe he still suffers. Less resolute men would have slowed down or backed away from the challenges of political life. It made him a bit cranky. But he stuck with it.

Dick was going into opposition just as I was taking over as editor. He wrote me a warm note wishing me well. And we were to run across each other over the next few years fairly regularly at public events or State occasions. Yet we had little contact and met formally on few occasions. Paradoxically, looking back, I probably had fewer conversations with Spring than with any other political leader. I had more regular contact with his successor as leader of the Labour Party, Ruairí Quinn.

I wasn't unhappy that it should be so. Part of the reason was that *The Irish Times* and the Labour Party were close in a number of ways that needed watching if the paper's impartiality were not be compromised.

Many aspects of the newspaper's editorial policy were *ad idem* with Labour

Party policy. Quite a few journalists were members of the party or were active supporters. Several had been Labour Party candidates, although only one, John Horgan, had succeeded in being elected to the Oireachtas—and that after he had left the staff. And there were a great many personal friendships between *Irish Times* journalists and Labour Party figures.

There was a firm friendship between Dick Walsh, whom I appointed as political editor, and Fergus Finlay, Dick Spring's political adviser and *guru*. Dick and Fergus would talk by telephone several times each week and, indeed, much more frequently if there was something big in the air. It was a good line of communication and information and there seemed little advantage in me replicating it. The interests and view of the Labour Party and its leader were more than well represented by Dick in our own internal conferences and discussions. He could be very critical of them, of course. But he was often more comfortable with Labour and with Fergus than with any other party or its officials.

It was perhaps this closeness, this sense of political kinship between the party and some of those within the paper, that caused occasional outbursts of anger and perhaps resentment when *The Irish Times* did not see things the Labour way —and said so.

In his book *Snakes and Ladders*, published in 1998, Fergus Finlay pondered on the lack of 'understanding' in *The Irish Times* over what Labour was trying to achieve when it went into government with Fianna Fáil in 1992. He put the question to a 'senior person' in *The Irish Times*.

> You have to understand, I was told, that we (*The Irish Times*) regard the Labour Party like the daughter to whom we've given every advantage. We've put you through the best finishing school, we've taught you etiquette and decorum and how to entertain our visitors in the parlour. And now you've gone and married the boy from the wrong side of town when there were some nice polite boys from good schools to choose from.

I would have put it another way. I would have said there was a sense in which elements of the Labour Party regarded the columns of *The Irish Times* as their personal fiefdom. It had no right to dissent from Labour Party orthodoxy and if it did it was *ipso facto* wrong or acting in bad faith.

I do not think Dick Spring took this view. But I believe it was held to a degree by some of those close to his thinking. It probably played a part in the build-up of anger between party and newspaper when Labour decided in 1992 to go into coalition government with Fianna Fáil. On 5 November 1992, in the closing days of the Fianna Fáil-Progressive Democrat Government of 1989–1992, Dick Spring made a memorably brilliant speech in the Dáil, setting out in the most cogent terms how and why Labour could not support Fianna Fáil in government. It was the adjournment debate, the closing hours of the 26th Dáil.

It was not merely a question of the party leadership, he stressed. It was impossible for Labour to contemplate any alliance with Fianna Fáil until it was thoroughly reformed, root and branch. Fianna Fáil as a party was characterised by 'low standards' and the 'debasement of political life'.

> We will not get involved in any government that are willing to bring politics into disrepute as this government has done . . . I believe that one political party in this House has gone so far down the road of blindness to standards, and of blindness towards the people they are supposed to represent, that it is impossible to see how anyone could support them in the future without seeing them first undergo the most radical transformation. We will not support any government with the track record of this one.
>
> [Dáil Report, 6 November 1992.]

It was powerful stuff, entirely in keeping with the reputation that Dick had built up over the previous four years of opposition, as the scourge of corruption, the Paladin of honesty in public life and the man who might—if he were given the opportunity by the electorate—rid public life of the Haughey legacy and its venalities.

This was the note upon which Dick Spring bade farewell to the 26th Dáil. He then went out into the electoral marketplace, seeking a mandate from the voters. To my mind, the basis upon which he went before the electorate could not have been clearer. He was going to put Fianna Fáil out. That was a view very widely held across middle-Ireland. In Dublin South, for example, the Labour Party candidate, Eithne FitzGerald, got two quotas—sufficient votes to have her elected twice over. That did not happen because Mount Merrion had become socialist.

But when the votes were counted, it became clear that forming a government was not going to be a simple thing. The arithmetic of a working majority for the 27th Dáil was capable of being computed in a variety of ways. One thing, however, was clear: Spring and Labour were the kingmakers. The shape of the incoming government would be determined by their choices.

It shortly emerged that things were not going well between John Bruton, the Fine Gael leader, and Spring. There were inconclusive meetings between the two at which, it was reported, the body-language was poor. After a few days, the political correspondents began to write about what they had assumed heretofore to be an impossibility—a Fianna Fáil/Labour government.

In his account of these events, Fergus Finlay writes of Dick Spring being forced by circumstances into the alliance with Fianna Fáil. Fine Gael had declared they would not sit in government with the Workers Party/Democratic Left. Thus a Fine Gael-led coalition would have to comprise, in addition to their own deputies, the PDS and Labour. In that calculation, Finlay argues, Labour would have been seriously outnumbered by the right-of-centre grouping. Labour would have fewer ministers, less influence and therefore less of an impact on the agenda of the incoming administration.

No doubt that calculation was correct. But I could not understand, and never have understood, why it could not have been modelled before the election and its hypotheses drawn out. We in the media did not do it. Labour chose not to do it. Fine Gael failed to do it.

The idea of Spring swallowing his own words had seemed simply unthinkable. The media, and the electorate, took him at face value.

Nor did we in the media make sufficient allowance for the history of poor relations between Bruton and Spring. John Bruton was a political leader of immense integrity. He was never the most diplomatic of men although, like Spring himself, he could also be the best of company. It seems that in the previous FG–Labour administration he had frequently clashed with Spring who took the view that Bruton was condescending towards him.

As the discussions among the parties appeared to go on interminably, public opinion became impatient. So did the media. It seemed as if there was never going to be a government.

Spring rang me at the office one Sunday evening and told me that we, the media, should lay off the pressure. It was a very cordial exchange. 'Give us a chance to get it right,' he said. 'If we rush into anything you'll be the first to criticise us when it goes wrong.'

I told him I understood but that people could not understand why he and Bruton did not bury their differences and get on with a deal. 'I'm teaching John about manners,' he replied tetchily. 'It's something he needs to learn about.'

When it finally emerged that Dick Spring and Albert Reynolds were about to form a government I decided the most eloquent statement *The Irish Times* could make was simply to re-publish in full and without comment, Dick's speech during the adjournment debate at the end of the 26th Dáil. When he invited me to lunch at Iveagh House three years later he was still annoyed!

Fergus Finlay wrote subsequently in hurt and almost baffled terms about the public and media reaction to Labour's decision to keep Fianna Fáil in government in 1992. He had great difficulty in understanding why the public and the media were so obsessed with who Labour chose for their partners in government and so little concerned with the capacity of the party to advance its agenda of change and social reform.

Spring was right when he told the Dáil that Fianna Fáil's problems did not begin or end with its leader. Elements within the party were seriously dysfunctional. When the Duggan case broke two years later, Spring was forced to the conclusion that there was widespread knowledge throughout the Fianna Fáil ministers that the full truth was not being told.

Had Dick Spring and Labour kept their word, the country would have been spared another two years with the hands of senior Fianna Fáil figures in the pork-barrel. That was what they were voted into office to do. They chose instead to swallow their words on Fianna Fáil on the basis that they could advance their reform agenda.

It was little wonder that the public and the media savaged them. Indeed, the wonder is that they got off so lightly. That wonder became greater when it emerged that Labour was just as adept as Fianna Fáil at packing every board and every job with its own lackeys.

But I stand by my adjudication that Spring was arguably the most significant, reforming figure on the political scene over these years. And ironically, much of his success in this was to be given effect in the years in which he served with John Bruton as Taoiseach in the Rainbow Coalition.

It was his political *nous* that created the presidency of Mary Robinson. Whether one takes the view that Robinson was a catalyst or merely a mirror of the age, there can be no denying the sense of transformation that swept through Irish society over the years of her presidency.

The legislative programme in Spring's years shaped an Ireland that was to be much more accountable and transparent, in which powerful institutions found themselves obliged to be more open. It included a Freedom of Information Act. He sponsored the Ethics in Public Life Act. He ensured the reappointment of an excellent Ombudsman in Michael Mills, when Albert Reynolds wanted to appoint a former Fianna Fáil backbencher, Eileen Lemass.

When Ruairí Quinn succeeded Dick Spring as leader of the Labour Party in 1997, he asked me to come and talk over a meal. He told me he wanted to 'normalise' relations between *The Irish Times* and Labour. He made it clear there were many in the party who felt it had got a hard time from *The Irish Times*.

I reflected on that. I could see no substance to it then and I cannot see it now. If anything Labour, more than any other party, had a fair wind from *The Irish Times*, at least initially.

Perhaps it simply proved that there can be no cosy relationship between a party in government and a newspaper that values its independence.

| ROUGH TIMES

The Irish Times *is over-reliant on two sources of advertising—*
property and recruitment. If anything happens to either of those,
you're in big trouble. You've got to broaden the base.
—Newspaper consultant JIM CHISOLM in 1999

The unease that flowed through *The Irish Times* after Tom McDowell's initiative on the commercial succession did not, unfortunately, abate even when the agreement had been struck for the procedures to be followed in the appointment of a new managing director.

Resentment and doubts endured. Louis O'Neill's commercial staff still felt that an unacceptable situation had been foisted on them. The journalists were suspicious. Some senior personnel on the commercial side were dismayed that the editor should have a role in the selection of a future managing director. (Paradoxically, they saw no reason why the managing director should not have a role in the selection of a future editor.)

Relations between Louis and Tom McDowell had grown tense. And the working relationship between Louis and Karen Erwin was difficult, even though Louis was tasked with 'bringing Karen on', in Tom's words.

It was impossible not to feel sympathy for Karen. She worked very hard at being pleasant to everybody. She had a good sense of humour, which she sometimes employed quite cleverly at her own expense. She had quickly been given the nickname 'Major Minor' and she sometimes took some delight in using it to introduce herself.

But she seemed to find the patterns and pace of a newspaper difficult after the very different environment of the law. This led to tensions between herself and Louis. She also seemed to find it difficult to absorb all the multitudinous complexities of an organisation that appeared homogenous and orderly on the outside but where each 24-hour cycle was a series of crisis-solving operations. Nobody could blame her for that. It was difficult enough even for those of us who had worked there for years.

As tensions rose all round, more and more of the organisation's agenda began to fall behind the pace at which it should have been moving.

The Irish Times had come through the hard years of the late 1980s and early

1990s into the lushness of the Irish economic boom. The 'Celtic Tiger' had arrived. The company had paid off the debts incurred in the formation of the Trust in 1974 and was earning significant profits—as it was to continue to do right through the remainder of the decade.

Circulation continued to rise. Our website *www.ireland.com* was one of the most successful newspaper websites in Europe. The range of editorial services grew, but always within the budgets agreed by the board, in turn increasing readership.

Advertising revenues were strong. The Uniman colour press, now almost a decade in operation, had been expanded with the addition of new units and a new inserter. Everything was going well—for the moment.

But in newspapers, as in any other business, regardless of what has been achieved, to stand still is to fall behind. There was an acute awareness among the senior executives of the organisation, both editorial and commercial, that it was only a matter of time until our rivals would close the gap with us in printing and other technologies. There was also an awareness that the organisation had serious, inherent problems that needed to be addressed sooner rather than later. We were faced with a number of issues.

The Uniman colour press, commissioned in 1986, was reaching the end of its working life. It was being pushed to the limits of its capacities and beyond and was being asked to deliver a product for which it was not built. Each night's production became a struggle. Breakdowns and stops became frequent, in turn playing havoc with deliveries. It was to the credit of production directors Jim Cooke, Derek McCullagh and chief of printing, Fred Snowe, that there were so few disruptions.

A new press, with significantly greater capacity, almost certainly to be located at a remote site away from D'Olier Street, was going to have to be ordered and brought on stream.

Moreover, the Atex publishing system which had been introduced in 1990 was obsolete. We needed a new, fully automated system that allowed journalists to make-up and design their own pages. That posed significant human resource problems. Other departments apart from editorial also needed new IT systems to replace ancient procedures, sometimes hand-written, involving accounts, distribution, circulation and others.

There was a potentially serious vulnerability in our advertising revenue streams. Up to two-thirds of the newspaper's advertising revenues came from two areas—appointments and property. If anything were to happen to either of these, the implications would be catastrophic. Indeed, when the company was obliged to face into the restructuring of 2001–2002, it was because the appointments and recruitment advertising streams had dried to a trickle.

The Irish Times was a single-product business. The six days a week publication was hugely successful. But inherent in this was the risk of relying on one source of income. One way to break that dependency would have been to go ahead with a Sunday publication. Thus, a great deal of executive time and effort was put into exploring this concept at the time.

It was also clear that our Saturday editions needed to be beefed up. From a situation in which the Saturday *Irish Times* had been the biggest-selling day of the week, it had now fallen to second and sometimes third place after Friday and Thursday.

The *Irish Independent* had also improved its Saturday editions, replicating our formula with back-folded additional sections on sport and lifestyle.

There was a consensus across the organisation that we needed an additional section, probably a magazine, on Saturdays. I knew it would add to circulation and the sales staff, conscious that they were still carrying their advertising revenue eggs in too few baskets, needed an additional sales platform.

We needed a clear policy on *www.ireland.com*. It was a big success in numbers of viewers, but it had not been possible to turn it into a profitable business and opinion was deeply divided at executive level as to how its future might be shaped.

There were also serious issues in the way the organisation had grown. There were problems of overmanning, and restrictive and wasteful practices that had built up over the years. There were sinecures, jobs for old pals and too many posts held under various systems of patronage, going back over the decades. It was a problem in editorial. But editorial was by no means the worst department. It ran from one end of the organisation to the other.

We were carrying a large cost-base that was manageable in good times. But if the chill winds were to blow, it would become unsupportable.

Fortunately, there was no problem in relation to the sales and readership performance of the newspaper itself. Circulation rose steadily. Its 'profile'—the socio-economic grouping of its readers—was ideal for selling advertising. Our research told us that readers valued the newspaper and held it in high regard. Its place in the minds of its readership had never been more secure.

McDowell, Louis and I shared an awareness that the newspaper had to be constantly refreshed. This entailed a process that was ordered and very exact. Every September or October, after discussions with section editors, I would put up my programme for the year ahead. There would be some tussling between Eoin McVey, the managing editor who handled editorial budgets, and Louis's accountancy staff. Then there would be some give-and-take between Louis and myself. Finally a budget would be brought to the board for approval. There was never any serious disagreement and the overall budget figures were never exceeded. It worked well.

———

After Karen's appointment, Tom began to draw Don Reid more and more into the running of the organisation. Don had been a member of the Trust and board for six years at this point. Tom was grooming him to take over some of the functions he had traditionally discharged himself and ultimately to succeed him as chairman.

Tom and Don had Louis and myself draw up an action plan together, setting down the tasks that lay ahead of the organisation. Tom then appointed Don Reid to be the *de facto* chairman of that process.

Louis organised a series of 'away days' at the Killiney Court Hotel through late 1997 and 1998 at which the senior executive team, both editorial and commercial, examined tasks and challenges ahead, explored ideas and finally set out targets and objectives.

At one of these, in September 1997, Jim Chisolm and Warwick Brindle, two UK newspaper industry consultants, worked with us through the day. There was a six-point agenda. Items 4, 5 and 6 focused on 'major threats' for the future, 'major barriers to growth' and asked 'what forms of new activities and diversification should we consider?'

Chisolm was positive about the opportunities that were there for us to advance, particularly with a Sunday title. But he was also clear about the dangers we faced. Time and again he came back to two, in particular.

One, we had an extremely high cost-base. The payroll costs were far too high although individual employee earnings were in line with the industry generally. Basically, we had too many people.

Two, our advertising revenue was ominously over-dependent on property and appointments. We had not developed alternative revenue streams as we should. If the property market were to collapse or if the information-technology sector were to suffer a significant reverse, much of our advertising would disappear.

I urged the conference to accept the necessity for spreading our operations which, in turn, would enable us to open new revenue streams. We needed to develop new information-based products that were high-quality and authoritative, consonant with the standards and ethos of the newspaper. We could not hold our influence if we continued as a one-paper operation. We would be eased out by digital TV, the internet, niche magazines and the combined effects of Independent Newspapers for sheer weight of numbers.

But this spread of operations did not happen. Advertising sales continued to be dependent on the two great cash-cows of property and appointments. When the US IT sector collapsed four years later we were still essentially dependent on one product with two large revenue streams.

The thinking and analysis that emerged from these sessions fed into the action programme that Louis and I put together for Don Reid.

We needed to start the process of building a new print plant and acquiring a new press. We needed to replace the Atex system used by journalists. We needed to explore the concept of a Sunday title, and to strengthen the Saturday editions. And all the administrative functions on the commercial side of the house— accounts, sales, distribution and so on—had to be put on to modern IT systems.

This development programme, we believed, would give the advertising sales departments the additional selling platforms they needed. There would be a wider spread of revenue sources and the dependency on property and appointments would be lessened.

But our problems were not simply on the revenue side. There was an issue of costs and in particular of high payroll costs.

There were several reasons why this had come about. The culture of *The Irish Times* was traditionally tolerant and indulgent. There were very few performance measures for employees at any level. People who were ill, or having problems perhaps with alcohol or drugs, or who were burned out were generally tolerated and protected. This, of course, was humane. But it also placed additional burdens on other employees and it often meant that additional staff had to be put in place to compensate for non-performance by others.

The unions were protective of their members—rightly so. But the agreements between the company and the unions that saw *The Irish Times* through the 1970s, 1980s and well into the 1990s, were extremely restrictive. There were many costly and rigid demarcation lines. New technologies and work practices could not be brought into operation. Any changes could only be achieved at a high cost, creating more jobs and providing additional pay and allowances to employees.

The board and the senior management were always anxious to avoid any confrontation, especially with either printers or journalists. That reticence was understandable. The Irish Press group had closed after a bitter stand-off between unions and the company.

But in the long term this approach compounded the costs problem. With each year, the numbers of people on the payroll expanded and the wages and salaries bill grew. This was fine as long as rising circulation, modern technology and a buoyant economy enabled the advertising sales staff to draw in more revenue each year.

The newspaper business tends to cyclical. Boom is followed by slump is followed by recovery is followed by another boom is followed by another slump . . . and so on. Before ever I became editor, I recognised that the organisation could not sustain an indefinite process of product-expansion unless measures were taken to reduce or shed embedded costs.

But the editor had to have resources to refresh, replenish and develop the newspaper each year. Thus there would be additional spending. It seemed clear to me that while this was necessary it was also imperative that ways be found for shedding historical or accumulated costs.

The age-profile of the editorial staff was in serious imbalance. We had very few young journalists (under 30) and very few close to retirement (over 60.) The great majority were in their forties and fifties. Many had been working for more than 30 years. Some were as energetic and committed as the day they started. But quite a few were burned out by the pace of a tough career. Many had spoken to me about their desire to move on, to make a fresh start, or simply to disengage—if the terms were right.

I began an exercise with Grant Thornton Management Consultants to see if we could put together a programme that would make this possible. Pat Gillan of Grant Thornton had worked before with the company and he and I, along with Seán Olson, set to devising a programme that would have enabled up to one third of the staff to take early retirement on very favourable terms. Pat costed the scheme.

The proposal was that for every two jobs we took out, we could, in time, replace one. In this way, the numbers and costs would be reduced but the organisation would continue to have an input of fresh blood.

For reasons that I never fully understood, the commercial side of the company did not wish to proceed with the scheme. I thought it was a serious mistake. I argued with Tom McDowell that while I had a relatively simple mechanism for adding to costs, I was provided with no equivalent mechanism for shedding costs. There may have been a sense that if something like this were done in the editorial departments it would have to be matched by similar programmes across the organisation—and perhaps the feeling was that the time was not right for that.

The human resources function of the company—as distinct from traditional 'personnel' services—had not been fully-developed at this time. It was to be almost a decade later when flexible change agreements were finally put in place with the unions.

Whatever the case may have been, matters remained as they were. A year or so later Pat Gillan and I made a second attempt to put the proposal forward. Again it failed to take off. After that, I decided to leave well enough alone and get on with the main business of my editorship—the content and policy of the newspaper. The commercial operation of the company was not my responsibility as editor.

There was however agreement across editorial and commercial departments on advancing the idea of a Sunday title. I put a small team together from the editorial departments under the chairmanship of Gerry Smyth. The team produced several prototypes of a Sunday *Irish Times* and we had these printed and tested on panels of readers using Des Byrne's *Behaviour and Attitudes* company.

Des was excited by the results. 'There's a tremendous response to the test-papers,' he reported to Louis O'Neill and myself. 'This could be the big breakthrough for *The Irish Times* in establishing a national readership.'

The circulation and readership of the newspaper had grown steadily. But the growth was uneven, being concentrated largely on the Dublin and east coast area. I felt strongly that it was important for us to grow also in the regional cities and towns. In addition, significant changes were taking place in social demographics.

There were fewer farmers and many fewer in the unskilled and semi-skilled cohorts. The middle-class cohorts, the ABC1s, had almost doubled over the previous decade, as a result of rising educational standards, more employment opportunities and higher incomes. These were our natural readership. But our circulation was not growing at anything like the rate at which they were increasing. We were getting about 50 per cent of the ABC1s. If the *Irish Independent* were to succeed in getting the greater share of the other 50 per cent it would be bad news for *The Irish Times.*

I believed then and I have believed since that the failure by *The Irish Times* to enter the Sunday market was a lost opportunity. Had it done so, it would have opened a whole new range of opportunities, editorial and commercial, for itself. And the shape of the Sunday newspaper market in Ireland, dominated as it is by the *Sunday Independent* and the *Sunday Times,* would have been very different.

Louis O'Neill recognised the desirability of our expanding into the Sunday market. But he did not believe that the Uniman press could sustain the additional printing load that would be required on Saturdays. I accepted that, of course. But I always felt that other printing options might have been explored elsewhere on the island, or even in Britain, in order to get a toehold on the Sunday market while we still could. Any of these options would have been costly. But the long-term, strategic benefit would have been the breaking of our dependency on a single title.

Relations between Louis and Tom became increasingly strained. Tom seemed to draw the members of the Trust closer around him. Finally, Irish Times Publications Ltd, the 'outer' board that comprised most of the middle-ranking executives of the organisation, ceased to operate. After one stormy board meeting, at which editorial and commercial managers expressed their frustrations, the board ceased to meet. Later it was wound up.

In early 1999 the final blow-up occurred between Louis and Tom. This occurred after Tom had decided to stand down as chairman of the company but to remain in position as chairman of the Trust. The new chairman of the board was to be Don Reid. Louis saw Don Reid's appointment as an affront—he understood Don to have the powers of an executive chairman, although Don and Tom McDowell insisted this was not the case.

Louis took retirement and stood down at the end of June 1999. I made the farewell speech for him in the newsroom, stressing his long and successful career. It was an emotional occasion, presaging further difficulties yet to come.

| A LITIGANT CALLED ALBERT

Charles Haughey was being traduced as the epitome of all that was wrong with Fianna Fáil, Albert Reynolds was being touted as the acceptable face of the party.

—SEÁN DUIGNAN

A senior civil servant—a good friend of mine, although he did not broadcast the fact—once told me he was on a flight out of Dublin and found himself sitting beside Albert Reynolds, then some years out of his period in office as Taoiseach.

The civil servant opened his *Irish Times* and began to leaf through the pages, making an approving remark about some story on page 1. Albert nudged him in the ribs. 'That crowd at *The Irish Times*. They'd do you down if they could. They'd be out to get you. I don't understand them at all.' The civil servant did not seek to draw the former Taoiseach out any further. Had he done so, I suspect, he would have got little chance to read his newspaper during the flight.

Albert Reynolds came to office obsessed with the media and promising to 'let in the light' in his relations with them. Then he promptly set about suing them, and found himself wondering why he was getting a bad press. His relationship with *The Irish Times* was especially troubled. I am still unsure why this was. But I think he probably did not understand what made a newspaper like ours act in the way it did—I think there was a blind spot in his field of vision. In turn, I believe, we probably failed to understand certain sensitivities in his psychological make-up. There was a gap in understanding between his world and that of the newspaper.

When he did step down, I failed to be as generous as I should have been, in acknowledging his contribution, in particular, to the Northern Ireland peace process. In part, that was because his contribution was not then fully in the public domain. In part it reflected the abysmal relationship between him and the newspaper. When I left the editorship in 2002, I acknowledged that we had been less than generous to him in what we wrote when he was leaving office.

Perhaps the seminal moment in Albert Reynolds's relationship with *The Irish Times* was in May 1990 when Dáil Éireann established a judicial inquiry into the beef processing industry, under the chairmanship of the President of the High

Court, Mr Justice Liam Hamilton. It was said this would be one of the longest and biggest inquiries in the history of the State.

How was the newspaper to cover this behemoth? A group of us sat in the editor's office, growing ever more gloomy at the prospect of assigning relays of reporters and filling pages with descriptions of production processes in boning-factories. It was Maev-Ann Wren who came up with the idea of having Fintan O'Toole cover the tribunal. He had just returned to the newspaper after a year's leave of absence with the Abbey Theatre.

It was an intriguing notion. But could it work? Could a theatre critic and an opinion columnist do what was essentially a job of courtroom reporting? Maev-Ann was insistent. 'He'll be brilliant. He'll bring it alive in a way that nobody else could.'

The news editor was sceptical. 'He's never done hard news.' Journalists can be among the most conservative people on earth. But he agreed to give it a try.

And thus began one of the most complex yet effective exercises in Irish journalism that I can remember. Fintan installed himself in Dublin Castle. There, day after day, week in week out, he cut through the proceedings like a hot knife through butter. He reduced complex arguments to simple English and summarised tortuous evidence in a way that somehow rendered it palatable. His coverage changed what might have been a dull, impenetrable and boring process into daily, accessible theatre. And it set a standard for others to follow—which they did.

And, of course, Albert Reynolds was the star of the show. Any hope he might have had that the reporting of the tribunal might be lost in dull swathes of print was dashed.

Albert came to office in an aurora of media goodwill. He had dislodged Haughey and swept away many of his *apparatchiks* in appointing his new Cabinet. The mass-dismissal of Haughey's Ministers became known in political circles, not very imaginatively, as the 'night of the long knives'.

Albert promised an end to secrecy and 'Golden Circles'. His appointment of Seán Duignan as Government Press Secretary was taken as an indicator of a new openness and honesty. Duignan ('Diggy' to all) was RTÉ's popular and ultra-professional political correspondent. Nobody chosen from the Irish media corps could better personify Albert's declared intentions.

On his election as Taoiseach, 6 February 1992, I wrote a welcoming editorial:

Yesterday was a healing day for Fianna Fáil. Albert Reynolds became leader . . . Mr Reynolds handled himself with assurance, openness and showing just about the right amount of steel at his press conference . . . few, either within the party or outside of its ranks, will doubt that a significant new force is about to be felt in Irish public life.

The truth was that the national media had, at best, a partial understanding of what made Albert Reynolds tick. He had come from a background that few of the Dublin press corps understood or empathised with: show-bands, ballrooms and his successful pet-food factory near Longford.

Journalists had written many profiles of him, naturally, as he rose through the political ranks. They tended to concentrate on the factory, the show-business years and his brief proprietorship of a local newspaper, *The Longford News*. There was an insufficient attempt—by any of us—to read the mind of the man behind the story.

Albert also knew many journalists. He went to the Press Ball. He mixed affably with the Leinster House press gallery. He and his wife were friends with some of the more prominent social columnists, notably Angela Phelan of the *Sunday Tribune* and later of the *Irish Independent*.

But few journalists knew Albert Reynolds, beyond the superficialities of these encounters. They did not know that behind the wise-cracking, take-me-for-what-I-am conviviality, there was a man of complex uncertainties, with a gambler's streak, an intuitive ability to make a political compromise and a sometimes contradictory insistence on having things his own way.

Seán Duignan recalls the sense of foreboding with which he realised that Reynolds, in spite of his declared intentions of openness, was, in effect, going on the offensive against sections of the media, and against *The Irish Times* in particular.

Reynolds initiated a Thursday afternoon on-the-record briefing that might last up to an hour, with the political correspondents in Leinster House. Duignan was horrified. It could only end in disaster, he reckoned. He recalls explaining this arrangement to his Downing Street counterpart, Gus O'Donnell, who headed Prime Minister John Major's information and media services.

'It doesn't matter how you do it,' O'Donnell told Duignan. 'Find a way to break out of that system before it breaks the Taoiseach.' But the Thursday briefings endured. And in the event, neither they nor any other contact between Reynolds and the media had any direct part in his downfall. When he was obliged to resign it was because of failures within the administration and the government's lack of frankness with Dáil Éireann.

Duignan wrote subsequently of Reynolds in his book *One Spin on the Merry-go-Round*: 'To a large extent he had led a charmed media existence since bursting on to the national scene in 1977. Even his political opponents saw him as, at worst, a genial go-getting operator, an astute self-made millionaire with an impressive ministerial track record. When Charles Haughey was being traduced as the epitome of all that was wrong with Fianna Fáil, Albert Reynolds was being touted as the acceptable face of the party.'

The key to Reynolds's ill-fated relationship with the media is probably revealed in Duignan's recollection of a conversation he had with the Taoiseach soon after he took office.

'Soon after becoming Taoiseach, he told me how he felt about . . . allegations.

Irrespective of the cost, he was not prepared to abide by Haughey's acceptance of the conventional wisdom that it would be counter-productive for him (Haughey) to take legal proceedings against those who vilified and smeared him.

'I nervously tried to interrupt; "But Taoiseach . . ." Reynolds was adamant: "I don't care, Diggy. I'm not going to take that kind of thing lying down. Charlie felt there was nothing he could do about it, but if they tell lies about me, I will sue them, and to hell with the consequences."'

He was as good as his word to Diggy. Within a few weeks, he had three sets of libel proceedings in train with the promise of more to come. *The Irish Times* was first in the firing-line.

Reynolds's action against *The Irish Times* was on foot of an article contributed to the opinion page by the economist Raymond Crotty in the run-up to the Maastricht referendum. Crotty was a well-known and respected, if slightly eccentric, anti-European campaigner, who was opposed to the Single Market and the extension of the European Union.

In the course of his article, Crotty criticised Irish Ministers who were in favour of closer links with the EU, citing Albert Reynolds as one such Minister who had benefited from Europe by securing funding from Brussels for his pet-food factory, C & D Foods Ltd. It was in the closing days of Charles Haughey's leadership and it was clear that Albert Reynolds was a probable successor.

When Reynolds's solicitors wrote to us, claiming that the article defamed their client, we sent the article to senior counsel for an opinion. The answer came back that, yes, there was at least an innuendo that he had used his privilege to feather his own business interests. We consulted our solicitors again. Andrew O'Rorke, the partner at Hayes and Sons who now dealt with much of our libel business, could not act for us in this case. His close involvement with Fianna Fáil would have constituted a conflict of interest. The senior partner, Adrian Glover, took the case. It was agreed that he would talk to 'the other side' to see how the matter might best be dealt with.

Meanwhile the issue of who would be leader of Fianna Fáil, and Taoiseach, was about to be decided. At this point, the picture becomes cloudy. Albert won the contest to succeed Haughey. When Seán Duignan took over as Press Secretary, the cases against *The Irish Times* had not been resolved and appeared to be going ahead.

Seán Duignan quotes Albert Reynolds as saying that a prompt apology from *The Irish Times* would have satisfied him. 'The problem with *The Irish Times* was that there had been foot-dragging in D'Olier Street,' he wrote. 'The only way he could guard his reputation was by recourse to law. Neither would he be satisfied merely to go through the motions "for the optics". As part of any settlement, he would be seeking financial recompense and costs. "Otherwise they'll just laugh and go on as before."'

Diggy continues his account of what was clearly an unhappy encounter:

In vain I tried to point out that, in the eyes of the law, Albert Reynolds was no better than any man in the street, so that a rich newspaper like *The Irish Times* need have no compunction about defending themselves in court if they had a legal leg to stand upon (for the publicity and circulation boost alone) and that a Taoiseach would have infinitely more to lose (including possibly his job) should the verdict go against him. 'You're on a loser, Taoiseach,' I said, 'the media stick together on this kind of thing and they have long memories.' 'They would have come after me at any rate,' he responded, 'but this just might make them that bit more careful.'

It was then that I told him that Conor Brady had emphasised to me that *The Irish Times* bore him no ill-will, that they were prepared to pay substantial damages etc. but they would like to know the money went to charity. He reared up: 'They have a bloody cheek. That's their way of saying I should never have taken them on—that they're right and I'm wrong—tell them I'll spend every shagging penny of the money.'

At *The Irish Times* we saw the encounter with Reynolds in a very different light. Our advice from senior counsel was that the article was indeed defamatory of Albert Reynolds. *The Irish Times* in those days had a simple, and not always sensible, approach once we had formal advice that we had defamed someone. We owned up and took whatever steps we could to minimise the damage both to the offended party and to our own coffers.

So we recognised that we had to put things to rights for Albert Reynolds. We sent our lawyers to his to acknowledge this and to see how best it might be done. There was no reluctance on our part to make an apology and to do whatever else might be necessary, within reason, to put the issue to bed.

I did, however, view this defamation as being somewhat different from others. Neither *The Irish Times* itself in its editorial column, nor any of its employees, had made any allegation against Albert Reynolds. It had carried an article offered by a public figure, himself a candidate for office, on an issue of legitimate public interest in the run-up to a referendum. This is what newspapers and other media are there to do, when issues of importance are submitted to the test of the people's will within the democratic process.

The newspaper, I reasoned, had a duty to correct Raymond Crotty's allegation and to put the record straight, with equal prominence to the first article. It also had a duty to pay Mr Reynolds's legal costs. But it would be unjust, surely, for the newspaper to have to carry additional, heavy financial penalties for doing its duty.

The case had started while Albert Reynolds was a Minister. But now he was Taoiseach. And as Taoiseach he had promised to 'let in the light'. He had opened his doors to the political reporters. In time, he undertook to look anew on the National Newspapers of Ireland (NNI) campaign to have the libel law overhauled and changed. I could not believe that the same Albert Reynolds would wish to extract the maximum penalty from a newspaper that found itself, *bona fide*, in the position we were in.

I could hardly have made a greater miscalculation. Our lawyers talked to 'the other side'. The discussions were inconclusive. It was agreed however that any apology or retraction would be best held over until the contest for the leadership of the Fianna Fáil party was out of the way. I was asked if we would agree to this by Hayes and Sons and I did so.

Then it was suggested somewhere between the lawyers that the damage done to Mr Reynolds's reputation might be alleviated by having us publish *another* article about C & D Pet Food Ltd, setting out the correct details of its rise from small beginnings to being a market-leader in its field. This we also did and the article was duly published.

All of these moves I interpreted as signals of an amicable resolution to the problem, certainly a resolution that would stop short of court proceedings.

There was also a much wider context to this case, as far as a newspaper like *The Irish Times* was concerned. The NNI was continuing to press for libel reform and we needed a Taoiseach who would be onside in that issue. Perhaps naïvely, we believed that as a former newspaper proprietor, Albert would have some empathy with our condition. If a bitter row was slowed to drag on and end in court proceedings, it was likely that his goodwill to our cause would be lost.

————

I was not so much worried about the cash impact on *The Irish Times* of having to settle with Reynolds. By far my greater fear was that the example of a Taoiseach suing for damages in these circumstances would do serious damage to the relationship between the media and the political process. It would stifle debate and make publications extremely wary about carrying anything critical of one political figure, written by another. Nothing could be further from the hoped-for liberalisation of the laws that we had been pressing for.

I called Seán Duignan and talked him through my worries. As he wrote subsequently, I explained that we were not unwilling to make a cash donation somewhere as further earnest of our contrition. But, I warned, if Albert Reynolds goes along this path, no good will come of it for anyone—politicians or media.

'Diggy' was clearly embarrassed on the telephone. 'I know, I know,' he said, 'but this man just isn't taking my advice on this. But I'll do what I can. Maybe it'll fade away.'

It didn't, of course. With horror, I learned some months afterwards, Albert Reynolds was going ahead with the case and was claiming substantial damages. I felt we had been let down. We had done everything that was reasonably possible to undo the impact of Crotty's article.

The other media organisations had watched our encounter with Reynolds with a great deal more than academic interest. He was already suing others, including RTÉ, over comments on air by the witty and controversial John A. Murphy, the Cork historian.

Now they were bemused. I had numerous telephone calls and notes of support from editors, programme makers and journalists. At one fell swoop, Reynolds had succeeded in squandering the entire capital of media good will with which he had come to office.

Interestingly, the issue of investment in Albert Reynolds's pet-food company was to emerge again in circumstances that caused further grief for him. In June 1994, it became known that two members of a wealthy Arab family named Masri had been granted Irish citizenship under the little-known 'Business Migration Scheme' which had been set up to attract foreign investment to Ireland. It also emerged that the Masri family had invested £1 million in C & D Foods.

What became known as the 'Passports for Sale' row blew up between Fianna Fáil and their Labour partners in coalition. Reynolds protested that he no longer had any involvement in the day-to-day running of the company. Why should not C & D Foods take advantage of a scheme that was open to anyone else in business if they could find the opportunity of attracting investors?

Albert Reynolds insisted that the matter had been dealt with properly and at arm's length by the Department of Justice. Dick Spring examined the files and declared the deal to have been done in an 'ethical, above board and arm's length way'.

An outcry followed in the media and in the Dáil. Although some of the columnists were withering on the issue, I insisted that *The Irish Times* take a muted stance in its leader comment, lest we be accused of continuing some agenda from the Crotty case. In any event, I believed the facts spoke for themselves. Michael McDowell, the Progressive Democrats' spokesman, trained his fire on Spring in the Dáil, describing him as 'morally brain-dead'. Spring promised a reform of the scheme and in due course it was abandoned.

The high point of Reynolds's brief reign as Taoiseach was undoubtedly his securing of the 1993 Downing Street Declaration that cleared the way for the IRA ceasefire in 1994. It was arguably the very qualities that got him into so much trouble otherwise, that enabled Reynolds to barge and bluff his way through the quagmire of Anglo-Irish relations and to lever the Sinn Féin/IRA axis to a new level of dialogue with the two governments and with the constitutional political parties.

He had taken the wise and fruitful decision to invite Martin Mansergh to remain in position as his adviser on Northern Ireland. But it was his gambling instinct that enabled him to stay in the game of trying to lure the Sinn Féin/IRA leaders to the peace table, even when everything suggested that violence was set to continue more or less indefinitely. IRA bombs continued to blast London and elsewhere, taking innocent life. The John Major government could hardly be kept in the dialogue. The Hume-Adams process was under terrible pressure, as I gleaned from discussions with the British Ambassador, David Blatherwick, and with Anglo-Irish division officials at Iveagh House.

Paradoxically, *The Irish Times* was the only newspaper that consistently supported Hume–Adams at this crucial time. We got little credit or thanks for it from Reynolds or any of his political supporters. But we did get acknowledgment from the chief of Anglo-Irish section and later Secretary General of the Department of Foreign Affairs, Dermot Gallagher and, indeed, from John Hume.

Albert Reynolds's tenure in office was marked by controversies that appeared to come back, time and again, to issues of his credibility.

──────

Mr Justice Hamilton's report into the beef-processing industry was inconclusive in many respects and left some important questions unanswered. It was scarcely a model of clarity. Albert Reynolds was insistent that he had been 'vindicated' by the report. The taking of evidence during the inquiry had brought him into public confrontation with the PD leader, Des O'Malley. When the report was finally published, in July 1994, Labour had replaced the PDS as Fianna Fáil's coalition partners after a general election. Albert Reynolds nearly came to a terminal clash with Dick Spring over the release of Hamilton's report.

When he had to vacate his office as Taoiseach in November 1994 it was caused by his taking a calculated gamble that Labour would buckle over his appointment of Harry Whelehan as President of the High Court. Whelehan, as Attorney General, had come in for heavy criticism over the handling by his office of charges against the paedophile priest Brendan Smyth. When it emerged that there had been an earlier, similar case, involving another religious, named Duggan, the tensions between the coalition partners in government could not be contained.

Reynolds pressed ahead with his proposed appointment of Harry Whelehan to the second highest judicial post in the State. But Labour stood firm and Albert's brief period as Taoiseach passed into history.

For a time, it appeared that Fianna Fáil might remain in Government, albeit under a different leader. It was a report in *The Irish Times* that finally brought the Labour-Fianna Fáil alliance to an end. On 18 November I wrote the editorial that marked the resignations of Harry Whelehan and Albert Reynolds:

> With the resignations of Mr Albert Reynolds as Taoiseach and Mr Harry Whelehan SC as President of the High Court, a considerable measure of dignity has been retrieved in the public life of the State. The resignations came not a moment too soon. Words can only inadequately describe the mixed emotions of anger, bafflement and shame that have been aroused among the public at large by the chain of events that started with the revelations in the Brendan Smyth extradition case . . .

> Both men comported themselves with propriety and grace. Mr Reynolds is not silver-tongued. But he expressed himself with a direct and unvarnished

eloquence which might easily lead an uninformed observer to the belief that here was a straight-talking man, imbued with simple verities, caught by cruel mischance in the vortex of public events. He has some things to his credit which the shambles of recent weeks can never take from him: the moving forward of the peace process; the furtherance with Mr Spring of a laudable programme for government; the sustaining of a measure of economic growth. . . . On a personal level there will be sympathy for Mr Reynolds and there will be an acknowledgment that he performed his closing act well. But there will be no crocodile tears for a Taoiseach who was swiftly revealed as a political bully behind a smiling face, who showed a cynical indifference to those principles of public office which did not suit his purposes and whose actions, once in power, belied so much of the principle which he enunciated in his campaign to get there. Public life will not be greatly the poorer for his departure from office.

I later came to regret the last line. It was unnecessary.

Labour had, in effect, got the head of a Fianna Fáil Taoiseach. Spring had insisted when the government was first formed, that it would stand or fall on the issue of trust. Now, it appeared that Labour was still willing to do business with Fianna Fáil but under a new leader. For the second time, Dick Spring was about to recant on his declaration in the adjournment debate of the 26th Dáil.

On 19 November I editorialised:

There is a sense of déjà vu about the present proceedings in and about the Fianna Fáil parliamentary party. The script and narrative for the unmaking of Albert Reynolds are eerily reminiscent of those for the unmaking of Charles Haughey three years ago. Only the names are different . . .

But is it credible that the mere fact of his (Bertie Ahern) replacing Albert Reynolds as leader of Fianna Fáil can be sufficient to satisfy Labour once again that the party has been purged, purified, reformed? Is there nothing more to Labour's disquiet with Fianna Fáil than the personality and character of the outgoing leader, Mr Reynolds?

The Government that Dick Spring formed with Albert Reynolds was a good one in many respects. But in his undertaking to the electorate that he could police Fianna Fáil to higher standards of behaviour, Mr Spring failed dismally.

But the drama had not come to an end. By the first week of December it was clear that Spring was about to re-enter government with Fianna Fáil, now led by Reynolds's successor, Bertie Ahern.

The media, and the population in general, had grown weary of the weeks of bickering and wrangling. With Christmas approaching there was a general, almost desperate wish that Spring and Ahern would conclude their negotiations, get on with the business of government and allow the country to get back to normal.

On the morning of 4 December, as I was about to leave home for the office, I received a telephone call from our political correspondent, Geraldine Kennedy.

'They were all in on it,' she announced.

'Who? In on what?'

'Virtually the whole Fianna Fáil side of the Cabinet. They knew about the Duggan case all along. It wasn't just Albert misinformed the Dáil. The others knew and they said nothing.'

I knew that if Geraldine Kennedy said she had a story, she probably had a good source. The implications of what she was saying were serious. But I asked her anyway. 'You're sure of your source?'

'I wouldn't be ringing you if I weren't.' Brusque might be one word to describe her when she had a story.

I discussed the story with her for a few minutes and then made one or two telephone calls to my own contacts. Nobody seemed to be aware of anything. Clearly someone had been marking her cards.

We held a special conference in the early afternoon. When the main conference of the day opened at 3.30 we had a cryptic one-line note on page 1: *There will be a good political story.*

It seemed as if nothing now could save the Fianna Fáil-Labour government. Nonetheless, I opted for safety when I wrote an editorial to accompany the story.

Would any prudent businessman . . . act as Dick Spring is now about to do? Would he proceed to merge with another enterprise whose head had been driven from office for misleading the company's shareholders and whose fellow directors had knowingly supported him in so doing, in spite of detailed, contrary advice from their legal advisers?

It is now apparent that virtually all of Mr Reynolds's Cabinet colleagues were up to their necks in the misleading of the Dáil. It is beyond credulity that Dick Spring will take their sins upon his own head and carry them back into office.

The rest, as they say, is history. On 7 December, when it became clear that Spring and his colleagues were about to leave the Cabinet, I wrote:

Mr Spring's and Labour's judgment stand severely indicted in this sorry saga. The facts which forced them to finally abandon their plans to re-enter Fianna Fáil would have been available to them had they asked . . . up to yesterday morning it appeared that Labour was unwilling to face what virtually every other observer of the political scene could read only too clearly: that Fianna Fáil had not told the whole story. Better late than never.

Albert Reynolds passed into political history. His star appeared as if it might shine again when he emerged as a possible presidential candidate in 1997. But by then he was a liability to Fianna Fáil and his attempt to secure a nomination was scuttled in favour of Mary McAleese.

Albert Reynolds's days of suing newspapers did not end with *The Irish Times*. Ultimately he foundered on the rock of his own litigiousness, having sued *The Sunday Times* in the London courts. The jury found that indeed he had been defamed but assessed the damages to his reputation at 1 penny. He appealed the case and declared himself happy with the outcome. But the process had cost him dearly.

In retrospect, the relationship between Albert Reynolds and *The Irish Times* was perhaps predictable. We stood for many of the things that he was not and *visa versa*. But it was an unhappy episode and it did not bring out the best in us.

I have often wondered if the battle-lines were drawn during those first few weeks when Fintan O'Toole was dispatched to Dublin Castle and began a daily narrative that was one of the most telling exercises in Irish journalism in my professional lifetime.

Albert Reynolds was desperately worried about the outcome of Mr Justice Hamilton's inquiry. His entire reputation rested upon it. *The Irish Times's* assignment of one of its intellectual heavyweights to the coverage of the inquiry —and the searing analysis that flowed as a result—may have seemed a signal of hostile intent to the Taoiseach. It had not been intended as such.

Perhaps as much as we failed to understand the character and makeup of Albert Reynolds, he may have failed to understand that the newspaper was simply doing its job to the best of its ability.

23

BERTIE AND THE SUPERINTENDENT

*I may be 100. But I was born on February 29th. So I've only had
25 birthdays. No wonder I feel well.*
                                —Former Superintendent WILLIAM GEARY

After the bruising relationship between *The Irish Times* and Albert
Reynolds, I resolved that I would put my best foot forward with the new
Fianna Fáil leader, Bertie Ahern.

I did not know Bertie beyond occasional social encounters. He seemed a
genial, likeable man, if a bit shy and ill-at-ease. I had first met him at a charity
fund-raising dinner in the Burlington Hotel when he was Lord Mayor of Dublin.
Our table included Gay and Kathleen Byrne and the actor Peter Ustinov, so the
conversation was lively. But Bertie seemed ill-at-ease all evening, pulling
nervously at his mayoral chain.

When he was elected as leader of the party in succession to Albert Reynolds, I
resolved that he should be given a fair wind by *The Irish Times*. I described him
editorially as an 'accomplished and experienced Minister . . .' who was 'popular,
approachable and direct'.

Not all of the columnists were as kind and I intervened in one or two instances
to challenge some offensive adjectives in their copy. It was one of a relatively few
occasions in which I told a columnist that I was exercising my editor's prerogative
to change the content of an opinion piece. If they wished to withdraw the
column, they were at liberty to do so. But it did not come to that.

I extended an invitation to Bertie Ahern and his partner, Celia Larkin, to come
to the house for dinner one Saturday night shortly after he became leader. None
of the other guests were media people or politicians—in order to make the
evening as relaxing and non-threatening as possible. It was a very pleasant
encounter, with little serious discussion of politics but with a good deal of banter
and many funny stories.

Dealing with Bertie Ahern was certainly less problematic than with Albert Reynolds or Charles Haughey. He was undemanding in his approach to coverage. He was courteous when he got a good show in the columns but he did not sulk or show any irritation when things might be pitched against him, as they often were. He wisely drew on the skills of the experienced P.J. Mara who had served Haughey so well for so long. P.J. smoothed out misunderstandings and potential difficulties on many occasions.

The Irish Times and PA Management ran an annual award for management excellence and a tradition had grown up that the Taoiseach would make the presentations, usually at a champagne reception. In 1998 the word came back from the Taoiseach's office that he would not be available to do the honours this year. The civil servant who conveyed the news said something about the Taoiseach's schedule becoming very crowded and that he needed to shed commitments.

I met P.J. at a private event a few days later and mentioned the matter to him. The following day he called to say that the Taoiseach would, in fact, be glad to attend and do the honours.

We did not spare Bertie Ahern at *The Irish Times*. Dick Walsh and others gave him a hard time, especially as it became clear that he had seriously misjudged in the case of Ray Burke, appointing him as Minister for Foreign Affairs against a background of considerable suspicion.

But he remained invariably courteous and unflappable. There were regular invitations for an informal meal and chat. I was struck by his ability to remember names and faces and dates. No matter who I took with me from the senior staff he knew their spouse's name, what their children were doing and where they lived.

On one occasion Pat O'Hara, our executive editor, came with me to dinner to meet Bertie. Pat was (is) a great sports fan and he and Bertie struck it off well together. The next time they met, Bertie took up the conversation with Pat about racing, golf and football where they had left off as if they were the firmest friends. Pat was not a man easily impressed but he was mightily amused by this.

———

I can put no long-term adjudication on Bertie Ahern at this writing beyond my account of one instance in which I found him honourable, thoughtful and decent. It concerned a man called William Geary.

In November 1998 I received a letter from a retired superintendent of the Gardaí, Tim Leahy, who lived in Co Clare. Leahy set out details of a remarkable case concerning another former superintendent, of an earlier generation, who had been dismissed by order of the Executive Council (the Cabinet) in 1928. Geary had been superintendent in West Clare, based at Kilrush. It was a strong IRA district, with a high crime rate and there were frequent clashes between the

Gardaí and extreme republicans who refused to accept either the Treaty or Éamon de Valera's 1923 'dump arms' order to the IRA.

Geary was the son of a well-off farming family from Co Limerick. He had trained at Atlantic College and had been a merchant navy officer before joining the Gardaí and being commissioned as a young superintendent. But his career in the Garda had not gone well. In the summer of 1928, he was arrested by Special Branch officers from Garda Headquarters and accused of taking a bribe of £100 from the IRA.

He protested his innocence but he was ordered to headquarters where he was confined in the Officers' Mess for a number of days before being handed his official notice of dismissal. In disgrace, the 30-year-old Geary left for America, never to return to Ireland.

I had known of the Geary case in a vague way. In 1973, when I was researching for my post-graduate thesis at UCD, I interviewed the former head of the Special Branch, Colonel David Neligan, then living in retirement in Booterstown, Co Dublin. Neligan had arrested Geary and served him with his dismissal notice.

Neligan told me about William Geary, adding that he had never known for certain if he was guilty or otherwise. 'But he's probably long dead now,' he told me. 'He went off to America and was never heard of again.'

But what Tim Leahy had to tell me in 1998 was that William Geary was *not* dead. He was alive and well, in his 101st year and living in New York, still protesting his innocence of the charge that had been levelled against him more than 70 years previously.

Tim Leahy was planning to write an article for the *Garda Review* to highlight Geary's claims of innocence. He wanted to know if I had any additional information about the case. I found myself intrigued by the matter. Neligan was long dead, but I distinctly remembered his expression of uncertainty about Geary's guilt.

I wrote back to Tim Leahy and suggested that *The Irish Times* might be more likely to shake the cobwebs of officialdom than the *Garda Review*. I offered to put a reporter on the case and Tim Leahy readily agreed to help in any way he could.

It was coming up to Christmas. We had a young American reporter, Margaret Ward, from New York, working on contract at the newspaper. I knew she was planning to go home to New York for Christmas. I met Margaret in the newsroom. 'How would you like to pick up an interesting assignment in New York over Christmas and get *The Irish Times* to pay your fare home?' I inquired. She jumped at the idea when I outlined what I had learned from Tim Leahy. Then she telephoned him and briefed herself fully before her visit.

Two weeks later she was back with an extraordinary file of information and a compelling, if sad, tale to tell. She had visited William Geary at his apartment in New York. She had found a sprightly, bow-tied and impeccably-groomed centenarian, still insisting on his innocence as he had done from the day in July 1928 when he was first accused of taking a bribe. She outlined his life story.

Geary had emigrated to the US in 1928. He had concealed his story from a succession of employers. He had worked in various jobs and had eventually risen to a relatively senior position with Edison, the power company. He had enrolled at Columbia University and shown himself to have considerable academic ability. In World War II he had served with the US air force and was posted overseas although not in a combat role. He had married and now had two adult daughters who, in turn, had their own families. His wife had predeceased him by some years.

I questioned Margaret about what she made of William Geary. 'I think he's telling the truth,' she said. 'His story has been absolutely consistent since the day he was accused. What he wants now is to have the file on his case released from the Department of Justice. He says he's certain there's no evidence against him.'

What I had not known, until Margaret handed me a sheaf of photocopied letters, was that William Geary had been lobbying successive Ministers for Justice and TDs for more than 20 years, asking that his file be released in order to give him the opportunity to clear his name. A number of his petitions had been supported by a judge of the Supreme Court of the State of New York, John Collins, who was Geary's godson. There had even been some publicity for his case in the columns of *The Limerick Leader*. But it had all come to nothing. Now, in what had to be the closing years of his life, it seemed as if William Geary would go his grave without clearing his name.

The Department of Justice had, predictably, refused all previous requests for the release of the Geary file. It was graded under the highest levels of State secrecy. It could not be released, if at all, until 2017.

Margaret wrote her story. It was a judicious mixture of factual accuracy and colour writing. She repeated Geary's request that his file be released. The picture editor, Dermot O'Shea, arranged for a photographer to take shots of William Geary at his apartment. The photographs bore out Margaret's description. They showed a dapper, bright-eyed gentleman, erect and alert in spite of his years. We ran the story and the pictures in January 1999.

I met Bertie Ahern at a function the following week and raised the Geary case with him. 'Talk to my office tomorrow,' he said. 'I'll look into it.' The next day I wrote to Paddy Teahon, the Secretary General at the Department of the Taoiseach, and then called him. I was not going to take the risk of being fobbed off by a junior civil servant and I did not want to give officialdom the chance to reach for the Official Secrets Act. 'This file is going to be released anyway in 2017,' I explained to Teahon. 'Geary certainly isn't going to be around then. So they might as well open it up now while he's still alive.'

Margaret in the meantime was still following the story and maintaining contact with Geary and Judge Collins. Two days later she arrived at my office. She was grinning from ear to ear. 'They've agreed to release the file,' she said. 'It's on its way now to William Geary.'

'Can we get a copy of it?' I asked.

'Collins wants to see it first and go through it for Mr Geary. After that Collins says he will see if Mr Geary wants it made public. If he does, we get it first.'

William Geary may have felt certain that the file contained no evidence against him. But he was playing his cards close to his chest nonetheless. Or perhaps he was simply being cautious on the advice of his legally-trained godfather. But four or five days later when the file arrived by courier from the US, I realised that the case against William Geary simply did not stack up.

The file of evidence was little more than a narrative of events from Neligan, recounting that a mail intercept on a known IRA man in Clare contained information that Geary had taken a bribe. From there, it recounted how Neligan with other officers had travelled to Clare and confronted Geary. The file—crucially, in my view—recalled Geary's denial. But there was not a whit of evidence in support of the allegation against him.

It seemed to me that in contemporary circumstances it would be impossible to take action against anyone on what was contained in the file. There had been no process of natural justice for William Geary. There had not been any right of representation.

I decided to send the file to Professor Dermot Walsh at the law department of the University of Limerick. Dermot Walsh is the author of the definitive work on the legal framework within which the Garda Síochána operates and he is thoroughly familiar with its internal procedures. It took him only a few hours to put together, in article form, a powerful critique of the case against William Geary. We published it the next day. I wrote an editorial to accompany the story:

> The onus should not be on Mr Geary to disprove his guilt. It should now be upon the State to prove beyond a reasonable doubt that he was guilty as accused in 1928. If that cannot be done he is entitled to be exonerated, to have his name cleared and his honour restored. It is clear from the opinion of Professor Walsh, which is also published today, that Mr Geary was denied natural justice in the manner of his dismissal . . .

> Mr Geary will be 100 years old this month. He reconstructed his life successfully and bravely in the United States and he remains healthy, lucid and committed to clearing his name. The Taoiseach and the Government have responded with humanity to his request to have his files made available. It is now essential that they be examined swiftly and that an early determination be reached on Mr Geary's call for an exoneration of the charges laid against him in 1928. An injustice is an injustice, for all that it may have taken place more than 70 years ago. Mr Geary's longevity may not be unconnected with his determination to see his case resolved. But his time must be limited and the State's further actions must take account of that.

In the afternoon I had a telephone call from Paddy Teahon at the Taoiseach's office telling me that the Taoiseach was personally moved by Mr Geary's plight and by his sustained claim to innocence. The Government was going to announce that William Geary was cleared of any allegation of wrongdoing, that his pension was to be restored and that he was to be given an *ex gratia* payment of £100,000 in acknowledgment of the injustice done to him.

Later that day, I spoke to Judge Collins and then to William Geary, by telephone. Naturally, both men were delighted. Geary became emotional on the telephone. It was a small triumph, I felt, for the newspaper. But it was obviously an event of huge proportions for William Geary. Above all, I felt, it showed a humane streak to Bertie Ahern that had not been evident in previous politicians who had been asked to intervene in the case.

William Geary died in New York in 2004 aged 105 years. He never returned to Ireland, even though Garda Commissioner Pat Byrne had contacted him, sending him greetings and offering him the hospitality of Garda Headquarters if he were to travel.

In March 2003, when I was a visiting professor at John Jay College at the City University of New York, I received a message one day that William Geary knew I was in New York and wanted to invite me to his home to say 'thank you and to share a meal in friendship'.

Ann and I travelled to Queens to his apartment one sunny afternoon. He greeted us at the door, immaculately presented in his trademark bow-tie, shoes gleaming, his trousers in a knife-edge crease. One could still see in him the gildy young officer he once had been. It was an emotional encounter. We were joined by his daughter, Anne Wallace, a Washington DC lawyer, and we adjourned for lunch to a local restaurant.

When we were leaving he presented me with a walking-stick which he had fashioned himself from beech wood, with his name 'GEARY' stamped on the side. It is among my treasures.

24

ON IRISH JOURNALISM

All that is required for success in journalism is rat-like cunning, a plausible manner and basic literary ability.

—NICHOLAS TOMALIN

At its best, Irish journalism can probably be as good as any other in the English-speaking world. In some respects, it may actually *be* the best. The Irish facility for language that breeds Nobel laureates and acclaimed writers in every *genre* sometimes infuses the newspapers, the magazines and the airwaves. Writers like Maeve Binchy, Miriam Lord, Tom Humphreys, Gene Kerrigan, Kevin Myers, Eileen Battersby, Nuala O'Faolain, Kathy Sheridan and many others weave words in Irish newspapers that can rank with pure literature.

At its worst, Irish journalism can be parochial, sensational, unprincipled and unprofessional. Increasingly, in recent years, it has tended to reflect the absence of any mechanism of public accountability, along with the pressures of growing competitiveness and a drive to maximising profit by the operating companies.

It has played an important role, often with courage, in the exposure of corruption and other evils in Irish society. It has probed deeply and determinedly in order to unmask the evil of sexual abuse of the young and vulnerable. It has worked effectively, in undeclared alliance, with elected representatives, lawyers, judges and other figures, to reveal the bribery and corruption that infected elements of the political and business communities in the closing decades of the twentieth century.

It has also, in some instances, allowed itself to be abused by proprietors and publishers, intent on pandering to the lowest tastes of voyeurism and character assassination. In other instances it has dishonoured some of its fundamental principles and time-tested precepts. Sometimes this has arisen through laziness and indifference. Sometimes it has happened in order to satisfy the demands of profit-driven editors and publishers.

———

In order to understand modern Irish journalism, it is necessary to know something of where it came from. Its roots lie in the great political struggles between nationalism and unionism in the latter half of the nineteenth century.

There were newspapers and news-sheets long before that. The Belfast *News Letter* was founded in 1737 and claims the honour of being the oldest daily newspaper printed in Britain or Ireland. But it was the rising tide of Irish separatism that provided the impetus for the establishment of new daily newspapers in the big cities as well as some hundreds of local or regional newspapers in the towns, usually published weekly.

The Irish Times was founded in 1859, initially as a liberal Home Rule newspaper and promising to cater for 'the most progressive elements' in Irish society. *The Freeman's Journal* was founded in 1763 and survived until 1924. The *Limerick Chronicle* had been set up in 1766.

Economic, technological and social factors were also important. The modest prosperity that came in the decades after the Famine meant that small businesses, including printers, began to be established. The spread of literacy as a result of the development of the national education system meant there was a growing market for newspapers. Improvements in printing technology made it possible to produce newspapers faster and less expensively than in the past. The high taxes that had been imposed on newspapers were rescinded.

Most of the newspapers, both dailies and weeklies, had clear and strong political affiliations. Many areas had both unionist and nationalist newspapers, offering sharply differing perspectives and views on politics and public affairs.

There was a frequent overlap between politics and newspapers. The proprietor-editor of the local newspaper was often active in party politics and in some instances represented his constituency in the Westminster parliament.

Journalists or 'press men' (there were scarcely any women) had no formal training. A local editor or proprietor would put one or two intelligent young men on a pitiably low wage to report on local news, from the condition of the crops, to proceedings in the courts. Journalism was hardly a secure or well-remunerated avocation although it offered a, sometimes, interesting alternative to life on a small farm or behind a shop counter.

The proprietor-editor, or the hired editor, would have had a good level of education in some instances. There were solicitors and barristers among them. Some became judges.

A small cohort of Irish journalists transferred to Britain and many were successful, rising to eminence in the Fleet Street newspapers. William Howard Russell (1820–1907) who was born near Tallaght, Co Dublin, was without doubt the most celebrated war-correspondent of his time. His reports from Crimea brought down a Prime Minister and changed the way the British army was led and managed. He was knighted in 1895 and his bust stands in St Paul's Cathedral in London.

Standards of accuracy, literacy, grammar and punctuation were generally high across Irish newspapers. An editor's fiercest critic could be the local school-master, or clergy. Perfection of language in what was published was the first line of defence.

In the years leading up to the foundation of the State, Irish journalism had begun to change. The National Union of Journalists (NUJ), a British union, had extended its operations to Ireland by 1909 and was active in most newspapers. Basic pay rates and allowances had been secured and proprietors were restrained from the worst extremes of capriciousness in their hiring and firing practices.

The years between the attainment of Irish independence and the early 1950s saw a lively Irish journalism. *The Irish Press* was anti-establishment, challenging and vigorous. Many of its journalists were imbued with the radicalism that had driven the early Fianna Fáil organisation. *The Irish Times* declined commercially but maintained high editorial standards under John Edward Healy (editor from 1904–1934) and later under R.M. ('Bertie') Smyllie.

But like so many other aspects of Irish life, much of Irish journalism in the 1950s had become dull, passive, conventional and compliant. *The Irish Press* and the *Irish Independent* were two sides of the coin that represented conservative Fianna Fáil and Fine Gael orthodoxies. The liberalism of Smyllie's *Irish Times* and of one or two literary periodicals was exceptional.

There was still no formal training for journalists. And as a way of making a livelihood it was but poorly valued. The overwhelming majority of journalists entered by way of apprenticeship with local newspapers. Very few university graduates considered it as an alternative to teaching or the civil service.

The Irish Times always had a few Trinity College graduates on its staff. R.M. Smyllie, who did not have a university degree (apart from an honorary M. Litt. from TCD), recognised the benefits of having a small *cadre* of classicists and English scholars about him.

At *The Irish Press* and the *Irish Independent* it was not uncommon to find journalists who were also barristers or would-be barristers. Indeed, some of these went on to occupy the highest judicial positions in the land. *The Irish Press* alone was *alma mater* to half-a-dozen judges of the High Court and the Supreme Court.

Formal training for journalists began in the early 1960s as a collaborative effort between the NUJ and the Dublin Newspaper Managers Committee—the employers' combination. An 'Irish Council for the Training of Journalists' was set up, largely through the energies of Richard Roche, a former school-teacher from Co Wexford, who was later to be the deputy editor of the *Irish Independent*. A part-time diploma course was established through the agency of the Dublin City Vocational Education Committee. Based in the Rathmines College of Commerce, it later became a fulltime course. This was the forerunner of the degrees in journalism, at graduate and post-graduate level, that are now offered by the Dublin Institute of Technology.

In the late 1950s and early 1960s, journalism was not an avocation that was eagerly and widely sought-after, either by ambitious school-leavers or by university graduates. It was perceived as insecure, not very well-paid, and it had little of the glamour, influence or status that later accrued to it. It appealed mainly to young men of modest means, sometimes with a flair for English, a sense of curiosity and perhaps a streak of individualism.

But it was also often very dull. Ireland was an insular and still largely agricultural society. It was pious and conventional. Much of the journalist's work was routine attendance at church events, political meetings and farming occasions such as ploughing matches. The reporter's role was frequently that of a deferential stenographer. An occasional murder or an outbreak of agrarian crime might be a God-sent relief from routine. The journalists who had the best of times were the sports reporters.

Like so much else in Ireland, things began to change for Irish journalism through the surge that came in the early to mid-1960s with the adoption of T.K. Whitaker's first and second *Progamme(s) for Economic Expansion.*

Ireland began to become a more complex society. The language and the vocabulary of public life started to change. International linkages began to develop. Irish troops went abroad to the Congo and elsewhere to serve with the UN peace-keeping forces. President John F. Kennedy came to visit. So did Princess Grace of Monaco, the offspring of Irish immigrants to the US. Ireland made its first application to join the European Economic Community. The Roman Catholic Church was changing too, with the calling of the Second Vatican Council by Pope John XXIII. Values and assumptions that had remained unchallenged and unchanged since the Famine were now under scrutiny and review.

And there was television. Newspapers and journalists no longer held the monopoly on the presentation of news and comment. Journalism had to change in order to meet new realities at every level.

The changes in the lives and conditions of journalists were possibly most in evidence at *The Irish Times* and, a little later perhaps, at the other Dublin dailies. Douglas Gageby and Tom McDowell recognised the need to professionalise journalists, to pay them decent salaries and give them secure employment. Gageby saw the need for specialisation, in order to give journalists and their newspapers more authority and accuracy. He also knew that in addition to its core news service, a modern newspaper had to provide comment, guidance and analysis, as well as some entertainment.

Although Sunday newspapers had been experimenting with the genre for some years, the daily columnist—as distinct from the reporter—was born in *The Irish Times* in these years. The newspaper began to recruit trainee journalists from among the young graduates, now coming out of the universities in larger numbers than ever before. There was no formal training for them at *The Irish Times* but there was a *de facto* apprenticeship in which they learned the traditional skills of the business. *The Irish Press* under Tim Pat Coogan followed suit albeit on a smaller scale. The *Irish Independent* also changed, more slowly than *The Irish Times,* but was on the same path by the mid-1960s under the thoughtful editorship of Louis McRedmond.

This was the milieu that was forming when I joined *The Irish Times* in 1969 as one of a number of young graduates from various colleges around Ireland. John Armstrong came from Trinity. Joe Joyce came from UCG. Nell McCafferty came a little later from Queens.

We joined journalists who had come in through provincial newspapers, journalists who had been trained at Rathmines, journalists who had been in religious life, who had been civil servants, teachers, soldiers, lawyers, medics and so on.

In my first week at *The Irish Times* I was taken aside by the gentlemanly and punctilious FOC (Father of the Chapel) of the journalists' union, Pat Nolan. He congratulated me on being appointed to staff, albeit on a trainee basis. He asked me some questions about myself and my background. He queried me about my courses at UCD, nodding appreciatively as I set out details of my curriculum.

'Well,' he said, 'it's good to have young people like you coming into journalism. And you're coming at a time of improvement. We have just secured parity for journalists with clerical officers in some of the semi-state companies.' He saw this as a considerable achievement.

And, of course, it was an achievement, the first of many. Journalists' pay and conditions did not simply rise in the 1970s. They soared. By the late 1970s, as a specialist correspondent or a middle-ranking editor, I was being paid more than my college contemporaries who had entered academe or the civil service or who were still on the lower slopes of the professions.

For all of us there was still very much a sense of being involved in something that was *risqué* and outside of the establishment. We believed we were doing something useful but from a position remote from the centres of real power in Irish society—the Dáil, the Churches, the civil service and so on. I doubt if any of us had any sense of the growing power of the media and their coming influence at the very centre of daily decision-making, across the society they serve.

Very few people did. Those who were involved in the social and political engineering of the new Ireland did not stop to think about the role of the media at all. Even yet, in the twenty-first century, none of the traditional universities— as distinct from those chartered or established in the 1990s—has any department or faculty dedicated to the study of media.

The result was that the growth in influence of the media in contemporary Ireland came about almost unnoticed, almost by stealth. Nor did anyone understand or realise the circle of power that was being woven by the interaction of print, radio, TV and politics.

Rather than square up to it, the authority figures tried to slap it down. In the case of the print media, that was generally by way of libel suits. In the case of broadcasting, the bishops used the crozier and the politicians used the big stick of political power, applied or threatened. At RTÉ there was always a sense that the hand of government was never far away.

It was not until 1995, in the aftermath of the collapse of *The Irish Press*, that any government saw the need for Ireland to take a look at the health of the Irish print media, in the form of the Finlay Commission. The *Report of the Commission on the Newspaper Industry* was published in June 1996. It had sat for nine months under the chairmanship of former Chief Justice T.A. (Tom) Finlay. At this writing not one of its 16 recommendations has been implemented, although the Department of Justice, Equality and Law Reform is preparing legislation for a new Defamation Act and the establishment of some form of press council.

The power of the media in Ireland today may be measured by the proliferation of media consultants and 'spin doctors' employed in government and elsewhere and, indeed, by the growing numbers of firms specialising in media and corporate relations. Figures compiled early in 2005 indicate that the Government is spending in excess of €30 million a year on media consultants—over and above the legions of 'in house' media officers on the payroll of various government departments.

A more subjective measure of the high priority accorded to media management is provided in Seán Duignan's *One Spin on the Merry-go-Round*, p. 7:

> I had been long enough around politicians to appreciate the massive importance they attached to the media. However, it was not until I actually found myself inside the tent that I felt the full seismic force of this awesome phenomenon. The reality is that where politicians are concerned . . . the media is a constant all-consuming passion.

Duignan added in his 'Diary,' 'N.B. They are all media-mad here. This obsession with everything to do with the media cannot be over-emphasised—repeat—cannot be over-emphasised!

———

How and why the Irish media, and Irish journalists, moved from the relative quiescence and marginal role of the past, to their powerful, sought-after status of today could fill another book.

It is a well-documented phenomenon that the power and influence of media, of *represented* reality as distinct from *experienced* reality, increase as a society becomes more complex and more wealthy. Professor Todd Gitlin, of the Journalism School at Columbia University in New York, argues in his book *Media Unlimited*, that in contemporary society we must realise that 'the media' are not simply a collection of 'wondrous gadgets' but a 'central condition of an entire way of life'.

Some events, personalities and technological developments have been pivotal to that process in Ireland. The advent of Irish television and to a lesser extent the liberalisation/modernisation of radio had an immense impact. Politicians, church leaders and other authority figures who had heretofore been protected by their remoteness, could now be interrogated and held to account. If they chose not to engage with the media—and many did so choose—they generally became invisible, irrelevant or both.

The influence of *The Irish Times* was considerable. It was part of the establishment but it played the role of its conscience at the same time, frequently challenging the orthodoxies of the day.

Gay Byrne, for 35 years presenter of RTÉ's *Late Late Show* and latterly running a 5-days-a-week radio talk show, was the dashing herald of a new Ireland that would not be fobbed off with politicians' platitudes or silenced by an Episcopal reprimand.

The marriage of modern radio technology with the telephone, especially the mobile telephone, generated a new and powerful kind of radio. Any citizen could call the talk-shows and put opinions out on air. 'Citizen broadcasting' is inexpensive, influential, unpredictable and almost wholly beyond the control of the establishment.

John Healy was an important influence in bringing about a new relationship between journalism and politics. He wrote his 'Backbencher' column in *The Sunday Review* and later in *The Irish Times*. He abandoned the reverential, hushed tone in which journalists had heretofore referred to political figures and, in particular, members of the Government. He wrote about them using their first names and sometimes their nicknames, de-mythologising them and poking fun at their foibles and idiosyncrasies. His style was to be emulated, but never equalled, by many political commentators long after he had ceased writing the column.

But if the journalists and programme presenters were influential, they were minor forces by comparison with Tony O'Reilly, later Sir Anthony O'Reilly, who hit the somnolent Irish media scene like a storm in the years after he took over Independent Newspapers. From a sleepy, if nicely profitable, stable of three newspapers in Dublin's Abbey Street, O'Reilly expanded the Independent operation to what it is today—a multinational, multi-media phenomenon, operating in four continents and dominating the Irish media landscape.

Its world-wide operations have now been grouped into Independent News and Media. It had a turnover of €1.6 billion in 2004 with assets reckoned at €3.4 billion. It employs 11,500 people and owns 165 newspaper and magazine titles around the world. O'Reilly is by far the single largest private shareholder. In Ireland, it controls the *Irish Independent*, the *Sunday Independent*, the *Evening Herald*, *The Sunday World*, along with a string of provincial newspapers. It has an important holding in the *Sunday Tribune* and it had a 50 per cent share in the tabloid daily *Star*. In Belfast, it owns *The Belfast Telegraph*.

In the UK it owns *The Independent*. In South Africa it owns titles once held by the Argus group. It has interests in Hong Kong, Malaysia and Indonesia. It has extensive newspaper holdings in Australia. Also in Ireland, it has valuable holdings in cable and website companies.

But if Whitaker's new economy stimulated processes of gradual change in the media, two major developments in the late 1960s and early 1970s saw the horizons of Irish journalists' broaden while they faced unprecedented challenges to their professional capacities.

One was the accession of Ireland to the EEC in 1973. The other was the crisis that burst upon Northern Ireland in 1968–1969 and which led to more than three decades of violence and upheaval.

The numbers of journalists grew rapidly through the 1970s as the news media struggled to cope with unprecedented reporting tasks. More and more specialists were appointed—not just for politics, but for economics, business, religious affairs, crime, education, industrial relations, legal affairs, science, the arts and so on. Journalists, programme-makers and editors were increasingly being drawn from the pool of those with third-level education. Some had professional qualifications in law, science, economics, accounting, medicine and so on.

They became a formidable force, capable of taking on the professionals appointed by Government or the large corporations, on their own ground. A crucially important factor in the rise of the Irish media has been the breaking down of the political monoliths that had alternated in government since the foundation of the State.

Up to the 1970s, political power in Ireland had fallen either to Fianna Fáil in single-party government or to Fine Gael, in coalition with Labour and, on occasion, one or two smaller parties or independent deputies. Political power alternated along predictable lines.

All of this began to change from the 1970s as Fianna Fáil first split and then watched its core vote shrink. Fine Gael enjoyed a resurgence under the leadership of Garret FitzGerald in the years 1977–1987 but then went into another decline. The Greens and the PDs were born. Official Sinn Féin became Democratic Left and then joined Labour. Provisional Sinn Féin entered the Dáil. Single-issue candidates and an increasing number of independents began to be elected.

The uniquely sensitive system of proportional representation employed in Irish elections meant that a tiny margin at the polls could now make the difference between a party being in government and languishing in opposition. The system also meant that competing candidates from within the same party could win or lose seats by a handful of local votes. Thus as the numbers of floating voters grew, the media became crucially important. The support of big newspapers and the power of television, in particular, became central to a party's and to an individual's political ambitions.

The media developed enormous power and they knew it. Smart politicians began to figure out ways of turning that power to their own ends. The art of the 'leak' and the 'spin' became an essential element in most politicians' skill sets. Just as journalists sought out politicians whom they cultivated as sources, politicians for their part sought out journalists whom they could use to circulate information either to their own advantage or to the disadvantage of rivals. It was a far cry from the days when reporters stood silently in the wings, short-handing the words of Éamon de Valera or Archbishop John Charles McQuaid.

New relationships also began to develop among differing elements of the media themselves. A media cycle, an unspoken alliance of inter-dependency, whose existence is never formally acknowledged, emerged among the different elements of the media.

It worked—and still works—something like this. A newspaper breaks a story or raises an interesting issue, say, in *The Irish Times*. Before sunrise, programme-makers and researchers at the radio stations are scanning the story or the feature and seeking to bring it a step further. They put calls out to the principals involved in the story, inviting them to come on air.

Later, the journalist who wrote the story may be featured on radio programmes also. Alternatively, another journalist, whether from within the radio station or from another newspaper, specialising in the same area, may be invited to contribute.

The story will build during the day. If it is strong enough it may feature on the evening TV news or in the political/current affairs programmes later in the night.

With luck, a Minister or an opposition spokesman or some principal will have been drawn further by now, to the extent that the story has advanced to new revelations. It is now ready for a second run in the newspapers of the following morning. *The Irish Times* will be following up its exclusive but meanwhile the *Irish Independent* and the *Irish Examiner* will be desperately seeking to recover what it sees as lost ground and will be searching for their own angle.

Within hours of the story being first published, the principals will find themselves at the centre of a media vortex, involving reporters and possibly photographers from half a dozen daily and Sunday newspapers, radio broadcasters, TV crews and web-journalists.

In a relatively short span of years, Irish journalism moved centre stage in Irish public life, inhabiting influential circles. Its practitioners frequently became celebrities in their own right, almost like TV presenters and stars. Their status and their acceptability rose, almost as those of the priests went down.

It has been argued that media in the broad sense, and journalism in the particular, have become the new priesthood in Ireland. They have displaced the Roman Catholic Church and, to a lesser extent, other authority institutions that had held sway in the society that emerged out of the Great Famine.

The enthronement of media and journalism at the centre of public discourse and value-formation in the closing decades of the twentieth century was not unique to Ireland. It was a feature of many western societies, notably the United States, where television first emerged as the most influential medium of an urbanised, affluent society.

Like their religious predecessors, the priesthood of media practitioners and journalists in Ireland do much good. They make a valuable contribution to society. Indeed, they are essential if the democratic system is to work properly. They are indispensable in ensuring adequate accountability across the many activities that constitute 'public life'. But the parallels with the earlier priesthood of the Roman Catholic Church are striking.

Prior to the foundation of Maynooth College at the end of the eighteenth century, the Catholic priesthood in Ireland, apart from those priests who went to the continent to study, was poorly educated, poorly provided for in material wealth and held a lowly status in the community. With the foundation of Maynooth and the education of the priesthood to what was, in effect, university level, priests became significant figures in the community, living well in material terms and looked up to for their knowledge and learning.

Journalism has come through a not dissimilar process. As journalists have become better educated and better paid, their status in the community has risen. The journalist of earlier generations who was not always quite accepted in polite society has been replaced by one who often has quasi-celebrity status and who is warmly welcomed, indeed often sought out, by the wider establishment.

In large measure, the journalists and broadcasters have displaced the priests as the daily and weekly arbiters of morality, of values and other issues of public contention. Where politicians, business persons and private individuals faced the utterances from the pulpit or the altar, they are now likely to face the adjudication of the newspaper columnist, the broadcaster, the TV pundit or the editorial writer.

———

Yet, at the end of the 1990s most media organisations still had no formal structure through which members of the public, whether readers or individuals who had featured in reports, could get an assured hearing. While the influence of journalists and the media increased, there was no parallel development of accountability. Journalism in Ireland has been one of the last bastions of unaccountability in public life.

At this writing Ireland is unique among western European states in not having a press council, a press ombudsman or any other body to adjudicate on standards or to offer redress to the citizen who is aggrieved by the newspapers.

The situation in regard to Irish broadcasting is somewhat different. The Broadcasting Complaints Commission adjudicates on issues raised by members of the public in regard to the content of any broadcast material—not just material that is put out as news or current affairs. If it finds that broadcast material does not conform to the requirement of the Broadcasting Acts—for example if it lacks balance—it has the power to compel the offending company to make amends by publishing an apology, a clarification or balancing material.

Print journalists have no equivalent to contend with. All members of the National Union of Journalists (NUJ) are obliged, notionally, to adhere to the NUJ

Code of Conduct and the NUJ Schedule of Working Practices

It is a voluntary code. It enjoins journalists to 'maintain the highest professional and ethical standards', to 'strive to eliminate distortion, news suppression and censorship', to 'rectify promptly any harmful inaccuracies', and so on. It requires that journalists shall obtain information only by 'straightforward means' and that a journalist shall not do anything (subject to the over-riding consideration of the public interest) 'which entails intrusion into private grief and distress'.

Other provisions require a journalist to protect confidential sources of information, and to ensure that he/she does not 'originate material which encourages discrimination on grounds of race, colour, creed, gender or sexual orientation'.

The code requires that a journalist shall not accept bribes or inducements, shall not be influenced by 'advertising or other considerations' and shall not 'take private advantage of information gained in the course of his/her duties before the information becomes public knowledge'.

The NUJ's rules allow for members to be reprimanded, fined or even expelled for breaches of the Code. But members of the public cannot employ the Code to pursue a complaint against a journalist. It may only be utilised by one journalist against another.

Only one Irish journalist has been penalised as a result of a complaint. This was when a charge of plagiarism was brought against the then editor of the *Irish Independent*, Vincent Doyle. The complainant was another journalist, Frank McDonald, the environment correspondent of *The Irish Times*.

Shortly after taking office as Minister for Justice, Equality and Law Reform in 2002, Michael McDowell promised a reform of the law of defamation. He also opened discussions with newspaper publishers and the NUJ about the establishment of a press ombudsman and a press council. The publishers and the NUJ set up a working group, under the chairmanship of former Trinity College Provost, Tom Mitchell, to draw up a new code of conduct for editors and journalists.

But by summer 2005, it had still not proven possible to bring reform proposals before the Dáil. McDowell's Cabinet colleagues insisted that steps be taken in parallel to provide for a new privacy law to curb media intrusions. He undertook to bring his proposals forward by the end of the year.

Calls for reform of defamation law have been in the air for almost two decades. But it took the threat of a state-appointed press council from Michael McDowell to have the Mitchell group brought into being and activated. And while the publishers and the journalists' union have been engaged with these issues, it is my experience with journalist colleagues that the great majority are either nervous or indifferent about possible change.

This lack of enthusiasm for any accountability is a true paradox, for journalists are at the forefront, rightly, in demanding such re-evaluation from other elements in society. The absence of debate may perhaps be attributable in part to the absence of any extended training or academic study of journalism and the media in Ireland, beyond entry-level.

Until 1984 no university in Ireland provided any courses in journalism. The first professional training in the country was a diploma course, set up in the early 1960s at the College of Commerce, Rathmines. In 1984, Dublin City University instituted a one year Masters in Journalism course, aimed at giving would-be journalists, who were already university graduates, a good inculcation in the basics of journalism in theory and practice. Dublin City University also introduced an undergraduate degree in journalism.

The Rathmines course developed into a degree in journalism within the reconstituted Dublin Institute of Technology. In 1998, DIT added a Masters in Journalism to its curriculum. NUI Galway also now operates an MA in journalism.

These courses are excellent insofar as they go. They have met a real need in the educational market to give pre-intake training for journalists. Many of the craft's most talented and best-recognised practitioners today have come through these. A number of other journalism and media courses have since been set up, at private colleges, and at colleges run by VECs in Dublin, Dún Laoghaire and elsewhere.

These courses have also been a boon for media employers who have been remiss in not providing for training in Ireland. They generate a steady stream of young men and women who can operate productively in the newsrooms from the moment they are hired. These young people have a good grasp of publishing law, of the structures of the Oireachtas and other public bodies. They have had a sound inculcation in issues of media ethics and standards.

But all of these courses are, in effect, entry-level courses. For the overwhelming majority of Irish journalists, formal training stops at this point. There are no opportunities in Ireland for in-service training; there are no refresher courses; there is no provision for journalists to review their formation or to explore, in any rigorous or academic way, any of the issues that they encounter as their careers advance. If there is any further formal training in an Irish journalist's career it will be to learn new keyboard skills or perhaps to refresh their awareness of the laws of libel and contempt.

The only exception that I am aware of has been the setting up of a system of internships by the Cork-based Thomas Crosbie Holdings, publishers of the *Irish Examiner* and the Cork *Evening Echo* as well as *The Sunday Business Post*. Some editors at the Independent group have also been sent in recent years for short management-training courses.

Journalists are confronted with complex and challenging issues as they go through their careers. They are presented with ethical issues, with operational challenges and with important questions about how their role and function are defined. As their experience grows, they find that they have to respond almost instinctively or intuitively in these situations. There is no place in their career structure for reflection or analysis on them. There is no institution offering that facility. It is not encouraged by editors or publishers.

There are international organisations which link editors and journalists, many of them offering in-service or advanced training. The National Council for the Training of Journalists in the UK offers a range of mainly technical courses but Irish journalists rarely attend. The European Journalism Centre, at Maastricht in the Netherlands, offers a wide range of short courses, from news-gathering techniques, to ethical decision-making.

Many fine schools of journalism and media, offering advanced training and research beyond entry-level, operate in the UK, in mainland Europe and in the United States. Centres of excellence in Britain include London City University, Cardiff University and Sheffield University. In Europe, apart from Maastricht, a highly-regarded Faculty of Journalism is located at Aarhus University in Denmark.

Many courses in the EU use English as their working language. In the United States, many celebrated schools of journalism operate in a range of universities, from Columbia (home of the Pulitzer Prizes) to Northwestern, to the Poynter Institute in Florida, endowed by the *St Petersburg Times* company. In the 1990s, I sent more than a dozen *Irish Times* journalists at various levels of responsibility for short courses at Poynter.

Irish participation in these schools is very low. There is, in fact, no tradition of Irish journalists seeking to explore or measure their working methods against international best practices. As a result, there is very little if any self-critiquing in Irish media. There is little interest in exploring how news is covered, what procedures are followed, how standards are defined elsewhere.

There is no formalised training for journalists promoted to supervisory or executive decisions. Reporters or sub-editors who have perhaps been excellent writers or wordsmiths are promoted to be editors, often in charge of scores of people and responsible for millions of euro in resources.

What is much worse in its implications for journalism is the fact that these executives have no developed formal training either in media theory, in ethical decision making or in comparative systems of media elsewhere. The supervisor, to whom a young journalist will turn for guidance, has no body of knowledge or formation upon which to fall back—other than his or her own newsroom experience.

I had none myself, other than what I learned 'on the job' from other, more experienced journalists as I progressed. It was only after I became editor of *The Irish Times* and became involved in international media linkages that I began to realise how inadequate our arrangements were.

It would be difficult to name any other avocation which has to the same degree failed to professionalise in the twenty-first century. Even those without a very long tradition of academic formation, such as catering, hospitality workers, police, fire personnel, paramedics and so on, have extensive in-service training.

They constantly re-evaluate their operating standards and procedures, comparing them to best international practices.

Journalists, editors and publishers must take their share of the blame. But so too must the major universities. There are no linkages between the excellent schools of government, political science and social studies in the older universities and any course, department or faculty committed to journalism or media.

This is in sharp contrast to the UK, mainland Europe and North America, where faculties of journalism and media studies have operated for more than a century, in many cases, side by side with other disciplines. It was left to the new universities—DCU—and to the reconstituted DIT to fill the need for basic, entry-level education. The gap for more advanced, reflective study and analysis yet remains.

25

THE WORST DAY SINCE 1916

It's the worst day of my life . . . we're not publishing tomorrow.
— Executive editor of *The Irish Times*, PAT O'HARA

By the end of 1998, the standoff over the future management of the organisation had created conditions of palpable tension. Louis O'Neill believed that Don Reid was being invested with executive powers, rather than becoming a non-executive chairman. Although Tom McDowell and Don Reid insisted this was not so, Louis saw the move as a direct affront to his authority and announced that he would leave.

He made his views clear when he met representatives of the *Irish Times* Group of Unions and said he would no longer serve. There was a troubled air about the place. Little did any of us realise the extent of the trouble that lay ahead—and not too far ahead.

Although I knew, of course, that Louis would have to be replaced, I had become apprehensive of the day that he would go. The agreement that had been put in place in 1995 between the company and the unions for the appointment of his successor would now propel me into a no-win situation.

But to my surprise and relief, when the notice announcing the vacancy for managing director appeared, Karen Erwin let it be known that she would not be a candidate. I do not know what thought processes brought her to this decision. But it was, in all the circumstances, a wise one. My principal sentiment towards Karen over the years had been one of sympathy for the situation in which she had found herself.

The processes that had been agreed in 1995 were now put in train. An interview panel was assembled, to be chaired by Don Reid. Esther McKee, one of the members from Northern Ireland, was nominated by the Trust. In addition to myself, there was to be an external assessor. The individual selected was David Sneddon, a Scottish former newspaper executive. Brian Ward, the human resources professional from MERC consultants, who organised the interview process, also participated.

The short-list, whittled down by Brian Ward, was a mixed bag. I was struck by the absence of high-profile names from among the Dublin business community. It seemed to me that it would be an attractive option, perhaps even as a stepping stone, in which an aspiring manager might prove himself, or herself. Don Reid was more realistic. 'There's been too much adverse publicity about the organisation over the last few years,' he said.

There were some interesting applicants from within Ireland. But for one reason or another, it was felt, they did not seem to match *The Irish Times*'s needs. We also had some good internal applicants, one of whom, in particular, was more or less at the right stage of career development and seemed to be possessed of most of the necessary skills.

There were quite a few applicants from the UK. In the main they were middle-ranking managers at Fleet Street newspapers or in the regions. They appeared to be generally competent in a technical way. But we felt that many of them would have real difficulties transferring their thinking from regional UK dailies to an Irish national newspaper. They nearly all referred to Britain as 'the mainland', which grated badly with us.

One of the British applicants stood out from the rest. Nicholas Chapman was a former managing director of BBC Enterprises and a member of the BBC's executive board. A tall, angular man, with a shock of grey hair, he immediately came across as the quintessential, decent, Englishman—which he was.

Chapman had departed from the BBC, after a successful career there, in the regime of Director General John Birt. He had left with a handsome package, a good reputation and, at 50 years of age, the prospect of developing, perhaps, a second, fulfilling career.

He spoke about the role and the place of newspapers like *The Irish Times* with conviction. He had a track-record in developing the BBC's subsidiaries as profit-centres. I liked him. We had in common the fact that he too was a history graduate—Cambridge in his case. He came across as a good blend of commercial experience and sensitivity to the character of *The Irish Times*.

But I was seriously concerned about his capacity to adapt to a society and an organisation both of which were steeped in cultures that were profoundly different from what he had known.

The fact that the English and Irish speak a version of the same language lulls many of both races into the false assumption that they can understand each other. But the commonality of language often serves only to camouflage differences in temperament, approach and outlook.

I had difficulty seeing Nicholas Chapman adapting to or understanding the Irish way of doing things, of saying things, of approaching issues. In particular, I had difficulty in seeing any outsider adapt to the deeply-ingrained culture of *The Irish Times*.

Nonetheless, Nicholas Chapman was the first choice. It was important that he start with as much support as possible and it was certainly necessary that he should have the backing of the person with whom he would work most closely—the editor. He was offered the job, by the board of The Irish Times Ltd, as the unanimous choice of the selection panel.

'Nick' Chapman took over as managing director in September 1999. He fulfilled all of my best expectations and most of my apprehensions. He was courteous to a fault. He was absolutely respectful of the editor's autonomy on policy and content. He tried very hard to break into the thinking within the organisation at all levels. He consulted widely. He had an open-door policy at his office.

But, in reality, he did not have a chance. Try as he might, he could not get on the same wavelength as his executives. What he intended as a patient, painstaking approach, they often saw as dithering and lack of certainty. Where he simply did not understand an issue—and he could not be expected to know everything about the internal workings of the operation—they saw further proof of the fatuity of an external appointment.

He tried very hard. And in fairness to his senior staff, they gave him a chance to prove himself for a time, in spite of their misgivings. But it was an unhappy situation. It is important to record that he made some considerable progress, nonetheless, on the agenda for the development and modernisation of the company that had fallen behind over the previous years.

A number of important projects were in hand before Louis left. A new Geoman press had been ordered from Man-Roland in Germany to replace the Uniman colour press that had been installed in D'Olier Street in 1986. But the new press would be of a different order of magnitude and capacity. It would require to be built at a remote site, at Citywest, ending almost 100 years of printing of *The Irish Times* in Dublin city centre.

The editorial *Atex* system which was elderly technology when it was introduced in 1990 was to be replaced. A decision in principle had been made to opt for *Hermes*, a fully-electronic publishing system, operated by an Italian subsidiary of the Unisys computer company.

The commercial and service departments of the company had been operating on a variety of elderly computer systems (and some manual information systems) and these had to be replaced. It was proposed to amalgamate these into a modern SAP network. A separate system called *Matrix* was to be used for the task of distributing up to 150,000 copies of the newspaper each morning.

Having accepted that it was not possible to get a Sunday title off the ground, the executive team had proposed instead to publish a magazine to be provided with the newspaper each Saturday. This was a sizeable and a delicate undertaking. The aim was to broaden the newspaper's appeal to younger women, in particular, while in no way putting off male readers or older readers. Patsey Murphy, one of the most versatile editors on staff, got to work on the prototypes.

All of these projects had been costed at a total of almost IR£100 million. It would represent by far the single largest set of linked developments and investments in the company's history. But the remarkable thing was that it could be covered by the cash reserves that the company had built up during the mid-1990s, when strong circulation delivered high-yield advertising. It would bring

The Irish Times into the twenty-first century, set fair to prosper and grow.

But this programme of development would require much more than cash. It would require editorial skill and technological know-how and it implied a major programme of negotiation and agreement with the unions across the company.

Louis and I had put the basic frameworks into place, with cross-departmental teams at work on various aspects of the programme. Don Reid was a good facilitator, standing back and allowing us to get on with it. But progress had been slow and the programme was anything from two to three years behind where it might have been.

Nick Chapman took a methodical and organised approach to the programme in hand. He had a good strategic grasp of what we were at. He expanded the cross-departmental activity and set up a number of task-forces, including one on which I was especially keen, to explore ways and means of expanding our circulation in Northern Ireland.

Very slowly, things began to fall into place.

I believed it was now possible for me to move on from the editorship. In discussions with Tom and Louis during 1999 it had been agreed that I would have the option of standing down with full benefits at age 55. My normal retirement age would be 60 so the company was effectively offering me an additional five years pensionable service. It was not ungenerous. But I had been young—37—on appointment and the years had been onerous.

In the summer of 2001 I had discussions with Don Reid about starting the processes to find a replacement editor. Don drafted a retirement contract and gave it to me in July.

Meanwhile, the programme for change continued apace. Michael Austen was the director of human resources. With a background in IBEC and with experience in banking and other industries, Austen knew that the company had to move away from the old adversarial relationships that existed between management and unions into an era of partnership, with agreed goals and programmes.

By 2000 the company had hammered out an agreement with the journalists and the print unions for the introduction of *Hermes*. That agreement, at long last, provided an early-retirement/voluntary redundancy option for journalists, albeit on modest terms. But we were finally going to have a mechanism to enable us to shed costs—and not simply to build them up. Had I had such a mechanism 10 years previously when I sought it, matters might have turned out differently.

The Saturday magazine was launched with the talented Patsey Murphy as editor. We had put a great deal of preparatory work into it. Its tone and pitch had to be such that it would grow our younger female readership while not antagonising our more mature readers.

It was immediately successful. Readership and circulation expanded among younger women readers, precisely as we had hoped for, but without any loss of readership in other sectors. Apart from attracting new readers, the hope for the Saturday magazine was that it would provide the advertising sales staff with an alternative vehicle or platform through which to sell space. Later, we added a weekly guide to entertainment and the arts, 'The Ticket', the creation largely of Gerry Smyth.

Before Louis O'Neill left in 1999, the organisation had begun to square up to a big decision. It had large cash reserves in hand. And it needed to embark on a large-scale development programme. The development programme could not be avoided. But the issue was whether it was wise to put the cash that had been built up into the programme, effectively leaving the company without reserves.

Louis had believed it was best to pay for the new developments out of the cash in hand and the board fully supported this view. Nor did he pluck his conviction out of the air. Prudently, he sought the advice of a leading economic consultant, Peter Bacon.

I had no contact with Bacon but his report was circulated to all directors. His conclusion, reflecting the conventional wisdom, was that the economic climate could be expected to remain favourable. Thus the newspaper could reasonably count on a continuation of strong revenue streams. This was supported by an internal report compiled by Louis and Richard Gee, the company's financial controller.

The correct and prudent course for the company was to avoid borrowings; to put the cash into the development programme, including the new press development. Profit projections for 2001, 2002 and 2003 were strong.

It was not anticipated anywhere in the western economies that the information technology sector in the United States would go into freefall in 2001. The end of the longest bull market in the history of Wall Street was not foreseen. People could not have anticipated the near-collapse of the airline business and related industries in the aftermath of the terrorist attacks in the US on 11 September 2001.

——

The year 2001 opened on a high note. In the first quarter, January to March, revenues for appointments advertising were historically at their highest ever in *The Irish Times*. It seemed as if the year was set to repeat—and exceed—the bumper revenues that had accrued steadily since the mid-1990s. The reports to the board from the commercial directors were upbeat and optimistic.

But in April the first signs of a downturn became apparent. Advertising bookings dropped sharply as American IT firms suddenly slammed on the brakes in their recruitment. New IT systems were not selling as fast as they had anticipated. People were content to work with the systems they had and were not prepared to invest thousands of dollars, maybe millions, in what they saw as unnecessary upgrades.

The organisation went into the Easter holiday break with apprehension mounting. The advertising sales departments would fall well short of revenue targets in the first quarter. The question was whether the business would come back in May. It didn't.

There was a glum mood across the commercial departments. May and June were weak. July and August were always slack and there were no expectations of any pick-up there. The only good news on the radar screen was a continuing strong performance in circulation.

Perhaps things would come right for the advertising in the autumn. But even if they did, it now appeared that there would be some period in which the company would go 'cash negative'. We would be into modest borrowings. 'Not much borrowing', the newly-appointed financial controller, Liam Kavanagh, told me one day at lunch. 'A few hundred thousand at most. Just to tide us over.'

Before Easter, Nick Chapman—rightly—believed it was time to call in the unions and tell them how things were looking. A meeting of the Joint Consultative Council was arranged with Nick, Michael Austen and myself representing the company. Three employees, one each representing NUJ, SIPTU and the print unions, attended.

Chapman set out the deteriorating trading situation. There would be a hiring freeze, he said, until things improved and existing vacancies across a number of departments would remain unfilled. Chapman asked the staff representatives to convey these moves to their members.

There were gasps of incredulity from the staff representatives. Eugene McEldowney, representing the journalists, did manage to respond. He raised his hands in a gesture of disbelief.

'Nick, you know what you're asking us to tell our colleagues? That with all this investment going on, with the paper more successful than ever, we're going to start losing money? They won't believe me, I'm telling you that.'

'That seems to be the reality, Eugene,' I said.

'Well, I'll pass it on,' he shrugged. 'But I can't guarantee the reaction.'

The staff member representing the SIPTU employees was more blunt. 'I won't do it,' she said. 'I'm not going to bring that sort of news. Do it yourself.'

The man representing the printers said nothing. It augured badly for what lay ahead.

———

In September I went to San Francisco for a family wedding. I would be absent for about two weeks, leaving Pat O'Hara, the executive editor, in charge as usual in my absence.

The visitor to San Franscico in the early autumn of 2001 could not fail to be struck by the empty restaurants, the amount of prime real estate for sale and the dropping rental prices. The bottom was falling out of the IT industry. The implications for media companies, I knew, would be serious, not least for *The Irish Times*.

On the morning of 11 September we woke to TV images of passenger jets slamming into the Twin Towers and the Pentagon. I had a couple of hours telephone contact with Pat O'Hara in Dublin and with our staffers and correspondents around the US, principally Conor O'Clery in New York and Paddy Smyth in Washington. I was dialling Elaine Lafferty, our correspondent in Los Angeles, when the telephone system began to crash under volume-usage.

All exits from the US were blocked. The airports were shut. The border with Canada was closed. I could only sit and wait out events.

Contact with Dublin was intermittent. The cellphone system became overloaded. At the lodge outside San Francisco where we were staying, the staff had abandoned the switchboard, unable to cope with the intermittent failure of the system and, when it functioned, the tremendous volume of calls as Americans sought desperately to make contact with family and friends or to arrange travel home. There were no flights. Every hire car was snapped up. Buses were filled to capacity and with long queues of hopeful travellers at the depots.

I was out of contact for perhaps 14–15 hours. When I eventually got through again to Pat O'Hara, he sounded deeply distressed. 'It's the worst day of my life,' he said. 'I've got bad news for you.'

This was not like Pat. He was the calmest of men, the most solid person one could have in charge of a newspaper. I had no idea what was coming next. 'We're not publishing tomorrow,' he said.

I was unable to find words, beyond asking him to repeat himself. He explained that the Government had called a national day of mourning to express solidarity with the US. It had been decided not to publish. Advertising for the newspaper had collapsed for that day. Don Reid had called the directors together, Pat explained. There would have been major problems with distribution and the editions of subsequent days could have been jeopardised, Don said.

Two hours later, still disbelieving, I got through to Don Reid after constant re-dialling. He confirmed what Pat told me. I believed that if we had to bring in every staff member with a car and a bicycle, we should get a paper out. If people had to carry copies of the paper in their teeth and sell them at the street-corners, we should do it.

But it was too late. The staff had been sent home. No pages had been prepared. He believed that he had no choice but to shut down. If we did publish on the day of mourning, the distribution system would be so disrupted that publication of the newspaper over subsequent days might be jeopardised, he told me.

The other Irish newspapers were publishing. *The Irish Times* would be off the streets for the first time since the Rising in 1916, apart from an industrial stoppage that closed all the Dublin newspapers simultaneously in 1963.

It was devastating news. In my view, it ran against everything a newspaper should do at a time of crisis. Whatever it cost, I felt, *The Irish Times* should have been on the streets. It is a news medium's overwhelming duty to be there for its readers, listeners or viewers.

Three days later, with the air services beginning to return to normal, we managed to get seats on an Aer Lingus flight to Dublin out of Los Angeles. We sacrificed our BA tickets back from San Francisco and queued for a day at the Hertz office to rent a car to drive to Los Angeles.

It was a miserable journey and a grim homecoming. The only consolation was that all four of us were upgraded by Aer Lingus from economy to a virtually empty executive class. Champagne and canapés never seemed so unappetising.

26

HERE COMES THE FUTURE . . .

This was the signal achievement—the newspaper came through the period July to December 2001 with the highest ever circulation figures in its history.

Advertising revenues in recruitment and appointments flat-lined in September and into October. It was clear that there was going to be a big shortfall in the revenues that were required to meet the company's operating costs.

The warnings issued by Jim Chisolm and others had come to pass. The newspaper's vulnerable dependency on one or two major areas of advertising was now apparent. The commercial departments had been warned to broaden their revenue base. They had not been able to do so. Now we were in trouble. Don Reid announced the establishment of a 'working party' to respond to the looming crisis.

I knew that at very least we were in for big cutbacks in resources. I knew that editorial services and spending would have to be severely curtailed. In addition, the newspaper was moving into a period of organisational change. *Hermes* was being brought on-stream to replace the *Atex* system. We would shortly be moving the printing of the newspaper to the new plant at Citywest. That would involve new processes of facsimile transmission of plates and it would present new challenges for the editorial departments and for quality control in the production departments.

What was crucial, I knew, was that the quality and standard of the newspaper had to be maintained in this difficult time. If they fell, so too would circulation. If circulation fell, revenue would drop further. A vicious, downward spiral of decline would develop. It would require huge effort all round and it would need all of my attention and energy as editor.

Nonetheless, I knew I would also have to play my role in Don Reid's working party. Or so I thought. Don told me the composition of the working party. It was composed exclusively of commercial staff. In addition he was asking Alex Burns, the former auditor of the company and a former partner at the KMPG accountancy firm, to 'help out'.

The air of crisis grew through September and early October. The advertising order books were shrinking. Meanwhile, the working party worked on. I became aware that groups of executive directors were meeting regularly to discuss the situation. Neither I nor Pat O'Hara, my deputy, was asked to attend these meetings.

When the working party concluded its deliberations it painted a grim scenario. A gap was about to open up between income and costs. The only way to bridge the gap was by cost-reduction. The payroll would have to come down—jobs would have to go. Operational costs would have to be reduced by one third across the board.

When these facts were put to the unions there was a predictable reaction. Unhappily, I was left to face it. Tom McDowell resigned as chairman of the Trust and handed over to David McConnell, a Trinity College genetics professor who had been Vice-Provost at the College. Don Reid did not engage with the media or, after the initial meetings, with the unions. Nick Chapman went on leave.

Naturally, the other media—and in particular the Independent group newspapers—were delighted at the opportunity to kick *The Irish Times*. The adjectives 'crisis-ridden', 'stricken' and 'ailing' became *de rigeur* in any story written about the newspaper.

Much of the medicine prescribed for the company by the working party was overdue. The cost-structure had been allowed to grow inordinately, principally through not engaging with payroll issues. The organisation was overstaffed across all departments.

Now the company proposed a fairly generous parting package for those who wished to leave voluntarily. Those in their 55th year or over were to have an additional five years added to their pensionable service.

The plan called for a reduction of 250 in staff numbers. In the event, there were more applications than the company wished for and all departures were voluntary. For many of those who did depart, it was an opportunity to make a fresh start in a new career or a business or to leave behind a lifestyle that made heavy demands on personal resources and family.

At an early stage of the process, Michael Austen, the director of human resources, told me: 'People don't realise it yet. Those who will have difficulties in all of this won't be the people who choose to leave. It will be those who stay behind who will find it harder to deal with.' I disagreed with Michael Austen on many issues. But he had been over this course elsewhere as a human resources consultant.

About 112 jobs were to go in the editorial departments. It would be a difficult task, but by no means impossible, to maintain the newspaper at its normal standard. It would be necessary to retain the key editorial services and at the same time to restructure every section.

Not only that, we were facing into a referendum on Europe and a general election. *The Irish Times* always performed well when important electoral tests were under way. This time we would have to be better than ever.

I decided it was necessary to create what were effectively two 'divisions' within the editorial structure. For the next few months Pat O'Hara would head the content function—the news, the presentation and the overall shape of the newspaper on a day-to-day basis. He was an editor of rock-solid judgment and sharp editorial instincts. Eoin McVey would have day-to-day responsibility for handling the restructuring process. Both would report to me as frequently as necessary. In effect that meant daily and usually several times daily.

The restructuring group within the editorial departments, chaired by Eoin McVey and supported by Cliff Taylor, did excellent work. I consulted widely and then laid out the general principles.

There were moments of terrible tension. The process did not bring out the best in everybody. I had a succession of department heads visiting me, in which the conversation went something like this.

Head of Department. There's terrible waste and feather-bedding, you know.
Me: Yes I do. We have to eliminate it.
Head of Department: Well, of course we're down to the bone in my section. But there are places in the (naming) Nth . . . floor that are run like holiday camps.
Me: Really?
Head of Department: Oh yes. There's enormous scope to cut back there.

I had to arbitrate between home news, foreign, sport, features and so on. It was not a pleasant process.

I suffered at this time because of my visibility. I was prepared to talk to journalists from other newspapers. I went on TV and radio and tried to explain what was going on. Nobody else did so. In consequence I came to be seen as the face of the crisis at the 'ailing' and 'stricken' *Irish Times*.

A bizarre aspect of this was the manner in which the editorial departments were singled out for criticism. They were overstaffed in some places. But the problems of surplus numbers and of carrying colleagues who, for one reason or another, were not performing optimally, were universal across the organisation.

There was feather-bedding in many places, editorial, commercial, service departments and so on. The organisation's policy had generally been one of benign indulgence. It rarely applied the sort of intervention measures that are now part and parcel of human-resources management.

Not a penny had ever been spent by the editorial departments that was not approved by the directors. Spending had always been in line with budget. The problem now was that one of the two principal advertising streams had dried up —as the commercial departments had been warned. That was hardly the fault of the editor or the journalists. Yet that was where the focus of criticism appeared to fall.

For example, at an early stage, reports were put about concerning the numbers of journalists who were 'assistant editors'. This quickly made its way into the Sunday newspapers and was the subject of many jibes.

The reality was that 'assistant editor' was a grade, not a function. The terminology was a hangover and an administrative convenience. All department heads, such as the features editor, Sheila Wayman; the literary editor, Caroline Walsh; the business editor, Paul O'Neill; the sports editor, Malachy Logan and so on, were paid as 'assistant editors'. So too were the senior overseas correspondents —Conor O'Clery, Séamus Martin, Frank Millar and others. The senior political staff, Geraldine Kennedy, Dick Walsh and Denis Coghlan, were paid as 'assistant editors'. So too were the design editor, Andy Barclay, the chief-sub editor, Noel Costello and the editor of the website, Deirdre Veldon. And there were others.

On the commercial side of the house a similar formula was employed. Numbers of people were nominally 'managers' or 'executives' but carried neither managerial nor executive responsibility. They were generally paid the same as the 'assistant editors' or department editors—sometimes more. Yet there was no mention of these, either internally or externally, when the troubled state of the organisation was being described.

————

The restructuring was traumatic. The collapse of the US IT sector and the aftermath of 9/11 were simply the catalyst. It was clear that the organisation could not continue indefinitely as it had been doing. It would emerge leaner and fitter, if not necessarily healthier or happier.

I was satisfied, when the exercise had been completed, that while stringencies would be necessary in all areas, virtually all editorial functions and service were in a position to operate at much the same level as before. But there were some costly areas in which retrenchment would hurt and I agreed to these changes with reluctance.

The hardest blow was the dismantling of the structure of regional correspondents which we had put in place over the previous three or four years. For all its growth, The Irish Times was still viewed by many people as a newspaper of the Dublin middle-classes alone. But with the growth in many regional urban centres I believed it would be possible to extend readership. I also believed it was necessary to give city-dwellers a more accurate view of the country outside of the capital.

The Irish Times had traditionally maintained staffers in Cork, Galway and Belfast. From the mid-1990s on, we added Limerick, Waterford, Sligo and the midlands. We sent a talented young feature writer, Róisín Ingle, to Belfast, to work alongside the news team there. At the same time, I converted page 2 each day into a regional news page, with the focus alternating daily from one region to another. Regrettably, we had to haul back, closing the more recent offices.

The other area of significant cutback was in the foreign coverage. We had opened an Asia bureau in Beijing four years previously under Conor O'Clery. In 2000 he had been assigned to New York to work as the newspaper's first Wall Street correspondent and had been replaced in China by Miriam Donohue. Beijing was very costly. So it closed.

We also had to close one of the US bureaux—either Washington or New York. I decided that Conor O'Clery should remain and with enormous regret called Paddy Smyth back from Washington. Paddy had been making great strides there but on his return he became a successful and effective opinion page editor. Later he became foreign editor.

What happened in the period 2001–2002 was a shock to a newspaper that had generally experienced nothing but plain sailing for 25 years and that had been buoyed up by a rising circulation graph for almost 40 continuous years.

Perhaps, in retrospect, the company over-reacted and slammed the brakes on too hard. True, it was facing into a period of trading losses. But it had an extraordinarily strong balance sheet, and still does. By mid-2002 it had trimmed its costs and its workforce by a third. It had a brand-new, state-of-the-art press complex at Citywest.

It had installed ultra-modern technologies across all of its operations. And it was completely free of debt, apart from a relatively small funding it secured from the banks to finance the restructuring and voluntary severance programme.

Most remarkable of all—and this was the signal achievement of the team—the newspaper came through the period July to December 2001 with the highest ever circulation figures in its history—just over the 120,000 barrier. In the following period, January to June 2002, it was a fraction under that figure, at 119,726. It was a satisfying outturn, considering the upheaval, disruption and loss of resources that had to be absorbed over these periods.

But it would be easy to be wise after the event. The company came back into profit in 2003. Staff got their annual percentage increases. Executive directors got sizeable bonuses. Some modest re-hiring began. In 2004 the company announced that it was investing a further €20 million in additional systems and developments at the Citywest printing plant.

In reality what happened at *The Irish Times* in 2001–2002 was a precursor of what was to happen worldwide to media companies over the coming two to three years. RTÉ, Reuters, Independent, The Daily Telegraph, Pearsons, *Le Monde*, even the BBC, found themselves caught in a trap of historically-high costs and rapidly diminishing revenues. Restructuring, downsizing, re-deploying and retrenching became the order of the day in the media industries.

Nonetheless, the company was fortunate at this time, that years of investment and hard work had built *The Irish Times* into the fine newspaper that it was. It was these strengths that carried it through a difficult period. The organisation may have had a revenue problem. It may have had a cost-structure problem. It did not have a quality newspaper problem.

| TIME TO GO

Everyone who works in a newspaper plays a vital part. But never forget that the heart of The Irish Times *is its journalism.*
                          — Parting words in the newsroom, 12 October 2002

With the restructuring programme agreed between the unions and the company, it was apparent that the organisation was going to take on a new shape for the future. David McConnell had already taken over as chairman of the Trust from Tom McDowell. Don Reid announced that he would retire as chairman of the company in April. Nick Chapman stepped down as Managing Director and later camee to a parting settlement with the company.

Before Christmas, I spoke with Don Reid and David McConnell about my intention to stand down. We put aside the document with the proposed severance terms that Don had given me the previous year. It was agreed instead that I would disengage when the restructuring process would have been completed.

A complication arose in regard to my pension. Tom McDowell and Louis O'Neill had agreed two years previously that I could step down at 55 years with full benefits. Since I was now short of my full pensionability, I wanted the company to add some years to my service—as was being done for other employees.

Don Reid proposed that instead of this, the company would pay me the difference each year to my 65th birthday. In return, I was to enter into a 'non-compete' clause that would prevent me from working for any competitor of *The Irish Times* in the national newspaper market. 'We don't want you going across the river,' he said to me cryptically when he made the proposal.

It left me somewhat disadvantaged. I had some attractive offers from other quarters, including one from within Independent News and Media, after I stepped down. But I agreed to the 'non-compete' clause. In every other respect, the financial terms of my parting were identical *pro rata* to those of every other employee who had left during the restructuring process.

The original proposed agreement, drawn up by Don Reid in the summer of 2001, provided that I would have the title *Editor Emeritus*. The company again agreed to give me this title to reflect my 'long and successful editorship', as the letter of offer expressed it. The terms of my departure were agreed, ratified by the remuneration committee and in April I received a letter of offer, signed both by

Don Reid and the managing director. I was happy with that although the formal contract was not signed until the following August.

I had six challenging months ahead from April. So it was important to me to get these personal matters wrapped up and out of the way. We were facing into a crucial referendum and a general election. I needed to be free from personal concerns to concentrate on the content of the newspaper over these months. It was a trying time. I was coming to the end of an association with the newspaper that I had joined at 20 years of age, fresh from UCD. But I was also glad to be going. Things had changed.

When the company put the restructuring proposals to the unions, an agenda emerged that was wider than the immediate issues of staff numbers, costs and redeployment. The union representatives had insisted on having their own accountants verify the state of the company's finances before they would agree to support the restructuring programme. The company offered to pay the costs of this and the unions chose the firm of Farrell Grant Sparks (FGS) to examine the situation on their behalf. One of its principals, Greg Sparks, had been a programme manager for Labour in the John Bruton-led 'Rainbow Coalition'. The company was neither surprised nor displeased with the unions' choice of advisers.

When Don Reid's working party produced its restructuring plan it had been put to the union representatives. There was some minor give-and-take but in general the unions accepted what was proposed—with FGS endorsing the financial picture that the company painted. The staff voted on the plan and accepted it. The board of the company and the Trust resolved to accept it also.

A series of joint committees was established in which union representatives and management sat down to address different aspects of the restructuring plan. In the long term, the most far-reaching of these was to be the committee on corporate governance. I had no role in this committee. But I had a lunch meeting with Greg Sparks and a further 30-minute meeting one morning at the firm's offices in Dublin.

The corporate governance committee agreed that the powers of the Trust should be significantly reduced. It would no longer have a majority on the board of The Irish Times Ltd and the 'A' share, which had been held by Tom McDowell and which underpinned his unassailable position, was to be eliminated. Effectively, the Trust was to be displaced by the board as the ultimate operating authority within the organisation.

I could readily understand the sense of animus against the *ancien régime*. But I was fearful that the baby was being thrown out with the bath-water. I tried to point out to the editorial committee and other representatives that in the long term, journalism's best interests were not to be served by disempowering the Trust.

Things would be different in the future, I knew. People were increasingly talking about 'the business' or 'the brand' rather than 'the newspaper'. I would be something of a disruptive influence in the new environment.

In the meantime, we had to appoint a new chairman of the board, to succeed Don Reid. A sub-committee, on which I sat, was appointed in March to identify suitable candidates. It was not an easy task. Some unsuitable proposals were made—which were slapped down very quickly by the redoubtable Dervilla Donnelly, former Professor of Microbiology at UCD, who was a member of the Trust. Finally it was agreed that an approach should be made to Brian Patterson. He was a former director of the Irish Management Institute and a former chief executive of Waterford-Wedgwood. David McConnell was asked to talk to Patterson and came back to say that Brian would be happy to accept the offer.

The way was now clear for me to go. In August I announced my intention to step down as soon as a successor could be appointed. The company employed a Dublin-based 'head hunter', Mike Lehman, to assist with the interview process. This began in late September and it followed the formula agreed, first in 1977 after Douglas Gageby's return and modified in 1995 after the discussions which had followed Karen Erwin's appointment at the company. It was a big, rather unwieldy panel. But it was handled well by Brian Patterson who chaired the process.

I was happy that we had a good field of candidates, both internal and external. There were half a dozen credible candidates from within and as many again from outside. We had two front-rank applicants from the UK. I had made a range of training experiences available to senior editors in the years leading up to this. Thus, every one of the senior internal candidates had a broad view of the editorship to put before the panel. In the end, the decision of the board was to offer the editorship to Geraldine Kennedy.

————

On 12 October I called the staff together in the newsroom and told them that the new editor had been selected. She would be the twelfth person to hold the editorship since the newspaper's foundation in 1859. I had prepared a farewell address for colleagues and used the opportunity to express personal convictions that had been developed over many years of working at the paper.

I told them never to take for granted the fact that they worked with *The Irish Times*—a newspaper that controlled its own destiny, that stood for honest, principled journalism, that was not in anybody's pocket and that paid its own way. I reminded them that the heart of the paper was its journalism; and while it was wonderful to have a state-of-the-art plant at Citywest and the lion's share of the quality advertising market, nevertheless the engine that pulled the whole train was the journalism of *The Irish Times*.

As journalists we had an immense capacity for doing good. We also had an immense capacity to damage, to injure, to hurt if we used our power carelessly, without regard to basic fairness, or in ways that were partisan or biased. Likewise we should never forget that we worked for our readers. If we looked after them, they would look after us. If we took them for fools, or if we underestimated their ability to discern fact from supposition, analysis from polemic, they would cease to have faith in us.

As journalists we were among the more privileged people in society. That obliged us to keep the focus on the marginalised, on those who could not get their cancer treatment because they lived in the wrong place, on the mothers who could not get the right education for children with learning difficulties, on the immigrants, on the widows, on the addicts and the alcoholics, on the victims of abuse, on those who thought that life wasn't worth living any more.

And we had to keep pouring the boiling oil on those who evaded their responsibilities, those who exploited their positions and those who victimised the weakest in society. I asked them all to be continually aware of three things:

To beware the mindset of partition; it was deeply rooted in Ireland and it had to be resisted always. *The Irish Times* was a 32-county newspaper for one hundred years before there was a Border. This was too small an island to allow one part of it to fester forever in sectarianism and hate.

To beware of the mindset of metropolitanism; the conviction that civilised life didn't exist beyond Templeogue and Malahide. *The Irish Times* should never be a newspaper for the Dublin middle classes alone.

To beware the 'Little Irelanders'. These were people who thrived on triviality; they were everywhere and they were dangerous. The global village was a full and present reality. The great issues of our time were not the foibles of stars and celebrities; they were the poisoning of the planet, the spread of nuclear weapons, the tide of AIDS and the economic stagnation of the Developing World, with the accompanying evils of hunger, disease and ignorance. It was our job to be out there, reporting them.

I concluded by emphasising that the difficulties of the previous year did not originate from the fact that the journalists of *The Irish Times* built a newspaper that was too broad or too deep in its reach. If others had discharged their responsibilities with the same professionalism, commitment and competence as the journalists then the problems would have been significantly lessened.

———

I went back to my room, read the leaders and checked the layout for the next day's front page. I logged on to the BBC news website and to *www.Ireland.com*. I checked my messages on *Hermes*. I took my briefcase and went down for the last time to the parking bay where the vans loaded the newspapers at printing time.

I took the back-stairs, avoiding the newsroom, and I passed the old caseroom floor. I will not deny that I felt emotional. I met ghosts on the stairs—Jack Singleton, Paddy O'Leary, Johnny Grant, Malachy Logan—the men who got the newspaper out night after night. Somewhere in the gloom of the now silent floor

I might have seen the bulky figure of Bruce Williamson, the night's leading article in his hand.

At the door, I passed the switchroom where Tommy Higgins ran his communications nerve-centre. There were ghosts there too—'The Sergeant' Kelly, Harry Sutherland and even ghosts of some of those not dead, like Paddy Williams and Ambrose Kenny. Tony, the security man, shook my hand and wished me well. Caroline Walsh came down and waved me off.

I drove home. Later, Ann took me and the boys to dinner in The Commons restaurant on Saint Stephen's Green. We had a great meal, a bottle of champagne and a few laughs and reminiscences. Fr Tom Stack, a frequent contributor to the paper, was there with friends and he generously sent over a drink to our table.

At midnight, when my cellphone had not rung, I knew the edition had gone—the last *Irish Times* for which I had responsibility.

It was a new morning, my first morning of freedom in 16 years.

MOREOVER . . .

I always like reading the editorials in The Irish Times, *especially the ones beginning with the word 'moreover'.*

—PETER USTINOV

Stepping out from *The Irish Times* into the Ireland of 2002, I felt a bit like Rip Van Winkle or Oisín returning from Tír na nÓg. Although by definition one is at the epicentre of events as an editor, one can also be curiously isolated from those events. One can be aware of individual incidents and developments without always having the time or space in one's head fully to absorb their significance.

At the beginning of this book I used the metaphor of the express-train driver to describe the editor's condition. It is only when the train finally comes to a halt that one has the opportunity to gaze around, taking in the new landscape. I could list the major events—international and local—that had dominated the headlines over the 16 years. But it took me a while to realise the extent to which the processes of change had now made Ireland a different place in which to live.

That the Roman Catholic Church had lost its traditional power and influence, I knew. But it took me some time to understand the full extent of the vacuum that had been left behind. Nothing much seemed to have replaced it, beyond the pursuit of money and consumer goods.

I was aware that authority institutions in general had taken a battering—the churches, the politicians, financial institutions, the Garda, the teachers, the judiciary. But I had underestimated the degree to which authority of any kind had been reduced and the extent to which so many public institutions were held in poor esteem. Yet, paradoxically, the great majority of individuals within them continued to be held in high regard by those with whom they came into professional contact.

The heroes of the Ireland I stepped out into in 2002 were young business men and women who battered old industries into shape and made millions in profits by doing so. Or they were men and women who had harnessed new technologies to market demands for new consumer goods, from software to sandwiches to penthouse homes.

I had under-estimated the degree to which Irish society had moved to a transactional model. Institutions that had relied in considerable part on loyalties and a sense of vocational commitment for their operation, were now functioning on the basis of short-term contracts for services. There was a lot of work, but there seemed to be fewer jobs, as people of my generation had understood the term.

I realised, a short while after stepping down, the extent to which alcohol abuse and drugs permeated Irish society. They were there for as long as I could remember, but I had not understood the degree to which an alcohol culture had gripped so many younger people nor the ready availability of drugs through every city, town and village.

Internationally, I found myself marvelling at the ways in which United States influence had encircled the planet. The Soviet Union had gone and American capital was everywhere under the label of 'globalisation'. In a short space of time it seemed that people like Bill Gates and Rupert Murdoch had become more influential worldwide than most prime ministers or presidents.

The basis of Ireland's relationship with Europe had changed. Yes, I had seen each successive referendum and treaty. But there was also a cumulative effect. Europe had moved forward from being little more than a loose economic agreement. The EU now was a series of integrated and overlapping communities.

Because of the events in the US on September 11, 2001, I had been forced to a sudden awareness of the rise of militant Islam and the reality of terror as a daily threat around the world. But—like so many other editors and media leaders—I found myself wondering why it was we had been so unable to recognise its rise or to anticipate its emergence.

And technology had changed the planet. In 1986 when I became editor, a web was a place where spiders lived, a net was a thing that trawler men caught fish in and CNN was a struggling concept, created through the vision and energy of an American venturer called Ted Turner.

The relationship between the rich western world and the developing world seemed depressingly the same. I had become editor of *The Irish Times* when Bob Geldof's Band Aid appeared to have initiated a new consciousness of developed countries' responsibilities to their poorer neighbours. But by 2002 sub-Saharan Africa had been devastated by AIDS. Conventional development assistance had been proven to be of limited value, while its impact was often diminished by local corruption. Far from reducing disparities in wealth and eliminating human misery, it seemed that the closing years of the twentieth century had witnessed their accentuation. The adoption of a set of high-sounding Millennium Development Goals by the United Nations sounded fine in principle, but there was no prospect that they would be attained in the proposed time-scale.

Reluctantly, I came to the conclusion that editors and journalists and programme-makers—as the supposed gate-keepers of change—had been doing a pretty poor job. Obsessed with reporting the minutiae of our own societies and our own petty, consumer-focused lives, we were prone to losing the big picture of what was happening in the world around us.

I needed to engage with new realities. One of the curiosities of stepping out of an active career is that things you expect to happen often don't. And things that you don't expect to, do happen.

Art Cosgrove, President of UCD, invited me to undertake some academic work at the Michael Smurfit Graduate School of Business at Blackrock. I have been a senior teaching fellow there for the past two years.

Almost simultaneously, Gerald Lynch, the President of John Jay College at the City University of New York, asked me to come as a visiting professor. I could choose my period of attendance and the university generously provided me with a spacious apartment.

I leapt at both invitations. They would give me the ideal framework and discipline within which to distil whatever it was I had learned over more than 30 years in journalism and 18 years as a newspaper editor.

In addition, I was involved in a number of *pro bono* projects. My old school, the Cistercian College in Roscrea, was due to celebrate its centenary in 2005. Much work had been undertaken in assembling information on its history but there was a major job to be done in editing and finishing a centenary volume. I took that on.

I had been involved with the British-Irish Association (BIA) for almost 20 years and I had been a participant in its annual conferences at Cambridge or Oxford. Shortly after stepping down from *The Irish Times* I was asked if I would be willing to go forward for the chair in succession to the writer and historian Thomas Pakenham. I was happy to accept the challenge and was elected in April 2005.

The Minister for Justice, Equality and Law Reform, Michael McDowell, asked me to participate in the Remembrance Commission, set up under the Belfast Agreement to acknowledge and make payments to victims of the troubles. Along with four other commissioners and under the chairmanship of David Andrews I became engaged in assessing the testimony of these victims, bereaved and survivors. It has been harrowing but satisfying to be part of a process that at least acknowledges their suffering.

The former Unionist politician John Taylor—Lord Kilclooney of Armagh —asked me to contribute to his group of newspapers, based in the midlands. I gladly took up his offer to write a weekly column.

Vincent Browne asked me to become consultant editor to *The Village* magazine which he launched in October 2004.

And Michael Gill asked me to write *Up with The Times!*

If I had my years over again, I would still want to have been editor of *The Irish Times*. There were difficult passages, but my overwhelming sense is that I was privileged to have taken my place, eleventh in succession to Dr Shaw, steering a fine newspaper through 16 eventful years. I was privileged in my mentors and in many of my colleagues—journalists, printing craftsmen and those engaged in the business end of the organisation.

The Irish Times is only a newspaper. A newspaper does not carry the heavy responsibilities of government. Its virtues are not always as clear or apparent as those of other institutions that society has brought into being for its betterment. But at its best, it has a noble purpose. What is done at a good newspaper—what I endeavoured to do, with my colleagues—was well described by G.K. Chesterton:

> A poet writing in the silence of his study may or may not have an intellectual right to despise the journalist. But I greatly doubt that he would not be morally the better if he saw the great lights burning on through darkness until dawn and heard the roar of the printing wheels weaving the destinies of another day. Here at least is a school of labour and of some rough humility . . .

Nobody would accuse *The Irish Times* of undue humility. But as a school of labour it has always tried hard. As newspapers go, it has been a reasonably good one, imbued from its foundation with a sense of humanity and intelligence.

The people who ran it were not saints and their philanthropy was never a barrier to their ability to take a profit or make a good living from the operation. But they generally understood and accepted certain principles. And they saw themselves with public responsibilities. Even where an unduly commercial emphasis appeared, from time to time, to overshadow the newspaper's sense of public purpose, good journalism survived and sound principles endured.

That is part of the remarkable thing that is a good newspaper. There are many examples from the history of the industry. Newspapers in different places and at different times have had to draw on their intellectual and moral capital in order to survive managerial encroachment or proprietorial waywardness. Sometimes they have had to survive the influence of editors who are weak and indecisive or who lack vision or judgement. Sometimes they have to survive the failure of staff or unions to see the wider picture.

Sometimes a good newspaper may have to part company with its readers for a while, or a section of them, even while they endeavour to serve them. It may have to run against the tide of public opinion rather than merely reflecting it. It may have to challenge its readers' tastes, by refusing to dumb-down when the trend in the marketplace is towards trivialisation and vulgarity.

But to challenge readers is not to hector them. And seriousness of purpose does not have to equate to dullness of content. Simplification should not be at the cost of accuracy.

A good newspaper, by definition, will not please everyone. In the words of C.P. Scott, 'We can but try, ask pardon for our shortcomings, and there leave the matter.'

INDEX